Interpersonal Trust During Childhood and Adolescence

Since the beginnings of psychology as a discipline, interpersonal trust has been regarded as a crucial aspect of human functioning. Basic levels of interpersonal trust among people were believed to be necessary for the survival of society and the development of successful psychosocial functioning. Some research has shown that interpersonal trust is linked to physical health, cognitive functioning, and social functioning (including close relationships) across development. This book presents the current research in the growing field of interpersonal trust during childhood and adolescence (up to the onset of adulthood). It deals with the extent to which children and adolescents demonstrate the multiple facets of trust and trustworthiness, and how these multiple facets affect their social relationships with a wide range of social contacts: parents, peers, and social groups. It will be of interest to developmental, social, educational, and clinical psychologists.

Ken J. Rotenberg is Professor in the School of Psychology at Keele University. He is the editor of *Disclosure Processes in Children and Adolescents* (Cambridge, 1995) and co-editor of *Loneliness in Childhood and Adolescence* (Cambridge, 1999).

Interpersonal Trust During Childhood and Adolescence

Edited by Ken J. Rotenberg

 CAMBRIDGE
UNIVERSITY PRESS

CAMBRIDGE UNIVERSITY PRESS
Cambridge, New York, Melbourne, Madrid, Cape Town, Singapore,
São Paulo, Delhi, Dubai, Tokyo

Cambridge University Press
The Edinburgh Building, Cambridge CB2 8RU, UK

Published in the United States of America by
Cambridge University Press, New York

www.cambridge.org
Information on this title: www.cambridge.org/9780521887991

© Cambridge University Press 2010

First published 2010

Printed in the United Kingdom at the University Press, Cambridge

A catalogue record for this publication is available from the British Library

Library of Congress Cataloguing in Publication data
Interpersonal trust during childhood and adolescence / edited by
Ken J. Rotenberg.
    p.   cm.
ISBN 978-0-521-88799-1
1. Trust.   2. Children.   3. Teenagers.   I. Rotenberg, Ken J.   II. Title.
BF575.T7I577 2010
155.4′18–dc22   2010010736

ISBN 978-0-521-88799-1 Hardback

For Mooney Rotenberg

Contents

Figures

Tables

Contributors

BRIAN E. ARMENTA, Graduate Student, Department of Psychology, *University of Nebraska-Lincoln*

LUCY R. BETTS, Senior Lecturer, *Nottingham Trent University*

KAY BUSSEY, Professor, Department of Psychology, *Macquarie University*

GUSTAVO CARLO, Professor, Department of Psychology, *University of Nebraska-Lincoln*

JUNE M. CLAUSEN, Associate Professor and Department Chair, Department of Psychology, *University of San Francisco*

KATHLEEN CORRIVEAU, Graduate Student, Harvard Graduate School of Education, *Harvard University*

NANCY DARLING, Associate Professor, *Oberlin College*

BONNIE DOWDY, Training Coordinator – Consultant, *Boaz and Ruth, Inc.*

PATRICIA GILL, Executive Director, *Marin Brain Injury Network*

CHRISTINA HARMON, Student, Child Development and Family Science, *North Dakota State University*

PAUL L. HARRIS, Professor, Harvard Graduate School of Education, *Harvard University*

MILES HEWSTONE, Professor, Social Psychology, *University of Oxford*

SHIRLEY MCGUIRE, Professor, Department of Psychology, *University of San Francisco*

ELISSA MYERS, Postgraduate Student, Social Psychology, *University of Oxford*

MATILDA E. NOWAKOWSKI, Graduate Student, Department of Psychology, Neuroscience and Behavior, *McMaster University*

BRANDY A. RANDALL, Assistant Professor, Child Development and Family Science, *North Dakota State University*

SARAH-JANE RENAUD, Doctoral Student, Educational and Counselling Psychology, *McGill University*

MONICA ROCK, Graduate Student, Child Development and Family Science, *North Dakota State University*

KEN J. ROTENBERG, Professor, School of Psychology, *Keele University*

ATSUSHI SAKAI, Associate Professor, Division of School Education, Faculty of Education and Human Sciences, *University of Yamanashi*

LOUIS A. SCHMIDT, Professor and Associate Chair, Department of Psychology, Neuroscience and Behavior, *McMaster University*

NANCY L. SEGAL, Professor, Department of Psychology, *California State University, Fullerton*

JUDITH G. SMETANA, Professor, Department of Clinical and Social Sciences in Psychology, *University of Rochester*

HERMANN SWART, Postdoctoral Fellow, *Stellenbosch University*

VICTORIA TALWAR, Professor, Department of Educational and Counselling Psychology, *McGill University*

TANIA TAM, Lecturer, Social Psychology, *University of Oxford*

NICOLE TAUSCH, Postdoctoral Fellow, School of Psychology, *Cardiff University*

CASEY J. TOTENHAGEN, Graduate Student, Division of Family Studies and Human Development, School of Family and Consumer Sciences, *University of Arizona*

MARK TRUEMAN, Senior Lecturer, School of Psychology, *Keele University*

RHIANNON N. TURNER, Lecturer in Social Psychology, Institute of Psychological Sciences, *University of Leeds*

TRACY VAILLANCOURT, Associate Professor and Canada Research Chair, Faculty of Education and School of Psychology, *University of Ottawa*

BRIDGET WHITLOW, Clinical Psychotherapist Intern, Eating Disorders Treatment and Research Program, *University of California, San Diego*

Section I

Conceptual foundations and issues

1   Introduction

Ken J. Rotenberg (Keele University)

Scholars throughout the world have advanced the principle that society cannot survive unless individuals establish and sustain basic levels of interpersonal trust (O'Hara, 2004; Uslander, 2002; Volker, 2002; Warren, 1999). Furthermore, interpersonal trust has been regarded as a crucial facet of human functioning since the very beginning of psychology as a discipline (Erikson, 1963; Hartshorne, May, and Maller, 1929). There is a growing body of evidence demonstrating that interpersonal trust across the course of development is linked to: physical health (e.g., Barefoot, Maynard, Beckham, Brammett, Hooker, and Siegler, 1998), cognitive functioning (e.g., Harris, 2007; Imber, 1973), social functioning (e.g., Rotenberg, Boulton, and Fox, 2005; Rotter, 1980), and the development and maintenance of close relationships (e.g., Holmes and Remple, 1989). Certainly, interpersonal trust plays a crucial role for physical health and psychosocial functioning during childhood and adolescence. Furthermore, because of developmental trajectories, interpersonal trust during childhood and adolescence should affect individuals by adulthood both directly (i.e., early trust affects later trust) and indirectly (i.e., via earlier links to health and psychosocial functioning). Unfortunately, there is a dearth of research on this topic. Indeed, most contemporary psychology books on childhood, adolescence, or developmental psychology *fail* to include *any* reference to interpersonal trust at all.

The purpose of this book is to redress that oversight and establish interpersonal trust during childhood and adolescence as a priority within the discipline of psychology. The book includes a selective set of chapters that address interpersonal trust during onset of adulthood as well as late adolescence. Although these chapters push the age boundary, they help to provide a bridge between the research on interpersonal trust during the conventionally defined periods of childhood and adolescence and the research on interpersonal trust during the conventionally defined period of adulthood.

The goal of the book is threefold: (1) to present the *current* research in the *growing* field of interpersonal trust during childhood and adolescence (up to the onset of adulthood); (2) to highlight the fact that interpersonal trust during childhood and adolescence is a highly significant phenomenon for researchers from a wide array of nationalities and cultures (e.g., Australia, Canada, Northern Ireland, United Kingdom, United States, and Japan); and (3) to serve as an impetus for further research on this phenomenon. It is truly hoped that this book will encourage the future generation of researchers to examine interpersonal trust during childhood and adolescence. To my knowledge, this is the *first* academic book to comprehensively address that topic: an achievement that is, in my opinion, long overdue. The book should be valuable to a range of individuals, both from within and from outside of the discipline of psychology, such as: social psychologists, developmental psychologists, clinical psychologists, counselling psychologists, counsellors, educational psychologists, educators, health professionals, sociologists, politicians, and legal professionals.

This book is divided into three sections. Section I is devoted to broad issues confronting researchers, including this overview, the conceptualization of interpersonal trust, neurological factors contributing to interpersonal trust, and evolutionary approaches. The following two sections represent a developmental organization of work on the topic. Section II is devoted to interpersonal trust during childhood, and Section III is devoted to interpersonal trust during adolescence and early adulthood.

The following chapters appear in Section I. This introduction comprises Chapter 1. In Chapter 2, I (Ken J. Rotenberg) outline in detail the bases, domains, and targets (BDT) framework of interpersonal trust. The BDT framework represents a unified approach to interpersonal trust during childhood and adolescence (and adulthood) that comprises the complex array of trust and trusting behavior towards the range of persons, groups, and abstract groups in individuals' social worlds. The BDT framework has guided a number of chapters and corresponding research reported in this book. In Chapter 3, Matilda E. Nowakowski, Tracy Vaillancourt, and Louis A. Schmidt present the research on oxytocin and vasopressin acids, which are hormones and neurotransmitters. These researchers outline the role of oxytocin and vasopressin in the nurturance and bonding in nonhuman species (primarily rodents), and the role of oxytocin on adult humans' trust behavior in a game interaction. The implications of the findings for interpersonal trust during childhood and adolescence are discussed.

An evolutionary perspective guided, in part, the research carried out by Atsushi Sakai in Chapter 4. He examined children's sense of trust, which comprised their perceptions of trusting mother, father, sibling, and best friend, and their perceptions of being trusted by each of them.

In the first of two studies, 194 pairs of monozygotic twins (MZ) and 127 pairs of dizygotic twins (DZ) from 9 to 10 years and 11 to 12 years of age were tested. It was found that shared and non-shared environmental factors statistically accounted for the sense of trust in parents, sibling, and best friend. In Study 2, two waves of same-sex MZ and DZ twin pairs ranging from 9 to 13 years of age were tested. The findings showed that the sense of trust in parents buffered the effects of negative peer life events on depression. In particular, children with a low sense of trust in parents showed elevated depression as a function of negative peer life events.

The following chapters appear in Section II. In Chapter 5, Kathleen Corriveau and Paul L. Harris describe a series of studies on young children's reliance on the information provided by others as evidence of their trust. The researchers found that preschool children were generally more inclined to rely on the information from an informant who was familiar than from one who was unfamiliar. Nevertheless, it was found that preschool children's reliance on information was affected by the accuracy of the informant, the reliability of the information, and bystander assents of the informant. Furthermore, those patterns were found to be associated with the children's quality of attachment and theory-of-mind ability. In Chapter 6, Lucy R. Betts, Ken J. Rotenberg, and Mark Trueman report in detail the use of social relation and mutual influence analyses in examining young children's specific trust beliefs, peer-reported trustworthiness, and reciprocity of trust in social groups and best friend dyads. The chapter provides examples of the applications of social relation and mutual influence analyses for researchers in the field.

In Chapter 7, Shirley McGuire, Nancy L. Segal, Patricia Gill, Bridget Whitlow, and June M. Clausen examine sibling trust with data from the Twins, Adoptees, Peers, and Siblings (TAPS) study. The TAPS design contains four sibling dyads that vary in genetic relatedness: monozygotic twins (MZ), dizygotic twins (DZ), full sibling pairs (FS), and virtual twins (VT). The researchers found, for example, that there were appreciable correlations between children's trust beliefs in their mother and children's trust beliefs in their siblings. Furthermore, in support of evolutionary theory, the researchers found that MZ twins reported significantly higher trust beliefs in their sibling compared to DZ twins, full sibling pairs, and virtual twins. In Chapter 8, Kay Bussey examines the issues of interpersonal trust (specifically the role of promises) within the context of child victims of sexual abuse. Kay Bussey points out that child victims of sexual abuse are often caught in a dilemma in which they are required by the abuser to promise to keep the abuse secret, but are required to promise to tell the truth about the abuse in court. In Chapter 9,

Victoria Talwar and Sarah-Jane Renaud examine parents' detection of their children's untrustworthiness using a modified temptation resistance paradigm (i.e., resist peeking at a forbidden toy). It was found that parents were able to predict their child's peeking behavior and their lying about their behavior above a chance level.

The following chapters appear in Section III. In Chapter 10, Nancy Darling and Bonnie Dowdy examined the association between adolescents' reports of their own trustworthiness and mothers' trust beliefs in their adolescents. The data were derived from the Home:School Linkages project and comprised interviews with sixty-seven mother–adolescent dyads. The authors found a very modest association between adolescents' reports of their trustworthy behavior and mothers' trust beliefs. It was found that adolescents reported that they frequently used deception when they disagreed with their parents. In Chapter 11, Judith G. Smetana reports the findings from a series of studies designed to examine adolescents' willingness to disclose to parents about their activities as a function of both the domain of the activity and the quality of the parent–adolescent relationship. It was found in one study, for example, that adolescents' perceptions of trusting relationships with parents was more strongly associated with reported voluntary disclosure of personal issues than either of prudential or peer activities. In another study, it was found that adolescents were more willing to disclose to their parents when they perceived their parents as setting more limits on their behavior.

In Chapter 12, Brandy A. Randall, Ken J. Rotenberg, Casey J. Totenhagen, Monica Rock, and Christina Harmon describe the psychometric properties and the correlates of a new scale for assessing adolescents' trust beliefs. In Chapter 13, Gustavo Carlo, Brandy A. Randall, Ken J. Rotenberg, and Brian E. Armenta found that the relation between undergraduates' interpersonal trust beliefs and their prosocial behavior varied as a function of the type of prosocial activity. It was found that trust beliefs (emotional trust beliefs in mothers, honest trust beliefs in fathers and romantic partners) were negatively associated with *public prosocial behaviors*, but positively associated with *altruism*. In Chapter 14, Rhiannon N. Turner, Miles Hewstone, Hermann Swart, Tania Tam, Elissa Myers, and Nicole Tausch describe a series of studies on "intergroup trust," which comprises a positive expectation about the intentions and behavior, and thus trust, of an outgroup towards the ingroup. The findings yielded support for the hypothesis that having outgroup friendships promotes outgroup impersonal trust by adolescents and young adults from a range of cultures/races: Protestants and Catholics in Northern Ireland, White and Colored individuals in South Africa, and South Asian and White individuals in the UK.

In summary, this book provides a comprehensive review of the theory and research on interpersonal trust during childhood and adolescence. The work presented is by scholars from a range of countries. The book should be of value to individuals from a wide range of disciplines and serve as impetus for the investigation of interpersonal trust during childhood and adolescence in the years to come.

References

Barefoot, J. C., Maynard, K. E., Beckham, J. C., Brammett, B. H., Hooker, K., and Siegler, I. C. (1998). Trust, health and longevity. *Journal of Behavioural Medicine*, **21**, 517–526.

Erikson, E. H. (1963). *Childhood and society*. New York: W. W. Norton & Company.

Harris, P. L. (2007). Trust. *Developmental Science*, **10**, 135–138.

Hartshorne, H., May, M. A., and Maller, J. B. (1929). *Studies in the nature of character: Vol. II. Studies in self-control*. New York: Macmillan.

Holmes, J. G. and Rempel, J. K. (1989). Trust in close relationships. In C. Hendrick (ed.), *Review of personality and social relationships: Vol. X* (pp. 187–219). Newbury Park, CA: Sage.

Imber, S. C. (1973). Relationship of trust to academic performance. *Journal of Personality and Social Psychology*, **28**, 145–150.

O'Hara, K. (2004). *Trust: From Socrates to spin*. Cambridge: Icon Books.

Rotenberg, K. J., Boulton, M. J., and Fox, C. L. (2005). Cross-sectional and longitudinal relations among children's trust beliefs, psychological maladjustment and social relationships: Are very high as well as very low trusting children at risk? *Journal of Abnormal Child Psychology*, **33**, 595–610.

Rotter, J. B. (1980). *Interpersonal trust, trustworthiness and gullibility. American Psychologist*, **35**, 1–7.

Uslander, E. M. (2002). *The moral foundations of trust*. Cambridge University Press.

Volker, B. (2002). The politics of social networks: Interpersonal trust and institutional change in post-communist East Germany. *Organizational Studies*, May–June.

Warren, M. (ed.) (1999). *Democracy and trust*. New York and Cambridge: Cambridge University Press.

2   The conceptualization of interpersonal trust: A basis, domain, and target framework

Ken J. Rotenberg (Keele University)

The notion that trust is crucial to psychosocial functioning has been advanced since the beginning of contemporary psychology (see Simpson, 2007). Erikson (1963) proposed that trust is formed during infancy and affects psychosocial functioning during the life-course. Similarly, attachment theorists propose that infants' trust is a product of their interactions with caregivers that, via its role in a cognitive model (the internal working model [IWM]), affects subsequent social functioning (Armsden and Greenberg, 1987; Bridges, 2003; Waters, Vaughn, Posada, and Kondo-Ikemura, 1995). Researchers have emphasized the role that trust plays in relationships with parents and peers across childhood and adolescence (see Bernath and Feshbach, 1995; Harris, 2007). Also, trust has been regarded as a critical facet of romantic relationships during adulthood (e.g., Holmes and Rempel, 1989; Mikulincer, 1998; Miller and Rempel, 2004).

A major problem confronting a researcher is how to conceptualize and assess interpersonal trust. This type of problem is frequently encountered in the discipline of psychology, where researchers examine constructs that correspond to commonly understood terms or concepts: ones that tap into individuals' naïve notions of psychosocial functioning. As a consequence, the conceptualization of trust is a very thorny problem, because a researcher's conceptualization may not match those commonly held by a social community, thus appearing to be disconnected from social reality. Researchers might attempt to avoid such problems by assessing individuals' perceptions or reports of trust per se. Unfortunately, this method is very limited because the meaning of the measure is unclear. Specifically, individuals likely hold somewhat different notions of trust, and consequently such judgments may not serve as a meaningful measure of a given construct (i.e., exactly what are individuals judging?). Furthermore, the definition of such a construct is essentially teleological: "trust is what individuals perceive it to be." Finally, individuals' perceptions of trust likely tap into their naïve notions of psychosocial functioning and therefore may be associated with other measures by *implicit association*.

One potential resolution of this "struggle" is to conceptualize trust in a fashion that is compatible with the concept of it held by the social community – thus maintaining its social meaningfulness – but that can be operationalized and measured by an array of precepts and behaviors. Moreover, such a conceptualization should be optimally compatible with other lines of research on the topic. One such resolution is Rotenberg and his colleagues' 3 (bases) × 3 (domains) × 2 (target dimensions) interpersonal trust framework – the BDT (Rotenberg, 1994, 2001; Rotenberg, Boulton, and Fox, 2005; Rotenberg, Fox, Green, Ruderman, Slater, Stevens, and Carlo, 2005; Rotenberg, MacDonald, and King, 2004; Rotenberg, McDougall, Boulton, Vaillancourt, Fox, and Hymel, 2004). The purpose of this chapter is to: (1) clarify the BDT framework; (2) describe how BDT is similar to, and differs from, other relevant theories and related research; (3) discuss the extent to which the research supports its utility; and (4) discuss the implications of the BDT framework as an impetus for future research. The chapter will include a description of some of the limitations of the BDT framework.

The BDT interpersonal trust framework is shown in Figure 2.1. The framework includes the following three bases of trust: (1) reliability, which refers to a person fulfilling his or her word and promise; (2) emotional trust, which refers to a person refraining from causing emotional harm, such as being receptive to disclosures, maintaining confidentiality of them, refraining from criticism, and avoiding acts that elicit embarrassment; and

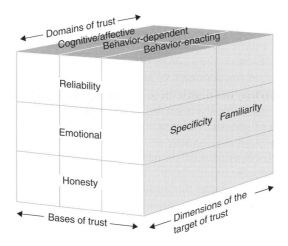

Figure 2.1 The bases × domains × target dimensions interpersonal trust framework

(3) honesty, which refers to a person telling the truth and engaging in behaviors that are guided by benign rather than malicious intent, and by genuine rather than manipulative strategies. The three domains are: (1) cognitive/affective, which comprises individuals' beliefs and feelings that others demonstrate the three bases of trust; (2) behavior-dependent, which comprises individuals behaviorally relying on others to act in a trusting fashion as per the three bases of trust; and (3) behavior-enacting (trustworthiness), which comprises individuals behaviorally engaging in the three bases of trust.

Finally, the framework includes the components of the specificity dimension of the target of trust (ranging from general category versus a specific person) and familiarity of the target of trust (ranging from slightly familiar to highly familiar). The framework highlights reciprocal qualities of trust whereby a person's trust in his or her partner within a dyad tends to be matched by the partner.

Relation of the BDT to other lines of research on trust

The three bases of trust as beliefs have been examined in some forms within various lines of investigation: reliability beliefs by adults (e.g., Rotter, 1980) and by children (Hochreich, 1973; Imber, 1973), emotional trust beliefs by adults (Johnson-George and Swap, 1982), and honesty beliefs by adults (Giffin, 1967). Similarly, the three bases of trust as behavior-dependency have been examined as: (1) reliability trust in the form of relying on promises in the Prisoner's Dilemma game by adults (Schlenker, Helm, and Tedeschi, 1973) and by delay of gratification by children (Lawton, 1966); (2) emotional in the form of the willingness to disclose personal information by adults (Steel, 1991); and (3) honesty in the form of relying on the accuracy of information by children (Harris, 2007). Finally, the three bases of trust as behavior-enactment have been examined as: (1) reliability behavior by adults fulfilling their promises (Simons, 2002); (2) emotional behavior by children keeping secrets (Carlson, 2007) and adults keeping secrets; and (3) honesty behavior by children in the form of truthful communication (Wilson and Carroll, 1991).

The specificity and familiarity dimensions of the target of trust encompass the partner, network, and generalized levels of trust described by Couch and Jones (1997), and the distinction between general and specific trust beliefs made by Johnson-George and Swap (1982). The reciprocal/dyadic nature of trust has been examined by a range of researchers, notably for romantic relationships by adults (Bartle, 1996; Holmes, 1991; Holmes and Remple, 1989; Larzelere and Huston, 1980; Wieselquist, Rusbult, Foster, and Agnew, 1999). The BDT framework includes individuals' perceptions or attributions of trust per se as a measure of the cognitive/ affective basis of trust, but the framework fosters a multi-measure assessment of interpersonal trust.

The BDT framework and perceived risk

The BDT framework bears on other facets of interpersonal trust. Giffin (1967) defined trust as "reliance upon the communication of another person in order to achieve a desired but uncertain objective in a *risky situation*" (p. 105, italics mine). Dunn and Schweitzer (2005) define trust as "the willingness to accept vulnerability based upon *positive expectations* about another's behavior" (p. 736, italics mine). The perception of risk and positive expectations play significant roles in the BDT framework. Consider, for example, the possibility that a target person's behavior is fixed as reliable, emotionally trustworthy, and honest because of some *apparent* external conditions (e.g., threat, enforced legal obligation). In that situation, an individual's trust beliefs about the target person, behavior-dependent trust towards him or her, and behavior-enacting trust towards him or her would be *irrelevant*. An individual's cognitive-affective behavior orientation to others, as outlined by the BDT framework, is *activated* when the individual perceives or apprehends risk and uncertainty of the situation for him or her: the greater the risk/uncertainty, the greater the activation. The cognitive-affective behavior orientation is designed to reduce risk and uncertainty, as well as to establish positive outcomes from social interaction.

Regarding the aforementioned definitions, researchers have found that trustworthiness comprising honesty, dependability, and loyalty is the most constantly desirable attribute in others (Cottrel, Neuberg, and Li, 2007). Ascribing those attributes to persons presumably gives rise to positive expectations about their behavior. Nevertheless, other attributes are ascribed to persons (e.g., cooperativeness, agreeableness, emotional stability) (see Cottrel, Neuberg, and Li, 2007) that presumably give rise to positive expectations about their behavior. The BDT framework posits that trust includes a *defined set* of beliefs (expectations) about persons – reliability, emotional, and honesty – which comprises (at the trusting end of the continuum) positive expectations of their behavior. This entire issue can be highlighted with reference to attachment theory. According to the BDT framework, trust by children and adolescents as beliefs is *distinct* from other forms of expectations, such that others are affectionate, loving, protective, supportive, kind, cooperative – attributes that may contribute to attachment and the IWM. How these distinctions are made during early development warrants consideration.

In summary, the BDT approach highlights that the three domains of trust (trust beliefs, behavior-dependent, and behavior-engaging) serve as potentials which become activated as a function of perceived or apprehended risk or uncertainty of a social situation. Furthermore, the domains serve to reduce risk and uncertainty, and increase the likelihood of positive outcomes of social interaction.

These principles may be best clarified by an example. Consider a child who holds high versus low beliefs that his or her parents are reliable, emotionally trustworthy, and honest. The child is walking down a street in their neighborhood with his or her parent, when suddenly a large dog approaches the child and starts barking. The parent instructs the child to try to be relaxed, not to pet the dog, and not to run away (likely wise advice); the child agrees to do so. Because this child holds high trust beliefs in his or her parent, the child would likely show trust-dependent behavior by relying on the parent's word to remain calm, and engage in trust-enacting behavior by not petting the dog and not running away – as promised by the child. In this example, the child displayed a given sequence of cognitive-affective behavior reactions in response to a risky and threatening situation, predicated, in part, on pre-existing trust beliefs in his or her parent. A very different sequence of reactions would have been demonstrated by a child who held low trust beliefs in his or her parent. It may not be possible to distinguish between this child and the child who held high trust beliefs in his or her parent while walking down the street, but differences would emerge when the large dog approached. Although the parent may give the same advice, this child would not be comforted by his or her parent's communication, would show anxiety, and might attempt to pet the dog or run away (likely the latter) – despite the child likely agreeing with the parent's recommended behavior. It should be emphasized that in both cases (i.e., high or low trust beliefs), the children's trust beliefs and corresponding behavior serve to result in positive outcomes from the interaction, such as avoiding being harmed by the dog.

In the aforementioned example, it is apparent how reciprocity and dyadic patterns emerge in parent–child interactions. When confronted by another risky or threatening situation, the child with high trust beliefs might hold even higher trust beliefs than before, be more likely to behaviorally rely on the parent, and show behavior-enacting trust. Importantly, as a result of such events, the parent would hold high trust beliefs in the child, depend on the child to rely on his or her (the parent's) word (as behavior-dependent trust), and rely on the child to show behavior-enacting trust in the form of demonstrating the recommended behaviors. The *opposite* pattern would emerge for the parent of the child who held low trust beliefs: the parent would hold low trust beliefs and expectations of behavior dependent and behavior enactment towards the child. The cognitive-affective behavior orientation of each partner is dyadic and therefore converges during the course of social interactions. According to the framework, this comprises the development *of social histories.*

In the aforementioned example, the parent's own behavior-enacting trust (i.e., trustworthiness) plays a crucial role in the preceding interactions. If the parent was not conveying the truth about how to deal with a potentially aggressive dog, perhaps as an act of deception, the entire sequence of the high trusting child's cognitive-behavior reactions would likely change. After being harmed or truly frightened by the dog, the child's trust beliefs, behavior-dependent trust, and behavior-enacting trust would suffer: he or she would not believe in the parent's word, be reluctant to depend on it, and be unlikely to fulfill his or her own promises to the parent. In effect, the child would have felt betrayed. What is important to note here is that these patterns should hold if the other person in the interaction was someone else: an older sibling, a relative, a peer, a teacher, a neighbor, a policeman, a crossing guard, or even a stranger (although the affect reactions contributing betrayal would certainly vary as a function of the nature of the relationship with the person). These events serve to establish social histories of interpersonal trust between the children and others.

The significance of interpersonal trust for children and adolescents

The BDT framework provides a perspective on why interpersonal trust is critical for children and adolescents – as has been advanced by various authors (e.g., Bernath and Feshbach, 1995; Erikson, 1963). Again, an example may clarify this point. Imagine that a child believes that the persons in his or her social world (parents, teachers, peers, siblings, and doctors) do not fulfill their promises or keep their word, do not keep information confidential, are critical to disclosure, are not honest in their communication, but are deceptive and manipulative. The child would withdraw from social contact and fail to attain or achieve, for example, social skills, social support, peer group relationships, close relationships, academic achievement, and medical treatment for illnesses.

Consistent with the aforementioned conclusion, it has been found that children's trust beliefs are positively associated with: low depression (Lester and Gatto, 1990), delay of gratification (Hochreich, 1973), helping others (Rotenberg, Fox, Green, Ruderman, Slater, Stevens, and Carlo, 2005; also see Chapter 13 of this book), social status (Buzzelli, 1988), low loneliness (Rotenberg, MacDonald, and King, 2004), academic achievement (Imber, 1973), absence of emotional disorders (Meltzer, Vostanis, Goodman, and Ford, 2007), and adherence to prescribed medical regimes (Rotenberg, Cunningham, Hayton, Hutson, Jones, Marks, Woods, and Betts, 2008; for a review see Bernath and Feshbach, 1995). As will be discussed, this conclusion warrants qualification.

Distinction between attachment theory and the BDT framework

According to attachment theory, the internal working model includes trust within the parent–child relationship and serves as a prototype of relationships; the latter, in turn, affects the formation of subsequent social relationships (see Bowlby, 1969, 1973, 1980). The BDT framework is distinct from attachment theory because it: (1) highlights the establishment of unique levels of trust towards various targets – who are not necessarily caregivers – varying in familiarity and generality; (2) treats trust as a multifactor phenomenon comprising different bases, rather than as a single factor implied by IWM; (3) emphasizes that trust in given targets emerges from social histories comprising reciprocal interactions among beliefs, behavior-dependent, and behavior-enacting; and (4) emphasizes that trust is a phenomenon that is separate from other relationship measures (e.g., love or affection, satisfaction, proximity-seeking), and its antecedents, correlates, and consequences can be uniquely examined. The BDT does accommodate some effects of early attachment bonds via IWM on individuals' trust in other targets. Nevertheless, the BDT does not represent a stance regarding the strength or time-dependent nature of such effects. In general, the BDT framework represents a unified approach to trust during childhood and adolescence (as well as adulthood) that comprises the array of trust and trusting behavior towards the range of persons, groups, and abstract groups in the individual's social world.

Direct empirical support for the utility of the BDT

The BDT has provided the basis for the development of six psychometrically established scales designed to assess the cognitive/affective domain – trust beliefs. The scales are (1) the Early Childhood Trust Belief Scale (Betts, Rotenberg, and Trueman, 2009a); (2) the Children's Interpersonal Trust Belief Scale (Rotenberg, Fox, Green, Ruderman,

Slater, Stevens, and Carlo, 2005); (3) the Children's Trust in General Physicians Scale (Rotenberg, Cunningham, Hayton, Hutson, Jones, Marks, Woods, and Betts, 2008); (4) the Children's Trust-Value Basis of Friendship Scale (Rotenberg and Morgan, 1995); (5) the Adolescents' Interpersonal Trust Belief Scale for adolescents and adults (Chapter 12 of this book); and (6) A Trust in Legal Professionals Scale for adults (Rotenberg, Emerson, Faulkner-Dunn, Gawn, Goswell, Ghumra, Shaikh, and Litvak, under review). All of these scales assess the three bases of trust beliefs. The targets of the scales are modestly familiar and general targets that include general categories of: mothers, fathers, teachers, peers, peer friends, physicians, and legal professionals.

The BDT framework has also provided the basis for assessing children's trust beliefs in more specific individuals or social groups: peer group (Rotenberg, 1986; Rotenberg, Boulton, and Fox, 2005; Rotenberg, MacDonald, and King, 2004), peer friend (Rotenberg, Boulton, and Fox, 2005; Rotenberg, MacDonald, and King, 2004), and siblings (see Chapter 6 of this book). In the research, children judge the extent to which peers, peer friends, or siblings keep promises (i.e., reliability trust beliefs) and keep secrets (i.e., emotional trust beliefs). In one study, Rotenberg (1986) found that children showed greater trust beliefs in same-sex than in opposite-sex peers, and that pattern emerged over the course of the early elementary school years. As another application, Rotenberg and Cerda (1994) examined 9- to 11-year-old Native and non-Native children's reliability, emotional, and honesty trust beliefs in different- as opposed to same-race hypothetical peers (i.e., either Native or non-Native). It was found that the children showed greater trust beliefs in same-race than different-race hypothetical peers, but that difference was attenuated when the children were enrolled in mixed-race schools. Finally, the BDT has guided the assessment of children's trustworthiness by peers and teachers judging the extent to which children kept promises and kept secrets (Betts and Rotenberg, 2007, 2008; Rotenberg, McDougall, Boulton, Vaillancourt, Fox, and Hymel, 2004; Rotenberg, Michalik, Eisenberg, and Betts, 2008).

As an examination of the domains of the BDT framework, Betts and Rotenberg (2008) carried out a social relations analysis of 5- to 7-year-old children's reports of promise-keeping and secret-keeping of peers. The study yielded significant "actor effects," demonstrating that there were significant individual differences in children's trust beliefs in peers. It also yielded significant "partner effects," demonstrating that there were significant individual differences in children's behavior-enacting trust as reported by peers. Finally, the study yielded evidence for dyadic reciprocity, which was more clearly shown among girls than among boys. The analyses provided evidence for the cognitive/affective domain, behavior-enacting domain, and dyadic quality of trust, respectively, as outlined by the BDT framework.

Behavior-enacting trust (trustworthiness): A BDT view of early findings

As noted, interpersonal trust has been a focus of interest since the beginning of contemporary psychology. In that vein, Hartshorne and his colleagues (Hartshorne and May, 1928; Hartshorne, May, and Maller, 1929; Hartshorne, May, and Shuttleworth, 1930) reported finding that children did not demonstrate coherent honesty traits. These researchers found, for example, low correlations (average .23) among thirty-three different tests of three types of deceit: cheating, lying, and stealing. It is worthwhile to note, though, that the researchers found stronger correlations among the tests of deceit in similar situations (e.g., in tests of cheating in the schoolroom). The BDT framework implies that there should be *modest* coherence or consistency of trustworthiness across a range of behaviors, as was found. In particular, though, the BDT framework leads to the expectation that there should be greater consistency within each basis of trustworthiness as opposed to across bases, and when shown towards a common as opposed to a different target. The finding that there were elevated levels of consistency among measures of deceit in the classroom is compatible with the expectations from the BDT framework that consistency in trustworthiness would be shown when the same basis of behavior is shown towards the same target – in this case, teachers or the category of school. The children who deceived in this case may have established a given history of social interaction with teachers and schools.

A number of researchers have focused on lying as part of a broader range of conduct disorders (see Waldman, Singh, and Lahey, 2006). Guided by the BDT framework, Betts and Rotenberg (2007) found that trustworthiness as assessed by peer reports of promise-keeping and secret-keeping longitudinally predicted school adjustment in 5- to 7-year-old children. Also, Rotenberg, Michalik, Eisenberg, and Betts (2008) found that trustworthiness (similarly assessed) was associated with school adjustment in 4- to 6-year-old children, and that trustworthiness served as a mediator, in part, of the relation between inhibitory control and school adjustment. The latter findings yielded support for the conclusion that inhibitory control is required for children to keep promises and keep secrets, and that this link partially accounts for how inhibitory control contributes to children's adjustment to school (also see Carlson, 2007). Finally, Betts,

Rotenberg, and Trueman (2009b) found that discrepancy between young children's self-perceptions of trustworthiness and reports of trustworthiness by peers/teachers was associated with poor school adjustment in the children. The findings supported the realistic principle prescribing that better psychological adjustment results from congruence between self-perceptions and reality – as marked by peer and teacher reports.

Are there consequences of children or adolescents being too trusting?

There is some evidence that being too trusting has negative consequences for children. Rotenberg, Boulton, and Fox (2005) carried out a short-term (8-month) longitudinal study with children initially of 9 years of age. The researchers proposed that children with very low trust beliefs and those with very high beliefs violated peer norms of trust (e.g., cynical or naïve, respectively) and that would result in peer rejection. In support of that hypothesis, the researchers found that children with very low trust beliefs and those with very high trust beliefs in peers (or in peer friends) had lower self-perceived social acceptance, and were more excluded by peers and less preferred than were children with the middle range of trust beliefs. Furthermore, the researchers found some evidence that those forms of peer rejection resulted in increases in internalized maladjustment. There was a negative linear longitudinal relation between children's trust beliefs in peers and internalized maladjustment (loneliness, depressive symptoms, and anxiety): the lower the children's trust beliefs, the more they demonstrated increases in internalized maladjustment. The observed linear relation was qualified, however, by a quadratic curvilinear pattern: children with very low trust beliefs and those with very high trust beliefs show greater increases in internalized maladjustment than that expected by a linear relation. The observed pattern was asymmetric, with children with very high trust beliefs being less disadvantaged than children with very low trust beliefs. The findings supported the conclusion that the peer rejection of children with high trust beliefs resulted in some elevation of their psychological maladjustment.

The role of discrepancy among the bases, domains, and targets of trust

The BDT framework posits that the bases, domains, and targets are all related facets of trust and thus are modestly associated – often as a sequence (e.g., trust beliefs promote behavior-dependent trust). Nevertheless, one of the defining features of the framework is its distinction among the bases, domains, and targets: this offers the opportunity of examining the discrepancy or conflicts among all components of the framework. As one example, Rotenberg, Fox, and Boulton (2009) examined the discrepancy between trust beliefs and their behavior-enacting trust (as reported by peers) in 9- to 11-year-old children. It was found that the more the children demonstrated trust beliefs that exceeded their behavior-enacting trust, the more they showed low levels of peer preference, high levels of peer victimization, and high levels of social disengagement. Furthermore, discrepancy between trust beliefs and behavior-enacting trust was predictive of increases in loneliness in girls, which was partially mediated by peer victimization. The findings supported the conclusion that the discrepancy between trust beliefs in peers and behavior-enacting trust in children was cross-sectionally and longitudinally associated with low psychosocial functioning.

The issue of discrepancy or conflict in the bases, domains, and targets of trust is exemplified in Chapter 8 of this book, by Kay Bussey, on the victims of sexual abuse. The chapter describes the dilemma in which a child is asked to reveal sexual abuse to legal professionals, but has promised the perpetrator of the sexual abuse – a parent or guardian – not to reveal those activities to others. This dilemma represents the conflict between reliability behavior-dependent trust towards modestly familiars (i.e., legal professionals) and emotional behavior-enacting trust towards a very familiar and specific target (i.e., the father). Such conflicts may be prevalent in human interaction. For example, a leader of a country may be involved in a conflict between telling the truth to his or her public (i.e., behavior-enacting honesty trust to unfamiliar and general others) and maintaining confidentiality of information to his or her advisors (i.e., behavior-enacted emotional trust to a very familiar and specific target). The complex issues surrounding trust in politicians within the United Kingdom has been discussed by O'Hara (2004).

Affect, emotional states, and interpersonal trust

Various researchers have discussed the emotional or affective components of interpersonal trust. For example, Lewis and Weigert (1985) distinguished between cognitive, emotional, and behavioral dimensions of trust. The cognitive dimension entailed a rational knowledge structure that included a leap of inference that permitted the identification of trustworthiness in the social world. The emotional trust dimension comprised the emotional bond established in relationships that was shown by an individual as emotional outrage when betrayed. Behavioral trust consisted of an individual undertaking a risky course of action that reflected confidence in others to act competently and dutifully. These distinctions bear a resemblance to the domains outlined in the BDT framework. According to Lewis and Weigert (1985), "Trust in everyday life is a mix of feeling and rational thinking" (p. 972).

Guided by a different theoretical orientation, Dunn and Schweitzer (2005) investigated the influence of emotional states on the judgments of trust. These researchers found that the induction of positive emotional states (e.g., gratitude, pride, happiness) increased trust in an unfamiliar person, and that the induction of negative emotional states (e.g., anger, sadness) decreased trust in that person. It was further found that the effects of the emotional states on trust were stronger when they were characterized by other-person control (e.g., anger and gratitude) and weak control appraisal (e.g., happiness) than when they were characterized by personal control (pride) or situation control (e.g., sadness). The emotional states were not found to appreciably affect trust judgments in a familiar person.

The BDT framework was based on the premise that trust beliefs include a substrate of affect that was primarily reflected in the *intensity or strength* of conviction (e.g., gut feelings) that others showed reliability, emotional trustworthiness, and honesty. Although this affective component was originally conceptualized as complementing trust beliefs, there is some possibility that they may not correspond precisely. For example, some individuals have reported the experience that they have a *feeling* they cannot trust a given person, but they are unable to articulate why. These experiences may reflect a gap between the cognitive representation of others (i.e., beliefs) and affective reactions to them, perhaps because of limits to the conceptualization of persons or events, or social desirability effects on cognitive representations of trust beliefs.

Because trust beliefs are affect-laden expectations of others' behavior, according to the BDT framework, violations of those expectations would be expected to evoke intense emotional reactions. Moreover, those are embedded in the closest bonds in human relationships (i.e., attachment, romantic) and therefore are linked to strong emotional reactions. Researchers have examined the emotional states associated with trust confirmation and trust violations in adult romantic relationships. For example, Mikulincer (1998) examined in a series of studies the differences between undergraduates varying in romantic attachment types: secure romantic attachment style, avoidant, and anxious-ambivalent.

In Study 1, Mikulincer (1998) assessed undergraduates' reaction time for recalling episodes regarding the behavior of father or mother or romantic partner which were positive (i.e., in a way that he or she increased the trust you felt towards him or her) or negative (in a way that he or she violated the trust you felt towards him or her). It was found that individuals with a secure romantic attachment style were quicker in retrieving positive trust-related memories than those with avoidant or anxious-ambivalent romantic attachment styles: the latter two types were quicker in retrieving negative trust-related memories than the former. In Study 2, Mikulincer (1998) required undergraduates to report their behavior when their romantic partner had violated trust placed in him or her. It was found that talking with the romantic partner was more frequently described by individuals with secure romantic attachment style; taking distance from the partner was more frequently described by individuals with avoidant romantic style; and ruminative worry was more frequently described by individuals with anxious-ambivalent romantic style. Similar patterns were found when undergraduates reported events regarding their romantic partners in diaries (Study 3). In a related study, Feeney (2005) found that violations of trust in romantic relationships, including infidelity and other forms of deception, were primarily associated with anger, but also with anxiety and lack of security (see also Jones, Couch, and Scott, 1997).

Research supports the conclusion that children prefer peers as friends when they keep rather than break promises and keep rather than reveal secrets (Buhrmester and Furman, 1987; Furman and Bierman, 1984; Rotenberg, 1991), and dislike peers who engage in trust-violating behavior (Rotenberg, 1991; Rotenberg and Morgan, 1995). Nevertheless, there is a scarcity of research on emotional states accompanying trust violations for children in peer friendships. In one study, Kahn and Turiel (1988) investigated the conceptualization of trust in 6- to 7-year-olds, 8- to 9-year-olds, and 10- to 11-year-olds. The children were presented with hypothetical dilemmas depicting deception, violations of conventional dress, and violations of emotional support by a casual peer friend or a close peer friend. The researchers found that the children reported that they would be upset by a deceptive act by a close friend or a casual peer friend: older children (10- to 11-year-olds) reported being more upset by the close friend's deceptive behavior. Very few children reported that they would re-establish reliance on a close friend if he or she had apologized or promised not to repeat the deceptive act. The researchers found that that pattern of judgments and justifications were distinctly different from those when the friends apparently engaged in violations of conventional dress or violations of providing emotional support. In future, researchers might be interested in assessing the precise emotional states of children in response to violations of honesty (i.e., deception) rather than promises or secret-keeping (i.e., the other bases of trust). Research could include assessments of children's reactions to naturally occurring events and include an examination of the role of children's use of secondary appraisal of the events, such as blame.

Theory of mind and beliefs about beliefs

Reliability trust beliefs (as conceptualized by the BDT framework) depend upon children comprehending the link between words and *intended* behavior. The honesty trust beliefs depend upon children inferring and comprehending that others engage in lying guided by deceptive and malevolent intent. Furthermore, behavior-enacting forms of reliability, emotional trust, and honesty depend in part on the child comprehending the thoughts and feelings of others. As a consequence, children's beliefs, behavior-dependent and behavior-enacting trust are likely linked to the development of theory of mind (ToM) (see Chandler and Hala, 1991; Maas, 2008; Polak and Harris, 1999; Talwar, Gordon, and Lee, 2007). Researchers have distinguished between first-order and second-order false-belief reasoning (Hogrefe, Wimmer, and Perner, 1986; Maas, 2008). First-order false-belief reasoning refers to children's reasoning about another person's representation of the world and has been found to emerge during the preschool years (3 to 4 years). Second-order false-belief reasoning refers to children's reasoning about another person's representation of a third person's representation of a given state of affairs and has been found to emerge during the early elementary school years. Associations between ToM and interpersonal trust have been found. Researchers have found that first-order false-belief reasoning is associated with preschool-aged children's deception about a transgression (Polak and Harris, 1999), perceptions of promises and lying as intended acts (Maas, 2008), and acceptance of informant choices following bystander assent (see Chapter 4 of this book). Also, researchers have found that, by early school age (after 6 years), second-order false-belief reasoning is associated with children's verbal concealment of deception (Talwar, Gordon, and Lee, 2007) and perceptions of a listener's perceptions of promises and lying as intended acts (Maas, 2008).

Trust beliefs may also serve as part of a perspective-taking system known as recursive thinking (Miller, Kessel, and Flavell, 1970; Veith, 1980). When applied to trust, a child could think about: (1) parents' trust beliefs in him or her (the child); (2) parents' thoughts about the child's trust beliefs in the parents (them); and (3) parents' thoughts about the child's thoughts about the parents' trust in him or her. According to the BDT framework, trust has a reciprocal component. Therefore, it is possible that the recursive thinking could include the child thinking about their thoughts and their parents' thoughts about trusting *each other*. Also, the content of the recursive thoughts would comprise the three bases of trust beliefs: reliability, emotional, and honesty. Given the tendency for children (and even adults) to assume that others hold similar beliefs to themselves (see Uleman, Saribay, and Gonzalez, 2008), recursive thinking might strengthen the link between the child's trust beliefs in others and their behavior-dependent trust. For example, a child who holds high emotional trust beliefs in parents would believe that parents: (1) hold similar beliefs in the child, and (2) hold those thoughts about the child's trust beliefs in the parents. This form of nested thinking would increase the likelihood that the child would show the corresponding behavior-dependent trust (e.g., disclose personal information as evidence of emotional trust beliefs). Broadly, theory-of-mind abilities in the form of second-order and recursive thinking may play a role in parent–adolescent interactions and relationships, as described in Chapters 10 and 11 in this book, and by other researchers (e.g., Finkenauer, Frijns, Engels, and Kerkhof, 2005; Ojanen and Perry, 2007).

Developmental issues

There is a scarcity of theory and research on the developmental course of interpersonal trust per se and the factors that affect the formation of trust in children and adolescents. I have advanced an account of how the bases, domains, and targets of the BDT framework change across the life-span (Rotenberg, 2001). According to these formulations, trust comprises: (1) behavior-dependent honesty during infancy; (2) honesty (predicated on inferring the intention not to deceive), reliability, and emotional bases, both as cognitions and as behavior-dependency during middle childhood; and (3) the manifestation of those facets of trust towards abstract targets and a broad range of targets during adolescence. Also, I have examined the parental antecedents of trust in children (Rotenberg, 1995). I found associations between maternal trust beliefs and children's trust beliefs in teachers. Also, associations were found between fathers' and their children's behavior-dependent trust towards strangers. Franklin, Janoff-Bulman, and Roberts (1990) found that parent divorce during childhood is associated with low trust in romantic partners during adulthood.

Summary

This chapter included a description of the BDT interpersonal trust framework, its links to other lines of theory and research, and its implications for psychosocial functioning for children and adolescents. The chapter will hopefully serve as an impetus for future research on a number of topics crucial to interpersonal trust during childhood and adolescence. The topics include the links between interpersonal trust and theory of mind, the role of perceived risk in interpersonal trust, the role of affect and emotional states in interpersonal trust, and the discrepancies or conflicts among the bases, domains, and targets of interpersonal trust as outlined by the BDT framework, the developmental course of trust from infancy through to adolescence, and antecedents of trust in children and adolescence.

References

Armsden, G. C. and Greenberg, M. T. (1987). The inventory of parent and peer attachment: Individual differences and their relationship to psychological well-being in adolescence. *Journal of Youth and Adolescence*, **16**, 427–454.

Bartle, S. E. (1996). Family of origin and interpersonal contributions to the interdependence of dating partners' trust. *Personal Relationships*, **3**, 197–209.

Bernath, M. S. and Feshbach, N. D. (1995). Children's trust: Theory, assessment, development, and research directions. *Applied and Preventive Psychology*, **4**, 1–19.

Betts, L. R. and Rotenberg, K. J. (2007). Trustworthiness, friendship and self-control: Factors that contribute to young children's school adjustment. *Infant and Child Development*, **16**, 491–508.

  (2008). A social relations analysis of young children's trust in their peers across the early years of school. *Social Development*, **17**, 1039–1055.

Betts, L. R., Rotenberg, K. J., and Trueman, M. (2009a). The Early Childhood Generalized Trust Belief Scale. *Early Childhood Research Quarterly*, **25**, 175–185.

  (2009b). An investigation of the impact of young children's self-knowledge of trustworthiness on school adjustment: A test of the Realistic Self-Knowledge and Positive Illusion models. *British Journal of Developmental Psychology*, **27**, 405–424.

Bowlby, J. (1969). *Attachment and loss: Vol. I. Attachment*. New York: Basic Books.

  (1973). *Attachment and loss: Vol. II. Separation: Anxiety and anger*. New York: Basic Books.

  (1980). *Attachment and loss: Vol. III. Loss*. New York: Basic Books.

Bridges, L. J. (2003). Trust, attachment, and relatedness. In M. H. Bornstein, L. Davidson, C. L. M. Keyes, and K. A. Moore (eds.), *Well-being: Positive development across the life course* (pp. 136–162). Mahwah, NJ: Lawrence Erlbaum Associates.

Buhrmester, D. and Furman, W. (1987). The development of companionship and intimacy. *Child Development*, **58**, 1101–1113.

Butler, J. K. (1986). Reciprocity of dyadic trust in close male–female relationships. *Journal of Social Psychology*, **126**, 579–591.

Buzzelli, C.A. (1988). The development of trust in children's relations with peers. *Child Study Journal*, **18**, 33–46.

Carlson, S.M. (2007). Inhibitory control and emotion regulation in preschool children. *Cognitive Development*, **22**, 489–510.

Chandler, M. and Hala, S. (1991). Trust and children's developing theories of mind. In Ken J. Rotenberg (ed.), *Children's interpersonal trust: Sensitivity to lying, deception, and promise violations* (pp. 135–159). New York: Springer-Verlag.

Cottrell, C.A., Neuberg, S.L., and Li, N.P. (2007). What do people desire in others? A sociofunctional perspective on the importance of different valued characteristics. *Journal of Personality and Social Psychology*, **92**, 208–231.

Couch, L.L. and Jones, W.H. (1997). Measuring levels of trust. *Journal of Research in Personality*, **31**, 319–336.

Dunn, J.J. and Schweitzer, M.E. (2005). Feeling and believing: The influence of emotions on trust. *Journal of Personality and Social Psychology*, **88**, 736–748.

Erikson, E.H. (1963). *Childhood and society.* New York: W.W. Norton & Company.

Feeney, J.A. (2005). Hurt feelings in couple relationships: Exploring the role of attachment and perceptions of personal injury. *Personal Relationships*, **12**, 253–271.

Finkenauer, C., Frijns, T., Engels, R., and Kerkhof, P. (2005). Perceiving concealment in relationships between parents and adolescents: Links with parental behavior. *Personal Relationships*, **12**, 387–406.

Franklin, K.M., Janoff-Bulman, R., and Roberts, J.E. (1990). Long-term impact of parental divorce on optimism and trust: Changes in general assumptions or narrow beliefs. *Journal of Personality and Social Psychology*, **59**, 743–755.

Furman, W. and Bierman, K.L. (1984). Children's conceptions of friendship: A multi-method study of developmental changes. *Developmental Psychology*, **20**, 925–931.

Giffin, K. (1967). The contribution of studies of source credibility to a theory of interpersonal trust in the communication process. *Psychological Bulletin*, **68**, 104–120.

Harris, P.L. (2007). Trust. *Developmental Science*, **10**, 135–138.

Hartshorne, H. and May, M.A. (1928). *Studies in the nature of character: Vol. I. Studies in deceit.* New York: Macmillan.

Hartshorne, H., May, M.A., and Maller, J.B. (1929). *Studies in the nature of character: Vol. II. Studies in self-control.* New York: Macmillan.

Hartshorne, H., May, M.A., and Shuttleworth, F.K. (1930). *Studies in the organization of character: Vol. III. Studies in the organization of character.* New York: Macmillan.

Hochreich, D.J. (1973). A children's scale to measure interpersonal trust. *Developmental Psychology*, **9**, 141.

Hogrefe, G.J., Wimmer, H., and Perner, J. (1986). Ignorance versus false-beliefs: A developmental lag in the attribution of epistemic states. *Child Development*, **57**, 567–582.

Holmes, J. G. (1991). Trust and the appraisal process in close relationships. In Warren H. Jones and Daniel Perlman (eds.), *Advances in personal relationships: A research annual: Vol. II* (pp. 57–104). Oxford: Jessica Kingsley Publishers.

Holmes, J. G. and Rempel, J. K. (1989). Trust in close relationships. In C. Hendrick (ed.), *Review of personality and social relationships: Vol. X* (pp. 187–219). Newbury Park, CA: Sage.

Imber, S. C. (1973). Relationship of trust to academic performance. *Journal of Personality and Social Psychology*, **28**, 145–150.

Johnson-George, C. and Swap, W. C. (1982). Measurement of specific interpersonal trust: Construction and validation of a scale to assess trust in a specific other. *Journal of Personality and Social Psychology*, **43**, 1306–1317.

Jones, W. H., Couch, L., and Scott, S. (1997). Trust and betrayal: The psychology of getting along and getting ahead. In Robert Hogan, John A. Johnson, and Stephen R. Briggs (eds.), *Handbook of personality psychology* (pp. 465–482). San Diego, CA: Academic Press.

Kahn, P. H., Jr. and Turiel, E. (1988). Children's conceptions of trust in the context of social expectations. *Merrill-Palmer Quarterly*, **34**, 403–419.

Kramer, R. M. and Carnevale, P. J. (2001). Trust and intergroup negotiation. In R. Brown and S. Gaertner (eds.), *Blackwell handbook of social psychology: Intergroup processes* (pp. 431–450). Malden, MA: Blackwell.

Larzelere, R. E. and Huston, T. L. (1980). The dyadic trust scale: Toward understanding interpersonal trust in close relationships. *Journal of Marriage and the Family*, **42**, 595–604.

Lawton, M. J. (1966). Delay of gratification as a function of characteristics of social agents. *Journal of Educational Psychology*, **57**, 246–252.

Lester, D. and Gatto, J. L. (1990). Interpersonal trust, depression, and suicidal ideation in teenagers. *Psychological Reports*, **67**, 786.

Lewis, D. and Weigert, A. (1985). Trust as social reality. *Social Forces*, **63**, 967–983.

Maas, F. K. (2008). Children's understanding of promising, lying, and false belief. *Journal of General Psychology*, **135**, 301–321.

Meltzer, H., Vostanis, P., Goodman, R., and Ford, T. (2007). Children's perceptions of neighbourhood trustworthiness and safety and their mental health. *Journal of Child Psychology and Psychiatry*, **48**, 1208–1213.

Mikulincer, M. (1998). Attachment working models and the sense of trust: An exploration of interaction goals and affect regulation. *Journal of Personality and Social Psychology*, **74**, 1209–1224.

Miller, P. H., Kessel, F. S., and Flavell, J. H. (1970). Thinking about people thinking about people thinking about ... : A study of social cognitive development. *Child Development*, **41**, 613–623.

Miller, P. J. E. and Rempel, J. K. (2004). Trust and partner-enhancing attributions in close relationships. *Personality and Social Psychology Bulletin*, **30**, 695–705.

O'Hara, K. (2004). *Trust: From Socrates to spin*. Cambridge: Icon Books.

Ojanen, T. and Perry, D. G. (2007). Relational schemas and the developing self: Perceptions of mother and of self as joint predictors of early adolescents' self-esteem. *Developmental Psychology*, **43**, 1474–1483.

Polak, A. and Harris, P. L. (1999). Deception by young children following non-compliance. *Developmental Psychology*, 35, 561–568.

Rotenberg, K. J. (1986). Same-sex patterns and sex differences in the trust-value basis of children's friendship. *Sex Roles*, **15**, 613–626.

—— (1991). The trust-value basis of children's friendship. In Ken J. Rotenberg (ed.), *Children's interpersonal trust: Sensitivity to lying, deception, and promise violations* (pp. 160–173). New York: Springer-Verlag.

—— (1994). Loneliness and interpersonal trust. *Journal of Social and Clinical Psychology*, **13**, 152–173.

—— (1995). The socialization of trust: Parents' and their children's interpersonal trust. *International Journal of Behavioral Development*, **18**, 713–726.

—— (2001). Trust across the life-span. In Neil J. Smelser and Paul B. Baltes (eds.), *International encyclopedia of the social and behavioral sciences* (pp. 7866–7868). New York: Pergamon.

Rotenberg, K. J. and Cerda, C. (1994). Racially based trust expectancies of Native American and Caucasian children. *Journal of Social Psychology*, **134**, 621–631.

Rotenberg, K. J. and Morgan, C. J. (1995). Development of a scale to measure individual differences in children's trust-value basis of friendship. *Journal of Genetic Psychology*, **156**, 489–502.

Rotenberg, K. J., Boulton, M. J., and Fox, C. L. (2005). Cross-sectional and longitudinal relations among children's trust beliefs, psychological maladjustment and social relationships: Are very high as well as very low trusting children at risk? *Journal of Abnormal Child Psychology*, **33**, 595–610.

Rotenberg, K. J., Cunningham, J., Hayton, N., Hutson, L., Jones, L., Marks, C., Woods, E., and Betts, L. R. (2008). Development of a children's trust in general physicians scale. *Child: Health, Care and Development*, **34**, 748–756.

Rotenberg, K. J., Emerson, L., Faulkner-Dunn, H., Gawn, S., Goswell, S., Ghumra, A., Shaikh, M., and Litvak, A. (under review). A trust in legal professionals scale. Manuscript submitted for publication.

Rotenberg, K. J., Fox, C., and Boulton, M. (2009). The cross-sectional and longitudinal relations between the coherence of interpersonal trust and psychosocial functioning during childhood. Manuscript submitted for publication.

Rotenberg, K. J., Fox, C., Green, S., Ruderman, L., Slater, K., Stevens, K., and Carlo, G. (2005). Construction and validation of a children's interpersonal trust belief scale. *British Journal of Developmental Psychology*, **23**, 271–292.

Rotenberg, K. J., MacDonald, K. J. and King, E. V. (2004). The relationship between loneliness and interpersonal trust during middle childhood. *Journal of Genetic Psychology*, **165**, 233–249.

Rotenberg, K. J., McDougall, P., Boulton, M. J., Vaillancourt, T., Fox, C., and Hymel, S. (2004). Cross-sectional and longitudinal relations among relational trustworthiness, social relationships, and psychological adjustment during childhood and adolescence in the UK and Canada. *Journal of Experimental Child Psychology*, **88**, 46–67.

Rotenberg, K. J., Michalik, N., Eisenberg, N., and Betts, L. R. (2008). The relations among young children's peer-reported trustworthiness, inhibitory control, and preschool adjustment. *Early Childhood Research Quarterly*, **23**, 288–298.

Rotter, J. B. (1980). Interpersonal trust, trustworthiness and gullibility. *American Psychologist*, **35**, 1–7.

Schlenker, B. R., Helm, B., and Tedeschi, J. T. (1973). The effects of personality and situational variables on behavioral trust. *Journal of Personality and Social Psychology*, **75**, 419–427.

Simons, T. (2002). Behavioral integrity: The perceived alignment between managers' words and deeds as a research focus. *Organization Science*, **13**, 18–35.

Simpson, J. A. (2007). Foundations of interpersonal trust. In A. W. Kruglanski and E. Tory Higgins (eds.), *Social psychology: Handbook of basic principles* (2nd edn.) (pp. 587–607). New York: Guilford Press.

Steel, J. L. (1991). Interpersonal correlates of trust and self-disclosure. *Psychological Reports*, **68**, 1319–1320.

Talwar, V., Gordon, H. M., and Lee, K. (2007). Lying in the elementary school years: Verbal deception and its relation to second-order belief understanding. *Developmental Psychology*, **43**, 804–810.

Uleman, J. S., Saribay, A., and Gonzalez, C. M. (2008). Spontaneous inferences, implicit impressions and implicit theories. *Annual Review of Psychology*, **59**, 329–360.

Veith, D. I. (1980). Recursive thinking and the self-concepts of preadolescents. *Journal of Genetic Psychology*, **137**, 233–246.

Waldman, I. D., Singh, A. L., and Lahey, B. B. (2006). Dispositional dimensions and the causal structure of child and adolescent conduct problems. In Robert F. Krueger and Jennifer L Tackett (eds.), *Personality and psychopathology* (pp. 112–152). New York: Guilford Press.

Waters, E., Vaughn, B. E., Posada, G., and Kondo-Ikemura, K. (eds.) (1995). Caregiving, cultural, and cognitive perspectives on security-based behavior and working models. *Monographs of the Society for Research in Child Development*, **60** (2–3, Serial No. 244).

Wieselquist, J., Rusbult, C. E., Foster, C. A., and Agnew, C. R. (1999). *Commitment, pro-relationship behavior, and trust in close relationships. Journal of Personality and Social Psychology*, 77, 942–966.

Wilson, J. M. and Carroll, J. L. (1991). Children's trustworthiness: Judgments by teachers, parents, and peers. *Children's interpersonal trust: Sensitivity to lying, deception, and promise violations* (pp. 100–117). New York: Springer-Verlag.

3   Neurobiology of interpersonal trust

*Matilda E. Nowakowski (McMaster University),
Tracy Vaillancourt (University of Ottawa), and
Louis A. Schmidt (McMaster University)*

The study of trust has a long and rich history in the field of human development (Erikson, 1963; Rotenberg, 2001). Over four decades ago, Erikson (1963) argued that the first experiences an infant has with his/her mother or primary caregiver are based on trust. According to Erikson, successful navigation of the infant through the trust versus mistrust stage of development is critical for the infant's future emotional and social functioning. Attachment theory further proposes that the *quality* of the early mother–infant interaction influences the infant's cognitions about future social relationships. Thus, a caregiver who is sensitive and responsive to his/her infant has a child who in turn develops a cognitive model of social relationships that include trustworthiness and dependability (Schore, 2001a, 2001b, 2005). In contrast, if a caregiver is insensitive to the needs of the infant and fails to respond to the infant's needs, or responds in an inappropriate manner, this will result in the infant developing a cognitive model of relationships as being unsafe and unreliable (Schore, 2001a, 2001b). Given these developmental trajectories, it is clear that the early mother–infant relationship plays a crucial role in the infant's development of trust towards the world.

Trust has also been shown to be an essential aspect in the development of friendships during childhood. Children who show a low level of trust beliefs towards their same-aged peers are less likely to engage in close relationships with their peers, which, in turn, places them at risk for future internalizing (i.e., anxiety and depression) and externalizing (i.e., truancy, oppositional-defiant disorder, conduct disorder) difficulties. Children who are low in trust beliefs report fewer friendship and increased levels of loneliness (Rotenberg, Boulton, and Fox, 2005; Rotenberg, MacDonald, and King, 2004). The relation between trust beliefs and psychosocial functioning has been shown to be curvilinear – children extremely high or extremely low in their trust beliefs have been shown to be high on internalizing difficulties and social exclusion, and low on social acceptance and social preference (Rotenberg, Boulton, and Fox, 2005). These findings highlight the important role that trust plays in the development and maintenance of friendships, which, in turn, play an important role in children's psychosocial functioning. Any deviances in trust behaviors from the norm (i.e., extremely high trust or extremely low trust) can compromise the development of friendships and the child's psychosocial functioning (Rotenberg, MacDonald, and King, 2004).

Most of the research that has been conducted to date on trust and its development has focused on *behavioral* and cognitive studies. These studies have shown that there is a great deal of variability among individuals in the extent to which they trust others. Although much attention has been given to the behavioral and cognitive aspects of trust, there is a lack of studies focusing on the neurobiological bases of trust. Understanding the behavioral and biological factors associated with interpersonal trust is important in order to develop a more comprehensive and accurate picture of mechanisms and processes involved in trust. There is a burgeoning field of inquiry that was spawned from recent theoretical and methodological advances in neuroscience that now informs how we view trust from a neurobiological perspective. In the present chapter, we review the literature that has been conducted to date on this issue, with a focus on understanding mechanisms, identifying future areas for research, and the implications of this research for clinical practice.

The present chapter comprises six sections. First, we provide a conceptualization of trust. We then discuss the issue of honesty and deception in studies with nonhuman animals, especially primates. Next, we present an overview of the two neuropeptides that have been identified as contributing to variations in social bonding and interpersonal trust: oxytocin and vasopressin. We then review the animal models that have been used in the study of social bonding and affiliative behaviors. A review of the recent studies that have investigated the influence of oxytocin on human trust is then presented, followed by a discussion of the implications that a neurobiological model of interpersonal trust has for increasing our understanding of psychological disorders, as well as directions for future research.

Conceptualizing trust

Trust has been conceptualized and defined in the literature in a number of different ways. One conceptualization that has been suggested by Rotenberg (1994, 2001) and referred to throughout this chapter is a 3 (bases) × 3 (domains) × 2 (dimensions) model. The three bases of trust are: (1) *reliability*, which refers to keeping one's promise or word; (2) *emotional*, which refers to the belief that other individuals will not cause harm by doing things like breaking confidentiality, purposely embarrassing an individual, or passing criticism; and (3) *honesty*, which consists of telling the truth and having a person's best interests in mind (Rotenberg, 1994, 2001). These three bases of trust are further defined by three dimensions: (1) *cognitive/affective*, which involves an individual's beliefs about and emotional reactions to the three bases of trust; (2) *behavior-dependent*, which is defined by the behavioral tendency to expect others to behave in ways that are reliable, emotional, and honest; and (3) *behavior-enacting* (i.e., trustworthiness), which is defined by behaviorally acting reliably, emotionally, and honestly. Finally, the three bases and the three dimensions are further defined by the following two domains of the "target of trust": (1) *specificity*, which refers to the differing responses for a person in general versus a specific individual; and (2) *familiarity*, which refers to the differing response to a person with whom one is unfamiliar or only slightly familiar versus a person with whom one is very familiar.

The model articulated by Rotenberg (1994, 2001) is essential to gain a better understanding of human behavior and provides researchers with a theoretical platform from which to understand the neurobiological mechanisms underlying trust. Although biological factors in the explanation of individual differences in interpersonal trust have all but been ignored in the trust literature to date, especially as it relates to children, there is mounting evidence from nonhuman animal research that the behavioral manifestation of trust has a biological basis. This idea has further been supported by recent novel studies in humans, which have involved collaborations among the fields of economics, psychology, and neuroscience. Thus, there is a need to integrate across disciplines to gain a better understanding of the complexity of interpersonal trust. Incorporating a neurobiological aspect to the model of interpersonal trust will enable researchers to gain an even better and more in-depth understanding of trust.

Honesty and deception: Nonhuman animal studies

There has been much interest in the question of whether nonhuman animals, especially primates, understand the psychological states of others. Nonhuman animals, such as chimpanzees, have been shown to engage in deceptive behaviors like emitting a false alarm call in order to attain a desired food. However, it is not clear whether these animals perform such behaviors because they have learned the relation between events, such that conspecifics flee when they hear an alarm call, or whether they understand the cognitive and psychological consequences of the behaviors. Up until less than a decade ago, researchers believed that the former explanation was correct, as studies investigating the ability of chimpanzees to react correctly to different psychological and cognitive states both in humans and in conspecifics had all yielded negative results (see Tomasello, Call, and Hare, 2003, for a review). However, recent and more naturalistic studies have suggested that, although chimpanzees do not have a true theory of mind, they are able to understand some psychological processes. For instance, when experimenters placed food in two locations – one that was visible to both the dominant and the subordinate chimpanzees, and another that was visible only to the subordinate chimpanzee – the subordinate chimpanzee took the food that was out of view of the dominant chimpanzee and would not pursue the food that was visible to both chimpanzees (Call, 2001). Furthermore, when the observation of the placement of food by the dominant chimpanzee was varied, such that at some points the door was open and the dominant chimpanzee saw the food being placed behind the barrier and at other times the door was closed, the subordinate chimpanzee would only pursue the food if it knew that the dominant monkey had not seen its placement. These results suggest that chimpanzees are able to know what others have or have not seen.

These findings are relevant to the study of trust in nonhuman animals as the ability to have some degree of understanding about others' mental states is an important aspect of the formation and maintenance of trust in relationships. However, the research in this area has largely focused on behavioral studies, and there has been no investigation of the underlying neural mechanisms behind these behaviors. Consequently, our review of nonhuman animal studies from a neurobiological perspective will focus on research that has largely utilized rodent models. Although these studies are limited by the fact that it is not possible to study trust directly in rodents, much research has been done on the behavioral and neurobiological bases of the formation of social relationships and social bonding, which are relevant to the trust literature.

Role of oxytocin and vasopressin in trust

Oxytocin is a peptide that consists of nine amino acids. It functions both as a hormone in peripheral circulation and as a neurotransmitter in the central nervous system. With regard to peripheral circulation, oxytocin is produced by the magnocellular neurons in the paraventricular and supraoptic nuclei of the hypothalamus (Sofroniew, 1983). These nuclei have extensions to the posterior pituitary, which is responsible for the release of oxytocin into peripheral circulation. In the central nervous system, oxytocin is produced by parvocellular neurons in the paraventricular nucleus of the hypothalamus. These neurons have projections to the limbic system, including the amygdala, hippocampus, and striatum, as well as to nuclei in the midbrain and hindbrain (Sofroniew, 1983). Oxytocin is widely known for its hormonal role in uterine contractions during labor and in the release of milk during lactation (Burbach, Young, and Russell, 2006; Gainer and Wray, 1994). However, as a neurotransmitter, it has been implicated in social bonding and affiliative behaviors in animals (Ferguson, Young, and Insel, 2002; Insel 2000; Lim and Young, 2006; Young, 2002; Young, Lim, Gingrich, and Insel, 2001; Young and Wang 2004), as well as interpersonal trust in humans (Kosfeld, Heinrichs, Zak, Fischbacher, and Fehr, 2005).

A second closely related peptide is vasopressin. Like oxytocin, vasopressin also consists of nine amino acids and functions as both a hormone in peripheral circulation and as a neurotransmitter in the central nervous system. In its peripheral circulation, vasopressin is produced by magnocellular neurons in the paraventricular and supraoptic nuclei of the hypothalamus and released by the posterior pituitary into peripheral circulation (DeVries and Miller, 1998; DeVries and Panzica, 2006). In the central nervous system, vasopressin is synthesized by both parvocellular and extrahypothalamic neurons. Parvocellular neurons are responsible for the production of vasopressin in the paraventricular and suprachiasmatic nuclei, while extrahypothalamic neurons synthesize vasopressin in the bed nucleus of the stria terminalis and the medial amygdala (DeVries and Miller, 1998; DeVries and Panzica, 2006). While vasopressin is best known for its role in the peripheral circulatory system as an antidiuretic hormone (Gainer and Wray, 1994), nonhuman animal models have also found that as a neurotransmitter in the central nervous system it plays a role in social affiliative behaviors and social bonding (Ferguson, Young, and Insel, 2002; Lim and Young, 2006; Young, 2002; Young and Wang, 2004). Thus, both oxytocin and vasopressin have been implicated as being involved in the formation and maintenance of social relationships.

Nonhuman animal models of social bonding

Given the complexity of human relationships and the invasiveness of neurobiological processes to study the phenomenon, much of the research on the neurobiological basis of bonding and social relationships has been based on nonhuman animal models. These models have shown that oxytocin and vasopressin are associated with a number of aspects of social behavior, including maternal care (Leng, Meddle, and Douglas, 2008; Nelson and Panksepp, 1998), social bonding (Lim and Young, 2006; Young and Wang 2004), attachment (Insel 2000; Young, Lim, Gingrich, and Insel, 2001), and social memory and recognition (Ferguson, Young, and Insel, 2002). As discussed above, the development of trust begins with the first relationship that the infant experiences, which in most cases is the mother–infant relationship. The quality of this early relationship is crucial for many aspects of development, including the development of the infant's ability to trust others and the world. The early mother–infant relationship can be parsed into separate components, including the onset of maternal behaviors and the development of attachment. Research using animal models has shown that oxytocin is essential for the development of both of these aspects of the early mother–infant relationship.

During pregnancy, the hormones estrogen and progesterone increase the levels of oxytocin and the number of oxytocin receptors in the brain of the mother rat, leading to an increased sensitivity to oxytocin (Amico, Thomas, and Hollingshead, 1997; Young, Munn, Wang, and Insel, 1997). In turn, oxytocin is responsible for the onset of maternal behaviors (Pedersen, Caldwell, Walker, Ayers, and Mason, 1994). While virgin female rats tend to avoid rat pups or even attack them, female rats after giving birth are attracted and nurturing towards rat pups (Fleming and Anderson, 1987; McCarthy, 1990). They engage in behaviors such as licking and grooming of the rat pups, arched-back nursing, nest building, and crouching to provide the pups with warmth. Research has shown that the central administration of oxytocin in virgin female rats results in these rats showing maternal behaviors towards rat pups (Pedersen, Ascher, Monroe, and Prange, 1982), while the blockage of oxytocin, through such methods as central injection of oxytocin antagonists or lesions of oxytocin cells, inhibits maternal behaviors in pregnant rats (Fahrbach, Morrell, and Pfaff, 1985; Insel and Harbaugh, 1989; Pedersen, Caldwell, Walker, Ayers, and Mason, 1994).

A similar pattern of results has been found in the prairie vole. Although the appearance of maternal behaviors occurs spontaneously in juvenile prairie voles and is not dependent on pregnancy, the spontaneous expression of these behaviors does require oxytocin (Olazabal and Young, 2006). Prairie voles injected with oxytocin antagonists into the central nervous system lack the spontaneous expression of maternal behaviors (Olazabal and Young, 2006).

Together, the findings from rats and prairie voles highlight the important role of oxytocin in the development of early mother–infant relationships, which are crucial for the infant's development of trust and security in the world. This is illustrated by the findings that natural variations in maternal licking and grooming in the rat are associated with stress responsivity in the offspring, as measured through cortisol levels (Caldji, Tannenbaum, Sharma, Francis, Plotsky, and Meaney, 1998; Francis, Diorio, Liu, and Meaney, 1999; Liu, Diorio, Tannenbaum, Caldji, Francis, Freedman, Sharma, Pearson, Plotsky, and Meaney, 1997). More specifically, as adults, offspring who had mothers who engaged in high rates of licking and grooming showed a decreased stress response. Conversely, offspring whose mothers engaged in low rates of licking and grooming behavior showed an increased and prolonged stress response (Caldji, Tannenbaum, Sharma, Francis, Plotsky, and Meaney, 1998; Francis, Diorio, Liu, and Meaney, 1999; Liu, Diorio, Tannenbaum, Caldji, Francis, Freedman, Sharma, Pearson, Plotsky, and Meaney, 1997). Thus, offspring whose mothers engage in low rates of licking and grooming tend to be more fearful and to produce higher stress responses – an indication that these animals may view the world and their environment as untrustworthy and unpredictable.

In addition to the importance of the onset of maternal behaviors, the development of an attachment between the mother and infant is an essential characteristic of the mother–infant relationship in most mammals. Attachment relationships are characterized by longevity and selectivity, such that individuals seek out specific individuals with which to interact, rather than just showing a general, non-selective tendency towards approaching others. Although rats and mice tend not to show attachment behaviors, sheep have been widely used as a nonhuman animal model for the study of mother–infant attachment. Much like the rat, the onset of maternal behaviors in the ewe occurs during pregnancy and birth, and involves oxytocin (Kendrick, DaCosta, Broad, Ohkura, Guevara, Levey, and Keverne, 1997; Kendrick, Keverne, Baldwin, and Sharman, 1986; Levy, Kendrick, Keverne, Picketty, and Poindron, 1992). In contrast to the rat, however, the ewe shows a high degree of selectivity in her attachment behaviors only a few hours after giving birth, a process that appears to be influenced by oxytocin. The vagino-cervical stimulation that occurs during birth results in an increase in the levels of a number of neurotransmitters in the olfactory bulb, including oxytocin, noradrenaline, acetylcholine, and glutamate (Kendrick, Keverne, Chapman, and Baldwin, 1988a, 1988b; Keverne, Levy, Guevara-Guzman, and Kendrick, 1993). The release of oxytocin triggers the release of these other neurotransmitters, leading to a reorganization of the olfactory bulb such that the ewe's olfaction increases in sensitivity and allows her to discriminate her own lamb from those of others (Levy, Guevara-Guzman, Hinton, Kendrick, and Keverne, 1995). Accordingly, the formation of a responsive and nurturing mother–infant relationship, which is largely mediated by the mother's oxytocin levels, is crucial for the offspring's future social success, including the offspring's ability to feel secure in the world. The mother–infant relationship is special and prominent in the child's development, as it forms the basis for future social relationships, including the extent to which the offspring will view future social partners as trustworthy.

As reviewed above, the mother–infant relationship, which plays an important role in the development of the infant's trust, is strongly influenced by oxytocin. Looking beyond the mother–infant relationship, oxytocin and vasopressin have also been shown to play a role in a number of behaviors that are essential for the establishment of adult social relationships and interpersonal trust. The formation of trust between individuals requires a number of criteria to be met, including the motivation to approach social partners, the ability to recognize and distinguish between familiar and unfamiliar conspecifics, and the ability to engage in social bonding and attachment formation. Both oxytocin and vasopressin have been implicated as playing roles in each of these processes (see Lim and Young, 2006, for a comprehensive review).

With regard to the first criterion (possessing the motivation to seek contact with other social partners), the central administration of oxytocin has been shown to increase the time that two adults spend together, in rats (Witt, Winslow, and Insel, 1992) and in gerbils (Razzoli, Cushing, Carter, and Valsecchi, 2003), while the central administration of vasopressin increases contact time between adult frogs (Marler, Chu, and Wilczynski, 1995), hamsters (Ferris, Albers, Wesolowski, Goldman, and Leeman, 1984), and birds (Maney, Goode, and Wingfield, 1997). Further investigations in nonhuman primates have shown that the two macaque species that show natural differences in affiliative behaviors show differences in cerebrospinal fluid levels of oxytocin (Rosenblum, Smith, Altemus, Scharf, Owens, Nemeroff, Gorman, and Coplan, 2002). That is, the highly sociable bonnet monkey shows significantly higher cerebrospinal fluid levels of oxytocin compared to the more solitary pigtail monkey.

Second, the ability to recognize a familiar individual is a crucial aspect for the development and maintenance of trust. Ferguson, Young, and Insel (2002) note that both oxytocin and vasopressin play important roles in the recognition of individuals and the formation of social memories. Although humans use their sense of sight to recognize familiar individuals, rodents rely on olfaction. When rodents are first exposed to an unfamiliar individual, they examine them by sniffing. It is assumed that this action enables them to collect information specific to that individual that will aid them in recognizing the individual in the future. Upon repeated exposures to a conspecific, the rodent examines it for decreased amounts of time, indicating that the rodent recognizes the conspecific and has formed a memory for it (Gheusi, Bluthe, Goodall, and Dantzer, 1994; Winslow and Camacho, 1995). In mice, oxytocin appears to play a role in the formation of social memories. Mice in the wild are unable to recognize conspecifics they encounter if an oxytocin antagonist is administered immediately before exposure to the target individual. Oxytocin administration in these same mice after the initial exposure does not restore the ability to recognize the conspecific in future exposures, suggesting that oxytocin is essential for the initial formation of the memory (Ferguson, Young, and Insel, 2002). Furthermore, mice that do not possess the oxytocin gene are unable to recognize target individuals after repeated exposures, despite being able to identify non-social familiar scents (Ferguson, Young, Hearn, Matzuk, Insel, and Winslow, 2000). However, injecting these mice with oxytocin immediately before exposure to the unfamiliar conspecific reverses this such that over repeated exposures to the unfamiliar individual, the mice exhibit decreased exploratory behavior, indicating the formation of a memory for that individual (Ferguson, Aldag, Insel, and Young, 2001).

A similar pattern of results has been found for vasopressin in rats. The central injection of a vasopressin antagonist results in a lack of recognition of familiar conspecifics in rats, while the central administration of vasopressin increases social recognition in rats (Everts and Koolhaas, 1999; Landgraf, Gerstberger, Montkowski, Probst, Wotjak, Holsboer, and Engelmann, 1995; Landgraf, Frank, Aldag, Neumann, Sharer, Ren, Terwilliger, Niwa, Wigger, and Young, 2003). This pattern of results is found despite the fact that the ability to recognize non-social stimuli is intact in the rats (Bielsky, Hu, Szegda, Westphal, and Young, 2004). Ferguson, Young, and Insel (2002) have suggested that oxytocin and vasopressin may play different roles in social recognition and memory, such that oxytocin may play a role in the formation of memory, while vasopressin may play a role in the retention and consolidation of memory. Ferguson, Young, and Insel (2002) suggest that it is unclear whether the differing roles of vasopressin and oxytocin in social memories are truly a reflection of different roles or a reflection of studying different rodents (i.e., the rat and the mouse) with different receptor distributions. Nevertheless, despite this lack of clarity, both oxytocin and vasopressin appear to play roles in the development of social memories, which are important factors for the development and maintenance of trust.

Once an animal has approached and formed a social memory of another conspecific, social bonding can occur. We have already discussed the role of oxytocin in the formation of selective and enduring mother–infant relationships. However, oxytocin and vasopressin are also involved in the formation of attachment relationships in adults. The prairie and montane voles provide excellent models for studying the neurobiological basis of social bonding, as they are genetically similar but differ greatly in their affiliative behaviors. While the prairie vole is highly sociable, forms enduring attachments, and is monogamous, the montane vole is solitary, does not form enduring attachments even with its own offspring, and tends to avoid social contact (Insel, Preston, and Winslow, 1995; Lim, Wang, Olazabal, Ren, Terwilliger, and Young, 2004; Wang and Insel, 1996). Research has shown that these two species of voles differ in the distribution of their oxytocin and vasopressin receptors, especially in neural circuits associated with reward and reinforcement. While the prairie vole has high concentrations of oxytocin and vasopressin receptors in these neural circuits, the montane vole has low concentrations (Insel and Shapiro, 1992; Insel, Wang, and Ferris, 1994; Lim and Young, 2004; Lim, Murphy, and Young, 2004). This pattern suggests that social bonding may be more rewarding for the prairie vole.

For the prairie vole, mating, which has been shown to release oxytocin, is necessary for the formation of partner preference (Williams, Catania, and Carter, 1992). However, central administration of oxytocin and vasopressin results in the development of partner preference in female and male prairie voles, respectively, without mating (Insel and Hulihan, 1995; Insel, Preston, and Winslow, 1995; Williams, Insel, Harbaugh, and Carter, 1994; Winslow, Hastings, Carter, Harbaugh, and Insel, 1993). Blocking oxytocin or vasopressin receptors through central injection of oxytocin or vasopressin antagonists eliminates pair bonding after mating in female and male prairie voles, respectively (Cho, DeVries, Williams, and Carter, 1999; Insel and Hulihan, 1995; Winslow, Hastings, Carter, Harbaugh, and Insel, 1993).

In summary, nonhuman animal models suggest that oxytocin and vasopressin play important roles in social bonding and affiliative behaviors. As mentioned previously, although the specific concept of interpersonal trust cannot be studied through animal models, trust plays an important role in affiliative behaviors and social bonding (Kosfeld, 2007). Thus, the neurobiological mechanisms that underlie these relationship processes in animals most likely also play a role in interpersonal trust in humans. This idea has been adopted by researchers over the last few years, as they have attempted to extend the work on the role of oxytocin on affiliative behaviors in animals to interpersonal trust in humans.

Interpersonal trust in humans

Social sciences research on interpersonal trust in humans has utilized a number of procedures, including tasks developed by game theory. These tasks measure individuals' willingness to take risks and trust individuals whom they do not know. Game theory, developed by Oskar Morgenstern (1944), proposes social interactions between humans as a strategic game consisting of three elements: (1) the individuals who participate in the game by interacting with one another; (2) a set of actions from which the individuals can choose; and (3) a pay-off for the participants (see Kosfeld, 2007, for a review). Importantly, although the actions that individuals choose are based on their own interests, the outcome of the game is determined by the behavior of all the players combined.

One widely used game theory task in the study of human trust is the trust game (Berg, Dickhaut, and McCabe, 1995; Camerer and Weigelt, 1988). In this game, participants are each given a certain number of monetary units that they can exchange for real money at an established exchange rate following the completion of the task. Participants are then randomly assigned to one of two roles, investor or trustee, and paired into investor–trustee dyads in which neither of the two participants in the dyad knows the identity of the other participant. Using a computer program, the investor is prompted to select a certain number of monetary units (including 0) to transfer to the trustee, with the knowledge that the amount that is transferred will be tripled and put into the trustee's account (Fehr, Kirchsteiger, and Riedl, 1993). Once this transfer is complete, the trustee is notified of the amount that has been transferred and is given the option to transfer a certain amount (including 0) to the investor (see Kosfeld, 2007, for a comprehensive review of the trust game).

In this task, the investor and trustee are each placed in very different roles. The investor has to approach the interaction and take the risk of transferring money to the trustee, without any guarantee that the trustee will reciprocate the transfer. Research has shown that humans tend to avoid such risks (Bohnet and Zeckhauser, 2004; Fehr and Schmidt, 1999; Holt and Laury, 2002). Thus, the investor has to overcome his/her aversion to betrayal in order to trust the trustee and exchange his/her monetary units. The behavior of the trustee, conversely, is a measure of trustworthiness, as the trustee knows the amount of money that has been transferred to him/her (Smith, 1998). Therefore, his/her behavior determines the extent to which he/she is trustworthy and will reciprocate according to the amount that he/she received. If both the investor and the trustee show trust and trustworthiness, respectively, they will each end up with more monetary units than they started with. Importantly, in order to reduce confounds, neither the investor nor the trustee knows the identity of the other participant with whom they are trading, and only one exchange is conducted with any one participant. This behavior is crucial as it prevents the results from being confounded by individuals' desire to make a positive impression on another person (Fehr, 2008).

There are a number of parallels between the trust game and Rotenberg's (1994, 2001) model of trust, especially in the behavioral dimension. The behavior of the trustee represents the bases of reliability and honesty, since the extent to which the trustee reciprocates the transfer received by the investor is representative of how reliable and honest the trustee is. In contrast, the behavior of the investor and his/her decision as to the amount of monetary units to transfer to the trustee is reflective of the *behavior-dependent* dimension, as the amount of monetary units that the investor transfers is a reflection of the extent to which he/she expects the trustee to behave reliably and honestly. It is important to note that the trust game does not encompass the *emotional* basis or the *cognitive/affective* basis of Rotenberg's (1994, 2001) model of trust. With regard to the emotional base, there is no direct assessment in the trust game of the extent to which one of the social partners believes that the other individual will not cause harm by doing things like breaking confidentiality, purposely embarrass him/her, or pass criticism. Also, there is no assessment of the *cognitive/affective* basis, as the task does not assess the investor's or trustee's cognitive or emotional reactions to the other social partner's monetary unit transfers. That is, the trust game does not assess cognitive or emotional reactions that individuals have to the three bases of trust, namely reliability, emotional, and honesty.

A complementary task, meant to tap whether the investor's performance on the trust game is truly a reflection of trust and is specific to social situations rather than just a reflection of risk-taking behavior, is the risk game (Kosfeld, Heinrichs, Zak, Fischbacher, and Fehr, 2005). The risk game has the same set-up as the trust game, except that there is no trustee and the investor is told that the exchange he/she receives will be randomly determined by a computer program. As a result, there is no social component in this task, and trust is not possible.

The use of game theory in social science research has provided much insight into the complexity of human interactions, specifically with regard to the issue of trust. However, research solely based on game theory has provided insight only into the behavioral aspects of human trust. Only recently have the areas of economics and cognitive neuroscience merged to create the field of neuroeconomics and the first studies investigating the neural bases of human interactions and trust (Adolphs, 2003; Lieberman, 2007). Much of the research in this area has utilized a combination of laboratory tasks based on game theory (e.g., the trust and risk games), and neuroscience techniques (e.g., functional resonance magnetic imaging and the administration of neuropeptides).

In their study of the role of oxytocin on trust behavior, Kosfeld, Heinrichs, Zak, Fischbacher, and Fehr (2005) administered either a nasal spray of oxytocin or a placebo to a group of undergraduate males who were then randomly assigned to either the trust game ($n = 128$) or the risk game ($n = 66$), and either the role of investor or trustee. The authors found that the investors in the oxytocin group transferred significantly more monetary units to the trustees compared to the investors in the control group during the trust game. Additionally, 45 percent of the investors in the oxytocin group transferred the maximum number of monetary units (i.e., 12) to the trustees during the trust game, compared to only 21 percent of the investors in the control group. Importantly, there were no statistically significant differences between groups in the amount the investors transferred during the risk game, indicating that oxytocin specifically influences trust in social situations and does not influence general risk-taking behaviors. Also, questionnaire data revealed that there were no statistically significant differences between investors in the two groups in their expectations about the back-transfer from the trustee, in their mood, or in their alertness. There was also no significant difference between the trustees in the two groups in terms of the number of monetary units that they transferred back to the investors. Kosfeld et al. (2005) interpreted these results as indicating that oxytocin specifically influences trusting behaviors, and not trustworthiness, by aiding individuals in overcoming their natural aversion to betrayal, thus increasing their level of trust.

The study by Kosfeld, Heinrichs, Zak, Fischbacher, and Fehr (2005) found that oxytocin only influenced the behaviors of the investors and did not influence the behaviors of the trustees. However, Zak, Kurzban, and Matzner (2005) and Morhenn, Park, Piper, and Zak (2008), using blood samples taken before and after making a decision in the trust game, found that endogenous oxytocin levels in the peripheral circulation system were related to the trustworthiness of the trustees and not to the investors' behaviors. Zak et al. (2005) found that oxytocin levels were positively related to the number of monetary units that were received by the trustee during the trust game, and to the number of monetary units that the trustee transferred back to the investor. The authors suggested that oxytocin was related to receiving a signal of trust, which was then positively related to the amount that was transferred back to the investor. Morhenn et al. (2008) took the findings of Zak et al. (2005) a step further and investigated how oxytocin mediated the influence of touch on trust behaviors. They found that oxytocin levels increased only for those individuals who received a massage and played the trust game, and not for those who only received a massage or who only played the trust game. While there were no statistically significant differences in the amount of monetary units transferred by the investors whether they received touch, the trustees who received touch transferred significantly more monetary units compared to the trustees who did not receive touch (Morhenn,

Park, Piper, and Zak, 2008). Further, with regard to the trustees, increases in oxytocin levels from pre- to post-decision were positively related to the amount that the trustees transferred back to the investors, such that larger increases in oxytocin levels predicted higher monetary value transfers. The authors interpreted these findings as suggesting that touch may prime oxytocin, resulting in increased responsiveness to signs of trust from others, thus leading individuals to be more generous and to sacrifice more of their monetary possessions (Morhenn, Park, Piper, and Zak, 2008).

Although the results reviewed above appear to be contradictory, with some studies finding that oxytocin influences investor behaviors and others finding that it influences trustee behaviors, it is important to note that the measurement and treatment of oxytocin differed between the studies. Zak, Kurzban, and Matzner (2005) and Morhenn, Park, Piper, and Zak (2008) both measured oxytocin levels through blood tests, which means that oxytocin levels were measured from the peripheral circulation and were not a direct measure of oxytocin levels in the brain. In contrast, research has shown that intranasally administered oxytocin can cross the blood–brain barrier (Born, Lange, Kern, McGregor, Bickel, and Fehm, 2002). Thus, the study by Kosfeld, Heinrichs, Zak, Fischbacher, and Fehr (2005) measured the influence of oxytocin on the brain. This point is an important distinction to make, as research has not investigated the concordance between oxytocin levels in the peripheral circulation and oxytocin levels in the brain, and, based on the nonhuman animal research reviewed above, it appears that oxytocin levels in the brain have the greatest influence on trust behaviors. Second, the study by Kosfeld, Heinrichs, Zak, Fischbacher, and Fehr (2005) measured the influence of synthetic oxytocin, while Zak, Kurzban, and Matzner (2005) and Morhenn, Park, Piper, and Zak (2008) measured non-synthetic oxytocin. It is likely that different mechanisms underlie synthetic and non-synthetic oxytocin. Non-synthetic oxytocin is derived from a complex neurocircuitry involving cognition, emotion, and behavior. In contrast, the administration of synthetic oxytocin is not associated with any specific behavioral or emotional situations. Thus, the contrasting and unclear findings between the studies in terms of whether oxytocin influences investor or trustee behaviors may be partially explained by differences in the measurement of oxytocin, as well as the different neural mechanisms that underlie synthetic and non-synthetic oxytocin.

It is also important to note that the ecological validity of the studies reviewed above is limited by the way in which the trust games were organized. In the trust games, the investor and trustee did not see one another, had no information about one another, and the investor played with a different trustee each time. This procedure is not reflective of social interactions in real life, where individuals usually see who they are interacting with and often have some background information, either based on previous interactions or based on what others have said about the social partner, regarding the morality and trustworthiness of the individual. Consequently, physical appearance and morality influence the individual's decisions of trustworthiness. In addition, in most cases, individuals do not interact with a person only once. Rather, social relationships are usually characterized by multiple back-and-forth interactions that aid in the formation and maintenance of relationships, including the formation and maintenance of trust.

A number of studies have been conducted that have attempted to account for these issues. First, to account for the issue of morality, Delgado, Frank, and Phelps (2005) provided participants with three hypothetical written descriptions of individuals with whom they would be playing the trust game; these descriptions differed in the extent to which they presented the individuals as being high, low, or neutral in moral character. As expected, prior to the task, investors rated the partners who were described as high in morality and those who were described as low in morality as high and low in trustworthiness, respectively. During the task, when investors interacted with the partners they viewed as being trustworthy, they shared significantly more monetary units and made their decisions of how much to transfer much more quickly compared to when they interacted with the partners they viewed as untrustworthy or neutral. This pattern was found despite the fact that all trustees provided the same amount in back-transfers. Thus, it appears that prior information on moral character influences investor's social decisions such that they rely more on the background knowledge in making their decisions than on the actual feedback they receive from back-transfers. Second, King-Casas, Tomlin, Anen, Camerer, Quartz, and Montague (2005) addressed the issue of using one-round games by employing a modified version of the trust game that involved the same investor and trustee playing ten rounds of the trust game together. The authors found that the best predictor of the maintenance of trust was reciprocity by the trustee. Any deviances from reciprocity resulted in a decrease in trust, reflected by a decrease in the number of monetary units that were transferred during the next round.

In addition to investigations focusing on the influence of the neuropeptide oxytocin and other behavioral factors on trust, a number of lesion and brain-imaging studies have focused on the brain-based mechanisms underlying trust. The majority of these studies can be grouped into two categories: (1) those focusing on brain activity during the ratings of the trustworthiness of faces, and (2) those focusing on brain activity during completion of game theory tasks. In general, these studies have implicated similar brain areas as being involved in these processes, and in trust behaviors in general, including the amygdala, striatum, and midbrain.

Several lesion and imaging studies have implicated the amygdala as being involved in the processing of the trustworthiness of faces. For instance, using a patient population of individuals with bilateral amygdala damage, Adolphs, Tranel, and Damasio (1998) found that patients with this type of neurological damage experienced disruptions in their ability to accurately rate the trustworthiness of faces. Although there were no differences on ratings of trustworthy faces between patients with bilateral amygdala damage and control patients with brain damage in different areas, patients with bilateral amygdala damage rated untrustworthy faces as significantly more approachable and trustworthy than controls with brain damage in different areas, including unilateral amygdala brain damage. Winston, Strange, O'Doherty, and Dolan (2002) extended these findings by investigating brain activity during both explicit and implicit judgments of the trustworthiness of faces. Regardless of whether the decisions were implicit or explicit, there was an increase in activity when processing untrustworthy faces in the bilateral amygdala and right insula. Furthermore, when the judgments were explicit, there was an increase in activity in the superior temporal sulcus. Importantly, the activity in the amygdala was still significant even when the statistical analyses controlled for the emotional expressions of the faces, indicating that activation of the amygdala provides a unique contribution to the assessment of the trustworthiness of faces, independent of emotional expression (Winston, Strange, O'Doherty, and Dolan, 2002). The amygdala is widely known as being involved in the processing of fear and danger (Adolphs, Tranel, and Damasio, 1998; Amaral, 2003). Consequently, it appears to make an important contribution to the ability of individuals to distinguish between trustworthy and untrustworthy faces.

Studies investigating the brain mechanisms involved in the negotiation of social relationships – specifically the determination, through multiple interactions with an individual, of whether the person is trustworthy – have implicated the striatum area, especially the caudate nucleus. Researchers, using a modified version of the trust game in which the investors played with the same trustees over a number of trials, found that, over time, activity in the striatum decreased (King-Casas, Tomlin, Camerer, Quartz, and Montague, 2005). The researchers interpreted this as suggesting that over repeated interactions, the investors made their decision as to the trustworthiness of the trustee. Consequently,

subsequent trading decisions were based more on the internal knowledge that the trustee was or was not trustworthy rather than the results
of the preceding trading round (King-Casas, Tomlin, Camerer, Quartz,
and Montague, 2005). Interestingly, studies in which investors did not
base their future trading decisions on the feedback they received through
back-transfers from the trustees have also shown decreased activity in
the striatum, among other areas. For instance, Delgado, Frank, and
Phelps (2005) found that when investors received back-transfers from
trustees who they had previously rated as being low, high, or neutral in
trustworthiness based on hypothetical biographical sketches, the caudate nucleus showed an increase in activity when playing with the neutral trustees, and this increase in activity differentiated between positive
and negative feedback. In contrast, there was no increase in activation
in the caudate nucleus when playing with the trustees the investors had
rated as trustworthy, and a weak increase when playing with the trustees
the investors had rated as untrustworthy. Delgado, Frank, and Phelps
(2005) suggested that these findings reflect different approaches to playing with neutral trustees (i.e., trustees about whom one has no information regarding moral character) and bad or good morality trustees, such
that when individuals have an opinion on the morality of the trustee,
they appear not to react as strongly to feedback information regarding
that person's trustworthiness compared to when they do not have such
information.

In another recent study, Baumgartner, Heinrichs, Vonlanthen,
Fischbacher, and Fehr (2008) administered either an intranasal spray
of oxytocin or a placebo intranasal spray to their participants, and randomly assigned participants to the roles of either investor or trustee.
After playing twelve games (six trust games and six risk games) with
different trustees, the investors were given feedback on the return rates
for their investments, being told that only 50 percent of their investments
resulted in a return. The investors then played another set of twelve randomly sequenced games (six trust games and six risk games). Following
the feedback, the investors in the control group decreased the number of
monetary units they transferred, while the investors in the oxytocin group
did not change the amount they transferred (Baumgartner, Heinrichs,
Vonlanthen, Fischbacher, and Fehr, 2008). With regard to brain activity,
investors in the oxytocin group had decreased activity in the amygdala,
midbrain, and striatum during the post-feedback trust game.

In summary, the brain-imaging research done to date, focusing on
trust behaviors, has implicated the amygdala, striatum, and midbrain
as playing roles in these processes. These brain areas are involved in
the experience of fear and behavioral adaptation to feedback (Adolphs,

Tranel, and Damasio, 1998; Amaral, 2003). Bringing together the research on the brain areas involved in the processing of the trustworthiness of faces, as well as in the making of decisions during the trust game, when individuals are administered oxytocin intranasally, it appears that oxytocin works on brain areas responsible for fear responses in order to decrease betrayal aversion, thus increasing trust. As pointed out by Baumgartner, Heinrichs, Vonlanthen, Fischbacher, and Fehr (2008), the amygdala, midbrain, and striatum are all subcortical brain structures whose functions are automatic and unconscious. Thus, oxytocin appears to work on brain areas that are responsible for automatic, unconscious processes in the making of decisions regarding trustworthiness.

Conclusion and clinical implications

We reviewed the human and nonhuman animal literature on the neurobiological bases of social relationships, with a special focus on interpersonal trust. The literature in this area suggests that the intranasal administration of oxytocin increases individual's risk-taking behaviors in social interactions involving the transfer of monetary units. This increase in risk-taking behaviors in social situations appears to be mediated through a decrease in activity in brain structures that are involved in the experience of fear. Thus, it appears that oxytocin enables humans to overcome their aversion to betrayal such that they increase their trust in social relationships. Preliminary imaging and behavioral studies suggest that oxytocin functions at a subconscious level, such that individuals do not knowingly report feelings of increased trust towards others when administered oxytocin. Rather, they exhibit increased trust behaviorally. Returning to Rotenberg's (1994, 2001) trust model that we presented at the beginning of this chapter, the literature on interpersonal trust in humans suggests that oxytocin influences the *behavior-dependent domain of the model*, especially the *reliability* and *honesty* behavior.

Past research and models of interpersonal trust in humans have largely focused on behavioral and cognitive approaches. Incorporating a neurobiological perspective to the current study of interpersonal trust in humans can add a missing piece to the puzzle and provide greater insight into a complex behavior that pervades the lives of all humans, and is especially important in child development. Trust is associated with a variety of developmental outcomes in children, including honesty (Wright and Kirmani, 1977), academic success (Imber 1973; Wentzel, 1991), and friendships (Rotenberg, 1986), with children who show high levels of trust showing higher levels on all of these qualities. Given the important role that trust plays in the development of children, the identification of factors that underlie individual variations in trust is essential in the development of appropriate interventions for children who show low levels of trust.

As discussed previously, the quality of the early mother–infant relationship has an influence on the infant's future ability to trust and feel secure in the world. However, although children who experience impoverished mother–infant interactions early in life are at an increased risk for later relational and psychosocial difficulties, there is a great deal of variability in outcome, such that some children who experience early disadvantaged environments through compromised mother–infant attachments go on to develop normal social relationships. Indeed, some children show resiliency towards impoverished early environments, including impoverished mother–infant relationships, while other children are greatly affected (Black and Lobo, 2008; Horning and Rouse, 2002; Masten, 2001; Murry, Bynum, Brody, Willert, and Stephens, 2001; Vanderbilt-Adriance and Shaw, 2008). A neurobiological view of interpersonal trust can help to explain this heterogeneity among children in developmental outcomes. That is, neurobiological differences, specifically at the level of oxytocin and oxytocin receptors, may underlie these individual differences, such that children who show resiliency to impoverished early relationships may have higher levels of oxytocin, resulting in more willingness to approach future social relationships and trust others, even after experiencing previous negative relationships. Conversely, children who are developmentally affected by the impoverished early interactions may have lower levels of oxytocin, thus decreasing their tendency to approach and form new relationships. Furthermore, even without compromised early mother–infant interactions, some children may simply be more hesitant and experience difficulties establishing close relationships due to naturally lower levels of oxytocin. This knowledge may inform and change the manner in which we intervene to assist children who have difficulties with trusting and forming friendships with their peer group. In addition to behavioral interventions, we may also consider interventions at the biological level, focused on oxytocin.

A neurobiological perspective of interpersonal trust also provides insight into psychological disorders that are associated with difficulties in social relationships, such as social phobia and schizophrenia, as well as early individual differences in temperament that have been implicated as precursors to internalizing and externalizing disorders, such as behavioral inhibition and disinhibition. Social phobia is characterized by a persistent, functionally impairing, and intense fear of being judged negatively by others or doing something humiliating in social situations (American Psychiatric Association, 2000) while behavioral inhibition, which is found in 10 to 15 percent of typically developing children, is characterized by a tendency to withdraw and show a high level of distress in response to novel situations, individuals, and objects (Garcia-Coll, Kagan, and Reznick, 1984). The defining characteristics of both social phobia and behavioral inhibition resemble difficulties with trust in social situations. Rotenberg, MacDonald, and King (2004) have reported significant relations between trust and loneliness in middle-school-age children. Also, very high and very low levels of trust have been shown to be associated with internalizing difficulties (Rotenberg, Boulton, and Fox, 2005). Thus, a biologically based understanding of trust can enhance researchers' and clinicians' understanding of social phobia and behavioral inhibition, aiding in the development of more effective treatments and interventions. Kosfeld (2007) suggested that the intranasal administration of oxytocin, in conjunction with cognitive behavioral therapy, may be an effective future treatment for individuals suffering from social phobia. Similarly, a neurobiological perspective on interpersonal trust can provide further insight into the biological mechanisms responsible for this tendency to avoid novel situations, individuals, and objects, and can add biological interventions focusing on the oxytocin system as a possible treatment option to help these children overcome their extreme avoidance behaviors. Most recently, low levels of oxytocin after trust-related interactions predicted negative symptoms (i.e., social withdrawal, isolation, and flattened affect), but not positive symptoms (e.g., depression, anxiety, and neuropsychological functions) in individuals with schizophrenia (Keri, Kiss, and Kelemen, in press).

It is important to note that all of the human studies that have investigated the neurobiological basis of interpersonal trust to date have focused on a very specific and narrow population: young adults and undergraduate students. Thus, studies focusing on children as well as older adult populations are necessary to understand the biological basis of interpersonal trust in these populations, and whether there are developmental changes that occur in these processes. Furthermore, recent research in the field of epigenetics has shown that genes are not destiny and that environmental factors can influence genetic expression. For instance, the work of Meaney and his research team has shown that differences in the rate of maternal licking and grooming can lead, through methylation (Weaver, Cervoni, Champagne, D'Alessio, Sharma, Seckl, Dymov, Szyf, and Meaney, 2004), to changes in the responsiveness of mice to stressors (Caldji, Tannenbaum, Sharma, Francis, Plotsky, and Meaney, 1998;

Liu, Diorio, Tannenbaum, Caldji, Francis, Freedman, Sharma, Pearson, Plotsky, and Meaney, 1997). That is, mice that experienced high rates of licking and grooming showed decreased responsiveness to stressors, while mice that experienced low rates of licking and grooming showed increased responsiveness to stressors (Caldji, Tannenbaum, Sharma, Francis, Plotsky, and Meaney, 1998; Liu, Diorio, Tannenbaum, Caldji, Francis, Freedman, Sharma, Pearson, Plotsky, and Meaney, 1997). These findings show that the environment can influence genetic expression and the behavior of individuals. Although the work of Meaney and his research team focused on stress responsivity, the general finding that the environment influences genetics is encouraging, as it suggests that if appropriate interventions are provided in a timely manner, individuals still have a chance for normal development. Thus, if we extrapolate this to the issue of trust, the possibility exists that individuals, who have difficulties with trust, possibly due to low levels of oxytocin, may still be able to form successful relationships in the future if they receive appropriate interventions in a timely manner.

As is clear from the complex model of trust proposed by Rotenberg (1994, 2001), trust is a multifaceted aspect of human relationships. Consequently, there is a high likelihood that the neurobiological basis of interpersonal trust is influenced by more than one neuropeptide. This idea is suggested by the fact that the current research appears to explain only one dimension of Rotenberg's model (1994, 2001) – that of the *behavior-dependent domain*. It is likely that there are a number of neuropeptides that work in conjunction and possibly even interact with environmental factors to determine trust behaviors in humans. The beginning of such a complex neurobiological model is evident in the findings that it is the combination of oxytocin-binding to oxytocin receptors and dopamine release that drives social bonding and affiliative behaviors (Young and Wang, 2004). It is highly likely that future research will further reveal such complex and interactive models.

As pointed out earlier, although current models of interpersonal trust are complex and highlight the behavioral, cognitive, and affective domains of interpersonal trust, these models have failed to consider neurobiology. Incorporating neurobiology into the model of interpersonal trust can help to add further explanatory power. The importance of considering the neurobiological basis of human behaviors and not just focusing on a behavioral level is highlighted by the disorder of autism. Early work that focused on explaining autism behaviorally viewed autism as being caused by what researchers termed "refrigerator mothers," defined as mothers who were cold and withdrawn towards their children (Bettelheim, 1967). It was not until research moved away from a solely behavioral perspective and incorporated biology that a genetic basis for autism was discovered, and appropriate interventions targeting the child rather than the parenting style of the mother were applied. This history highlights the need to develop a comprehensive model of interpersonal trust that incorporates both behavioral and neurobiological domains in order to appropriately aid children who struggle with trust and, consequently, experience difficulties in the formation and maintenance of social relationships. As the field of neuroeconomics continues to grow and develop, future research that applies the methods of game theory and neuroscience to both typically and atypically developing children will provide insight that will not only increase our understanding of various disorders, but will also help to inform intervention.

Acknowledgments

The writing of this chapter was supported by an Ontario Graduate Scholarship and operating grants from the Social Sciences and Humanities Research Council of Canada, the Canadian Institutes of Health Research, and the Natural Sciences and Engineering Research Council of Canada.

References

Adolphs, R. (2003). Cognitive neuroscience of human social behavior. *Nature Reviews Neuroscience*, **4**, 165–178.

Adolphs, R., Tranel, D., and Damasio, A. R. (1998). The human amygdala in social judgment. *Nature*, **393**, 470–474.

Amaral, D. G. (2003). The amygdala, social behavior, and danger detection. *Annals of the New York Academy of Sciences*, **1000**, 337–347.

American Psychiatric Association (2000). *Diagnostic and statistical manual of mental disorders* (4th edn., Text Revision [DSM-IV-TR]). Washington, DC: American Psychiatric Association.

Amico, J. A., Thomas, A., and Hollingshead, D. J. (1997). The duration of estradiol and progesterone exposure prior to progesterone withdrawal regulates oxytocin mRNA levels in the paraventricular nucleus of the rat. *Endocrine Research*, **23**, 141–156.

Baumgartner, T., Heinrichs, M., Vonlanthen, A., Fischbacher, U., and Fehr, E. (2008). Oxytocin shapes the neural circuitry of trust and trust adaptation in humans. *Neuron*, **58**, 639–650.

Berg, J., Dickhaut, J., and McCabe, K. (1995). Trust, reciprocity and social history. *Games and Economic Behavior*, **10**, 122–142.

Bettelheim, B. (1967). *The empty fortress*. New York: Free Press.

Bielsky, I. F., Hu, S. B., Szegda, K. L., Westphal, H., and Young, L. J. (2004). Profound impairment in social recognition and reduction in anxiety in vasopressin V1a receptor knockout mice. *Neuropsychopharmacology*, **29**, 483–493.

Black, K. and Lobo, M. (2008). A conceptual review of family resilience factors. *Journal of Family Nursing*, **14**, 33–55.

Bohnet, I. and Zeckhauser, R. (2004). Trust, risk and betrayal. *Journal of Economic Behavior & Organization*, **55**, 467–484.

Born, J., Lange, T., Kern, W., McGregor, G.P., Bickel, U., and Fehm, H.L. (2002). Sniffing neuropeptides: A transnasal approach to the human brain. *Nature Neuroscience*, **5**, 514–516.

Burbach, J.P., Young, L.J., and Russell, J. (2006). Oxytocin: Synthesis, secretion and reproductive functions. In J.D. Neill (ed.), *Knobil and Neill's physiology of reproduction* (pp. 3055–3128). London: Elsevier.

Caldji, C., Tannenbaum, B., Sharma, S., Francis, D., Plotsky, P., and Meaney, M. (1998). Maternal care during infancy regulates the development of neural systems mediating the expression of fearfulness in the rat. *Proceedings of the National Academy of Sciences of the USA*, **95**, 5335–5340.

Call, J. (2001). Chimpanzee social cognition. *TRENDS in Cognitive Sciences*, **5**, 388–393.

Camerer, C. and Weigelt, K. (1988). Experimental tests of a sequential equilibrium reputation model. *Econometrica*, **56**, 1–36.

Cho, M.M., DeVries, A.C., Williams, J.R., and Carter, C.S. (1999). The effects of oxytocin and vasopressin on partner preferences in male and female prairie voles *(Microtus ochrogaster)*. *Behavioural Neuroscience*, **113**, 1071–1079.

Delgado, M.R., Frank, R.H., and Phelps, E.A. (2005). Perceptions of moral character modulate the neural systems of reward during the trust game. *Nature Neuroscience*, **8**, 1611–1618.

DeVries, G.J. and Miller, M.A. (1998). Anatomy and function of extrahypothalamic vasopressin systems in the brain. *Progress in Brain Research*, **119**, 3–20.

DeVries, G.J. and Panzica, G.C. (2006). Sexual differentiation of central vasopressin and vasotocin systems in vertebrates: Different mechanisms, similar endpoints. *Neuroscience*, **138**, 947–955.

Erikson, E.H. (1963). *Childhood and society* (2nd edn.). New York: W.W. Norton & Company.

Everts, H.G.J. and Koolhaas, J.M. (1999). Differential modulation of lateral septal vasopressin receptor blockade in spatial learning, social recognition, and anxiety-related behaviors in rats. *Behavioural Brain Research*, **99**, 7–16.

Fahrbach, W.E., Morrell, I.I., and Pfaff, D.W. (1985). Possible role for endogenous oxytocin in estrogen-facilitated maternal behaviour in rats. *Neuroendocrinology*, **40**, 526–532.

Fehr, E. (2008). The effect of neuropeptides on human trust and altruism: A neuroeconomic perspective. In D.W. Pfaff, C. Kordon, P. Chanson, and Y. Christen (eds.), *Hormones and social behavior* (pp. 47–56). Berlin and Heidelberg: Springer-Verlag.

Fehr, E. and Schmidt, K.M. (1999). A theory of fairness, competition, and cooperation. *Quarterly Journal of Economics*, **114**, 817–868.

Fehr, E., Kirchsteiger, G., and Riedl, A. (1993). Does fairness prevent market clearing? An experimental investigation. *Quarterly Journal of Economics*, **108**, 437–459.

Ferguson, J. N., Aldag, J. M., Insel, T. R., and Young, L. J. (2001). Oxytocin in the medial amygdala is essential for social recognition in the mouse. *Journal of Neuroscience*, **21**, 8278–8285.

Ferguson, J. N., Young, L. J., Hearn, E. F., Matzuk, M. M., Insel, T. R., and Winslow, J. T. (2000). Social amnesia in mice lacking the oxytocin gene. *Nature Genetics*, **25**, 284–288.

Ferguson, J. N., Young, L. J., and Insel, T. R. (2002). The neuroendocrine basis of social recognition. *Frontiers in Neuroendocrinology*, **23**, 200–224.

Ferris, C. F., Albers, H. E, Wesolowski, S. M., Goldman, B., and Leeman, S. (1984). Vasopressin injected into the hypothalamus triggers a stereotypic behavior in golden hamsters. *Science*, **224**, 521–523.

Fleming, A. S. and Anderson, V. (1987). Affect and nurturance: Mechanisms mediating maternal behavior in two female mammals. *Progress in Neuro-Psychopharmacology & Biological Psychiatry*, **11**, 121–127.

Francis, D., Diorio, J., Liu, D., and Meaney, M. J. (1999). Nongenomic transmission across generations of maternal behavior and stress responses in the rat. *Science*, **286**, 1155–1158.

Gainer, H. and Wray, W. (1994). Cellular and molecular biology of oxytocin and vasopressin. In E. Knobil and J. D. Neill (eds.), *The physiology of reproduction* (pp. 1099–1129). New York: Raven Press.

Garcia-Coll, C., Kagan, J., and Reznick, S. (1984). Behavioral inhibition in young children. *Child Development*, **55**, 1005–1019.

Gheusi, G., Bluthe, R. M., Goodall, G., and Dantzer, R. (1994). Social and individual recognition in rodents: Methodological aspects and neurobiological bases. *Behavioural Processes*, **33**, 59–87.

Holt, C. and Laury, S. (2002). Risk aversion and incentive effects. *American Economic Review*, **92**, 1644–1655.

Horning, L. E. and Rouse, K. A. G . (2002). Resilience in preschoolers and toddlers from low-income families. *Early Child Education Journal*, **29**, 155–159.

Imber, S. C. (1973). Relationship of trust to academic performance. *Journal of Personality and Social Psychology*, **28**, 145–150.

Insel, T. R. (2000). Toward a neurobiology of attachment. *Review of General Psychology*, **4**, 176–185.

Insel, T. R. and Harbaugh, C. R. (1989). Lesions of the hypothalamic paraventricular nucleus disrupt the initiation of maternal behavior. *Physiology & Behavior*, **45**, 1033–1041.

Insel, T. R. and Hulihan, T. (1995). A gender-specific mechanism for pair bonding: Oxytocin and partner preference formation in monogamous voles. *Behavioral Neuroscience*, **109**, 782–789.

Insel, T. R. and Shapiro, L. E. (1992). Oxytocin receptor distribution reflects social organization in monogamous and polygamous voles. *Proceedings of the National Academy of Sciences of the United States of America*, **89**, 5981–5985.

Insel, T. R., Preston, S., and Winslow, J. T. (1995). Mating in the monogamous male: Behavioral consequences. *Physiology & Behavior,* 57, 615–627.

Insel, T. R., Wang, Z. X., and Ferris, C. F. (1994). Patterns of brain vasopressin receptor distribution associated with social organization in microtine rodents. *Journal of Neuroscience,* 14, 5381–5392.

Kendrick, K. M., DaCosta, A. P. C., Broad, K. D., Ohkura, S., Guevara, R., Levy, F., and Keverne, B. E. (1997). Neural control of maternal behavior and olfactory recognition of offspring. *Brain Research Bulletin,* 44, 383–395.

Kendrick, K. M., Keverne, E. B., Baldwin, B. A., and Sharman, D. F. (1986). Cerebrospinal fluid levels of acetylcholinesterase, monoamines and oxytocin during labour parturition, vaginocervical stimulation, lab separation and suckling in sheep. *Neuroendocrinology,* 44, 149–156.

Kendrick, K. M., Keverne, E. B., Chapman, C., and Baldwin, B. A. (1988a). Intracranial dialysis measurement of oxytocin, monoamine and uric acid release from the olfactory bulb and substantia nigra of sheep during parturition, suckling, separation from lambs and eating. *Brain Research,* 439, 1–10.

(1988b). Microdialysis measurement of oxytocin, aspartate, gammaaminobutyric acid and glutamate release from the olfactory bulb of the sheep during vaginocervical stimulation. *Brain Research,* 442, 171–174.

Keri, S., Kiss, I., and Kelemen, O. (in press). Sharing secrets: Oxytocin and trust in schizophrenia. *Social Neuroscience.*

Keverne, E. B., Levy, F., Guevara-Guzman, R., and Kendrick, K. M. (1993). Influence of birth and maternal experience on olfactory memories mediated by nitric oxide. *Nature,* 388, 670–674.

King-Casas, B., Tomlin, D., Anen, C., Camerer, C. F., Quartz, S. R., and Montague, P. R. (2005). Getting to know you: Reputation and trust in a two-person economic exchange. *Science,* 308, 78–83.

Kosfeld, M. (2007). Trust in the brain. *European Molecular Biology Organization Reports,* 8, S44–S47.

Kosfeld, M., Heinrichs, M., Zak, P. J., Fischbacher, U., and Fehr, E. (2005). Oxytocin increases trust in humans. *Nature,* 435, 673–676.

Landgraf, R., Frank, E., Aldag, J. M., Neumann, I. D., Sharer, C. A., Ren, X., Terwilliger, E. F., Niwa, M., Wigger, A., and Young, L. J. (2003). Viral vector mediated gene transfer of the vole V1a vasopressin receptor in the rat septum: Improved social discrimination and affiliative behavior. *European Journal of Neuroscience,* 18, 403–411.

Landgraf, R., Gerstberger, R., Montkowski, A., Probst, J. C., Wotjak, C. T., Holsboer, F., and Engelmann, M. (1995). V1 vasopressin receptor antisense oligodeoxynucleotide into septum reduces vasopressin binding, social discrimination abilities, and anxiety-related behavior in rats. *Journal of Neuroscience,* 15, 4250–4258.

Leng, G., Meddle, S. L., and Douglas, A. J. (2008). Oxytocin and the maternal brain. *Current Opinion in Pharmacology,* 8, 731–734.

Levy, F., Guevara-Guzman, R., Hinton, M. R., Kendrick, K. M., and Keverne, E. B. (1995). Oxytocin and vasopressin release in the olfactory bulb of parturient ewes: Changes with maternal experience and effects of acetylcholine, gamma-aminobutyric acid, glutamate and noradrenaline release. *Brain Research*, **669**, 197–206.

Levy, F., Kendrick, K. M., Keverne, E. B., Piketty, V., and Poindron, P. (1992). Intracerebral oxytocin is important for the onset of maternal behavior in inexperienced ewes delivered under peridural anesthesia. *Behavioral Neuroscience*, **106**, 427–432.

Lieberman, M. D. (2007). Social cognitive neuroscience: A review of core processes. *Annual Review of Psychology*, **58**, 259–289.

Lim, M. M. and Young, L. J. (2004). Vasopressin-dependent neural circuits underlying pair bond formation in the monogamous prairie vole. *Neuroscience*, **125**, 35–45.

(2006). Neuropeptidergic regulation of affiliative behavior and social bonding in animals. *Hormones and Behavior*, **50**, 506–517.

Lim, M. M., Murphy, A. Z., and Young, L. J. (2004). Ventral striatopallidal oxytocin and vasopressin V1a receptors in monogamous prairie voles (*Microtus ochrogaster*). *Journal of Comparative Neurology*, **468**, 555–570.

Lim, M. M., Wang, Z., Olazabal, D. E., Ren, X., Terwilliger, E. F., and Young, L. J. (2004). Enhanced partner preference in promiscuous species by manipulating the expression of a single gene. *Nature*, **429**, 754–757.

Liu, D., Diorio, J., Tannenbaum, B., Caldji, C., Francis, D., Freedman, A., Sharma, S., Pearson, D., Plotsky, P., and Meaney, M. (1997). Maternal care, hippocampal glucocorticoid receptors, and hypothalamic-pituitary-adrenal responses to stress. *Science*, **277**, 1659–1662.

Maney, D., Goode, C., and Wingfield, J. (1997). Intraventricular infusion of arginine vasotocin induces singing in a female songbird. *Journal of Neuroendocrinology*, **9**, 487–491.

Marler, C., Chu, J., and Wilczynski, W. (1995). Arginine vasotocin injection increases probability of calling in cricket frogs, but causes call changes characteristic of less aggressive males. *Hormones and Behavior*, **29**, 554–570.

Masten, A. S. (2001). Ordinary magic: Resilience processes in development. *American Psychologist*, **56**, 227–238.

McCarthy, M. M. (1990). Oxytocin inhibits infanticide in female house mice (*Mus domesticus*). *Hormones and Behavior*, **24**, 365–375.

Morhenn, V. B., Park, J. W., Piper, E., and Zak, P. J. (2008). Monetary sacrifice among strangers is mediated by endogenous oxytocin release after physical contact. *Evolution and Human Behavior*, **29**, 373–383.

Murry, V. L., Bynum, M. S., Brody, G. H., Willert, A., and Stephens, D. (2001). African American single mothers and children in context: A review of studies on risk and resilience. *Clinical Child and Family Psychology Review*, **4**, 133–155.

Nelson, E. E. and Panksepp, J. (1998). Brain substrates of infant–mother attachment: Contributions of opioids, oxytocin, and norepinephrine. *Neuroscience and Biobehavioral Reviews*, **22**, 437–452.

Olazabal, D. E. and Young, L. J. (2006). Oxytocin receptors in the nucleus accumbens facilitate "spontaneous" maternal behavior in adult female prairie voles. *Neuroscience*, **141**, 559–568.

Pedersen, C. A., Ascher, J. A., Monroe, Y. L., and Prange, A. J., Jr. (1982). Oxytocin induces maternal behavior in virgin female rats. *Science*, **216**, 648–650.

Pedersen, C. A., Caldwell, J. D., Walker, C., Ayers, G., and Mason, G. A. (1994). Oxytocin activates the postpartum onset of rat maternal behavior in the ventral tegmental and medial preoptic areas. *Behavioral Neuroscience*, **108**, 1163–1171.

Razzoli, M., Cushing, B. S., Carter, C. S., and Valsecchi, P. (2003). Hormonal regulation of agonistic and affiliative behavior in female Mongolian gerbils (*Meriones unguiculatus*). *Hormones and Behavior*, **43**, 549–553.

Rosenblum, L. A., Smith, E. L., Altemus, M., Scharf, B. A., Owens, M. J., Nemeroff, C. B., Gorman, J. M., and Coplan, J. D. (2002). Differing concentrations of corticotrophin-releasing factor and oxytocin in the cerebrospinal fluid of bonnet and pigtail macaques. *Psychoneuroendocrinology*, **27**, 651–660.

Rotenberg, K. J. (1986). Same-sex patterns and sex differences in the trust-value basis of children's friendship. *Sex Roles*, **15**, 613–626.

 (1994). Loneliness and interpersonal trust. *Journal of Social and Clinical Psychology*, **13**, 152–173.

 (2001). Trust across the life-span. In N. J. Smelser and P. B. Baltes (eds.), *International encyclopedia of the social and behavioral sciences* (pp. 7866–7868). New York: Pergamon.

Rotenberg, K. J., Boulton, M. J., and Fox, C. L. (2005). Cross-sectional and longitudinal relations among children's trust beliefs, psychological maladjustment, and social relationships: Are very high as well as very low trusting children at risk? *Journal of Abnormal Child Psychology*, **33**, 595–610.

Rotenberg, K. J., MacDonald, K. J., and King, E. V. (2004). The relationship between loneliness and interpersonal trust during middle childhood. *Journal of Genetic Psychology*, **165**, 233–249.

Schore, A. N. (2001a). The effects of early relational trauma on right brain development, affect regulation, and infant mental health. *Infant Mental Health Journal*, **22**, 201–269.

 (2001b). Effects of a secure attachment relationship on right brain development, affect regulation, and infant mental health. *Infant Mental Health Journal*, **22**, 7–66.

 (2005). Back to basics: Attachment, affect regulation, and the developing right brain: Linking developmental neuroscience to pediatrics. *Pediatrics in Review*, **26**, 204–217.

Smith, V. (1998). The two faces of Adam Smith. *Southern Economic Journal*, **65**, 1–19.

Sofroniew, M. V. (1983). Morphology of vasopressin and oxytocin neurons and their central and vascular projections. *Progress in Brain Research*, **60**, 101–114.

Tomasello, M., Call, J., and Hare, B. (2003). Chimpanzees understand psychology states – the question is which ones and to what extent. *TRENDS in Cognitive Sciences*, **7**, 153–156.

Vanderbilt-Adriance, E. and Shaw, D. S. (2008). Conceptualizing and re-evaluating resilience across levels of risk, time, and domains of competence. *Clinical Child and Family Psychology Review*, **11**, 30–58.

Wang, Z. X. and Insel, T. R. (1996). Parental behavior in voles. *Advances in the Study of Behavior*, **25**, 361–384.

Weaver, I., Cervoni, N., Champagne, F., D'Alessio, A., Sharma, S., Seckl, J., Dymov, S., Szyf, M., and Meaney, M. (2004). Epigenetic programming by maternal behavior. *Nature Neuroscience*, **7**, 847–854.

Wentzel, K. R. (1991). Relations between social competence and academic achievement in early adolescence. *Child Development*, **62**, 1066–1078.

Williams, J., Catania, K., and Carter, C. (1992). Development of partner preferences in female prairie voles (*Microtus ochrogaster*): The role of social and sexual experience. *Hormones and Behavior*, **26**, 339–349.

Williams, J. R., Insel, T. R., Harbaugh, C. R., and Carter, C. S. (1994). Oxytocin administered centrally facilitates formation of a partner preference in prairie voles (*Microtus ochrogaster*). *Journal of Neuroendocrinology*, **6**, 247–250.

Winslow, J. T. and Camacho, F. (1995). Cholinergic modulation of a decrement in social investigation following repeated contacts between mice. *Psychopharmacology*, **121**, 164–172.

Winslow, J. T., Hastings, N., Carter, C. S., Harbaugh, C., and Insel, T. R. (1993). A role for central vasopressin in pair bonding in monogamous prairie voles. *Nature*, **365**, 545–548.

Winston, J. S., Strange, B. A., O'Doherty, J., and Dolan, R. J. (2002). Automatic and intentional brain responses during evaluation of trustworthiness of faces. *Nature Neuroscience*, **5**, 277–283.

Witt, D. M., Winslow, J. T., and Insel, T. R. (1992). Enhanced social interactions in rats following chronic, centrally infused oxytocin. *Pharmacology, Biochemistry, and Behavior*, **43**, 855–861.

Wright, T. L. and Kirmani, A. (1977). Interpersonal trust, trustworthiness, and shoplifting in high school. *Psychological Reports*, **41**, 1165–1166.

Young, L. J. (2002). The neurobiology of social recognition, approach and avoidance. *Society of Biological Psychiatry*, **51**, 18–26.

Young, L. J. and Wang, Z. (2004). The neurobiology of pair bonding. *Nature Neuroscience*, **7**, 1048–1054.

Young, L. J., Lim, M. M., Gingrich, B., and Insel, T. R. (2001). Cellular mechanisms of social attachment. *Hormones and Behavior*, **40**, 133–138.

Young, L. J., Munn, S., Wang, Z., and Insel, T. R. (1997). Changes in oxytocin receptor mRNA in rat brain during pregnancy and the effects of estrogen and interleukin-6. *Journal of Neuroendocrinology*, **9**, 859–865.

Zak, P. J., Kurzban, R., and Matzner, W. T. (2005). Oxytocin is associated with human trustworthiness. *Hormones and Behavior*, **48**, 522–527.

4   Children's sense of trust in significant others: Genetic versus environmental contributions and buffer to life stressors

Atsushi Sakai (University of Yamanashi)

The capacity to form trusting relationships is regarded as essential to the development and maintenance of healthy social relationships (Gurtman, 1992). Furthermore, trusting relationships and individuals' sense of trust regarding those relationships have been found to serve important psychosocial functions, such as promoting reciprocal cooperation in interpersonal exchanges (Deutsch, 1958, 1960; Rapaport and Orwant, 1962). Erikson (1963) was a pioneer in recognizing the importance of trust in early life. He argued that individuals' ability to establish basic trust with the significant others who care for them affects their psychological functioning throughout their life-span. Erikson (1963) viewed basic trust as encompassing an individual's sense that he or she can trust others and his or her confidence that he or she has the ability to form a relationship.

A similar perspective on the role of trust in interpersonal trust to that held by Erikson emerges from the attachment theory advanced by Bowlby (1969, 1973). Bowlby (1969) proposed that attachment is the emotional bond between an infant and its significant other (i.e., caregiver) and that the security of that bond substantively affects social functioning during the course of development. These principles guided the seminal work by Ainsworth and her colleagues (e.g., Ainsworth, Blehar, Waters, and Wall, 1978), as well as others.

The primary mechanism for the link between the attachment bond and social development is the internal working model (IWM). According to Bowlby (1973), the IWM has two components: (1) an internal working model of *others*, which pertains to subjective evaluation of the responsiveness of the attachment figure when help is sought; and (2) an internal working model of *self*, which refers to the sense of self-worth that leads an individual to be sure that it is acceptable to ask for help. There is a body of research that yields support for the other component of the IWM (Johnson, Dweck, and Chen, 2007) and the self component of the IWM (e.g., Goodwin, Meyer, Thompson, and Hayes, 2008), as well as the principle that those contribute to individuals' social functioning across their life-span (e.g., Allen, Porter, McFarland, McElhaney, and Marsh, 2007; Hazan and Shaver, 1987; Raikes and Thompson, 2008). Secure attachment and the corresponding IWM during infancy have been linked to elevated levels of trust in others during the course of the life-span (e.g., Armsden and Greenberg, 1987; Mikulincer, 1998; Waters, Vaughn, Posada, and Kondo-Ikemura, 1995).

An integration of the aforementioned theory and research on attachment and the IWM yields a view of the function and development of trust across the life-span (shown graphically in Figure 4.1). According to these formulations, trust that originates in the relationship between infant and its close caregivers is thought to extend to significant others outside the family. Through the stages of development, children's trust in family members may guide them to trust in teachers, peers, best friend, and romantic partner. In extending this theory, it is possible that trust in these significant others may become generalized to others in general. Figure 4.1 summarizes this notion of how trust may generalize to others outside the family. Previous studies of development of trust considered that two factors are involved in trust formation: the environmental factors surrounding an individual and the individual's intrapersonal factors. Parenting style (Bernath and Feshbach, 1995; Maccoby and Martin, 1983) and the quality of peer relationships (Rotenberg, 1986; Selman and Selman, 1979) have often been listed as primary environmental factors. Examples of intrapersonal factors are personality traits such as extraversion (Shikishima, Hiraishi, and Ando, 2005) and individual differences in information-processing (Rotenberg, 1991; Rotenberg and Pilipenko, 1983–1984). In this way, a close examination of the interrelationship between environmental factors and intrapersonal factors is required in order to better understand how trust towards caregivers develops among school-age children. However, if we take the approach of examining the effects of parenting style, peer relations, certain personality types, and so forth, there is a limit to the number of factors we can examine and we have to ignore the factors that we cannot include in the study. This issue can be overcome by adopting a behavioral genetic approach to developmental psychology, which endeavors to explain environmental and genetic contributions to human behavior (Kendler, 1996; Plomin, 1994). This approach, while not focusing on identifying specific genetic or environmental factors affecting behaviors, allows us to distinguish the effects of the family environment from the effects of genes.

This chapter includes research guided by the behavioral genetic approach. The research was designed to examine the development of a sense of trust by school-age children in significant others within the family as well as best friends. Consistent with Erikson's and Bowlby's theories, sense of trust in a significant other was conceptualized as having two

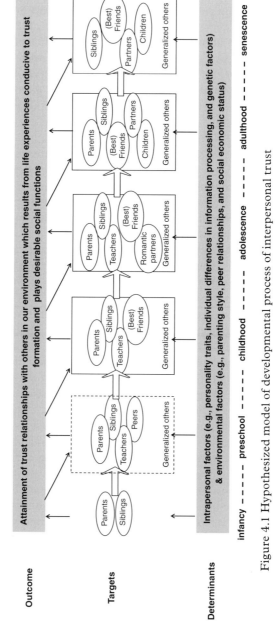

Outcome

Attainment of trust relationships with others in our environment which results from life experiences conducive to trust formation and plays desirable social functions

Targets

Determinants

Intrapersonal factors (e.g., personality traits, individual differences in information processing, and genetic factors) & environmental factors (e.g., parenting style, peer relationships, and social economic status)

infancy – – – – – preschool – – – – – childhood – – – – – adolescence – – – – – adulthood – – – – – senescence

Figure 4.1 Hypothesized model of developmental process of interpersonal trust

components: trust belief in a significant other and perceived trustworthiness from a significant other.

Behavioral genetics approach

Studies of human behavioral genetics aim to ascertain quantitatively the contribution made by two types of environments, namely "shared" and "non-shared," and by genes, in vast arrays of human behavior, by often observing twins and adopted children. A shared environment primarily pertains to a home environment where parenting style and siblings are shared, while a non-shared environment mainly exists outside the home environment, where peer relations differ for each child. Genetic factors include such things as individual differences in information-processing and personality.

Children's trust in others has thus far rarely been studied using the behavioral genetic approach. Having said that, considering that keeping promises and secrets are typical childhood behavior based on trust (Rotenberg, McDougall, Boulton, Vaillancourt, Fox, and Hymel, 2004), a behavioral genetic study of self-disclosure by Manke and Plomin (1997) can be considered an exception. In this study, self-disclosure has been regarded as trusting behavior (see Chapter 2 of this book). Manke and Plomin (1997) conducted a survey study of positive and negative self-disclosure to siblings among adopted and non-adopted children (aged between 8 and 17). They reported that there is only a weak genetic contribution in explaining self-disclosure, while shared and non-shared environment accounted for much of the self-disclosure. Twin studies that used the strange situation paradigm (Bokhorst, Bakermans-Kranenburg, Fearon, van Ijzendoorn, Fonagy, and Shuengel, 2003; O'Conner and Croft, 2001) to examine infant attachment to caregiver also found that stability of attachment was mostly accounted for by shared environment (52 percent) and little was explained by genetic factors. These results suggest that genes in fact explain a relatively small amount of variance in children's trust in significant others. Furthermore, the shared and non-shared environment has been found to be a better predictor of twins' behavior than genetic factors. In contrast to these studies, an adult study of trust relationships (Shikishima, Hiraishi, and Ando, 2005) reported that while the genes and non-shared environment accounted for trust in generalized others, shared environment did not. These findings might be interpreted to mean that what constitutes trust in others differs across age groups and who the target of trust is.

What would account for trust in parents, siblings, and best friend among children in the elementary school years? The studies of self-disclosure mentioned above (Manke and Plomin, 1997) would suggest that trust in parents and siblings is accounted for by shared and non-shared environment. For trust in a best friend, contradictory predictions can be made. If a best friend is considered to be a significant other in the same way that parents and siblings are, then it is likely to be accounted for by shared and non-shared environment. If, on the other hand, a best friend is considered to be important, but not significant in the same way the family members are, then trust in a best friend is more likely to be explained by the genes and non-shared environment – the same as shown in the study of trust in generalized others. The behavioral genetic approach guided the current investigation of the extent to which genes and the environment accounted for a sense of trust in parents, siblings, and friends in children in late childhood.

According to the theories of developmental psychology consistent with the concept of IWM (Bowlby, 1973; MacDonald, 1992; Sroufe, 1990), children's trust in significant others forms the basis of trust in others outside the family environment. This way of looking at trust development suggests that the factors that contribute to the development of trust in parents and siblings, particularly shared environmental factors such as parenting style, also affect trust in best friends and other non-family members.

There are, however, other theorists (Harris, 1995; Hurlock, 1964; Sullivan, 1953) and researchers (Hartup, 1983; Ladd, 1990) who maintain that peer relationship during school-age years affects child developmental outcome. According to their view, the children's unique social experiences with peers and agents outside of the family unit correspond to non-shared environment, and these are independent of factors influencing trust in parents and siblings. Moreover, these factors are implicated in the development of trust in non-family members. It can be said that children's relationships with their friends are marked by greater reciprocal and intimate properties of affiliation, which makes these experiences important for the acquisition of social skills. Learning to regulate emotions and coordinate activities with others hones competencies to form successful future relationships (Newcomb and Bagwell, 1996).

Harris's (1995) group socialization theory also emphasizes the importance of peer relationships in personality development during childhood. She (Harris, 1995) argued that children learn how to behave outside the home by becoming members of, and identifying with, a social group. Children acquire rules of the groups to which they belong (groups as defined by gender, age, classes at school, clubs, and so on), learn what acceptable behavior is, and how to speak to one another. Thus, it makes sense that peer relationships have an enormous influence over the child during the phase of development when they spend much time with friends. Furthermore, Rotenberg and Morgan (1995) suggested that children in the late elementary school years select friends based on the trust-related behavior (e.g., keep promises, do not lie) of prospective friends. It might be expected that children during these years make friends with those with whom they frequently exchange trust-related interactions. In fact, Ito (2000) showed that children tend to make those who happen to be found in physical proximity their close friends. This sharing of a similar physical environment might explain siblings having common friends.

Based on an integration of the research findings, the current investigation was guided by the expectation that development of a sense of trust in a best friend among children may be affected by an environment shared with siblings or unique to each child. In addition, it was also thought likely that there is still a possibility of genetic effect on the development of a sense of trust found for adults being relevant to children (Shikishima, Hiraishi, and Ando, 2005). This chapter includes a description of two studies designed to examine these expectations.

Study 1

This study is part of a longitudinal twin research project (Sugawara, Sakai, and Maeshiro, 2001) that began in 1999 for families who belong to a nationwide parents' circle for supporting multiple births. In this longitudinal research, the questionnaire surveys were conducted every two years, and families with twins aged between 0 and 15 years responded. Study 1 summarizes results collected from 2001 to 2005, when the twins were in the fourth grade, fifth grade and sixth grade (to 12 years of age).

The twins and mothers received a separate set of questionnaires; they were asked to complete them while not in the presence of others and return them in separate envelopes, provided by the researchers in order to protect their privacy. The total number was 194 pairs of monozygotic twins (MZ) and 127 pairs of dizygotic twins (DZ). Different-gender pairs were excluded from this study. In 1999, the mean age of participating twins' mothers and fathers was 36.17 years ($SD = 3.87$) and 39.16 years ($SD = 4.64$), respectively. Of the mothers surveyed, 78.8 percent had completed some college, and 69.7 percent of fathers had obtained a college degree or higher. The average income of the principal earner of participating families (generally, the father) was 7.34 million yen. While most families considered themselves to belong to the middle class, the participating families had an income slightly higher than the national male average in 1999 (5.67 million yen; National Tax Agency Japan, 2000), and maternal and paternal educational attainment was also slightly higher than the national average from 1975 to 1980 (Ministry of Education, Science, Sports and Culture of Japan, 1981). There were no significant differences between the MZ families and DZ families in parental age (mother: $t[316] = 1.2$, *n.s.*, father: $t[313] = 1.8$, *n.s.*), parental educational attainment (mother: $\chi^2 = .4$, *n.s.*, father: $\chi^2 = .2$, *n.s.*), and family income ($t[300] = 1.1$, *n.s.*). Zygosity was determined using the mother's report of doctor's diagnosis at birth and the questionnaire developed by Ooki, Yamada, Asaka, and Hayakawa (1990). This three-point scale questionnaire consisted of three items assessing the extent of similarity in physical features of the twins and the occurrence of people mistaking one twin for the other. A total score on this scale of five or less was used to categorize the twin to be considered MZ.

Measures

Building on the work of Bowlby (1973) and studies of trust in close relationships (Couch, Adams, and Jones, 1996; Mikulincer, 1998; Rempel, Holmes, and Zanna, 1985), Sakai (2005) developed the Sense of Trust in Significant Others Scale (STS), which assesses children's sense of trust in attachment figures, including parents, best friend, and romantic partner. The STS addresses both the sense of trust or the individual's belief that others do not intend to betray him/her and that others would like him/her to be happy, and the sense of being trusted or the individual's desire not to betray others and to make them happy. The trustworthiness subscales and self-disclosure subscales of the STS were used in the current study to assess children's sense of trust because those were most compatible with other measures of that construct (e.g., Rotenberg, McDougall, Boulton, Vaillancourt, Fox, and Hymel, 2004). Participants were asked to rate on a four-point scale their mother, father, sibling, and best friend on the following four items: (1) Do you think _____ trusts you the most? (2) Does _____ tell you everything? (3) Can you trust _____ more than anyone else? (4) Can you tell _____ everything? The subscale scores were summed to obtain a sense of trust score, with a higher score indicating a greater sense of trust. Principal Component Analysis of these items showed that sense of trust in all attachment figures studied was unidimensional, in that only the first factor had the eigenvalue of greater than one. The first principle component accounted for 58.9 percent of sense of trust in mother, 64.89 percent of sense of trust in father, 72.5 percent of sense of trust in siblings, and 61.6 percent of sense of trust in best friend. Moreover, the correlation between any of the items and the first component was greater than .70. Cronbach's alpha coefficient for the scale of sense of trust in mother, father, sibling, and best friend were .76, .82, .87, and .79, respectively. As the sense of trust score for mother and father had high intercorrelation ($r = .73$), these scores were added to obtain a sense of trust score for parents.

Results

Variations in sense of trust associated with demographic characteristics Two-way analyses of variance (ANOVAs) were conducted to examine individual differences in sense of trust in significant others by gender and zygosity. The results showed the significant main effects of gender on sense of trust in sibling, $F(1,626) = 48.00, p < .01$), and in best friend, $F(1,602) = 8.7, p < .01$. On average, the girls' sense of trust ratings for sibling, $M = 12.3$ ($SD = 3.5$), and best friend, $M = 12.4$ ($SD = 2.7$), were higher than those of boys for sibling, $M = 10.2$ ($SD = 3.8$), and best friend, $M = 11.8$, ($SD = 2.9$). The results also produced a significant main effect for zygosity in sense of trust ratings for siblings, $F(1,626) = 4.7$, $p < .05$. The sense of trust rating of sibling by the MZ twins was higher than that of the DZ twins, as shown in Table 4.1. While some gender differences in sense of trust ratings were observed, the gender effect was not related to the effect of zygosity, $\chi^2 = 2.9$, $n.s.$ Because of this outcome, the following analyses were carried out by collapsing gender categories and focusing on zygosity.

Univariate behavioral genetic analysis When applying the behavioral genetic approach, Mx (Neale, Boker, Xie, and Maes, 2003) was used. The models were fitted to the raw data using the full-information maximum-likelihood estimation, which corrects for statistical biases resulting from missing values. The twin design relies on different levels of genetic relatedness between MZ twin pairs (who share 100 percent of their genes) and DZ twin pairs (who share on average 50 percent of their genes). This difference is used to estimate the contribution of genetic and environmental factors to individual differences in the phenotypes of interest (Plomin, DeFries, McClearn, and McGuffin, 2001), which in this study is the sense of trust in various significant others.

In comparing the fit of the models, first, the standard biometrical twin method (Neale and Cardon, 1992) decomposed the total phenotypic variances of an observed trait into additive genetic (A), shared environmental (C), and non-shared environmental (E) variances. The additive genetic effect is the sum of the average effects of the individual genes. Shared environmental effects refer to the environmental influences that make twin siblings similar, regardless of whether they are MZ or DZ. The correlation between MZ twin pairs is assumed to be due to both additive genetic and shared environmental influences (i.e., A + C). In contrast, since DZ pairs share only half of their genes, the within-pair correlation for DZ twins is assumed to be due to the sum of half the additive genetic effects and the shared environmental factors. Non-shared environmental effects refer to the environmental influences that cause twin pairs to differ from each other after the effects of A and C have been removed. As such, non-shared environmental variance also includes measurement error. The relative contribution of the A, C, and E variance components of sense of trust in significant others (parents, sibling, and best friend)

Table 4.1 *Descriptive statistics, intraclass correlation and univariate model fitting results for sense of trust in significant others (MZ = 194 pairs, DZ = 127 pairs)*

Target	Descriptive Statistics MZ Mean (S.D.)	DZ Mean (S.D.)	Intraclass correlation model MZ	DZ	model	A	C	E	-2LL	df	AIC	-2$_\Delta$LL	$_\Delta$df	p
							Parameter estimate (95% CI)		Model fit			Compared with ACE model		
Parents	24.34 (5.31)	23.96 (5.35)	.65**	.63**	ACE	.05 (.00–.29)	.60 (.38–.70)	.35 (.28–.43)	3681.97	615	2451.97			
					CE	—	.64 (.57–.70)	.36 (.30–.43)	3682.13	616	2450.13	.16	1	.69
					AE	.67 (.60–.73)	—	.33 (.27–.40)	3701.77	616	2469.77	19.80	1	.00
					E			1.00	3843.39	617	2609.39	161.42	2	.00
Sibling	11.63 (3.77)	10.87 (3.75)	.62**	.65**	ACE	.00 (.00–.20)	.63 (.44–.69)	.37 (.30–.44)	3296.37	623	2050.37			
					CE	—	.63 (.56–.69)	.37 (.31–.44)	3296.37	624	2048.37	.00	1	.99>
					AE	.65 (.57–.71)	—	.35 (.29–.43)	3320.31	624	2072.31	23.94	1	.00
					E			1.00	3455.81	625	2205.81	159.44	2	.00
Best friend	12.20 (2.81)	11.98 (2.84)	.29**	.49**	ACE	.00 (.00–.16)	.37 (.21–.47)	.63 (.53–.73)	2931.08	599	1733.08			
					CE	—	.37 (.27–.47)	.63 (.53–.73)	2931.08	600	1731.08	.00	1	.99>
					AE	.37 (.25–.47)	—	.63 (.53–.75)	2942.28	600	1742.28	11.20	1	.00
					E			1.00	2974.09	601	1772.09	43.00	2	.00

Notes: ** p < .01

were estimated in univariate genetic analyses. The significance of the contribution made by each of the three components was examined by comparing fit statistics of three models: (1) additive genetic and both shared and non-shared environmental model (ACE model); (2) shared environment and non-shared environmental model (CE model); and (3) additive genetic and non-shared environmental model (AE model). The fit statistics used were the chi-square index and Akaike's Information Criteria (AIC) (Akaike, 1987). A significant decrease in AIC value when a specific variance component was removed indicated a worse fit.

Intraclass correlation was used to compare sense of trust in various significant others among MZ twins and DZ twins; the result is summarized in Table 4.1. While moderate to high intraclass correlation was found for sense of trust in parents and siblings between both MZ twins and DZ twins, DZ twins showed stronger intraclass correlation for sense of trust in best friend. The model fit comparison (ACE model, CE model, and AE model) summarized in Table 4.1 showed that the CE model, which takes into account shared and non-shared environmental factors, fitted the data the best (that is, the result of χ^2 test is not significant; the value of AIC is the smallest; and the RMSEA value is less than .05). This result can be interpreted to mean that both shared and non-shared environmental factors, but not genetic factors, underlie sense of trust in various significant others. The result also showed that while shared environmental factors accounted for more variance in sense of trust in parents and siblings, sense of trust in best friend was better accounted for by non-shared environmental factors (63 percent; 95 percent CI of 53 to 73 percent) than by shared environmental factors (37 percent; 95 percent CI of 27 to 47 percent). In order to assess more accurately the relative strength of contributions from the two environmental factors, the element of measurement error contained in the variance for the non-shared environment needed to be controlled. Thus, the alpha coefficient value (in this case .79) was subtracted from 1 to estimate the error variance. In this way, the variance attributable to non-shared environment was adjusted to 42 percent (i.e., 63–21=42%) (95 percent CI: 32 to 52 percent). Even with this adjusted estimate, a greater variance of sense of trust rating for best friend is attributable to non-shared environment.

These results of the present study are at odds with the general findings in behavioral genetics studies of intelligence, psychiatric disorders, and personality, which play down the involvement of shared environment while maintaining that these behaviors are the result of genetics and non-shared environment. For example, Turkheimer (2000) noted that the law of behavior genetics posits that while genes are involved in the emergence of phenotypes of individual differences and in the psychological make-up of humans, the impact of shared environment in this is inconsequential. Interestingly, the studies of human relationships and social behavior which have used the behavioral genetic approach reported findings similar to the present study. The above-mentioned study of self-disclosure by school-aged children (Manke and Plomin, 1997) and the studies of attachment in infants (Bokhorst, Bakermans-Kranenburg, Fearon, van Ijzendoorn, Fonagy, and Shuengel, 2003; O'Connor and Croft, 2001) recognized the relatively strong role played by shared environment. It can be said that Study 1 adds to the emerging body of evidence showing the pivotal role played by shared environment in the development of relationship-building capabilities in young children, as evidenced in their sense of trust.

The present study showed that environment also plays a part in development of sense of trust in others outside of family members. While the shared environment accounted for a greater amount of variance in sense of trust for parents and sibling than non-shared environment did, the reverse trend was observed for sense of trust in best friend. This finding is consistent with the findings by Rotenberg and Morgan (1995), which indicated that trust in friends develops through interaction with them.

Thus, this study showed that it is environmental factors rather than genetic factors that affect sense of trust in significant others such as parents, siblings, and best friends. Moreover, the relative contribution coming from shared environment is greater when the object of sense of trust is a family member, while non-shared environment contributes more to explaining sense of trust in non-family members. In the next section, we will examine whether it is the case that the factors affecting sense of trust in parents also influence sense of trust in best friend, or if sense of trust in best friend depends on factors independent of sense of trust in parents.

Multivariate behavioral genetic analysis The degree to which variance in A, C, and E was shared among sense of trust in three types of significant others (parents, sibling, and best friend) was explored using correlation analysis for genetic and environmental factors. These coefficients are estimated by comparing MZ and DZ cross-twin correlations (e.g., between sense of trust in parents in Twin 1 and sense of trust in best friend in Twin 2). If MZ cross-correlations are greater than DZ cross-correlations, then genetic contributions to the covariance of measures are indicated. A standard Cholesky decomposition model (Neale and Cardon, 1992) was used to decompose phenotypic covariances among three variables into genetic and environmental sources.

Table 4.2 *Multivariate model fitting results for sense of trust in significant others (MZ = 194 pairs, DZ = 127 pairs)*

Model	Model fit			Compared with ACE model		
	−2LL	df	AIC	−2$_d$LL	$_d$df	p
Cholesky decomposition full model	9697.73	1837	6023.73			
CE Cholesky decomposition model	9698.70	1843	6012.70	.97	6	.99
Best model: Model dropping paths from C2 to trust in best friend from CE Cholesky decomposition model	9699.83	1844	6011.83	2.10	7	.95

To find out which of the models tested in this study fitted the data the best, we first examined the fit of the full Cholesky model using the Cholesky decomposition method, and then compared it to the model from which the non-significant paths were removed.

To decompose covariance into genetic and environmental components, there must be at least a moderate correlation between the variables of interest at the outset (Pike, McGuire, Hetherington, Reiss, and Plomin, 1996). Phenotypic correlation (correlation between the observed variables) between sense of trust score was as follows: $r = .49$ ($p < .01$) between parents and sibling, $r = .34$ ($p < .01$) between parents and best friend, and $r = .28$ ($p < .01$) between sibling and best friend. The presence of positive significant correlation between sense of trust in family member and in best friend can be interpreted as an indication that there are some common components that contribute to both sense of trust in family members and people outside the family. Cholesky decomposition analysis was conducted to evaluate this interpretation. Cholesky decomposition analysis was applied to the ACE model (i.e., including all three components: genes, shared environment, and non-shared environment) as well as to the CE model (which had the best model fit to the data). The result of this analysis (summarized in Table 4.2) showed that the modified CE model, or the model with only environmental factors, excluding non-significant paths, best explained the data based on the values of χ^2 and AIC.

Figure 4.2 depicts the modified CE model and the relative contributions made by shared and non-shared environment in estimation

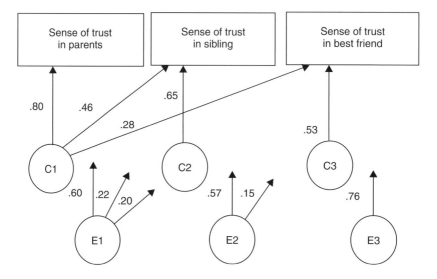

C: Factor arising from shared environment that contributes to sense of
   trust in siginificant others
E: Factor originating from non-shared environment that accounts for
   sense of trust in significant others

Figure 4.2 Multivariate model of best fit, showing shared and
non-shared environmental influences on sense of trust in
significant others

of sense of trust in various significant others. The results showed that
C1 and E1 (i.e., the shared and non-shared environmental factors that
account for the sense of trust in parents) also explained sense of trust
in sibling and best friend. This result is consistent with the IWM in
that environmental factors which contribute to sense of trust in family members were shared with sense of trust in significant others outside of the family environment. The amount of variance explained by
C1, $c^2 = 7.8\%$, is relatively small. However, this shared environmental
contribution requires attention, as Fraley (2002) suggested that shared
environment provides temporal continuity that gives rise to different
attachment types.

Sense of trust in best friend was statistically significantly accounted
for by environmental factors unique to sense of trust in best friend,
$e^2 = 57.8\%$ (i.e., E3 did not account for sense of trust in parents or sibling). Late childhood is a period of time when children spend much of
their time at school, with various others in their environment, and hone

their social skills. In this way, and consequently, the findings yield some support for the conclusion that the unique and non-shared environment exerts a greater effect on trust-related behavior among friends, and this in turn affects development of sense of trust in best friend.

Moreover, the results indicated that shared environment (C3) also played a role in sense of trust in best friend. In considering this result, we need to examine carefully what constitutes shared environment. When the effects of shared environment are found in individual differences in psychological attributes, it is often assumed that shared environment refers to within-family environment. Rutter (2002) cautioned against this assumption. He discussed the studies that examined the effects of genetics and environment on psychological characteristics and pointed out errors in interpretation. One of the sources of errors, he noted, comes from the tendency to use narrow definitions of what is considered to be a shared and non-shared environment. Rutter (2002) argued that shared environment for twins should not be restricted to family environment, but should include all environments that are common for the twins. Many twins attend the same school in Japan, as they both live in the same catchment area for public schools. Almost all the twins in Study 1 (99.4 percent) in fact attended the same school. Furthermore, 80.7 percent of the twins have found their best friend from the school they attended. These statistics show that school environment (not just family environment) is common to twins and thus should be considered part of the shared environment. It appears, therefore, that one needs to be cautious when interpreting findings from behavioral genetic studies, as they often do not specify what constitutes shared environment and non-shared environment. We need to keep in mind that the shared environment may include family as well as non-family elements of twins' environment, and at the same time, that some elements of the family environment may not be shared by the twins.

The present study showed that sense of trust in best friend is statistically accounted for by factors that contribute to sense of trust in parents, but also by factors outside of family environment. Furthermore, siblings may share within the family environment as well as outside of the family environment. The existence of shared environmental factors unique in accounting for sense of trust in best friend arise from the fact that most of the twins attended the same school, had the same, or at least similar, sets of friends, and knew each other's best friends quite well. Before leaving the discussion on this subject, it might be important to view this finding in the context of development rather than focusing only on the fact of being twins. Studies that examined formation of friendship in childhood showed that those who happen to be found in physical proximity tend to become close friends in childhood. In adolescence and beyond, in contrast, those who share the same interests and activities are more likely to become close friends (Ito, 2000). In this way, it might be predicted that the older the twins, the more likely they will acquire close friends through individual differences in preferred activities and values. This trend might then reduce the relevance of shared environment in trust formation with close friends in older children.

The use of the behavioral genetic approach in studying sense of trust in children who are in their late elementary school years and beyond would help us to understand better how children develop in an environment unique to themselves as they grow up. Moreover, we would be able to examine in what ways the environment unique to each child affects how they develop a sense of trust in their significant others. It would be interesting to study twins beyond the age of middle school years and explore how they form a sense of trust with best friend and boyfriend or girlfriend.

Sense of trust as a buffer of life stressors

The previous section examined how sense of trust in significant others within and outside of the family environment develops during the school-age years. The results showed that sense of trust in best friend is accounted for by environmental factors that contribute to family environment. It appears, therefore, that even during the time in child development when time spent with peers increases considerably, children's sense of trust in their parents still makes a major contribution to their trust development in friends and their peer relationships. In what ways, then, does trust in parents influence peer relationships?

In recent years, Japan has seen an increase in depression among children in early adolescence (e.g., Denda, Kako, Sasaki, Ito, Kitagawa, and Koyama, 2004; Tsujii, Yuki, and Honjyo, 1990). This phenomenon has led those involved in psychiatry and education to search for the causes of this unwelcome trend (Murata, Shimizu, Mori, and Oushima, 1996). A number of studies that examined school-age children and their attachment style have shown that secure and stable attachment is associated with lower levels of depression, anxiety (Allen, Moore, Kuperminc, and Bell, 1998; Nada-Raja, McGee, and Stanton, 1992; Papini and Roggman, 1992), and attenuated symptomatic responses to stressful life events (Armsden and Greenberg, 1987). Consistent with these studies, a study that used the STS (Sakai, Sugawara, Maeshiro, Sugawara, and Kitamura, 2002) also found an association between sense of trust in parents and lower level of isolation at school. A good parent–child relationship, characterized by a secure attachment, not only has the main effect of reducing the child's internalizing problems, but also moderates the effects of adverse life events on psychological well-being. Social support studies (Rutter, 1983; Wagner, Cohen, and Brook, 1996) have shown that intimacy with parents and parental care may act as a moderating buffer when children encounter negative life events, and protect them from depression.

One of the factors among many that are considered to be implicated in the onset of childhood depression is negative life events, as is the case in adult depression (Hammen, 1992; Kovacs, 1997). Studies have shown that children are likely to be exposed to a high rate of stressful life events in their network of friends in class and other places where they spend time with peers (Compas, 1987; Seiffge-Krenke, 1995). The Japanese national statistics (Ministry of Education, Culture, Sports, Science and Technology of Japan, 2007) showed that the highest rate of bullying occurs in the first and second years of junior high school. In the study dealing with the relationship between life events and social support of school-age children, there is a tendency to count life events cumulatively and simply represent the total severity of them (Herman-Stahl and Petersen, 1996; Jackson and Warren, 2000). Thus, these studies did not differentiate the types of life events. As a result of this trend, parental support has been identified to have a universal positive effect on a rather broad range of life events. In order to better understand how parental support works to alleviate the effects of negative life events, the types of life events need to be defined more specifically. An examination of peer-related life events that children go through in their late elementary school years to adolescence, and what effect parental support has on these, would be worthwhile, as the risk for childhood depression increases in those years. Explicating how parental support functions to protect children from the effects of life events that happen outside of the family environment will help inform parents and teachers what interventions can be implemented to help youngsters.

Research so far has not examined how children's trust or sense of trust in their parents might protect them from the effects of peer-related negative life events such as bullying. The next study (Study 2) embarked on this topic. The study used a longitudinal design, which allowed us to see the causal relationship between sense of trust, negative life events, and depressive symptoms. The study explored how sense of trust in parents affects change in depressive symptoms when children encounter peer-related negative life experiences.

Previous research has indicated significant gender differences in the effects of social support in early adolescence. This difference has been explained in terms of differences in social support availability for boys and girls. It has been noted that boys are likely to have wider and more extensive social support networks, whereas girls are more likely to have closer and more intimate social support networks (Buhrmester and Furman, 1987). Girls are also more likely than boys to engage in self-disclosure with the source of support, because they tend to expect the source of support to provide them with actual assistance (Belle, Burr, and Cooney, 1987). Gender differences reported in the above studies are likely to be seen in the trust boys and girls have in their parents. Based on the above-mentioned studies, it is hypothesized that girls score higher on the sense of trust scale than boys do. Moreover, the effect of sense of trust in parents on depressive symptoms will be stronger among girls.

Study 2

This study included 184 same-sex twin pairs (115 pairs of MZ and 69 pairs of DZ) who participated in two consecutive questionnaire surveys, two years apart (the study required data to be collected from the same individuals at two data points). Although the individuals in this study were twins, their data were treated as "individual" data rather than "twin" data (i.e., 156 boys and 212 girls). The first data set was obtained from the participants who were in fourth, fifth, sixth, and seventh grades in 2001 (ranging from 9 to 13 years of age), and who were in the sixth, seventh, eighth, and ninth grades in 2003. The second data set was obtained from the participants who were in the fourth, fifth, sixth, and seventh grades in 2003 (ranging from 9 to 13 years of age), and who were in the sixth, seventh, eighth, and ninth grades in 2005, and they were not included in the first set. The current study combined the data of the fourth-, fifth-, sixth-, and seventh-graders in 2001 in the first set with the data of the fourth-, fifth-, sixth-, and seventh-graders in 2003 in the second set, and used them as Time 1 data; and combined the data of the sixth-, seventh-, eighth-, and ninth-graders in 2003 in the first set with the data of the sixth-, seventh-, eighth-, and ninth-graders in 2005 and used them as Time 2 data.

Measures

Depressive symptoms self-rating scale (Time 1 and Time 2)   Depressive symptoms were assessed by the Japanese version (Murata, Shimizu, Mori, and Oushima, 1996) of the Depression Self-Rating Scale for children (DSRS) (Birleson, 1981). The eighteen items of the DSRS describe the signs and symptoms associated with childhood depression. The individuals

Table 4.3 *Gender differences in frequency of events occurring in the last 12 months*

Negative life events	Boys	Girls
Peer-related events		
You were bullied at school.	15 (9.7%)*	22 (10.4%)
You were spoken ill of by your friends behind your back.	19 (12.2%)	34 (16.0%)
You suffered from peer pressure/you were ostracized.	6 (3.8%)	22 (10.4%)
You did something embarrassing and were made fun of at school because of it.	12 (7.7%)	19 (9.0%)
Your best friend made a new friend and did not play with you very often.	12 (7.7%)	38 (18.0%)
You argued with your best friend and did not speak with him/her after that.	8 (5.1%)	41 (19.4%)

Notes: *Number of participants who experienced the event (% of participants in each gender group)

were asked to rate each item to indicate how often they experienced the condition described, using a three-point scale: 2 = "describes me most of the time"; 1 = "describes me some of the time"; 0 = "does not describe me at all." Cronbach's alpha coefficient for the DSRS was .82 for Time 1 and .86 for Time 2.

Life events scale (Time 2) We developed a scale that measures life events in the past year based on the two widely used scales in Japan: Stressful Life Events Scale for Childhood (Kakazu, Nakazawa, Inoue, Toyama, and Shimabukuro, 1997) and the Life Events Scale for Adolescence (Newcomb, Huba, and Bentler, 1981). In this study, we used the items which measure peer-related negative life events in a school context. The examples include "being bullied at school" and "having trouble getting along with best friend at school events." Individuals were asked to rate events on a five-point scale, ranging from 1 for most pleasant to 5 for most unpleasant. The average score for fourteen events was above the mid-point of 3, and thus considered stressful life events. Table 4.3 summarizes the number of participants who experienced the stressful life events defined above. Score on the life events was obtained by aggregating the number of events experienced (a score of 1 was given to the event experienced). Cronbach's alpha coefficient for this scale was .62 for peer-related events.

Sense of trust scale (Time 2) Consistent with Study 1, the STS scale (Sakai, 2005) was used to measure sense of trust in mother and father. As the sense of trust score for mother and father had high intercorrelation ($r = .80$, p < .01), as was the case in Study 1, these scores were added to obtain a sense of trust score for parents. Cronbach's alpha coefficient for this scale was .88.

Results

Gender differences

To examine whether children differed in their depressive symptoms, experience of negative life events, and sense of trust in parents by gender, t-tests were conducted on each of the variables. These analyses revealed a significant gender difference in peer-related events. On average, the girls' rating of the number of events experienced was higher than that of boys, as shown in Table 4.3. Based on the results of preliminary analysis described here, the subsequent analysis was conducted considering gender differences.

Effects of life events and sense of trust in significant others in moderating depressive symptoms

Correlations between depressive symptoms, experience of negative life events, and sense of trust in each significant other is summarized in Table 4.4. The peer-related events were correlated with the depressive symptoms score, and the depressive symptoms score correlated negatively with sense of trust in parents.

In order to examine how sense of trust in parents affects the experience of negative life events, a series of hierarchical multiple regression analyses were conducted. In each of these analyses, gender of the child, zygosity, school grade, and depressive symptoms at Time 1 were entered in Step 1; negative life events and sense of trust in parents were entered in Step 2; the interaction between sex and sense of trust in parents, as well as the interaction between negative life events and sense of trust in parents, were entered in Step 3; and the interaction of sex, negative life events, and sense of trust in parents were entered in Step 4. In order to minimize the problem of multicolinearity, the scores for each variable (except dummy-coded variables such as sex and zygosity and interaction variables) were centered (Aiken and West, 1991). As summarized in Table 4.5, the results showed that there was a statistically significant main effect of sense of trust in parents on change in depressive symptoms. This result is in agreement with previous studies that reported that a close relationship with a supportive parental atmosphere at home diminishes depressive symptoms (Herman-Stahl and Peterson, 1996; Kraaij, Garnefski, Wilde,

Table 4.4 *Correlations among children's depressive symptoms, sense of trust in parents, and peer-related events (N=368)*

	Boys		Girls									
	Mean (S.D.)	n	Mean (S.D.)	n	t-value	1	2	3	4	5	6	
1. Depressive symptoms: Time 2	10.25 (5.96)	149	11.26 (6.67)	207	1.48							
2. Sex (1=Boy, 0=Girl)						-.08 (n=356)						
3. Zygosity (1=MZ[a], 0=DZ[b])						.03 (356)	-.06 (368)					
4. Grade						.16** (356)	-.06 (368)	-.03 (368)				
5. Depressive symptoms: Time 1	10.28 (5.88)	151	10.08 (5.27)	200	.35	.53** (340)	.02 (351)	.02 (351)	.12* (351)			
6. Peer-related events	.46 (.91)	155	.83 (1.21)	208	3.31**	.37** (352)	-.17** (363)	.03 (363)	.05 (363)	.20** (347)		
7. Sense of trust in parents	21.52 (6.25)	153	20.53 (6.68)	208	1.42	-.48** (352)	.08 (361)	-.03 (361)	-.22** (361)	-.36** (345)	-.18** (356)	

Notes: *p<.05; **p<.01
a-b MZ refers to monozygotic twins and DZ refers to dizygotic twins

Table 4.5 *Hierarchical regression analysis for predicting depressive symptoms at Time 2: Main effect and buffering effect of sense of trust in parents on peer-related events (n=333)*

	Depressive symptoms: Time 2							
	Model 1		Model 2		Model 3		Model 4	
Variables	b	β	b	β	b	β	b	β
Step 1								
Sex (1=boy, 0=girl)	−1.25	−.10*	−.34	−.03	−.31	−.02	−.28	−.02
Zygosity (1=MZ, 0=DZ)	.38	.03	.21	.02	.26	.02	.21	.02
Grade	.51	.09	.23	.04	.27	.05	.25	.04
Depressive symptoms: Time 1	.59	.51**	.41	.35**	.41	.35**	.40	.35**
Step 2								
Peer-related events			1.38	.24**	1.30	.23**	1.24	.22**
Sense of trust in parents			−.32	−.32**	−.33	−.33**	−.33	−.33**
Step 3								
Sex × Sense of trust in parents					.04	.03	.06	.04
Peer-related events × Sense of trust in parents					−.07	−.08**	−.09	−.11**
Step 4								
Sex × Peer-related events × Sense of trust in parents							.10	.06
R^2		.28**		.43**		.44**		.44**
R^2 *change*				.15**		.01		.00

Notes: *$p<.05$; **$p<.01$

Dijkstra, Gebhardt, Maes, and Doest, 2003; Sandler, Miller, Short, and Wolchik, 1989).

Because the interaction effect of life events and sense of trust in parents was also significant (Table 4.5), we ran a further analysis in which we forced the regression model to account for Time 2 DSRS scores among those whose sense of trust score varied between 1 standard above or below the mean. This method is consistent with Aiken and West (1991). The analysis conducted this way showed that the effect of peer-related events was negative and significant for children who have low sense of trust in their parents, $b=1.82$, $\beta=.32$, $p<.01$ (see Figure 4.3). Moreover, the effect of

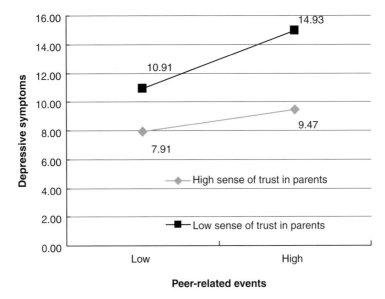

Figure 4.3 Interaction between peer-related events and sense of trust in parents predicting depressive symptoms

peer-related events was not statistically significant among children who had a high sense of trust in their parents, $b = .07$, $\beta = .12$, *n.s.* As is shown in Table 4.5, the interactions including gender did not explain change in depressive symptoms, and thus we conclude that there is no gender difference in the effect of sense of trust on reactions to negative life events.

In this way, the results of this study showed that the sense of trust in parents can function as a buffer against an increase in depressive symptoms when children experience peer-related negative life events, such as being bullied and excluded from a group. While there are not many studies that have looked at the domain-specific effect of parental support on children's reactions to stressful events at school, the one study that did (Gore and Aseltine, 1995) reported that parental support does not protect children from the effects of negative life events at school. Thus, the findings from the present study and Gore and Aseltine (1995) do not agree. The explanation given in Gore and Aseltine (1995) was that at high-school age, the youth may consider family and friends to be separate and independent sets of relationships, and, as such, the effect of social support in one domain (family) does not cross over to the other (friends). This explanation concurs with the stressor-resource matching theory (Cohen and Wills, 1985), which was developed based on adult studies.

One main factor that may account for the discrepancy between this study and Gore and Aseltine (1995) is age. The children in the present study were considerably younger than those in the Gore and Aseltine (1995) study. It can be argued that many children in late childhood and early adolescence are just beginning to start the journey into adulthood, at the onset of puberty and sexual maturity, and they are still in need of adult care and supervision. Thus, it can be said that the present study showed that in early adolescent years, during which the youths are subjected to the increasing power of influence by their peers, parents are still able to provide psychological support to help them deal with peer-related problems. Future studies should examine whose support effectively alleviates the effects of negative life events during different stages of child development by studying children of a wider age range and in various domains of life events. The discrepancy between the studies may also reflect cultural differences. Future studies should examine whether there are cultural differences in terms of who can alleviate the effect of negative life experiences among adolescents.

In the present study, gender difference was not found in the sense of trust score, the main effect of sense of trust on depressive symptoms, or the buffering effect of sense of trust on depressive symptoms. These findings contradict those from previous studies (Belle, Burr, and Cooney, 1987; Buhrmester and Furman, 1987) which found gender difference in social support in late elementary school years to adolescence. This finding of the present study, that parental support is equally important to both genders, may be something that is unique to Japanese parent–child relationships and child-rearing attitudes. This should be investigated further in future studies.

Conclusion

The first study used the genetic behavioral method to examine factors that affect sense of trust in significant others, within and outside the family environment, among children in their late elementary school years. This study showed that sense of trust in parents, siblings, and best friend is accounted for by environmental factors, but not by genetic factors. The study also showed that sense of trust in best friend is accounted for by factors that contribute to family environment, as well as by environmental factors that are unique to individuals. In fact, the latter explained sense of trust in best friend even better than the former. These findings are in agreement with Bowlby's (1973) IWM theory, which emphasizes the importance of child–carer relationships, as well as with theories that underscore the importance of peer relationships in late elementary school years

(Hartup, 1983; Sullivan, 1953). What is more notable in the findings from the first study is that environmental factors have a stronger role to play in sense of trust development than genetic factors. This finding conflicts with the study by Shikishima, Hiraishi, and Ando (2005), which found that general interpersonal trust in others is accounted for by genetic and non-shared environmental factors, but not by shared environment. The two studies differ in terms of: (1) whether the target of trust was a significant other or generalized other; (2) the age of the participants (present study examined children); and (3) the trust scales used to measure trust (present study used STS scale). By taking these differences into account, we might be able to explain the discrepancy in the findings as follows. The shared environment, which would strongly affect trust formation in significant others in early life, may diminish as children grow up and expand their interpersonal relationships outside the home. Increasing multiplicity of relationships and increasing individuation in adolescence then leads children to spend more time in their unique environment, which is not shared with their family. During the period of adolescence and beyond, the genetic influence may increase as children mature and their unique individual characteristics start to become more pronounced. In this way, shared environmental factors may account for trust formation in earlier childhood, while the genetic factors and non-shared environmental factors start to matter increasingly more in children in post-adolescence periods. Future studies should examine the changes in trust formation in children by following them from early adolescence to young adulthood, to explore changes in relative contribution coming from the shared and non-shared environment and genetic factors.

The second study examined how children's sense of trust in their parents may protect them from the adverse effects of negative life events. The study showed that sense of trust in parents has a main effect of lowering the depressive symptoms which may result as a reaction to negative life events. In addition to the main effect, sense of trust in parents also had a buffering effect on reaction to negative life events. Bullying is a widely recognized social problem across a broad range of studies, including in Canada, Norway, the USA, and Japan (Morita, Smith, Junger-Tas, Olweus, Catalano, and Slee, 1999). Given the widespread issues of bullying, it is notable that sense of trust in parents does curb the effect of peer rejection and bullying at school. Adolescent children may be characterized as rebellious, and their strengthening sense of self-identity can make many youths defiant towards adults. While these adolescent symptoms can make maintaining positive relationships with youths difficult, it is important to note that trusting relationships with adults within the home environment can protect them from the risks of psychological maladjustment.

In the second study, the focus was on how parental support can help children experiencing stress stemming from peer relationships (i.e., we focused on the effect of support available outside of the domain of the stressors). Future studies should examine what effect support available in the same domain as the stressors has on the reactions to stress. For example, teachers' support in dealing with peer-related issues would be interesting and worthwhile to examine. We may find that teachers' support also has a buffering effect on peer-related negative events (Torsheim and Wold, 2001). We encourage further expansion of the current studies in order to better understand the role that trust or sense of trust plays in maintaining children's mental health in various circumstances.

References

Aiken, L. S., and West, S. G. (1991). *Multiple regression: Testing and interpreting interactions*. London: Sage.

Ainsworth, M. D. S., Blehar, M. C., Waters, E., and Wall, S. (1978). *Patterns of attachment: A psychological study of the strange situation*. Hillsdale, NJ: Lawrence Erlbaum Associates.

Akaike, H. (1987). Factor analysis and AIC. *Psychometrika*, **52**, 317–332.

Allen, J. P., Moore, C., Kuperminc, G., and Bell, K. (1998). Attachment and adolescent psychosocial functioning. *Child Development*, **69**, 1406–1419.

Allen, J. P., Porter, M., McFarland, C., McElhaney, K. B., and Marsh, P. (2007). The relation of attachment security to adolescents' paternal and peer relationships, depression, and externalizing behavior. *Child Development*, **78**, 1222–1239.

Armsden, G. C. and Greenberg, M. T. (1987). The Inventory of Parent and Peer Attachment: Individual differences and their relationship to psychological well-being in adolescence. *Journal of Youth and Adolescence*, **16**, 427–454.

Belle, D., Burr, R., and Cooney, J. (1987). Boys and girls as social support theorists. *Sex Roles*, **17**, 657–665.

Bernath, M. S. and Feshbach, N. D. (1995). Children's trust: Theory, assessment, development, and research directions. *Applied & Preventive Psychology*, **4**, 1–19.

Birleson, P. (1981). The validity of depressive disorder in childhood and the development of a self-rating scale: A research report. *Journal of Psychology and Psychiatry*, **22**, 73–88.

Bokhorst, C. L., Bakermans-Kranenburg, M. J., Fearon, R. M. P., van Ijzendoorn, M. H., Fonagy, P., and Shuengel, C. (2003). The importance of shared environment in mother–infant attachment security: A behavioral genetic study. *Child Development*, **74**, 1769–1782.

Bowlby, J. (1969). *Attachment and loss: Vol. 1. Attachment*. New York: Basic Books.
    (1973). *Attachment and loss: Vol. 2. Separation: Anxiety and anger*. New York: Basic Books.

Buhrmester, D. and Furman, W. (1987). The development of companionship and intimacy. *Child Development*, **58**, 1101–1113.

Cohen, S. and Wills, T. A. (1985). Stress, social support, and the buffering hypothesis. *Psychological Bulletin*, **2**, 310–357.

Compas, B. E. (1987). Stress and life events during childhood and adolescence. *Clinical Psychology Review*, 7, 275–302.

Couch, L. L., Adams, J. M., and Jones, W. H. (1996). The assessment of trust orientation. *Journal of Personality Assessment*, **67**, 305–323.

Denda, K., Kako, Y., Sasaki, Y., Ito, K., Kitagawa, N., and Koyama, T. (2004). Depressive symptoms in a school sample of children and adolescents: Using the Birleson depression self-rating scale for children (DSRS-C). *Japanese Journal of Child and Adolescent Psychiatry*, **45**, 424–436.

Deutsch, M. (1958). Trust and suspicion. *Journal of Conflict Resolution*, **2**, 265–279.

(1960). Trust, trustworthiness, and the F scale. *Journal of Abnormal and Social Psychology*, **61**, 138–140.

Erikson, E. H. (1963). *Childhood and society* (2nd edn.). New York: W. W. Norton & Company.

Fraley, R. C. (2002). Attachment stability from infancy to adulthood: Meta-analysis and dynamic modeling of developmental mechanisms. *Personality and Social Psychology Review*, **6**, 123–151.

Goodvin, R., Meyer, S., Thompson, R. A., and Hayes, R. (2008). Self-understanding in early childhood: Associations with child attachment security and maternal negative affect. *Attachment & Human Development*, **10**, 433–450.

Gore, S. and Aseltine, H., Jr. (1995). Protective processes in adolescence: Matching stressors with social resources. *American Journal of Community Psychology*, **23**, 301–327.

Gurtman, M. B. (1992). Trust, distrust, and interpersonal problems: A circumplex analysis. *Journal of Personality and Social Psychology*, **62**, 989–1002.

Hammen, C. (1992). Cognitive, life stress, and interpersonal approaches to a developmental psychopathology model of depression. *Development and Psychopathology*, **4**, 189–206.

Harris, J. R. (1995). Where is the child's environment? A group socialization theory of development. *Psychological Review*, **102**, 458–489.

Hartup, W. W. (1983). Peer relations. In P. H. Mussen (series ed.) and E. M. Hetherington (vol. ed.), *Handbook of child psychology: Vol. IV. Socialization, personality, and social development*. New York: Wiley.

Hazan, C. and Shaver, P. (1987). Romantic love conceptualized as an attachment process. *Journal of Personality and Social Psychology*, **52**, 511–524.

Herman-Stahl, M. and Petersen, A. C. (1996). *The protective role of coping and social resources for depressive symptoms among young adolescents*, **25**, 733–753.

Hurlock, E. B. (1964). *Child development*. New York: McGraw-Hill.

Ito, Y. (2000). *The developmental psychology of gender*. Kyoto: Minerva Shobo.

Jackson, Y. and Warren, J. S. (2000). Appraisal, social support, and life events: Predicting outcome behavior in school-age children. *Child Development*, **71**, 1441–1457.

Johnson, S.C., Dweck, C.S., and Chen, F.S. (2007). Evidence for infants' internal working models of attachment. *Psychological Science*, **18**, 501–502.

Kakazu, A., Nakazawa, J., Inoue, A., Toyama, R., and Shimabukuro, T. (1997). Children's life events and psychological stress: Differences between Chiba and Okinawa. *Bulletin of Faculty of Education Center for Educational Research and Development*, **5**, 73–80.

Kendler, K.S. (1996). Parenting: A genetic-epidemiologic perspective. *American Journal of Psychiatry*, **153**, 11–20.

Kovacs, M. (1997). Depressive disorders in childhood: An impressionistic landscape. *Journal of Child Psychology and Psychiatry*, **38**, 287–298.

Kraaij, V., Garnefski, N., Wilde, E.J., Dijkstra, A., Gebhardt, W., Maes, S., and Doest, L. (2003). Negative life events and depressive symptoms in late adolescence: Bonding and cognitive coping as vulnerability factors. *Journal of Youth and Adolescence*, **32**, 185–193.

Ladd, G.W. (1990). Having friends, keeping friends, making friends, and being liked by peers in the classroom: Predictors of children's early school adjustment. *Child Development*, **61**, 1081–1090.

Maccoby, E.E. and Martin, J.A. (1983). Socialization in the context of the family: Parent–child interaction. In P.H. Mussen (series ed.) and E.M. Hetherington (vol. ed.), *Handbook of child psychology: Vol. 4. Socialization, personality, and social development* (4th edn.) (pp. 1–102). New York: Wiley.

MacDonald, K. (1992). Warmth as a developmental construct: An evolutionary analysis. *Child Development*, **63**, 753–773.

Manke, B. and Plomin, R. (1997). Adolescent familial interactions: A genetic extension of the social relations model. *Journal of Social and Personal Relationships*, **14**, 505–522.

Mikulincer, M. (1998). Attachment working models and the sense of trust: An exploration of interaction goals and affect regulation. *Journal of Personality and Social Psychology*, **74**, 1209–1224.

Ministry of Education, Culture, Sports, Science and Technology of Japan (2007). *A survey on all problems in the student education including problematic behavior of children or students*. Retrieved from www.mext.go.jp/b_menu/houdou/21/08/__icsFiles/afieldfile/2009/08/06/1282877_1_1.pdf on January 5, 2010.

Ministry of Education, Science, Sports and Culture of Japan (1981). *The report of School Basic Survey 1980*. Tokyo: National Printing Bureau.

Morita, Y., Smith, P.K., Junger-Tas, J., Olweus, D., Catalano, R., and Slee, P. (eds.) (1999). *Sekai no ijime*. Tokyo: Kaneko Shobou.

Murata, T., Shimizu, A., Mori, Y., and Oushima, S. (1996). Childhood depressive state in the school situation: Consideration from the Birleson's scale. *Japanese Journal of Psychiatry*, **1**, 131–138.

Nada-Raja, S., McGee, R., and Stanton, W.R. (1992) Perceived attachments to parents and peers and psychological well-being in adolescence. *Journal of Youth and Adolescence*, **21**, 471–485.

National Tax Agency Japan, Commissioner's Secretariat Planning Division (2000). The actual state of salary in private sector seen from the taxation statistics: The result report of National Tax Agency statistical survey for actual status for salary in the private sector. Tokyo: Printing Bureau of the Ministry of Finance.

Neale, M. C. and Cardon, L. R. (1992). *Methodology for genetic studies of twins and families*. London: Kluwer Academic Publishers.

Neale, M. C., Boker, S. M., Xie, G., and Maes, H. H. (2003). *Mx: Statistical modeling* (6th edn.). Richmond, VA: Department of Psychiatry. Retrieved from www. vipbg.vcu.edu/~vipbg/software/mxmanual.pdf on January 5, 2010.

Newcomb, A. F. and Bagwell, C. L. (1996). The developmental significance of children's friendship relations. In W. M. Bukowski, A. F. Newcomb, and W. M. Hartup (eds.), *The company they keep:; Friendship in childhood and adolescence*. Cambridge University Press.

Newcomb, M. D., Huba, G. J., and Bentler, P. M. (1981). A multidimensional assessment of stressful life events among adolescents: Derivation and correlates. *Journal of Health and Social Behavior*, **22**, 400–415.

O'Connor, T. G. and Croft, C. M. (2001). A twin study of attachment in preschool children. *Child Development*, **72**, 1501–1511.

Ooki, S., Yamada, K., Asaka, A., and Hayakawa, K. (1990). Zygosity diagnosis of twins by questionnaire. *Acta Geneticae Medicae et Gemellologiae*, **39**, 109–115.

Pike, A., McGuire, S., Hetherington, E. M., Reiss, D., and Plomin, R. (1996). Family environment and adolescent depressive symptoms and antisocial behavior: A multivariate genetic analysis. *Developmental Psychology*, **32**, 590–603.

Plomin, R. (1994). The Emanuel Miller Memorial Lecture 1993: Genetic research and identification of environmental influences. *Journal of Child Psychology and Psychiatry*, **35**, 817–834.

Plomin, R., DeFries, J. C., McClearn, G. E., and McGuffin, P. (2001). *Behavioural genetics* (4th edn.). New York: Worth Publishers.

Raikes, H. A. and Thompson, R. A. (2008). Attachment security and parenting quality predict children's problem-solving, attributions, and loneliness with peers. *Attachment & Human Development*, **10**, 319–344.

Rapaport, A. and Orwant, C. (1962). Experimental games: A review. *Behavioral Science*, **7**, 1–37.

Rempel, J. K., Holmes, J. G., and Zanna, M. P. (1985). Trust in close relationships. *Journal of Personality and Social Psychology*, **49**, 95–112.

Rotenberg, K. J. (1986). Same-sex patterns and sex differences in the trust-value basis of children's friendship. *Sex Roles*, **15**, 613–626.

(1991). Children's cue use and strategies for detecting deception. In K. J. Rotenberg (ed.), *Children's interpersonal trust: Sensitivity to lying, deception, and promise violations* (pp. 43–57). New York: Springer-Verlag.

Rotenberg, K. J. and Morgan, C. J. (1995). Development of a scale to measure individual differences in children's trust-value basis of friendship. *Journal of Genetic Psychology*, **156**, 489–502.

Rotenberg, K. J. and Pilipenko, T. A. (1983–1984). Mutuality, temporal consistency, and helpfulness in children's trust in peers. *Social Cognition*, **2**, 235–255.

Rotenberg, K. J., McDougall, P., Boulton, M. J., Vaillancourt, T., Fox, C., and Hymel, S. (2004). Cross-sectional and longitudinal relations among relational trustworthiness, social relationships, and psychological adjustment during childhood and adolescence in the UK and Canada. *Journal of Experimental Psychology*, **88**, 46–67.

Rutter, M. (1983). Stress, coping, and development: Some issues and some questions. In N. Garmezy and M. Rutter (eds.), *Stress, coping, and development in children*. New York: McGraw-Hill.

   (2002). Nature, nurture, and development: From evangelism through science toward policy and practice. *Child Development*, **73**, 1–21.

Sakai, A. (2005). *Development of sense of trust: From childhood to adolescence*. Tokyo: Kawashima Shoten.

Sakai, A., Sugawara, M., Maeshiro, K., Sugawara, K., and Kitamura, T. (2002). Parent–child relations of mutual trust, trust in one's best friend, and school adjustment: Junior high school students. *Japanese Journal of Educational Psychology*, **50**, 12–22.

Sandler, I. N., Miller, P., Short, J., and Wolchik, S. A. (1989). Social support as a protective factor for children in stress. In D. Belle (ed.), *Children's social support*. New York: John Wiley & Sons.

Seiffge-Krenke, I. (1995). *Stress, coping, and relationships in adolescence*. Mahwah, NJ: Lawrence Erlbaum Associates.

Selman, R. L. and Selman, A. P. (1979). Children's ideas about friendship: A new theory. *Psychology Today*, October, 71–80.

Shikishima, C., Hiraishi, K., and Ando, J. (2005). Genetic and environmental influences on general trust: A test of a theory of trust with behavioral, genetic and evolutionary psychological approaches. *Research in Social Psychology*, **22**, 48–57.

Sroufe, L. A. (1990). An organizational perspective on the self. In D. Cicchetti and M. Beeghly (eds.), *The self in transition: Infancy to childhood* (pp. 281–307). University of Chicago Press.

Sugawara, M., Sakai, A., and Maeshiro, K. (2001). *Developmental psychopathology: A behavioural genetic approach*. Poster presented at meeting of 10th International Congress on Twin Studies, London, July.

Sullivan, H. S. (1953). *The interpersonal theory of psychiatry*. New York: W. W. Norton & Company.

Torsheim, T. and Wold, B. (2001). School-related stress, school support, and somatic complaints. *Journal of Adolescent Research*, **16**, 293–303.

Tsujii, M., Yuki, J., and Honjyo, S. (1990). A study on depression with normal population in childhood and adolescence. *Bulletin of the Faculty of Education, Nagoya University (Educational Psychology)*, **37**, 129–139.

Turkheimer, E. (2000). Three laws of behavior genetics and what they mean. *Current Directions in Psychological Science*, **9**, 160–164.

Wagner, B. M., Cohen, P., and Brook, J. (1996). Parent/adolescent relationships: Moderators of the effects of stressful life events. *Journal of Adolescent Research*, **11**, 347–374.

Waters, E., Vaughn, B. E., Posada, G., and Kondo-Ikemura, K. (eds.) (1995). Caregiving, cultural, and cognitive perspectives on security-based behavior and working models. *Monographs of the Society for Research in Child Development*, **60** (2–3, Serial No. 244).

Section II

Childhood

5 Young children's trust in what other people say

Kathleen Corriveau (Harvard University) and
Paul L. Harris (Harvard University)

Young children's trust in what other people say

When we trust someone in the context of a close relationship, we expect them to act in a thoughtful, sensitive fashion. For example, we expect them to keep their promises, to provide help and solace when asked to do so, and to be discreet if we confide in them. In a series of studies, Rotenberg and his colleagues have shown that children vary in the expectations that they routinely bring to close interpersonal relationships, such as friendships with peers. Some children are unduly optimistic about other children's interpersonal trustworthiness, some are unduly pessimistic, and some strike more of balance between optimism and realism. In this chapter, we focus on a potentially related but different aspect of trust – on epistemic trust rather than interpersonal trust. As adults, we are often aware of our own lack of expertise or information on a given topic and we turn to others for guidance. For example, we seek information about medical, financial, and culinary matters, to name but a few areas. Yet we also recognize that individuals differ in the extent to which they provide reliable and accurate information: some informants are more trustworthy than others – in this epistemic sense.

It could be argued that interpersonal trust and epistemic trust are simply two different aspects of the same package. For example, if we are prepared to share private information about ourselves with someone – to trust them interpersonally – we are also often willing to trust and act on the advice that they offer – to trust them epistemically. The image of the trusted family doctor typically includes both interpersonal and epistemic aspects. He or she is a person to whom we confide, but also an expert whose medical advice we trust. Yet there are clearly cases where the adherence – or non-adherence – of a particular informant to the norms that apply to close interpersonal relationships does not affect our judgments of the person's epistemic trustworthiness. Consider our preferences among cookery writers. The extent to which a given chef is trustworthy in interpersonal relations need not concern us here. For all we know or care, Gordon Ramsay might be a sweet-tempered angel and Nigella Lawson might be a tyrant. When we look to them for culinary advice, the key issue is which person will give us a reliable recipe for osso buco, and not whom we would be willing to confide in. So, although there are certainly occasions when interpersonal and epistemic considerations overlap, as in the case of the family doctor, this overlap between the epistemic and the interpersonal is contingent rather than necessary. The two dimensions of trustworthiness are empirically separable. A bank manager might offer eminently trustworthy financial advice, but still divulge our secrets to the tax inspector. Conversely, even if we confide our financial woes to a best friend, we might still ignore their well-intentioned advice when it comes to deciding where to invest.

In short, it is a mistake, and sometimes a costly one, to assume that a person's trustworthiness in the interpersonal domain is a guide to their trustworthiness in the epistemic domain, and vice versa. That certainly does not mean that children always distinguish appropriately between the two domains. Indeed, as we shall discuss, there is some evidence that young children fail to make that distinction – they are inclined to extrapolate from the interpersonal to the epistemic. Nevertheless, from a conceptual standpoint, interpersonal trustworthiness is not the same as epistemic trustworthiness. In the next section, we consider the epistemic domain in more depth.

Children's epistemic dependence

It is evident that young children are highly dependent on other people in learning about the world. There are many areas – such as history, science, and religion – where it is difficult for them to gather the relevant information from their own first-hand observations. For example, children cannot ordinarily observe historical events and figures for themselves. They rely on parents and teachers to supply them with relevant information. It is interesting to note that such trust in the information provided by other people does not have a very respectable epistemological pedigree. Instead, philosophers have often emphasized the need for knowers to gather and check information for themselves. Trusting others is seen as lazy, or even risky. This emphasis on the need for knowers to be autonomous rather than dependent on others is especially evident in early, classic writings on cognitive development. For example, Rousseau (1762/1957) counselled against answering a pupil's questions. The learner, he alleged, should be encouraged to seek out his own answers:

To nourish his curiosity, never hasten to satisfy it ... Ask questions that he can handle and leave them to him to resolve. Let him not know anything because you have told him but rather because he has understood it for himself: Let him not learn science, let him invent it. If you ever substitute authority for reason in his mind, he will no longer reason; he will only be the plaything of other people's opinions.

This same emphasis on the need for cognitive autonomy is apparent in much of Piaget's writings. He was dubious about whether children's questions were truly intended to gather valuable information, and he asserted that children who learned on the basis of other people's say-so – as opposed to their own active exploration and observation – were prone to "verbalism," a superficial rather than a deep understanding of the phenomenon in question. English educators, such as Nathan and Susan Isaacs, who were markedly influenced by Piaget's theory, followed his guidelines. Wherever possible, they sought to encourage children to find their own answers to the questions that they posed. Indeed, teachers in their progressive, experimental school, Malting House in Cambridge, were discouraged from answering pupils' questions directly (Isaacs, 1930).

Still, it is important to recognize that children and adults very often do trust the information that other people provide, and they could scarcely survive if they did not do so (Harris and Koenig, 2006). We rely on others to tell us important facts about ourselves – for example, when and where we were born. We rely on them to tell us about historical events, to tell us about contemporary events outside of our immediate ken, and to introduce us to the many claims of science and technology. Neither as children nor as adults could we gather this vast harvest of information via our own first-hand observation. In recognition of our wide-ranging dependence on what other people tell us, philosophers have recently taken an increasing interest in our wide-ranging trust in the information that we acquire from other people, and in its epistemic status (Coady, 1992; Lackey, 2008).

In this chapter, we look at the origins of such epistemic trust. In Part I, we ask if young children are selective about their informants – do they trust the claims of some informants more than others or are they indiscriminately credulous? In Part II, we ask whether young children are prone to trust people who are in agreement with one another – even in cases where that consensus flies in the face of what children would conclude if left to their own devices. Finally, in Part III, we seek to draw the various empirical studies together in a speculative discussion of how children weigh various different indices of epistemic trustworthiness. We conclude, contrary to the Rousseau-Piaget tradition, that cognitive autonomy – a distrust of the testimony provided by others – is problematic for cognitive development. Trust in the claims made by other people is warranted, particularly when it provides children with access to expert information that has been accumulated over generations.

Part I: Selective trust or indiscriminate credulity? Trust in familiar informants

From birth, infants show a preference for the familiar. They prefer familiar faces (such as the face of their mother) to faces of strangers. They prefer infant-directed speech when spoken in their native tongue over infant-directed speech in other languages. More generally, by 9 months, infants show a bias to familiar markers such as race, language, and so on (Kinzler, Dupoux, and Spelke, 2007). Does this preference for the familiar affect children's decisions about which informants to trust? We explored this question in two experiments. First, we asked whether children prefer the information provided by their mother rather than a stranger, and whether this preference for the mother varies as a function of their mother–infant attachment relationship. Next, we explored children's trust in familiar caregivers more generally, by asking if they prefer information from a preschool teacher whom they had frequently met before, as compared to an unfamiliar preschool teacher.

In our first study, we presented 4- and 5-year-old children with a variety of novel objects – for example, an unfamiliar tool from the hardware store – and asked their mother and a stranger to supply conflicting names (Corriveau, Harris, Meins, Fernyhough, Arnott, Elliott, Liddle, Hearn, Vittorini, and de Rosnay, 2009). Children were then invited to say which name they thought the object was called. Not surprisingly, children typically showed a preference for the names supplied by their mother, choosing the name that she had provided 65 percent of the time.

However, this preference for the information provided by the mother varied in strength depending on the perceptual features of the object. In addition to the unfamiliar items from the hardware store, we also presented children with pictures of two types of hybrid creatures created by Jaswal (2004). Each picture combined features of two animals – for example, a rabbit and a squirrel. As can be seen from inspection of Figure 5.1, the hybrids were either symmetric – equally resembling both creatures (e.g., a cow and a horse) – or asymmetric – mostly resembling one creature (e.g., a squirrel), but with some features belonging to the other creature (e.g., a rabbit).

When the hybrid pictures were asymmetric, the mother named the creature with the less likely name – "rabbit" – whereas the stranger named it with the more likely name – "squirrel." When the hybrid pictures were symmetric, so that the perceptual evidence was equally consistent with both names, children once again displayed a preference for the name provided by the mother, choosing her 62 percent of the time. However, in the asymmetric condition, when the mother provided a name that was less consistent with the perceptual information, trust in the mother was

(a)

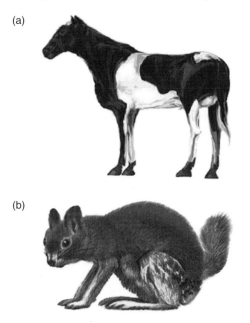

(b)

Figure 5.1 Examples of the (a) symmetric hybrids (cow-horse) and (b) asymmetric hybrids (squirrel-rabbit)

undermined. Under these circumstances, children endorsed the name supplied by the mother only 43 percent of the time, preferring instead to endorse the name supplied by the stranger, which was more consistent with the overall appearance of the hybrid.

Overall, this experiment suggested that children use two strategies: when the perceptual evidence is equally consistent with either name, as was the case for the novel items from the hardware store and the symmetric hybrids, children preferentially accept their mother's claim; when the perceptual evidence is less consistent with their mother's claim, as was the case for the asymmetric hybrids, children are inclined to reject that name and to favor the name supplied by the stranger, which is more consistent with the perceptual evidence. This flexible approach – sometimes relying on a trusted informant, sometimes relying on the perceptual evidence – makes good, adaptive sense. If children lack any basis for judgment, they would do well to turn to a familiar informant, such as their mother, for guidance. On the other hand, if most of the available information points to a different conclusion, they would do well to accept that conclusion, even if it goes against what a familiar informant says.

As a further probe of children's pattern of trust in the information provided by their mother, we subdivided them according to the type of attachment that children had with their mother. Children's attachment had been assessed in the conventional way, namely on the basis of their behavior in the strange situation when they were 15 months old. At that point, most of the children (65 percent) had been classified as securely attached. According to attachment theory (Ainsworth, Blehar, Waters, and Wall, 1978), secure children are characterized both by their ability to gain reassurance from their mother's availability when they are apprehensive or uncertain, and by their willingness to engage in sensorimotor exploration of the world around them. Thus, they are quite flexible – sometimes turning to their mother for reassurance, but also capable of using her as a secure base and engaging in independent observation. In broad terms, secure children displayed a similar pattern of flexibility in our study (see Figure 5.2). More specifically, they were likely to be guided by their mother when they experienced uncertainty in the face of ambiguous perceptual evidence – as in the case of the novel objects and the symmetric hybrids. On the other hand, they were more likely to register and be guided by the perceptual evidence when it ran counter to the name supplied by their mother – as in the case of the asymmetric hybrids.

According to attachment theory, insecure children are less flexible than secure children. Insecure-ambivalent children seek reassurance from their mother, but are less likely than secure children to engage in exploration. Insecure-avoidant children, by contrast, engage in exploration but, unlike secure children, rarely seek or gain reassurance from their mother. Interestingly, we observed similar patterns of inflexibility with respect to children's epistemic trust. Ambivalent children behaved like secure children for the novel hardware items and for the symmetric

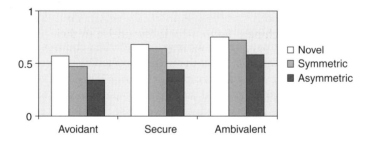

Figure 5.2 Proportion of trials on which children chose their mother by task and attachment group compared to chance performance

hybrids – they trusted their mother. However, for the asymmetric hybrids such as the squirrel-rabbit, they responded differently from secure children. Even if it was supported by more of the perceptual evidence, they showed no tendency to favor the claim made by the stranger. Avoidant children, by contrast, showed no systematic preference for their mother's claims, even in the case of the novel hardware items or the symmetric hybrids. On the other hand, like the secure children, they mistrusted her input in the context of the asymmetric hybrids – when the evidence ran counter to the mother's claim. Thus, both groups of insecure children were less likely to adjust their strategy as compared to secure children. The ambivalent children had difficulty in distancing themselves from their mother's input, even when the perceptual evidence suggested that it was appropriate to do so. The avoidant children showed no systematic preference for her input, even in circumstances where there was no countervailing perceptual evidence.

Why exactly did children's attachment status influence the pattern of epistemic trust that they displayed in the information supplied by their mother? Classic attachment theory implies that infants and young children seek out their mother primarily in the context of emotional distress – they turn to her for comfort and reassurance. Our results suggest, however, that, depending on the nature of their attachment, children also turn to their mother for information or guidance when faced with perceptual uncertainty. There are two ways in which this parallel between comfort-seeking and information-seeking might come about.

One possibility is that mothers who are sensitive and responsive to their child's emotional needs are also sensitive to the child's epistemic needs. For example, a mother who attends promptly to her infant's signals of distress, such as crying and whimpering, might also be the kind of mother who responds promptly to her infant's "social referencing" – the inquiring glances that her infant makes towards her when confronted by a novel or ambiguous situation (Ainsworth, 1992). Thus, infants might learn that an attachment figure who is responsive to their bids for emotional reassurance is equally responsive to bids for epistemic guidance. A second possibility is that – notwithstanding the conceptual distinction between interpersonal trust and epistemic trust set out at the beginning of the chapter – infants treat them as a package. They assume that someone who is trustworthy in the context of a close, interpersonal relationship is also trustworthy in the epistemic domain. In due course, when we consider young children's sensitivity to the accuracy of their informants, we will return to the question of whether young children differentiate between interpersonal and epistemic trustworthiness.

In our second study (Corriveau and Harris, 2009b), we again showed preschool children novel objects. However, in this study, children received conflicting input from a familiar teacher working in their preschool and an unfamiliar teacher working in a different but comparable preschool. The study was run in each preschool so that, for half the children, teacher A was familiar and teacher B was unfamiliar, whereas for the other half, teacher A was unfamiliar and teacher B was familiar. Again, we found a preference for the information supplied by the familiar informant. This preference emerged in both preschools and across all three age groups tested, with 3-, 4-, and 5-year-olds preferring the information provided by the familiar informant 68 percent, 64 percent, and 78 percent of the time, respectively.

The consistent preference for a familiar informant underlines the paradoxical response of the insecure-avoidant children described earlier. Recall that even though a highly familiar person, namely their mother, supplied them with names for unfamiliar objects, avoidant children showed no preference for the name supplied by their mother as compared to the one supplied by a stranger. By implication, mere familiarity with an informant is not sufficient to elicit trust. The quality of the relationship is also critical. According to attachment theory, insecure-avoidant children come to the conclusion that their mother is not emotionally available and responsive to their needs. By contrast, when we interviewed them, the teachers at the two preschools claimed to have a warm, non-conflictual relationship with most of the children in their charge, consistent with the level of trust that they elicited from them.

Summing up across these two studies, it is evident that young children are not indiscriminate in their choice of informants. They prefer information from people who are familiar to them – for example, their mother and their preschool teacher. The one dramatic exception to this generalization is the case of avoidant children. That exception underlines the conclusion that familiarity per se is insufficient to elicit trust – it only does so when it is associated with a positive stance towards the person in question. When it is associated with the deliberate distancing behaviors that are characteristic of avoidant attachment, selective trust is not observed. The familiar informant is trusted no more than a stranger.

Trust in accurate informants

Children's sensitivity to the familiarity of an informant, or more precisely to the *quality* of their relationship with a familiar informant, suggests the possibility that they select among informants primarily on the basis of socio-emotional rather than cognitive factors. As just noted, such findings are consistent with the possibility that preschool children generalize from a person's trustworthiness in the context of a close, interpersonal relationship to their trustworthiness in the epistemic domain.

However, several recent studies suggest that preschoolers also pay close attention to an informant's past record in the epistemic domain. More specifically, if one informant has made obvious errors in naming familiar objects, whereas another informant has named them correctly, 3- and 4-year-olds are more likely to seek and accept information about the names, and indeed the functions, of unfamiliar objects from the hitherto accurate informant (Birch, Vauthier, and Bloom, 2008; Clément, Koenig, and Harris, 2004; Corriveau and Harris, 2009b; Jaswal and Neely, 2006; Koenig and Harris, 2005; Koenig, Clément, and Harris, 2004; Pasquini, Corriveau, Koenig, and Harris, 2007).

Two further aspects of this basic phenomenon have recently been established. First, preschoolers' monitoring of informant accuracy appears to be spontaneous rather than something they need to be prompted to engage in. In some studies, children have been explicitly questioned about which of the two informants named objects accurately, possibly sensitizing them to variation between the informants. In other studies, however, children were not explicitly questioned about the informants' accuracy, or were only questioned at the end of the experiment (Birch, Vauthier, and Bloom, 2008; Corriveau and Harris, 2009a). In either case, children proved sensitive to prior accuracy, as reflected in their selective trust in the more accurate informant.

The second finding is that not only do children spontaneously attend to and utilize accuracy information, they retain and use that information for some time. For example, when 3- and 4-year-olds returned for further test trials 4 days after they had first encountered the differential accuracy of two informants, they still displayed preferential trust in the more accurate informant on those delayed trials. Indeed, when children returned approximately one week later, they still displayed more trust in the previously accurate informant (Corriveau and Harris, 2009a). Taken together, these two findings suggest that accuracy monitoring is a robust strategy among preschoolers. It is not something that they need to be coaxed into via explicit questioning about informant accuracy, nor is it a transient phenomenon – children encode and act on an informant's prior accuracy several days later.

How do children weigh familiarity and accuracy?

The previous two sections have demonstrated that children trust familiar informants with whom they have a positive, non-avoidant relationship over strangers, and they also trust more accurate informants over inaccurate informants. It could be argued that these two aspects of epistemic trust are causally related. For example, it is plausible that children typically find that a familiar informant makes accurate rather than inaccurate claims. Therefore, faced with a choice between a familiar informant and a stranger, they invest greater trust in the familiar person because they know that that person has a history of prior accuracy, whereas they have no information about the stranger's past accuracy. Although this interpretation can explain most of the data just reviewed, there is one outstanding problem. Recall that children with an insecure-avoidant relationship towards their mother did not favor the information that she supplied over that supplied by a stranger – in contrast to secure and insecure-ambivalent children, who generally favored their mother. Although there is good evidence that mothers of insecure-avoidant children are less emotionally available, it is doubtful that they make more inaccurate claims than other mothers. For example, we can reasonably assume that they name common objects accurately. Granted the vast number of accurate claims that all mothers routinely make in the course of everyday life, it is unlikely that any differences among mothers in their perceived trustworthiness is due to variation in their history of accuracy.

To the extent that children can independently monitor their relationship to an informant as well as his or her past record of accuracy – treating them as potentially distinct aspects of the person – we may ask what children do when those cues are placed in conflict with one another. In particular, what stance do they adopt towards a familiar informant who proves vulnerable to error, or an unfamiliar informant who proves to be accurate?

To examine this issue, we engaged in additional testing of the preschoolers at the two preschools mentioned earlier. We knew that they preferred to gather information from whichever teacher was familiar to them, but what would happen if one of the two teachers proved to be inaccurate? Following the initial test trials with unfamiliar objects described above, half the children received four "accuracy/inaccuracy" trials, in which the teacher who was familiar to them named a well-known object such as a ball correctly, whereas the unfamiliar teacher named it incorrectly. The remaining children received the reverse arrangement: four "accuracy/inaccuracy" trials in which the familiar teacher was inaccurate and the unfamiliar teacher was accurate. Finally, all children received four additional test trials in which the two teachers provided conflicting names for unfamiliar objects, just as they had done in the first set of test trials. This enabled us to examine whether preschoolers' initial trust in a familiar informant is tempered by subsequent accuracy/inaccuracy information.

The results are shown in Figure 5.3, which indicates the proportion of test trials in which children trusted the familiar teacher as a function of

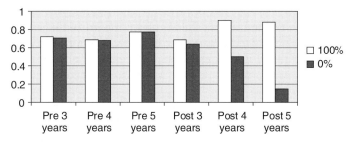

Figure 5.3 Proportion of choices directed at the more familiar teacher by age, type of trial (pre-test versus post-test), and type of accuracy experience (familiar = 100 percent accurate versus familiar = 0 percent accurate)

age, type of test trial (before versus after the accuracy/inaccuracy trials), and type of accuracy/inaccuracy trials (familiar accurate + unfamiliar inaccurate versus familiar inaccurate + unfamiliar accurate). Scrutiny of the pre-test trials – those that took place before the provision of any accuracy information – confirms that children in all three age groups preferred the more familiar teacher. Moreover, they did so irrespective of whether she was destined to prove accurate or inaccurate.

There was a marked age change in the post-test trials: 3-year-olds were scarcely affected by the relative accuracy information; 4-year-olds displayed a modest impact, preferring the familiar teacher even more if she had proven accurate, but showing no preferential trust in her if she had not; 5-year-olds displayed a more potent impact, showing a marked preference for the familiar teacher if she had proven accurate, but considerable mistrust of her (and a preference for the unfamiliar teacher) if she had proven inaccurate.

Why does children's sensitivity to accuracy information increase with age? In particular, why were 3-year-olds so little affected by accuracy information about their preschool teacher? For the moment, we suspect that two factors are involved – the "protective" role of a positive attachment for younger children, and their ability to code not just inaccuracy but also accuracy. We consider each factor in turn.

As discussed earlier, when 3-year-olds are presented with new and hitherto unfamiliar informants, they rapidly encode information about their relative accuracy and display selective trust in the more accurate of the two unfamiliar informants. Moreover, this appraisal endures in the sense that 3-year-olds, as well as 4-year-olds, continue to display selective trust in light of it several days and even a week later (Corriveau and Harris,

2009a). By implication, having a prior relationship with an informant helps to protect or immunize children from the impact of relative accuracy. Thus, 3-year-olds, unlike 5-year-olds, overlook or filter out the mistakes that a familiar informant makes, especially if it is someone who is personally known to them – such as a familiar preschool teacher – rather than a stranger.

Still, other findings point to an additional factor that likely contributes to the age change. When children meet two unfamiliar informants – one who names objects accurately and one who names them inaccurately – how do they end up differentiating between them? One possibility is that they increasingly come to mistrust the inaccurate informant; a second possibility is that they increasingly come to trust the accurate informant; still a third possibility is that both of these processes operate more or less concurrently. To examine these various alternatives, 3- and 4-year-olds were tested under three different conditions (Corriveau, Meints, and Harris, 2009). In the accuracy-inaccuracy condition, children heard one informant consistently name objects accurately and the other name them inaccurately. In the accurate-neutral condition, one informant consistently named objects accurately, whereas the other made a neutral remark – for example, "Let me look at that." Finally, in the inaccurate-neutral condition, one informant consistently named objects inaccurately, whereas the other made a neutral remark. Our aim was to assess how far children monitored for accuracy, for inaccuracy, or for both.

In the subsequent test trials, children's pattern of trust varied both by condition and age, as can be seen in Figure 5.4. In the accurate-inaccurate condition, both age groups were more likely to trust the accurate informant, although this effect was stronger for 4-year-olds than for 3-year-olds. This finding is consistent with previous studies showing that when they meet two unfamiliar informants, both 3- and 4-year-olds

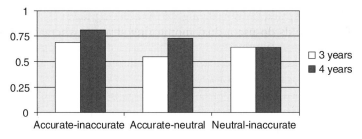

Figure 5.4 Proportion of choices directed at the more trustworthy informant by age and condition

trust an accurate informant rather than an inaccurate informant, and that the effect is more robust among 4-year-olds than 3-year-olds. In the neutral-inaccurate condition, both age groups were likely to trust the neutral informant more than the inaccurate informant and did so to the same extent. In the accurate-neutral condition, only the 4-year-olds were selective, showing greater trust in the accurate informant. By contrast, 3-year-olds were indiscriminate between the two informants.

A simple and plausible explanation for this pattern of results is that 3-year-olds monitor for inaccuracy but not for accuracy. Errors reduce their trust in an informant, but accuracy does not increase it. Thus, in the two conditions where one of the two informants clearly made errors (accurate-inaccurate, neutral-inaccurate), 3-year-olds preferred to trust the informant who had not been inaccurate. By contrast, 4-year-olds monitor for both inaccuracy and accuracy. Inaccuracy reduces their trust in an informant, but, in addition, accuracy increases it. Thus, when both cues are available, as in the accurate-inaccurate condition, their differentiation between the two informants is maximized; when only one cue is available, they are selective, but less markedly so.

Why might 4-year-olds differ from 3-year-olds in displaying dual monitoring of both accuracy and inaccuracy? A plausible interpretation is that 4-year-olds realize that accurate claims should not be taken for granted – informants do sometimes make false claims, so an informant who is accurate should thereby earn trust. Arguably, this realization is facilitated by children's developing insight into false beliefs, an insight that improves markedly between 3 and 4 years (Wellman, Cross, and Watson, 2001). Thus, 4-year-olds, realizing that people often have false beliefs and end up making false claims, will be less likely than 3-year-olds to take true claims for granted. They will be more alert to the possibility that an informant will say something false. Hence, not only will they build up mistrust in an inaccurate informant as 3-year-olds do, they will also build up trust in an accurate informant – giving the informant credit, so to speak, for not having said something false.

If 4-year-olds do use a dual monitoring strategy whereas 3-year-olds monitor for inaccuracy only, the preference for the more trustworthy informant should be stronger among 4-year-olds. This age difference in the accurate-inaccurate condition is evident in Figure 5.5. Although both age groups invested greater trust in the more trustworthy informant, that preference is more pronounced among 4-year-olds. This observed age difference also corresponds to the pattern of results obtained by Pasquini, Corriveau, Koenig, and Harris (2007) in an earlier study using similar methods.

Returning, then, to the pattern of selective trust following accuracy information about familiar informants, it is likely that two factors are at work. Although 3-year-olds monitor for inaccuracy – and take accuracy for granted – they also overlook or discount errors made by an informant whom they know personally. By contrast, 4- and 5-year-olds monitor for both accuracy and inaccuracy, and they do so with respect to both familiar and unfamiliar informants. Thus, when older preschoolers are deciding whom to trust, information about past accuracy and inaccuracy "trumps" familiarity information.

More broadly, the age changes evident in Figures 5.3 and 5.4 suggest that the relationship between interpersonal trust and epistemic trust gradually changes in the preschool years. Among 3-year-olds, interpersonal trust based on a positive relationship with a familiar informant guides their decisions in the epistemic domain, even in the face of negative feedback about the epistemic reliability of that person. By contrast, older preschoolers appraise even familiar informants in light of their record of accuracy or inaccuracy. They accept the claims of a stranger over those of a familiar informant if the former has proved more accurate.

Part II: Sensitivity to agreement and disagreement group effects

So far, we have asked about children's trust in individual informants who vary in terms of their relationship to the child or their history of accuracy. However, children do not always obtain information by focusing on a single individual. Indeed, there are many instances in which information about the potential epistemic trustworthiness of an informant is not available to children. Under these circumstances, they can seek or gather information from several informants, monitoring whether those informants are in agreement with one another or not. For example, informants may or may not agree about the name or identity of a given object. Are children attentive to such variation? In particular, do they trust an informant whose claims are endorsed by other people? To examine this issue, 4-year-olds were presented with two informants who provided conflicting names for novel objects (Fusaro and Harris, 2008). Two bystanders greeted the names provided by one informant with assent – they smiled and nodded their heads. The same two bystanders greeted the names provided by the other informant with dissent – they frowned and shook their heads. Children were then consulted and asked which name they thought was correct. Both age groups differentiated very sharply between the two informants. They endorsed the apparently more reliable informant on just over 90 percent of the trials. By implication, children noticed, and were markedly influenced by, the reactions of the bystanders in what was otherwise an ambiguous situation, because the objects themselves offered no clue as to which of the conflicting names was correct.

In the next phase of the study, the two bystanders withdrew and testing continued as before, with the two informants providing conflicting names for novel objects. Considered as a group, children continued to place more trust in the informant who had previously attracted bystander assent. However, some interesting individual differences emerged. Children had been given a test of mental state understanding and were divided into two groups – those with high and low scores. High scorers showed a marked preference for the informant who had previously received bystander assent – they accepted the names she offered at virtually the same high rate as before (89 percent). By contrast, low scorers showed only a non-significant trend towards a greater preference for the previously endorsed informant (57 percent).

What was it about children's mental state understanding that accounted for this difference? High scorers showed an understanding of false beliefs, whereas low scorers did not. This difference fits the analysis above concerning the sensitivity of 4-year-olds (but not of 3-year-olds) to the possibility that an informant deserves credit for being right. The 4-year-olds who understood that someone might hold a false belief treated the bystanders' assent as a kind of extended warranty or character reference. They construed the bystanders as saying: "This informant gets things right." The remaining 4-year-olds – those who did not understand that someone might hold a false belief – were also guided by the bystanders' reactions in the first phase of the experiment, but they did not appear to interpret them as a character reference. They simply chose the name that had received assent rather than dissent. By implication, they focused primarily on the names themselves rather than on the mental states or character of the informants supplying the names. So, when the two bystanders withdrew and no longer supplied cues of assent and dissent, these children did not know which informant to trust.

The agreement and disagreement in the above study was conveyed by means of nonverbal cues – nods and smiles versus head-shaking and frowning. Such nonverbal signals might have been interpreted by children as expressions of approbation or liking (in the case of nods and smiles) and as disapprobation or dislike (in the case of head-shaking and frowning). To counter the likelihood of this type of interpretation, agreement and disagreement were conveyed in a more tacit fashion in two follow-up studies (Corriveau, Fusaro, and Harris, 2009). Three- and 4-year-olds watched as four informants were invited to indicate which of a set of objects was, for example, "a modi." Three of the four informants all silently pointed to the same object, but a lone dissenter pointed to a different object. Asked for their judgment, both 3- and 4-year-olds typically agreed with the majority verdict rather than with the lone dissenter. This bias was not as strong as the one observed in the previous experiment, but it was significant for each age group (3-year-olds: 67 percent; 4-year-olds: 70 percent).

In the next stage of the experiment, two of the majority of three left the room. The remaining member of the majority and the lone dissenter supplied conflicting names for additional, novel objects. Both 3- and 4-year-olds were more likely to endorse the names supplied by the previous member of the majority as opposed to the lone dissenter. A similar pattern of results emerged in a follow-up study in which there were only three informants present at the beginning of the experiment, with two in agreement (they again pointed silently to the same object) and one lone dissenter, who pointed silently (with both hands) to a different object. Children again endorsed the claims of the majority (of two) and even when one of that majority left the room, they were more likely to endorse names supplied by the remaining member rather than the lone dissenter.

Taking all three studies together, it is evident that preschoolers are very sensitive to agreement and disagreement among informants. When they are asked to adjudicate between conflicting claims, they go with the flow. They typically agree with claims that are endorsed or echoed by other people. Moreover, they continue to trust an informant whose claims have coincided with those of other people.

One puzzle warrants further reflection. Recall that the transfer of selective trust in a given informant from initial to later trials in the study of Fusaro and Harris (2008) was quite circumscribed. It was only displayed by 4-year-olds who showed an understanding of false belief, despite the fact that on the initial test trials, the tendency to endorse the names supplied by the informant who received bystander assent as opposed to dissent was very marked across the entire group of 4-year-olds. Recall that the informant who had been greeted with bystander assent was preferred on over 90 percent of those initial trials. On the other hand, the selective trust observed by Corriveau, Fusaro, and Harris (2009) during initial trials was less marked (67 percent for 3-year-olds; 70 percent for 4-year-olds), but there was a more widespread transfer of trust during subsequent test trials. In particular, the tendency to endorse names supplied by the informant who had been part of a consensus was shown by 3-year-olds as well as by 4-year-olds, even though 3-year-olds typically fail standard false belief tests. Placing these studies alongside one another suggests that when an informant gains a reputation by being either a lone dissenter or part of a consensus, that reputation is more durable than the reputation that an informant gains on the basis of bystander reactions such as smiling or frowning. Moreover, the attribution of a reputation via the first route does not call for an understanding of false beliefs. One possibility is that the status of "lone dissenter" is rapidly acquired and relatively stable. Thus, even after the departure of all but one member of the consensus, the previous lone dissenter is still stigmatized. By contrast, an informant who has elicited bystander dissent might be given an honorable discharge as soon as the dissenting bystanders make their exit.

Future research on agreement and disagreement will benefit from the disaggregation technique applied by Corriveau, Meints, and Harris (2009) to children's processing of accuracy and inaccuracy. More specifically, it will be important to find out whether 3- and 4-year-olds are equally, or differently, attuned to information about the extent to which an informant is in agreement with other people, in disagreement, or both. For example, just as 3-year-olds monitor for inaccuracy whereas 4-year-olds monitor for both accuracy and inaccuracy, it might turn out that 3-year-olds monitor for disagreement whereas 4-year-olds monitor for both agreement and disagreement.

Asch revisited

In his classic study of conformity, Asch (1956) reported that when they make a simple perceptual judgment that would normally be error-free, adults defer to the opposing (but incorrect) judgment of the majority on approximately one-third of the trials. In the studies just described, children showed a good deal of sensitivity to the views of the majority in a situation that was quite ambiguous –the unfamiliar objects were just as likely to have one name as the other. We asked if young children also defer to – or display trust in – a consensual majority in cases where the perceptual evidence flies in the face of the majority judgment (Corriveau, 2010).

Three- and 4-year-olds were shown three lines differing in length and asked to pick out "the big one." They did this unerringly. In a subsequent phase of the study, children first watched a film in which they saw three adults pick out a different (and incorrect) line as the big one. The question was then asked once more of the child. At this point, children pointed to the incorrect line on about one-quarter of the trials, and when they did so they invariably picked the same line as the adult majority had just indicated. In a follow-up study, one more phase was added to the procedure. Children were invited to pick out the line (actually, a strip of foam-board) that would be long enough to form a bridge connecting two towers. Again, children responded without error.

The overall pattern of results suggests that children have two different modes of responding: a perceptually driven mode in which they trust their own eyes to deliver veridical information, and a socially driven mode in which they defer to a consensus – despite the conflicting perceptual evidence available to them. Children's initially correct judgments and their correct choices in the bridge-building task provide clear evidence for the perceptually driven mode. Their occasional agreement with the majority – despite their ability to identify the longest line – provides evidence for the socially driven mode.

Less clear is exactly how the socially driven mode should be construed. Two interpretations seem feasible. One possibility is that children are displaying what we may dub "respectful deference": they entertain the possibility, however tentatively, that the majority might be correct. Another possibility is that they are showing only superficial compliance:– they assume that the majority is wrong, but concur with its judgment to avoid trouble or embarrassment. Two pieces of evidence lend support to the first interpretation. First, when children were asked whether the adults were good or not very good at judging the lines, most children appropriately said that they were not very good. However, those children who occasionally said that the adults were good at judging the lines were more likely to be those who deferred. Second, when children were asked to remember which line the adults had chosen, they usually remembered that the adults had picked out the wrong line. However, some children misremembered the adults' choice and picked out the longest line, and, again, these were more likely to be children who had deferred. Both of these pieces of evidence suggest that even if children mostly dissented, remembered the adults' errors, and judged them negatively, when children did endorse the adult majority, it was due to respectful deference. More specifically, these deferential children were inclined to forget that adults had erred and did not judge them negatively.

Two additional findings fit this focus on respectful deference. First, if children were displaying only superficial compliance in order to avoid social discomfiture, there would be no reason to expect such compliance to decline in the course of the experiment. On the other hand, if children were conflicted – if they were weighing their own perceptual judgment against a respectful deference to the opinion of the adult majority, we might expect children to increasingly doubt that majority. After all, as discussed in Part I, 3- and 4-year-olds come to mistrust informants whom they believe to be in error, and in each trial children faced a conflict between deference to the adults and their own perceptual judgment. Inspection of children's replies across the four trials fits this latter prediction. The deferential pattern was less common as trials progressed.

Finally, one other, somewhat unexpected, finding is consistent with an emphasis on respectful compliance. Most of the children tested came from either Caucasian or Asian families. When children were divided by family of origin, the rate of deference was greater among Asian children than Caucasian children. The difference was not large (Asian children deferred on 31 percent of trials, whereas Caucasian children deferred on 18 percent of trials), but it was significant. In addition, scrutiny of replication studies using the original Asch paradigm, or variants of it, confirmed that exactly the same difference has been observed for adults (Bond and Smith, 1996). Again, when we ask what might be driving this cultural difference, it is plausible that respectful deference – rather than superficial compliance – is at work.

In summary, across three different studies, we have found that children notice who agrees with whom. If they are presented with a claim that is endorsed by several people, they are likely to favor that claim rather than one made by a lone dissenter. Indeed, individual members of a consensual majority are trusted even when those they agree with have made an exit. At the same time, children continue to weigh the claims of a majority against their own perceptual judgment and generally favor the latter if there is an evident conflict – increasingly so if they are presented with the same type of conflictual choice over several trials. Nevertheless, children do sometimes defer to the majority. For the time being, we interpret this deference as respectful or trusting and not as superficial compliance.

Part III: How do children weigh different indices of trustworthiness?

In Part I, we concluded that although younger preschoolers are mostly swayed by their relationship with an informant, older preschoolers are primarily guided by an informant's past epistemic reliability. Thus, older preschoolers are likely to invest more trust in an unfamiliar but accurate informant rather than a familiar but inaccurate informant. How do children decide who is an accurate versus an inaccurate informant? At first glance, this question seems easy to answer. When children hear an informant say, for example, that an object is one thing, but they themselves can readily see that it is another, they judge that the informant is making a false claim. By implication, preschoolers monitor informants for truth-telling – for "telling it like it is."

However, there is an alternative possibility. Suppose that children are natural sociologists or psephologists. They keep track of the degree of consensus that surrounds particular assertions. For example, they might note that all the speakers in their community call a spade by its appropriate name: "spade." When they hear a person deviate from that consensus by calling it a fork, they regard the person as an untrustworthy dissenter. The results from Part II underline the fact that children are, in fact, very observant sociologists. They notice when there is a consensus, and they trust informants who belong to a consensus. Hence, the findings from Part II raise the possibility that children do not genuinely monitor informants for their truth-telling but rather for their social conformity. Indeed, stated more broadly and provocatively, it is possible that children are not interested in obtaining information that is true. Instead, they are interested only in obtaining information that everyone agrees with.

Granted this possibility, the results presented in Part I on young children's accuracy monitoring call for cautious interpretation. At first sight, these results indicate that young children are not indiscriminate or credulous when they place their trust in others. Despite their reliance on other people's testimony, they keep track of which informant has told the truth and which has not. In this way, they would be likely to avoid being misled by false witnesses. However, if children monitor their informants primarily for their membership of a social consensus, there is clearly some risk that children will be misled. More specifically, they will be likely to accept claims that are part of a consensus and to trust the informants who belong to such a consensus, irrespective of whether their claims are true or not.

Is there any evidence showing that children are ultimately interested in the truth and trust those who tell it, notwithstanding their sensitivity to a social consensus? One tentative piece of evidence emerged in the final study, using the Asch-like paradigm. Recall that children faced a conflict between identifying the longest line on the basis of their own perceptual judgment and agreeing with the majority. If children were guided simply by social conformity, they would typically agree with the majority. We found that they did not – they agreed with the majority on only a minority of trials. In addition, in the course of the test trials, children were increasingly likely to go against the majority judgment. These findings are somewhat reassuring. At the very least, they show that when children have unequivocal perceptual evidence, they can and do resist the pressure to conform.

However, it is important to remember that children will encounter many contexts in which the available evidence is equivocal, or even nonexistent. For example, many young children believe in the existence of Santa Claus and the Tooth Fairy (Harris, Pasquini, Duke, Asscher, and Pons, 2006). From their perspective, the evidence for the existence of these two special beings is probably unimpeachable. Most adults in their immediate community endorse the existence of these beings – at least when interacting with young children – so children are led to believe that they do exist.

Only when they get older, perhaps when they hear dissenting voices in the schoolyard, will children come to doubt the existence of these beings. Second, many young children believe that the origin of species can be traced back to a Creator. This belief is both widespread and stable if children are growing up in fundamentalist communities where adults mostly endorse Creationism as opposed to evolutionary theory (Evans, 2000). Thus, in these two cases, children display an acceptance of the social consensus, but their trust can be questioned. After all, Santa Claus and the Tooth Fairy do not exist, and the Creationist account of the origin of species is debatable. At this point, it is tempting to sympathize with the plea for cognitive autonomy made by Rousseau and Piaget.

Consider, however, two further cases. When children see a whale for the first time, they will likely think that it is a fish. After all, many of its perceptual attributes resemble those of a fish. Yet most, if not all, children come to accept the consensus that a whale is not a fish but a mammal – despite appearances to the contrary. Second, when children hear people talk about germs, they might initially wonder whether germs really exist because they cannot be seen (Harris, Pasquini, Duke, Asscher, and Pons, 2006). Certainly, the historical record confirms that many adults, including those belonging to the medical profession, doubted the existence of germs (Rosenberg, 1962). Nevertheless, contemporary elementary school children and even preschoolers readily accept that germs do exist, and they also (rightly) assert that other people claim that they exist. So, in both of these cases, children display an acceptance of the social consensus, but – from an adult perspective – their trust is well founded. A whale is a mammal and germs do exist.

In conclusion, children's trust in the claims made by other people is not indiscriminate – it varies depending on the familiarity, the reliability, and the social conformity of their informants. The plea for cognitive autonomy made by Rousseau and Piaget may be appropriate in some cases, but it ignores the fact that children's trust in others' testimony allows them, in many contexts, to "see" further than they would on their own. Even Isaac Newton, whose capacity for cognitive autonomy is beyond dispute, recognized that: "If I have seen further it is by standing on the shoulders of giants."

Acknowledgments

The research described in this chapter was conducted with the support of a grant (no. 200700131) from the Spencer Foundation. We thank the preschools in Boston, MA and Buffalo, NY who enabled us to carry out the experiments.

References

Ainsworth, M. D. S (1992). A consideration of social referencing in the context of attachment theory and research. In. S. Feinman (ed.), *Social referencing and the social construction of reality in infancy* (pp. 349–367). New York: Plenum Press.

Ainsworth, M. D. S., Blehar, M. C., Waters, E., and Wall, S. (1978). *Patterns of attachment: A psychological study of the strange situation.* Hillsdale, NJ: Lawrence Erlbaum Associates.

Asch, S. E. (1956). Studies of independence and conformity. A minority of one against a unanimous majority. *Psychological Monographs*, **20** (9, Whole No. 416).

Birch, S., Vauthier, S., and Bloom, P. (2008). Three- and four-year-olds spontaneously use others' past performance to guide their learning. *Cognition*, **107**, 1018–1034.

Bond, R. and Smith, P. B. (1996). Culture and conformity: A meta-analysis of studies using Asch's (1952b, 1956) line judgment task. *Psychological Bulletin*, **119**, 111–137.

Clément, F., Koenig, M., and Harris, P. L. (2004). The ontogenesis of trust in testimony. *Mind and Language*, **19**, 360–379.

Coady, C. A. J. (1992). *Testimony.* Oxford University Press.

Corriveau, K. H. and Harris, P. L. (2009a). Preschoolers continue to trust a more accurate informant up to 1 week after exposure to accuracy information. *Developmental Science*, **12**, 188–193.

(2009b). Choosing your informant: Weighing familiarity and recent accuracy. *Developmental Science*, **12**, 426–437.

(2010). Preschoolers (sometimes) defer to the majority when making simple perceptual judgments. *Developmental Psychology.*

Corriveau, K. H., Fusaro, M., and Harris, P. L. (2009). Going with the flow: Preschoolers prefer non-dissenters as informants. *Psychological Science*, **20**, 372–377.

Corriveau, K. H., Harris, P. L., Meins, E., Fernyhough, C., Arnott, B., Elliott, L., Liddle, B., Hearn, A., Vittorini, L., and de Rosnay, M. (2009). Young children's trust in their mother's claims: Longitudinal links with attachment security in infancy. *Child Development*, **80**, 750–761.

Corriveau, K. H., Meints, M., and Harris, P. L. (2009). Early tracking of informant accuracy and inaccuracy. *British Journal of Developmental Psychology*, **27**, 311–342.

Evans, E. M. (2000). Beyond scopes: Why creationism is here to stay. In K. Rosengren, C. N. Johnson, and P. L. Harris (eds.), *Imagining the impossible: Magical, scientific and religious thinking in children.* Cambridge University Press.

Fusaro, M. and Harris, P. L. (2008). Children assess informant reliability using bystanders' non-verbal cues. *Developmental Science*, **11**, 781–787.

Harris, P. L. (2007). Trust. *Developmental Science*, **10**, 135–138.

Harris, P. L. and Koenig, M. (2006). Trust in testimony: How children learn about science and religion. *Child Development*, **77**, 505–524.

Harris, P. L., Pasquini, E. S., Duke, S., Asscher, J. J., and Pons, F. (2006). Germs and angels: The role of testimony in young children's ontology. *Developmental Science*, **9**, 76–96.

Isaacs, S. (1930). *Intellectual growth in young children*. New York: Harcourt, Brace & Company.

Jaswal, V. K. (2004). Don't believe everything you hear: Preschoolers' sensitivity to speaker intent in category induction. *Child Development*, **75**, 1871–1885.

Jaswal, V. K. and Neely, L. A. (2006). Adults don't always know best: Preschoolers use past reliability over age when learning new words. *Psychological Science*, **17**, 757–758.

Kinzler, K., Dupoux, E., and Spelke, E. S. (2007). The native language of social cognition. *Proceedings of the National Academy of Science*, **104**, 12577–12580.

Koenig, M. and Harris, P. L. (2005). Preschoolers mistrust ignorant and inaccurate speakers. *Child Development*, **76**, 1261–1277.

Koenig, M., Clément, F., and Harris, P. L. (2004). Trust in testimony: Children's use of true and false statements. *Psychological Science*, **10**, 694–698.

Lackey, J. (2008). *Learning from words: Testimony as a source of knowledge*. Oxford University Press.

Pasquini, E. S., Corriveau, K., Koenig, M., and Harris, P. L. (2007). Preschoolers monitor the relative accuracy of informants. *Developmental Psychology*, **43**, 1216–1226.

Rosenberg, C. E. (1962). *The cholera years: The United States in 1832 and 1866*. University of Chicago Press.

Rousseau, J.-J. (1762/1957). *Emile*. New York: Dutton.

Wellman, H. M., Cross, D., and Watson, J. (2001). Meta-analysis of theory-of-mind development: The truth about false belief. *Child Development*, **72**, 655–684.

6   Social relation and mutual influence analyses of children's interpersonal trust

Lucy R. Betts (Nottingham Trent University),
Ken J. Rotenberg (Keele University), and
Mark Trueman (Keele University)

Interpersonal trust has been viewed as a crucial aspect of social functioning that originates in infant–caregiver interactions and affects psychosocial functioning across the life-span (Armsden and Greenberg, 1987; Erikson, 1963; Waters, Vaughn, Posada, and Kondo-Ikemura, 1995). Researchers have found that children's interpersonal trust is associated with various aspects of their psychosocial functioning. Specifically, trustworthiness in children has been found to be associated with, and longitudinally predictive of, the number of their friendships (Rotenberg, McDougall, Boulton, Vaillancourt, Fox, and Hymel, 2004) and their adjustment to school (Betts and Rotenberg, 2007; Betts, Rotenberg, and Trueman, 2009; Rotenberg, Michalik, Eisenberg, and Betts, 2008). Children's trust beliefs have been found to be associated with honesty (Wright and Kirmani, 1977), lack of depression (Lester and Gatto, 1990), academic achievement (Imber, 1973), and lack of loneliness (Rotenberg, MacDonald, and King, 2004). Rotenberg, Boulton, and Fox (2005) found that the trust beliefs of elementary school children were negatively associated with, and longitudinally predictive of, internalized maladjustment (loneliness, depression, and anxiety). Also, a curvilinear relationship was found whereby children with very high and those with very low trust beliefs were at additional risk for internalized maladjustment. Some researchers (see Chapter 2) have highlighted that interpersonal trust during childhood is dyadic and reciprocal in nature, but there is a scarcity of research addressing this hypothesis.

The models and analyses guiding the aforementioned studies were limited. The purpose of the current chapter is to redress those limitations by describing the application of the social relations model (Kenny and La Voie, 1984) and the mutual influence model (Kenny, 1996; Woody and Sadler, 2005) to the examination of interpersonal trust during childhood. These models have been developed as a method of dealing statistically with the complexities of analyzing dyadic relationships. Specifically, the models have been developed in recognition of the principle that dyad members are likely to influence each other's scores, and, as such, problems may arise with more traditional statistical techniques because of the non-independence of dyadic data. Through the use of illustrative examples, the chapter will describe how these models can be applied to examine specific trust beliefs, peer-reported trustworthiness, and reciprocity of trust in young children's social groups and best friend dyads.

The social relations model

The social relations model (SRM) was developed by Kenny and colleagues (Kenny, 1994a, 1994b; Kenny and La Voie, 1984; Malloy and Kenny, 1986; Warner, Kenny, and Stoto, 1979) as a method of statistically examining behavior between two individuals engaging in a dyadic relationship. The underlying principles of the SRM are that: (1) the variance within dyadic relationships can be partitioned, and (2) an individual can be both the stimulus for, and the provider of, behavior ratings (Kenny, 1998; Malloy and Kenny, 1986). For example, an individual can rate, and also be rated by, the other member of the dyad. Importantly, both these aspects of an individual's behavior can be examined at the same time through the application of the SRM. Therefore, when a social relations analysis is performed, conclusions can be drawn regarding how much of the variance in dyadic behavior is due to: (1) the characteristics of the individuals within the dyadic relationship, and (2) the unique relationship between the two dyad members (Kenny, Kashy, and Cook, 2006).

The SRM has typically been used to answer three questions about behavior in dyadic relationships:

1. Whether individual A behaved with B in a particular way because A always engages in such behavior regardless of their interaction partner (i.e., it is something to do with A).
2. Whether individual A behaved with B in a particular way because everyone who interacts with B engages in that behavior (i.e., it is something to do with B).
3. Whether individual A behaved with B in a particular way because of the unique relationship between them.

According to the SRM, an individual's behavior in a dyadic interaction comprises a general mean, actor variance, partner variance, relationship variance, and error variance. The SRM also permits examination of reciprocity between dyad members – whether individuals match or complement their behavior in dyadic relationships (Kenny, 1994a). Therefore, the application of the SRM permits a "fuller" picture of the behavior between individuals in a dyad than more standard traditional methods that have been used to examine dyadic behavior.

The SRM has been used successfully by researchers to examine a range of children's dyadic behavior – for example, conflict in toddlers' peer relationships (Ross and Lollis, 1989), desirability as a playmate or work partner in first- to sixth-grade children (Simpkins and Parke, 2002; Whitley, Schofield, and Snyder, 1984), social status in first- to sixth-grade children (Malloy, Yarlas, Montvilo, and Sugarman, 1996), and aggression in third-grade children (Coie, Cillessen, Dodge, Hubbard, Schwartz, Lemerise, and Bateman, 1999; Hubbard, Dodge, Cillessen, Coie, and Schwartz, 2001). However, although the SRM is particularly suited to examine interpersonal trust (Kenny and La Voie, 1984), only one study to date has applied the SRM to the examination of children's trust (Betts and Rotenberg, 2008). The next part of the chapter will review each component of the SRM in turn, with particular regard as to how the analysis can be applied to the study of children's trust.

It is important to note there are some conventions governing the terminology used when discussing the SRM. First, when results across groups or studies using the SRM are described, the term *variance* is used, and when referring to an individual's score, the term *effect* is used (Kenny, Kashy, and Cook, 2006). Second, when the term *unique* is used, in the context of the SRM, it pertains to the relationship between the two members of the dyad when the other influencing factors have been statistically controlled for, and reflects that the effect may not be the same for both dyad members (Kenny and La Voie, 1984).

Group mean

The group mean represents the mean score for a given variable occurring within the individual dyads across the interaction group. Therefore, the group mean pertains to the extent to which an individual's behavior within a dyadic interaction may be a reflection of the general behavior of the group (Kashy and Kenny, 2000). It should be noted that the group mean is infrequently reported because the variance rarely differs across groups and, as such, only accounts for a small amount of variance within dyadic interactions (D. A. Kenny, personal communication, June 8, 2004).

Actor effects and actor variance

Actor variance within the SRM represents a measure of assimilation. Assimilation is the tendency for individuals to consistently rate their interaction partners at a similar level on a trait (Kenny, 1994a). Conversely, actor effects denote an individual's "average level of behavior in the presence of a variety of other partners" (Kenny and La Voie, 1984, p. 142). Therefore, actor effects and actor variance indicate an individual's pattern of behavior across all of their interaction partners. So the following question can be answered: does an individual behave consistently with all of their interaction partners? Dependent on the ratings awarded, individuals can have positive or negative actor effects (Kenny, Kashy, and Cook, 2006).

With regard to trust, actor effects serve to represent individual differences in the expression of specific trust beliefs in the interaction partners. So, if peers were chosen as the interaction partners, the actor effects would represent individual differences in how much a child trusted their peers. It is widely reported in the literature that adults (Couch and Jones, 1997; Rotter, 1967; Scott, 1980; Wright and Sharp, 1979) and children (Rotenberg, 1984, 1986; Rotenberg, MacDonald, and King, 2004) differ in their expression of specific trust beliefs. Specifically, some adults and some children have high trust in others, whereas some adults and some children have low trust in others, regardless of who they are interacting with. Therefore, when the SRM is applied to examine trust, it is likely that these differences will be evident, and, as such, there will be significant actor variance. In other words, the likelihood that children differ in the extent to which they trust their interaction partners can be determined as an outcome of a social relations analysis. Further, because of the nature of the SRM, this can be unconfounded. If a child rated all of their interaction partners as keeping their promises, she/he would have a positive actor effect, whereas a child who rated all of their interaction partners as not keeping their promises would have a negative actor effect.

Partner effects and partner variance

Partner variance within the SRM is a measure of consensus. Consensus pertains to the tendency for an individual to elicit characteristic ratings of a trait when interacting with others in a dyad, regardless of the interaction partner (Albright, Kenny, and Malloy, 1988; Kenny, 1994a). Partner effects are an indicator of the average level of response that an individual elicits from all of their interaction partners (Kenny and La Voie, 1984). So, partner variance and partner effects represent the ratings that an individual receives across their interaction partners, and indicates the extent to which an individual elicits a similar response regardless of their interaction partner. An individual's partner effect can be positive or negative, dependent on the ratings the individual elicits from their interaction partners (Kenny, Kashy, and Cook, 2006).

In the context of trust, partner effects and partner variance would be evidenced by consistent individual differences in the extent to which children elicit ratings of specific trust beliefs from their interaction partners (termed trustworthiness in previous research). Individual differences in the ratings of specific trust beliefs elicited from interaction partners have typically been examined in adults (Rotter, 1967; Wright and Sharp, 1979) and in children (Rotenberg, McDougall, Boulton, Vaillancourt, Fox, and Hymel, 2004) as peer reports of trustworthiness. Therefore, when specific trust beliefs are analyzed using the SRM, there can be individual differences in the ratings of trust elicited from interaction partners. Further, the SRM will make it possible to determine whether some children consistently receive ratings of being trustworthy whereas other children may not. If a child was rated by all of their peers as trustworthy, they would have a positive partner effect, whereas if a child was rated by all of their peers as less trustworthy, they would have a negative partner effect.

Relationship variance and relationship effects

As part of the SRM, relationship variance and relationship effect examine the unique pattern of behavior between two individuals in a dyadic relationship when the actor and partner effects for those individuals are statistically controlled for (Kenny and LaVoie, 1984).

When applied to trust, relationship variance represents the unique trusting relationship between the members of the dyad. There has been little previous research at the level of the relationship. However, research does suggest that children can identify different characteristics of the social relationships that they engage in. In particular, Furman and Buhrmester (1985) report that the qualities of 11- to 13-year-olds' relationships varied according to whether they were interacting with their parents or their peers. Although it remains unclear whether such a pattern would emerge with regard to trust, it is likely that the differences will emerge in the nature of the children's dyadic interactions, and this difference will be evidenced through the relationship variance. However, it is important to note that, dependent on how the variable of interest is assessed and the social relations analysis conducted, relationship variance can be confounded with error variance.

Error variance represents measurement error, "random noise," and unstable variance in the measured variable (Malloy and Kenny, 1986).

One way to overcome the problem of error variance confounding relationship variance in a social relations analysis is through the use of a construct. A construct can be created, as part of the social relations analysis, when two or more associated measures are used to assess the same domain and these measures are subsequently combined in the analysis. For example, promise-keeping and secret-keeping could be used as separate indicators of the overall variable of trust because these beliefs represent associated facets of trust (Rotenberg, 1994, 2001). In this example, children would be asked to separately report the extent to which their interaction partners keep their promises and the extent to which their interaction partners keep their secrets. Taken together, as a construct, these two variables would represent the children's trust in their peers. It is beneficial to create a construct when conducting a social relations analysis because it allows a clear picture as to the reliability of the results and allows conclusions to be drawn regarding the size of the relationship variance. This is particularly important with a variable such as trust, because it is likely that a large proportion of the variance within a dyad is due to the unique nature of the relationship between dyad members (i.e., relationship variance and relationship effects).

Reciprocity

The SRM permits investigation into two types of reciprocity: individual-level reciprocity and dyadic-level reciprocity. Reciprocity at the individual level examines whether individuals who rate their partners as possessing a particular trait consistently elicit similar ratings for the same trait from their interaction partners (Malloy and Kenny, 1986). Specifically, individual-level reciprocity correlates an individual's actor effect with their partner effect. Consequently, individual-level reciprocity focuses on the behavior of one of the dyad members. With regard to trust, individual-level reciprocity would correlate the extent to which an individual trusts their interaction partner and the extent to which the same individual elicits ratings of trust from their interaction partners. Although it remains unclear whether such a relationship occurs in children, a relationship is likely because specific trust beliefs tend to be associated with trustworthiness (Rotter, 1967).

Reciprocity at the dyadic level describes the extent to which one dyad member is rated by the second dyad member as uniquely displaying a trait, and the extent to which the second dyad member is rated by the first dyad member as displaying the same trait (Kenny, 1994a). Consequently, reciprocity between individuals within a dyad can be examined while the other components within dyadic relationships (actor and partner effects) are statistically controlled for. Ultimately, reciprocity at the dyadic level is the correlation between the relationship effect for each member of the dyad while controlling for actor and partner effects. In other words, dyadic reciprocity examines the unique pattern of behavior between the two individuals within the dyad.

With regard to trust, dyadic-level reciprocity would be consistent with the hypothesis that reciprocal trust is essential for the formation of close relationships in adults (Holmes and Rempel, 1989; Larzelere and Huston, 1980) and in children (Buzzelli, 1988; Moyer and Kunz, 1975). Further, empirical evidence of the reciprocal qualities of trust has been widely reported in the context of romantic relationships, especially those of married couples (Butler, 1986; Holmes and Rempel, 1989; Larzelere and Huston 1980; Zak, Gold, Ryckman, and Lenney, 1988). Also, there is limited evidence of reciprocity of fourth-grade children's specific trust beliefs (Rotenberg and Pilipenko, 1983). Therefore, the application of the SRM to children's trust allows the investigation of the reciprocal properties of trust while statistically controlling for the other components of dyadic relationships.

Due to the nature of social behavior, it is likely that for any individual, associations may occur between how he/she perceives others (actor effects) and how she/he is perceived by others (partner effects). Therefore, the social relations analysis permits examination of potential multivariate relationships between an individual's actor and partner effects. However, it is only possible to examine these multivariate relationships when multiple indicators of the same variable are used (i.e., when a construct is created). Through the creation of a construct, it is possible to examine the multivariate correlations between the actor, partner, and relationship effects for each of the variables of interest. These multivariate correlations between the actor and partner components are regarded as being at the individual level because only aspects pertaining to the individual are examined (Kenny, Kashy, and Cook, 2006). The four multivariate correlations that could be examined are: (1) actor–actor, (2) partner–partner, (3) actor–partner, and (4) partner–actor.

In the context of trust, if promise-keeping and secret-keeping were used as indicators of trust, the actor–actor correlation would examine the extent to which an individual who rates their interaction partners as keeping promises also rates their interaction partners as keeping secrets. These actor–actor multivariate correlations can provide a method of assessing the stability of the measures, if applied to a longitudinal study, and cross-measure consistency. Specifically, it is likely that if the components of the construct are assessing the same variable, then an individual's actor effects should be similar for both measures representing the stability of the measure. The partner–partner multivariate correlations represent the extent to which an individual elicits similar ratings across the measures used to create a construct – for example, the relationship between the extent to which an individual elicits ratings of promise-keeping from others and the extent to which the same individual elicits ratings of secret-keeping. Consequently, as with the actor–actor multivariate correlations, partner–partner multivariate correlations can be used as a method of assessing the stability of a measure and cross-measure consistency. The actor–partner multivariate correlation examines the extent to which the actor effect for one variable is associated with the partner effect for the second variable. In other words, the actor–partner multivariate correlation examines whether individuals who rate their interaction partners as possessing a trait, also elicit ratings of the same trait from their interaction partners. So, for example, the actor–partner multivariate correlation pertains to whether individuals who rate others as keeping promises elicit ratings of keeping secrets from others. The partner–actor multivariate correlation assesses whether individuals who elicit ratings of promise-keeping from others rate others as keeping secrets. The actor–partner and partner–actor multivariate correlations can be used as a method of assessing the consistency across measures.

Multivariate correlations can also be used to examine the relationship effects for two individuals in a dyadic interaction (Kenny, Kashy, and Cook, 2006). Specifically, at the relationship level, *intrapersonal* and *interpersonal* multivariate correlations can be examined. The intrapersonal multivariate correlation examines the association between the relationship variance when the perceiver and the target are the same for both variables. For example, the intrapersonal multivariate correlation represents the association between how much individual A uniquely reports that individual B keeps promises, and how much individual A uniquely reports that individual B keeps secrets.

The interpersonal multivariate correlation changes the role of the perceiver and the target for the variables – so the perceiver for one of the variables becomes the target for the second variable (Kenny, Kashy, and Cook, 2006). Therefore, the interpersonal multivariate correlation represents the association between how much individual A uniquely reports individual B as keeping promises and how much individual B uniquely reports individual A as keeping secrets.

Suitability of the SRM for examining trust

The suitability of the SRM to examine specific trust beliefs was first highlighted in Kenny and La Voie's (1984) review of the SRM. The application of the SRM to examine trust provides potentially "richer" results than the more traditional methods used to investigate children's trust. However, to our knowledge, there is very little empirical research that has used the SRM as a method of analyzing young children's trust (Betts, 2005; Betts and Rotenberg, 2008). Moreover, beyond the statistical advantages of the SRM, there are a number of practical reasons for examining specific trust beliefs using the SRM.

First, researchers examining children's specific trust beliefs have typically done so using children's classmates as the target of trust (e.g., Rotenberg, 1984, 1986; Rotenberg, MacDonald, and King, 2004). This approach, adopted in the previous research, makes sense because children tend to spend a high proportion of their time in school. Moreover, the time children spend in school is likely to be in the company of their classmates, and, as such, children are likely to develop "insider" knowledge of the other children's behavior. Further, because of its very nature, this "insider" knowledge is unlikely to be easily assessed through observations by others such as teachers or researchers (Malloy, Yarlas, Montvilo, and Sugarman, 1996; Malloy and Kenny, 1986). Moreover, it is widely acknowledged by researchers that peers are a valuable information source of a child's behavior within the classroom (Merrel and Gimpel, 1998; Perry, Kusel, and Perry, 1988; Schneider, 2000). Therefore, because it can be argued that one classroom of children comprises a group, by examining trust in a number of classrooms, these classrooms can then be entered as the separate groups within the social relations analysis. Alternatively, groups could be created within the classroom (e.g., Malloy, Sugarman, Montvilo, and Ben-Zeev, 1995; Malloy, Yarlas, Montvilo, and Sugarman, 1996). However, by creating arbitrary groups within classrooms, it may be that these groups do not accurately reflect the social groups. Therefore, the estimations from the SRM may not accurately reflect the group and dyadic dynamics.

Second, the application of the SRM and associated analysis is useful for the study of specific trust beliefs because the results of the analysis provide unconfounded measures of the various components of the SRM. For example, in the previous research that did not use the social relations analysis to partition the variance (e.g., Rotenberg, 1984, 1986; Rotenberg, Fox, Green, Ruderman, Slater, Stevens, and Carlo, 2005; Rotenberg, MacDonald, and King, 2004), the measurement of specific trust beliefs may have been confounded with the ratings of trust elicited by the target (i.e., partner effects) and with relationship effects (the unique trusting relationship between perceiver and target). Specifically, when the SRM is applied to the investigation of trust, specific trust beliefs could be investigated without the potential confounding effects of peer-reported trustworthiness. Further, trustworthiness could be examined without the potential confound of specific trust beliefs (i.e., actor effects) or the unique relationship between individuals (i.e., relationship effects). Therefore, using the social relations analysis to examine trust would permit a greater understanding of children's specific trust beliefs and trustworthiness at a dyadic level, without the potential confounding influence of the other factors important in a dyadic relationship.

Third, using the SRM allows reciprocity of trust to be examined empirically. Although previous research has sought to empirically examine reciprocity, there are limitations with some of the approaches adopted by researchers. For example, one method of examining reciprocity of specific trust beliefs has been through the use of individuals' scores within the dyad and attempting to match these scores (Rotenberg and Pilipenko, 1983). Such an approach has been criticized for not demonstrating the existence of actual reciprocity because the components of the relationship cannot be examined separately as awarded scores, received scores, and relative scores (Kenny and Nasby, 1980). Other methods of investigating reciprocity in trust have been criticized for similar methodological weaknesses. For example, when researchers have used two scores from dyad members to obtain an aggregate score, such an approach simply matches the scores (Kenny and Nasby, 1980; Malloy and Kenny, 1986). The SRM overcomes this issue by statistically controlling for the various components of the dyadic relationship while investigating dyadic reciprocity of trust and ultimately overcoming the limitations of previous studies.

As outlined earlier, the SRM is appropriate to analyze young children's trust as a dyadic behavior as part of a wider group context. When applied to the investigation of trust, the SRM allows examination of: (1) individual differences in specific trust beliefs; (2) individual differences in the rating of trust elicited from interaction partners (termed trustworthiness in previous research); (3) the unique trusting relationship between individuals; and (4) dyadic reciprocity of trust. Moreover, the SRM and associated analysis allows these components to be investigated separately. However, there are a number of factors that researchers must take into consideration when designing a study in which they plan to use the social relations analysis as a method of examining trust.

First, researchers need to decide which SRM design is most appropriate for their research: the block design or the round-robin design. These designs can be implemented separately or combined as part of a block round-robin design. The block design involves different individuals being rated to those who are providing the ratings. An example of a block design would be girls providing ratings of promise-keeping for boys but not for girls. In comparison, the round-robin design involves all members of a group providing ratings of each other. Therefore, each group member is rated by, and rates, all of the other group members on the same variable. An example of a round-robin design would be if all children in a classroom formed a group that provided ratings of promise-keeping of children within the same classroom. Consequently, the round-robin design allows all possible dyadic combinations within the group to be explored and, as such, this design offers potentially "richer" results than the block design (Kenny, Kashy, and Cook, 2006). Further, the round-robin design is also preferable because it has twice the power of the block design (Lashley and Kenny, 1998).

Second, researchers need to consider the issue of group size. Although, the SRM examines behavior at a dyadic level, it assumes that these dyads form a wider group. The social relations analysis can be used with different group sizes, but when researchers are expecting dyadic reciprocity, the group size must exceed four. With regard to examining trust, it is likely that dyadic reciprocity would occur and, as such, it is recommended that the group sizes for the analysis exceed four. If dyadic reciprocity is not expected, then the minimum group size needed for a social relations analysis is three (Kenny, 1998).

Third, when designing a study that involves the application of the social relations analysis, researchers need to decide how many groups to include. For the SRM to be effective in partitioning the variance, it is necessary that any study comprises a number of groups. However, there is an ongoing debate in literature as to whether it is preferable to have a small number of large groups or a large number of small groups. Lashley and Kenny (1998) endorse the approach of using fewer large groups, rather than a large number of small groups, when conducting a social relations analysis. Specifically, if larger groups are used in favor of smaller groups, more data per group are generated and this results in more stable SRM parameter estimates (Lashley and Kenny, 1998). Also, when larger group sizes are used, the distribution of the parameter estimates has less variance and, ultimately, more power (Lashley and Kenny, 1998). According to Kenny, Kashy, and Cook (2006), to achieve power of .80, for actor variance five groups of twelve are needed, and for partner variance three groups of twelve, when a round-robin design is implemented with larger groups. Conversely, if the group size is four to achieve a power of .80, for actor variance sixty-nine groups are needed, and for partner variance seventeen groups in a round-robin analysis (Kenny, Kashy, and Cook, 2006). In a block design to achieve power of .80, for actor variance 158 groups of four or seven groups of twelve are needed, and for partner variance thirty-three groups of twelve or four groups of twelve are needed (Kenny, Kashy, and Cook, 2006).

Fourth, the SRM assumes that dyadic reciprocity is linear, but the strength of the reciprocity is not assessed in the model (Kenny, Kashy, and Cook, 2006; Kenny and La Voie, 1984). This is a potential limitation because the strength of reciprocity may vary according to whether it is positive or negative reciprocity. However, to date there is little that can be done to address this issue when designing a study to examine young children's trust using the SRM, as the effects cannot be measured (Kenny, Kashy, and Cook, 2006).

Finally, the SRM does not take into account extradyadic effects that may influence the dyad members, but rather it assumes that individuals are not influenced by the actions of those dyads that they are not part of (Kenny and La Voie, 1984). For example, children may communicate with peers the nature of their specific dyadic interactions, which is not accounted for in the model (Kenny and La Voie, 1984). Therefore, as an attempt to try to lessen the influence of extradyadic effects, when designing a study, it is imperative that researchers ensure that participants do not communicate their responses to other children within the group.

An example

The next part of the chapter provides an illustrative example of a social relations analysis performed to examine young children's trust (Betts and Rotenberg, 2008). A social relations analysis was performed with a sample of 274 children (142 male and 132 female) with a mean age of 6 years 2 months (*SD* = 7 months). The children were asked to report how often they thought that their classmates kept their promises and secrets, using a five-point Likert scale, ranging from 1 (never ever) to 5 (always). High scores on these measures were treated as higher trust beliefs. Following Rotenberg's (1994, 2001) interpersonal trust framework, promise-keeping and secret-keeping reports were treated as separate indicators of the variable trust.

For the purpose of the analysis, all of the children's peers within each classroom served as a round-robin group. In total, there were sixteen groups and the group size ranged from five to twenty-eight. The data were analyzed using WinSoReMo (Kenny and Xuan, 2002) and SOREBIG (D.A. Kenny, personal communication, June 10, 2004). These programs were used to partition the variance within the dyads into actor, partner, and relationship variance, and because the group size exceeded twenty-five respectively. As two indicators of trust had been used, a construct of trust was created so that the error variance could be separated from the relationship variance.

The first part of the social relations analysis is an output of simple variance partitioning. This represents the proportion of the total variance that can be accounted for by actor, partner, relationship, and, if a

Table 6.1 *The relative variance according to SRM component*

Behavior	Actor	Partner	Relationship	Error
Promise-keeping	.14*	.15*	.71	—
Secret-keeping	.16*	.09*	.75	—
Trust construct	.12	.12	.26	.50

Notes: The analysis is based on a group size of 22.83. Also, significance tests cannot be performed on the variance partitioning for a construct or for relationship variance (Kenny, 1998).
*p<.05

construct is created, error variance for promise-keeping, secret-keeping, and the trust construct (see Table 6.1). By multiplying the figures presented in Table 6.1 by ten, it is possible to calculate the percentage variance accounted for by each component. The variance tests are one-tailed because the model assumes that the variance will be positive (Kenny, Kashy, and Cook, 2006) and the analysis only tests for significance of the variance at $p < .05$. As shown in Table 6.1, a significant amount of the variance in young children's promise-keeping and secret-keeping could be accounted for by the actor and the partner components. In other words, there were consistent individual differences in the children's ratings of specific trust beliefs and in the ratings of trust that the children elicited from their peers for both promise-keeping and secret-keeping. When the error variance is removed from the relationship variance, using a construct, the relationship variance accounts for approximately twice the amount of the variance as the actor and partner components. Therefore, young children's trust appears to be most strongly a dyadic phenomenon. However, it should be noted that a relatively high proportion of the variance in young children's trust can be attributed to error.

As previously noted, the social relations analysis also yields a series of individual multivariate correlations. The significance of these multivariate correlations is tested through a series of specialist multiple t-tests, with the group as the unit of analysis. The multiple t-tests do not test the correlations per se, but rather the underlying covariances, as a test of whether the correlations are significantly different from zero (Kenny, Kashy, and Cook, 2006). Also, in some instances, the correlation coefficient for these multivariate correlations is 1.00, or very close to 1.00, which indicates that the true correlation coefficient is close to 1.00 (Kenny, 1998).

When examining the individual-level multivariate correlations, there was a significant relationship between children's actor effect for promise-keeping and their actor effect for secret-keeping, *multivariate* $r(11)=.81, p<.001$. Therefore, children who reported that their peers kept promises also reported that their peers kept secrets. Additionally, there was a significant relationship between the partner effects for promise-keeping and the partner effects for secret-keeping, *multivariate* $r(11)=.98$, $p<.001$. Therefore, children who elicited ratings of promise-keeping also elicited ratings of secret-keeping from their peers. There was no evidence of significant actor–partner multivariate correlations. Consequently, the scores that the children awarded their peers for promise-keeping and secret-keeping were not related to the scores elicited from their peers for these variables.

The social relations analysis also yielded evidence of associations between promise-keeping and secret-keeping at the relationship level. Specifically, there was a significant intrapersonal correlation between promise-keeping and secret-keeping, *multivariate* $r(11)=.36$, $p<.001$. Therefore, when a child uniquely reported that a second child keeps their promises, the child also uniquely reported that the second child keeps their secrets. Also, there was evidence of interpersonal multivariate relationships between promise-keeping and secret-keeping: if child A rated child B as keeping their promises, child B uniquely rated child A as keeping their secrets, *multivariate* $r(11)=.09, p<.05$.

The social relations analysis revealed evidence of the reciprocal properties of trust. There was evidence of dyadic reciprocity for promise-keeping, *multivariate* $r(11)=.08$, $p<.05$, and secret-keeping, *multivariate* $r(11)=.10$, $p<.05$. Therefore, when child A uniquely reported that child B kept their promises or secrets, child B also uniquely reported that child A kept their promises or secrets. The strength of this reciprocity is comparable to reported dyadic reciprocity in previous research (e.g., Card, Hodges, Little, and Hawley, 2005). There was no evidence of individual reciprocity.

In summary, this application of the social relations analysis has provided evidence of the different components of dyadic relationships when applied to the variable of trust. In particular, the results reveal that young children: (1) differ in their ratings of trust awarded to their interaction partners; (2) elicit different ratings of trust from their interaction partners; and (3) reciprocate nominations of trust with their interaction partners. Also, the analysis reveals that trust is most strongly a dyadic phenomenon in young children. This pattern of findings is consistent with the previous research. However, it is important to note that these findings extend the previous research because this application of the social relations model provides unconfounded evidence of these facets of trust. Future research could extend this line of inquiry by examining individuals' actor and partner effects with other adjustment variables.

Dyadic data analysis: The mutual influence model

The chapter will now focus on a second type of dyadic data analysis: the mutual influence model. It is widely accepted that individuals within dyadic relationships influence each other's behavior (Campbell and Kashy, 2002; Woody and Sadler, 2005). Specifically, the behavior of one dyad member is likely to have a strong influence on the behavior of the other dyad member when they interact. When this principle is applied to trust in a dyad, the extent to which a child trusts their interaction partner influences the extent to which the interaction partner trusts the child in return. This is consistent with the principle of reciprocity of trust that has been highlighted as fundamental to social relationships (Rotenberg, 1994, 2001; Rotter, 1980).

The shared influence of behavior between the dyad members can have consequences for the method of analysis used to examine the behavior of individuals when engaging in dyadic interactions. Specifically, because individuals influence each other's behavior in dyads, this interdependence is likely to exist between dyad members (Kenny, Mannetti, Pierro, Livi, and Kashy, 2002). Further, interdependence violates one of the most important assumptions of statistical analysis: that of independence (Kenny, Mannetti, Pierro, Livi, and Kashy, 2002). Therefore, the issue of non-independence and the consequences of violating this principle is something that is becoming of increasing concern to researchers examining dyadic behavior and group interactions (Woody and Sadler, 2005). In particular, Woody and Sadler (2005) argue that interdependence must not be overlooked when analyzing dyadic data.

According to Kenny (1996), there are three sources of non-independence in dyads: partner effects, common fate, and mutual influence. Partner effects occur when one dyad member's behavior influences the behavior of the other dyad member (Kenny, 1996). Common fate occurs when the similarity in the dyad members' behavior is a result of an additional variable that influences both individuals (Kenny, 1996).

Mutual influence and the associated mutual influence model are of particular relevance to the study of children's trust between dyad members. According to the principle of mutual influence, one individual's score causes the other individual's score within a dyad, and the other individual's score causes the first individual's score (Kenny, 1996). Moreover, this pattern arises because a feedback loop exists between the two dyad members, and this feedback loop, in turn, results in the dyad members' scores reciprocally influencing each other (Kenny, 1996; Woody and Sadler, 2005). Therefore, within the context of trust, according to the mutual influence model, how much individual A trusts individual B influences how much individual B trusts individual A.

Although the concept of mutual influence within dyadic relationships is not a new one, it is only recently that a method has been proposed to examine mutual influence in dyadic relationships using structural equation modelling (see Woody and Sadler, 2005). Specifically, through the use of a phantom variable, Woody and Sadler (2005) outline a method of obtaining the necessary covariances and path strengths to test the reciprocal path between one dyad member and the other. A phantom variable is a latent variable that is unmeasured and is not important for the results of the model; rather, it provides a method of testing for additional paths and, ultimately, reciprocity between dyad members (Woody and Sadler, 2005). However, the mutual influence model and the associated analysis assumes that there is an absence of partner effects (Kenny, 1996; Woody and Sadler, 2005).

The mutual influence model is appropriate to examine trust because it is likely that reciprocal patterns of trust will emerge because researchers have hypothesized that the reciprocity of trust is important for relationship formation and maintenance (Rotter, 1980). Also, in dyadic relationships, trust is believed to be reciprocal, with both partners matching the other's expression of trust (Rotenberg, 1994). There is also limited empirical evidence of the reciprocal qualities of trust in fourth-grade children's friendship pairs (Rotenberg and Pilipenko, 1983). However, the previous research that has attempted to examine the reciprocal qualities of trust in dyadic relationships is limited because: (1) the methods used to examine reciprocity did not account for interdependence that occurs when two individuals interact (see Kenny, 1996; Woody and Sadler, 2005), and (2) the age of the sample studied was limited. In particular, no research has examined reciprocal trust in young children's friendships using appropriate methods to overcome the problems of interdependence. Through the use of the mutual influence model, these two issues with the previous research can be addressed.

An example

The next part of the chapter will present an analysis of young children's trust in best friend dyads using the mutual influence model (Betts, Rotenberg, and Trueman, 2006). Specifically, Woody and Sadler's (2005) SEM method of testing the mutual influence model will be used to examine whether young children's trust has reciprocal qualities in best friend dyads.

Initially, 211 children (103 male and 108 female) from nine year 2 and year 3 classrooms in the UK were asked to nominate their best friends using Parker and Asher's (1993) procedure. Specifically, children were asked to report which of their classmates were their best friends, and a reciprocal best friendship was coded when both children nominated each other as best friends. From these nominations, forty-six same-gender and three cross-gender best friend dyads were identified. The final sample comprised forty-seven boys and fifty-one girls, with a mean age of 7 years and 2 months (SD=6 months). The children also provided ratings of the extent to which they thought each classmate kept his/her promises and kept his/her secrets, using a five-point Likert scale (1=Strongly disagree to 5=Strongly agree). Subsequently, the promise-keeping and secret-keeping rating for each participant's best friend in the dyad were extracted.

The analysis of the mutual influence for secret-keeping revealed evidence of reciprocity between best friends within the dyads (see Figure 6.1). This is evidenced through the significant pathway between secret-keeping. Specifically, the propensity of one child to keep their secrets influenced the propensity of the other child to keep their secrets. However, the children's gender in the dyads did not predict secret-keeping reports. When the analysis of mutual influence was repeated from promise-keeping (see Figure 6.2) there was no evidence of reciprocity of promise-keeping for best friend dyads. Therefore, these findings suggest that young children tend not to match other in terms of the expression of promise-keeping

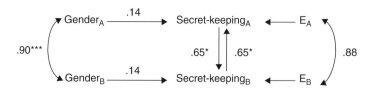

Figure 6.1 Reciprocity in secret-keeping in best friend dyads with standardized regression weights. Subscripts denote partner. *p<.05, ***p<.001 (one-tailed)

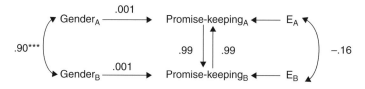

Figure 6.2 Reciprocity in promise-keeping in best friend dyads with standardized regression weights. Subscripts denote partner. ***p<.001 (one-tailed)

within their best friend dyads. Also, the gender of the child did not predict promise-keeping. Consequently, similar patterns of results emerged for boys and for girls, and also for same-gender and mixed-gender best friend dyads.

In summary, the results of the mutual influence analysis revealed evidence of dyadic reciprocity of secret-keeping in young children's best friend dyads. These findings support the claims that reciprocal secret-keeping is important for friendship and that best friends tend to engage in this behavior. Further, previous research has argued that children regard their peers as more desirable friends when they keep rather than reveal secrets (Rotenberg, 1991) and engage in trust behavior (Shannon and Kafer, 1984). However, the present findings extend previous research through using appropriate methods to account for interdependence in dyadic relationships, and empirically establishing reciprocity of secret-keeping in young children's best friend dyads.

This chapter has presented two statistical techniques: the social relations model and the mutual influence model as methods of analyzing children's trust. These techniques are part of a growing family of statistics that researchers can use to investigate dyadic relationships. Further, these methods are appropriate because they take into account interdependence that occurs between dyad members, and also permit separate investigation into the components of trust. The findings of the present chapter also contribute to the growing evidence that young children's relationships can be partitioned into different components (Betts and Rotenberg, 2008; Malloy, Sugarman, Montvilo, and Ben-Zeev, 1995; Malloy, Yarlas, Montvilo, and Sugarman, 1996; Ross and Lollis, 1989; Simpkins and Parke, 2002).

With regard to trust, the application of the social relations model has revealed that there are: (1) individual differences in children's ratings of trust awarded to others (identified as specific trust in previous research) and (2) individual differences in the extent to which children elicit ratings of trust from their peers (previously termed trustworthiness). Further, these differences have been identified as unconfounded effects and across different indicators of trust, suggesting that the measures used to assess young children's trust in peers are appropriate and reflect Rotenberg's (1994, 2001) conceptualization of trust. The findings also support the claim that trustworthiness is a personality characteristic that is observable in children, and the claim that children may develop cognitive schemas of trust (Rotenberg, Fox, Green, Ruderman, Slater, Stevens, and Carlo, 2005).

The social relations analysis has also underscored the importance of the relationship for children's trust. Specifically, the analysis has revealed

that children's trust is most strongly a dyadic phenomenon and a reciprocal process. Therefore, future research examining children's trust should
acknowledge the importance of the relationship. Further, the findings
suggest that the situational factors are important for children's trust and
their social relationships (see Betts and Rotenberg, 2008). The outcome
of the social relations analysis extends beyond the practicalities of future
research. For example, the finding that children's trust is a dyadic process
has implications for the number of interventions that have been developed to try to enhance children's social skills and friendship qualities.
Specifically, it may be that these interventions are only truly effective
when both interacting parties develop a shared understanding of trust.

The findings of the mutual influence analysis also revealed evidence
of dyadic reciprocity of secret-keeping in best friend pairs. This finding
reinforces the role of children's disclosure in friendships, and provides
evidence that young children engage in similar levels of disclosure in
the context of best friendships and that, even at a young age, children
prefer friends who keep secrets (Furman and Bierman, 1984). Further,
the finding is consistent with those researchers who have highlighted
the importance of disclosure and keeping information confidential for
the maintenance and continued survival of close relationships (Buzzelli,
1988; Moyer and Kunz, 1975).

In conclusion, the findings presented in this chapter further contribute to our understanding of the components of young children's
trust and clearly demonstrate the importance of reciprocal processes in
trust. The findings also demonstrate that trust is a dyadic phenomenon
that is underscored by the context of the unique relationship between
individuals.

References

Albright, L., Kenny, D. A., and Malloy, T. E. (1988). Consensus in personality judgments at zero acquaintance. *Journal of Personality and Social
Psychology*, **55**, 387–395.
Armsden, G. C. and Greenberg, M. T. (1987). The inventory of parent and
peer attachment: Individual differences and their relationship to psychological well-being in adolescence. *Journal of Youth and Adolescence*, **16**,
427–454.
Betts, L. R. (2005). *The relationship between young children's trust and their school
adjustment*. PhD thesis, Keele University.
Betts, L. R. and Rotenberg, K. J. (2007). Trustworthiness, friendship and self-
control: Factors that contribute to young children's school adjustment.
Infant and Child Development, **16**, 491–508.
   (2008). A social relations analysis of children's trust in their peers across the
early years of school. *Social Development*, **17**, 1039–1055.

Betts, L. R., Rotenberg, K. J., and Trueman, M. (2006). *Examining reciprocity of trust in young children's dyadic relationships*. Poster presented at the British Psychological Society Social Section Annual Conference, Birmingham.

(2009). An investigation of the impact of young children's self-knowledge of trustworthiness on school adjustment: A test of the Realistic Self-Knowledge and Positive Illusion models. *British Journal of Developmental Psychology*, **27**, 405–424.

Butler, J. K. (1986). Reciprocity of dyadic trust in close male–female relationships. *Journal of Social Psychology*, **126**, 579–591.

Buzzelli, C. A. (1988). The development of trust in children's relations with peers. *Child Study Journal*, **18**, 33–46.

Campbell, L. and Kashy, D. A. (2002). Estimating actor, partner, and interaction effects for dyadic data using PROC MIXED and HLM: A user-friendly guide. *Personal Relationships*, **9**, 327–342.

Card, N. A., Hodges, E. V. E., Little, T. D., and Hawley, P. H. (2005). Gender differences in peer nominations for aggression and social status. *International Journal of Behavioural Development*, **29**, 146–155.

Coie, J. D., Cillessen, A. H. N., Dodge, K. A., Hubbard, J. A., Schwartz, D., Lemerise, E. A., and Bateman, H. (1999). It takes two to fight: A test of relational factors and a method for assessing aggressive dyads. *Developmental Psychology*, **35**, 1179–1188.

Couch, L. L. and Jones, W. H. (1997). Measuring levels of trust. *Journal of Research in Personality*, **31**, 319–336.

Erikson, E. H. (1963). *Childhood and society* (2nd edn.). New York: W. W. Norton & Company.

Furman, W. and Bierman, K. L. (1984). Children's conceptions of friendship: A multimethod study of development changes. *Developmental Psychology*, **20**, 925–931.

Furman, W. and Buhrmester, D. (1985). Children's perceptions of the personal relationships in their social networks. *Developmental Psychology*, **21**, 1016–1024.

Holmes, J. G. and Rempel, J. K. (1989). Trust in close relationships. In C. Hendrick (ed.), *Review of personality and social psychology: Group processes and intergroup relations* (9th edn.) (pp. 187–220). Thousand Oaks, CA: Sage.

Hubbard, J. A., Dodge, K. A., Cillessen, A. H. N., Coie, J. D., and Schwartz, D. (2001). The dyadic nature of social information processing in boys' reactive and proactive aggression. *Journal of Personality and Social Psychology*, **80**, 268–280.

Imber, S. C. (1973). Relationship of trust to academic performance. *Journal of Personality and Social Psychology*, **28**, 145–150.

Kashy, D. A. and Kenny, D. A. (2000). The analysis of data from dyads and groups. In H. T. Reis and C. M. Judd (eds.), *Handbook of research methods in social personality psychology* (pp. 451–477). Cambridge University Press.

Kenny, D. A. (1994a). *Interpersonal perception: A social relations analysis*. New York: Guilford Press.

(1994b). Using the social relations model to understand relationships. In R. Erber and R. Gilmour (eds.), *Theoretical framework for personal relationships* (pp. 111–127). Hillsdale, NJ: Lawrence Erlbaum Associates.

(1996). Models of non-independence in dyadic research. *Journal of Social and Personal Relationships*, **13**, 279–294.

(1998). SOREMO version 2. Retrieved from http://davidakenny.net/srm/srmp.htm on December 17, 2009.

Kenny, D. A. and La Voie, L. (1984). The social relations model. *Advances in Experimental Social Psychology*, **18**, 141–182.

Kenny, D. A. and Nasby, W. (1980). Splitting the reciprocity correlation. *Journal of Personality and Social Psychology*, **38**, 249–256.

Kenny, D. A. and Xuan, A. (2002). WinSoReMo (computer software).

Kenny, D. A., Kashy, D. A., and Cook, W. L. (2006). *Dyadic data analysis*. New York: Guilford Press.

Kenny, D. A., Mannetti, L., Pierro, A., Livi, S., and Kashy, D. A. (2002). The statistical analysis of data from small groups. *Journal of Personality and Social Psychology*, **83**, 126–137.

Larzelere, R. E. and Huston, T. L. (1980). The dyadic trust scale: Toward understanding interpersonal trust in close relationships. *Journal of Marriage and the Family*, **42**, 595–604.

Lashley, B. R. and Kenny, D. A. (1998). Power estimation in social relations analyses. *Psychological Methods*, **3**, 328–338.

Lester, D. and Gatto, J. L. (1990). Interpersonal trust, depression, and suicidal ideation in teenagers. *Psychological Reports*, **67**, 786.

Malloy, T. E. and Kenny, D. A. (1986). The social relations model: An integrative method for personality research. *Journal of Personality*, **54**, 199–225.

Malloy, T. E., Sugarman, D. B., Montvilo, R. K., and Ben-Zeev, T. (1995). Children's interpersonal perceptions: A social relations analysis of perceiver and target effects. *Journal of Personality and Social Psychology*, **68**, 418–426.

Malloy, T. E., Yarlas, A., Montvilo, R. K. and Sugarman, D. B. (1996). Agreement and accuracy in children's interpersonal perceptions: A social relations analysis. *Journal of Personality and Social Psychology*, **71**, 692–702.

Merrel, K. W. and Gimpel, G. A. (1998). *Social skills of children and adolescents: Conceptualization, assessment and treatment*. Mahwah, NJ: Lawrence Erlbaum Associates.

Moyer, J. E. and Kunz, J. T. (1975). Trust in everything. *Young Children*, **30**, 107–112.

Parker, J. G. and Asher, S. R. (1993). Friendship and friendship quality in middle childhood: Links with peer group acceptance and feelings of loneliness and social dissatisfaction. *Developmental Psychology*, **29**, 611–621.

Perry, D. G., Kusel, S. J., and Perry, L. C. (1988). Victims of peer aggression. *Developmental Psychology*, **24**, 807–814.

Ross, H. S. and Lollis, S. P. (1989). A social relations analysis of toddle peer relationships. *Child Development*, **60**, 1082–1091.

Rotenberg, K. J. (1984). Sex differences in children's trust in peers. *Sex Roles*, **11**, 953–957.

(1986). Same-sex patterns and sex differences in the trust-value basis of children's friendship. *Sex Roles*, **15**, 613–626.

(1991). *Children's interpersonal trust: Sensitivity to lying, deception, and promise violations.* NY: Springer-Verlag.

(1994). Loneliness and interpersonal trust. *Journal of Social and Clinical Psychology*, **13**, 152–173.

(2001). Interpersonal trust across the lifespan. In N.J. Smelser and P.B. Baltes (eds.), *International encyclopedia of social and behavioral sciences* (pp. 7866–7868). New York: Pergamon.

Rotenberg, K.J. and Pilipenko, T.A. (1983–1984). Mutuality, temporal consistency, and helpfulness in children's trust in peers. *Social Cognition*, **2**, 235–255.

Rotenberg, K.J., Boulton, M.J., and Fox, C.L. (2005). Cross-sectional and longitudinal relations among children's trust beliefs, psychological maladjustment, and social relationships during childhood: Are very high as well as very low trusting children at risk? *Journal of Abnormal Child Psychology*, **33**, 595–610.

Rotenberg, K.J., Fox, C., Green, S., Ruderman, L., Slater, K., Stevens, K., and Carlo, G. (2005). Construction and validation of a children's interpersonal trust belief scale. *British Journal of Developmental Psychology*, **23**, 271–292.

Rotenberg, K.J., MacDonald, K.J., and King, E.V. (2004). The relationship between loneliness and interpersonal trust during middle childhood. *Journal of Genetic Psychology*, **165**, 233–249.

Rotenberg, K.J., McDougall, P., Boulton, M.J., Vaillancourt, T., Fox, C., and Hymel, S. (2004). Cross-sectional and longitudinal relations among relational trustworthiness, social relationships, and psychological adjustment during childhood and adolescence in the UK and Canada. *Journal of Experimental Child Psychology*, **88**, 46–67.

Rotenberg, K.J., Michalik, N., Eisenberg, N., and Betts, L.R. (2008). The relations among young children's peer-reported trustworthiness, inhibitory control, and preschool adjustment. *Early Childhood Research Quarterly*, **23**, 288–298.

Rotter, J.B. (1967). A new scale for the measurement of interpersonal trust. *Journal of Personality*, **35**, 651–665.

(1980). Interpersonal trust, trustworthiness and gullibility. *American Psychologist*, **35**, 1–7.

Schneider, B.H. (2000). *Friends and enemies: Peer relations in childhood.* London: Edward Arnold.

Scott, C.L. (1980). Interpersonal trust: A comparison of attitudinal and situational factors. *Human Relations*, **33**, 805–812.

Shannon, K. and Kafer, N.F. (1984). Reciprocity, trust and vulnerability in neglected and rejected children. *Journal of Psychology*, **117**, 65–70.

Simpkins, S.D. and Parke, R.D. (2002). Do friends and nonfriends behave differently? A social relations analysis of children's behavior. *Merrill-Palmer Quarterly*, **48**, 263–283.

Warner, R.M., Kenny, D.A., and Stoto, M. (1979). A new round-robin analysis of variance for social interaction data. *Journal of Personality and Social Psychology*, **37**, 1742–1757.

Waters, E., Vaughn, B.E., Posada, G., and Kondo-Ikemura, K. (eds.) (1995). Caregiving, cultural, and cognitive perspectives on security-based behavior and working models. *Monographs of the Society for Research in Child Development*, **60** (2–3, Serial No. 244).

Whitley, B. E., Schofield, J. W., and Snyder, H. N. (1984). Peer preferences in a desegregated school: A round-robin analysis. *Journal of Personality and Social Psychology*, **46**, 799–810.

Wright, T. L. and Kirmani, A. (1977). Interpersonal trust, trustworthiness, and shoplifting in high school. *Psychological Reports*, **41**, 1165–1166.

Wright, T. L. and Sharp, E. G. (1979). Content and grammatical sex bias on the interpersonal trust scale and differential trust toward women and men. *Journal of Consulting and Clinical Psychology*, **47**, 72–85.

Woody, E. and Sadler, P. (2005). Structural equation models for interchangeable dyads: Being the same makes a difference. *Psychological Methods*, **10**, 139–158.

Zak, A. M., Gold, J. A., Ryckman, R. M., and Lenney, E. (1988). Assessment of trust in intimate relationships and the self-perception process. *Journal of Social Psychology*, **138**, 217–228.

7   Siblings and trust

Shirley McGuire (University of San Francisco),
Nancy L. Segal (California State University, Fullerton),
Patricia Gill (Marin Brain Injury Network),
Bridget Whitlow (University of California, San Diego), and
June M. Clausen (University of San Francisco)

Developmental psychologist Judy Dunn (1996) called the sibling relationship "the first society." This is because many children first attempt to protect their territory, justify their actions, and negotiate deals in the context of this relationship. Given what is at stake – love, protection, toys – it is, perhaps, not surprising that books for parents about reducing sibling rivalry and sibling conflict are popular (e.g., Brazelton and Sparrow, 2005; Faber and Mazlish, 2004). Sibling research, however, shows that siblings can also be sources of social support for individuals, particularly for children who are experiencing problems with their parents or peers (e.g., East and Rook, 1992; Milevsky and Levitt, 2005), and for adults who are widowed or childless (e.g., Doherty and Feeney, 2004; Guiaux, van Tilburg, and van Groenou, 2007). Furthermore, many children and teenagers report warm and intimate relationships with their siblings, especially with their sisters (e.g., Brody, 1998; Buhrmester and Furman, 1987, 1990; Dunn and McGuire, 1992; McGuire, McHale, and Updegraff, 1996; Noller, 2005). In fact, Howe and colleagues have found links between sibling warmth and relying on siblings as confidants, suggesting that a close sibling relationship may nurture the development of trust (Howe, Aquan-Assee, Bukowski, Lehoux, and Rinaldi, 2001; Howe, Aquan-Assee, Bukowski, Rinaldi, and Lehoux, 2000).

Interpersonal trust is a crucial component to positive relationships that foster healthy development (Rotenberg, 1991; Simpson, 2007). Given that siblings are children's most constant social companions (McHale and Crouter, 1996) and, for many people, the sibling relationship is the longest one of their lives (Cicirelli, 1995), the development of trust between siblings may contribute to positive mental health across development.

The purpose of this chapter is to explore the nature of sibling trust with data from the Twins, Adoptees, Peers, and Siblings (TAPS) study. The research project is a collaboration between the University of San Francisco and California State University, Fullerton. The main purpose of the study is to use a biosocial perspective to move beyond the study of sibling rivalry to examine sibling socialization effects in middle childhood. The TAPS study incorporates a unique design that combines the traditional twin, adoption, and family designs with a novel addition. The investigation also includes same-aged, genetically unrelated sibling pairs called "virtual twins," who mimic the twin context without biological relatedness (Segal, McGuire, Havlena, Gill, and Hershberger, 2007). The design allowed us to test hypotheses concerning correlates of sibling trust based on attachment and evolutionary theories.

Sibling trust: Theoretical perspectives

Attachment theorists have proposed that a secure bond with a warm, reliable caregiver plays a central role in development (e.g., Bowlby, 1969). More recently, social scientists have argued that such a bond can develop between brothers and sisters under certain circumstances (e.g., Ainsworth, 1989; Bank and Kahn, 1997; Tancredy and Fraley, 2006). However, a model of trust based on the attachment paradigm alone is limiting because it does not provide a useful operational definition of interpersonal trust (Rotenberg, 1994) and does not consider possible genetic contributions to sibling relationship processes (Michalski and Euler, 2008), including trust in siblings. Consequently, the chapter continues with a review of Rotenberg's (1994) model of interpersonal trust, which served as the foundation for the TAPS trust measures, and a discussion of evolutionary theory. This review begins with attachment theory, however, because most research on trust between family members is embedded in this literature.

Attachment theory

Psychodynamic theorist Erik Erikson (1964) made trust a foundation of social-emotional development. He argued that the first year of life involved the decision to trust or mistrust others. Reliable caretakers who respond to children's needs foster faith in interpersonal relationships. Trust in the caretaker allows the child to feel safe, tolerate brief separations, and interact with the world independently of the parent. Attachment theorist John Bowlby (1969) also argued that a secure relationship with a consistent, accessible caregiver was crucial for healthy development. Attachment is the dynamic equilibrium between the caregiver and the child that balances the child's need for safety with the need to explore their world. The infant's trust in the caretaker is a key element of the attachment bond, but not all trusting relationships are attachment relationships. Attachment relationships differ from other close relationships in proximity-seeking behavior, levels of separation distress, and use of the relationship as a safe haven and secure base (Ainsworth, 1989). Secure relationships serve as a safe place where children feel protected and supported; these feelings allow children to explore their world, leading to cognitive as well as social-emotional development. Once children develop symbolic representation, the theory specifies that they construct mental representations or internal working models of relationships that are based on their attachment experiences with the parent; the model serves as a guide for other relationships. Thus, children with secure attachments to their caregivers will learn to trust others, including their siblings. Consequently, the TAPS study included measures of trust in the mother and in the sibling relationships. The first hypothesis was that children's trust beliefs in these two relationship contexts would be significantly correlated.

Bowlby (1969) also stated that children could have attachments to multiple caregivers, although none would be as central as the one with the mother. Studies of young children have shown that older siblings can serve as secure bases for their younger brothers and sisters (Stewart, 1983; Stewart and Marvin, 1984; Teti and Ablard, 1989). Studies of older adults have shown that siblings serve as attachment figures for them, especially individuals who do not have partners or children (Doherty and Feeney, 2004). Ainsworth (1989) and Bank and Kahn (1997) argued specifically for the development of an attachment bond between siblings independent of the caregiver bond, especially when parents were physically or emotionally unavailable. Tancredy and Fraley (2006) asserted that an attachment bond can develop independently in a twin relationship, because that bond contains many elements that promote attachment in the caregiver–child bond (i.e., shared experiences, proximity-seeking, feelings of interconnectedness, and empathy). They found that adult twins were more likely than adult non-twin siblings to report that their sibling was a primary attachment figure. Age interacted with dyad type, with siblings at the bottom of the attachment hierarchy for non-twins, and at the top, along with partners and friends, for twins. Still, attachment theory does not provide us with a useful model for defining trust itself and it requires a close, personal bond. Rotenberg (1991, 1994) has addressed both of these issues in his work on the development of interpersonal trust in children.

Rotenberg's interpersonal trust framework

Rotenberg's (1994) framework for conceptualizing children's interpersonal trust consists of a 3 (bases) × 3 (domains) × 2 (target dimensions) matrix. The three bases of trust are reliability (e.g., keeping promises), emotional trust (e.g., keeping disclosures confidential, not causing harm or embarrassment), and honesty (e.g., telling the truth, being genuine). According to Rotenberg's theory, there are three domains of trust: the cognitive/affective, behavior-dependent, and behavior-enacting. The cognitive/affective domain encompasses children's trust beliefs about the target person and the emotions accompanying those beliefs. Trust beliefs are manifested in behavior dependence in the form of the person relying on others to fulfill their promises, keep information confidential, and be honest. Also, behavior-enacting is a disposition that corresponds to how much a person engages in trustworthy behavior in the form of fulfilling promises, maintaining confidentiality, and being honest. Frequently, trustworthiness is assessed by peer reports of those behaviors in children (Rotenberg, McDougall, Boulton, Vaillancourt, Fox, and Hymel, 2005). The last element of Rotenberg's framework is the dimensions of the target of trust: targets may differ on specificity (from generalized trust to trust in a specific person) and familiarity (from somewhat unfamiliar to very familiar). This framework is described in detail in Chapter 3 of this book. According to this framework, trust is manifested in a range of persons in addition to the specific and highly familiar target person – the primary caregiver. This chapter focuses on school-age children's *trust beliefs* in two specific, very familiar relationships: with their sibling (or twin) and with their mother. All three bases of children's trust beliefs (i.e., reliability, emotional trust, and honesty) in these two people were assessed in the TAPS measures.

Rotenberg (1991) has argued that interpersonal trust is essential to the establishment and maintenance of relationships with others. According to his theory, children must learn to keep promises, to be reliable, and to participate in sharing confidences in order to be part of the social world. Indeed, he and his colleagues have found links between children's trust beliefs and their prosocial behavior, cooperative behavior, and psychological adjustment (e.g., Rotenberg, Boulton, and Fox, 2005; Rotenberg, MacDonald, and King, 2004). Studies of sibling disclosure, an element of trust beliefs, suggest that trust beliefs in the sibling may be linked to sibling intimacy (Howe, Aquan-Assee, Bukowski, Lehoux, and Rinaldi, 2001; Howe, Aquan-Assee, Bukowski, Rinaldi, and Lehoux, 2000). Trust beliefs promote disclosure because there is the belief that the person will keep the information confidential. Shared confidences, along with cooperation and helping behavior, may promote sibling intimacy and lower sibling conflict. Thus, it was predicted that trust beliefs in the sibling would be positively correlated with children's reports of sibling intimacy and negatively correlated with children's reports of sibling conflict in the TAPS sample.

Evolutionary theory

The TAPS design allows us to examine another potential correlate of children's trust beliefs in their siblings – genetic relatedness of the sibling pair. Evolutionary psychology is concerned with identifying characteristics and relationship processes that promote individual survival and reproduction (Buss, 2004). Evolutionary psychologists have begun using Darwinian concepts of natural selection and reproductive strategies to explain the development of psychological mechanisms that influence family functioning (Salmon and Shackelford, 2008). This perspective acknowledges the roles of adaptation and inclusive fitness in altruistic behavior towards others (Hamilton, 1964). According to this principle, people will act more favorably towards those with whom they share genes, compared to those with whom they do not share genes, because those individuals have the ability to pass on their common genes. Promoting the survival and reproductive capabilities of genetically related kin is one way of promoting the survival of one's own genes in future generations (Segal, Seghers, Marelich, Mechanic, and Castillo, 2007).

According to evolutionary theory, the quality of sibling interaction (and related beliefs about the relationship) would vary as a function of the genetic relatedness between the sibling pairs (Michalski and Euler, 2008). Monozygotic twins, who share all inherited genes, would experience more positive sibling relationships compared to dizygotic twins, who share on average 50 percent of their segregating genes. In addition, full siblings, who share on average 50 percent of their segregating genes, should experience more positive sibling relationships compared to half-siblings or genetically unrelated siblings. Some studies have found that MZ twins are more likely to experience closer, more intimate relationships compared to DZ twins (Segal, 2000), and that full siblings have warmer or more emotionally engaged relationships compared to half-siblings and genetically unrelated siblings in stepfamilies (Deater-Deckard, Dunn, O'Connor, and Golding, 2002; Hetherington and Clingempeel, 1992; Hetherington, Henderson, and Reiss, 1999). In their study of twin attachment, Tancredy and Fraley (2006) found that MZ twins were more likely to report being attached to their siblings than DZ twins, who were more likely to report sibling attachment compared to non-twins.

The TAPS design contains four sibling dyads that vary in genetic relatedness: (1) monozygotic twins (MZ), (2) dizygotic twins (DZ), (3) full sibling pairs (FS), and (4) virtual twins (VT). MZ twins result from the division of a single fertilized egg and, as mentioned above, share all inherited genes. DZ twins result from the separate fertilization of two eggs by separate sperm and share, on average, 50 percent of their segregating genes. FS pairs also result from the separate fertilization of two eggs, but at different time points, and share 50 percent of their segregating genes. Virtual twin pairs (VT) are same-aged, genetically unrelated pairs reared together since infancy (Segal, 1997; Segal, McGuire, Havlena, Gill, and Hershberger, 2007). They replicate the rearing situation of twins, but without genetic relatedness. If children's trust beliefs are associated with positive aspects of their relationships (e.g., closeness, cooperation, warmth), then mean levels in children's trust beliefs in their siblings would show the same pattern found in twin and sibling studies of sibling positivity. Evolutionary theory predicts that a child's trust beliefs in their sibling should vary positively with the genetic relatedness of the pair. That is, mean differences in children's trust beliefs should show the following pattern: MZ twins > DZ twins = FS pairs > VT pairs.

It is important to note that significant mean differences in children's trust beliefs would not necessarily indicate that individual differences in children's trust beliefs are heritable. Heritability is a statistic that estimates the proportion of variance in individual differences in behavior that can be contributed to individual differences in genetic relatedness between individuals (see Plomin, 1994; Reiss, Neiderhiser, Hetherington, and Plomin, 2000). Behavioral genetic studies would test for significant differences in sibling similarity in their reports of their trust beliefs across dyads varying in genetic relatedness. Evolutionary psychology studies test for significant mean differences in behavior or relationship processes across dyads varying in genetic relatedness. This chapter focuses on the etiology of mean level differences in children's trust beliefs across different sibling dyads.

Hypotheses

Based on attachment theory, it was predicted that children's trust beliefs concerning their siblings and mothers should be correlated. The next hypothesis was that children's trust beliefs would be positively correlated with sibling intimacy and negatively correlated with sibling conflict. This prediction was based on studies of children's interpersonal trust and self-disclosure (e.g., Howe, Aquan-Assee, Bukowski, Lehoux, and Rinaldi, 2001; Howe, Aquan-Assee, Bukowski, Rinaldi, and Lehoux,

2000; Rotenberg, 1994) – that is, a sibling relationship high in warmth and closeness would promote the development of feelings of trust in the sibling. The final hypothesis, based on evolutionary theory, was that mean differences in children's trust beliefs concerning the sibling would vary positively with the genetic relatedness of the dyad. That is, MZ twins would report higher beliefs compared to the other dyads, and DZ twins and FS pairs would report higher beliefs compared to the VT pairs.

The Twins, Adoptees, Peers, and Siblings (TAPS) study

The TAPS study incorporates a unique design that combines the traditional twin, adoption, and family designs with a novel addition, virtual twins. Friend–friend pairs were also added to the design to serve as a comparison group when testing socialization effects. This chapter includes only the twin and sibling pairs because it focuses on children's trust beliefs regarding their siblings.

Participants

The study included 870 participants (316 parents and 554 children) in 316 families. The families included 206 families with two twins or siblings in the study, 14 families with three or more siblings in the study, and 96 families with a child in a friend–friend pair. All analyses on dyads were conducted with and without the pairs containing repeated data and any changes in results were noted.

Several methods were used to recruit the families in order to reduce bias introduced by one technique alone. Thirty-eight percent of the families were recruited through school letters, community organizations, newspaper ads, and flyers posted in diverse neighborhoods. The sample comprised 13 percent recruited from a previous study of VT twins (Segal, McGuire, Havlena, Gill, and Hershberger, 2007); 6 percent recruited through parents of twins clubs; and the remaining 43 percent of the families recruited through referrals from participants and other community members knowledgeable about the study. Interested families went through a two-step screening process, first during the initial phone call, and again during scheduling of the home interview. Both participating children had to meet the following criteria: (1) be primary school-aged (i.e., between 7 and 12 years old); (2) be in a twin, full sibling, or friend relationship; and (3) be free of disabilities or handicaps that would prevent them from completing the measures. One interview had to be rescheduled until after the older sibling turned 13 years old;

Table 7.1 *Ethnic and racial background of TAPS participants*

Categories	Mothers		Children		Total sample	
	N	%	N	%	N	%
African American	9	2.9	18	3.3	27	3.1
Native American	1	0.3	0	0	1	0.1
Asian	16	5.1	21	3.8	37	4.3
White, not Hispanic	228	72.1	347	62.6	575	66.1
Hispanic, Latino	35	11.1	41	7.4	76	8.7
Mixed ancestry	13	4.1	112	20.2	125	14.4
Other	6	1.9	3	0.5	9	1.0
No response	8	2.5	12	2.2	20	2.3
Totals	316	100	554	100	870	100

Note: In one of the 316 families, the reporter was a father.

data for this pair were included in the TAPS study. Virtual twins had to meet additional strict criteria: (1) the siblings needed to be within 9 months of each other; (2) the children must have been raised together since they were 1 year of age; and (3) the children must have been in the same school grade, but could have attended separate classes or schools (see Segal, 1997 for more details).

Participating parents from the 316 families included one father and 315 mothers. Most families were two-parent households living near metropolitan areas in the Western United States. The VT families, however, were from multiple regions across the USA. TAPS families were predominantly middle-class, with the modal family income in the $75,001 to $100,000 range. However, family income for the sample ranged from less than $10,000 to $300,000 or higher, and parental education ranged from eighth grade to a graduate/postgraduate education. Table 7.1 shows the ethnic and racial background percentages for the mothers and the children participating in the TAPS study. The majority of the mothers (72.1 percent) and children (62.6 percent) were of White, non-Hispanic ancestry. The average age of the children was 9.6 years (*SD*=1.4 years) and a range of 7 to 13 years. Forty-six percent of the children were boys (*n*=254) and 54 percent were girls (*n*=300).

Design

The TAPS design included 300 child–child pairs in five dyad types: fifty-four monozygotic twin pairs; eighty-six dizygotic twin pairs (fifty-one

Table 7.2 *Characteristics of the dyad types in the TAPS study*

	MZ twins	DZ twins	VT pairs	FS pairs	FF pairs
No. of pairs	54	86	43	69	48
Genetic relatedness	100%	50%	0%	50%	0%
Chose to be together	No	No	No	No	Yes
Hypothesized closeness	High	Low	Low	Low	High
Sex composition	Same only	Same & opposite	Same & opposite	Same & opposite	Same only
Age differences in months	0	0	$X=3.0$ $(SD=2.6)$	$X=26.9$ $(SD=10.4)$	$X=6.3$ $(SD=6.4)$

Notes: MZ=monozygotic; DZ=dizygotic; VT=virtual twin; FS=full sibling; FF=friend–friend

same-sex pairs and thirty-five opposite-sex pairs); forty-three virtual twin pairs (sixteen same-sex pairs and twenty-seven opposite-sex pairs); sixty-nine full sibling pairs (thirty-six same-sex pairs and thirty-five opposite-sex pairs); and forty-eight friend–friend pairs (all same-sex). Table 7.2 gives the characteristics of each of the dyad types.

The zygosity of the same-sex twin pairs was established by comparative examination of thirteen short tandem repeat (STR) DNA markers. DNA extracted from buccal swabs was analyzed by Affiliated Genetics in Salt Lake City, Utah. The MZ–DZ twin comparison is the traditional twin design allowing us to investigate genetic and environmental contributions to attitudes, behavior, and relationship processes.

Of the forty-three VT pairs, forty-one were part of an ongoing longitudinal study of cognitive and social development (Segal, 1997; Segal, McGuire, Havlena, Gill, and Hershberger, 2007). The pairs replicate the rearing situation of twins, offering an opportunity to assess shared environmental contributions to behavioral traits. VT pairs consisted of either one adopted and one biological child or two adoptees. The average age difference for the VTs in the TAPS sample was 3 months (*SD*=2.6 months).

Full siblings (FS) were genetically related pairs within 4 years of age of each other. The average age difference between the siblings was 26.9 months (*SD*=10.4). Including full sibling pairs allowed us to test age-related correlates of behavioral traits, as well as generalizability of the findings from the twins.

Procedures

After obtaining consent from the participating children and parents, the family members were interviewed and videotaped in structured situations in their homes as part of a 2- to 3-hour assessment of children's personal characteristics and family experiences. Children and one parent were interviewed on the telephone 7 days after the interview to assess daily activities. Only the children's interview data were used in the analyses included in the present chapter.

The children were given the designation of "Child 1" and "Child 2" before the interview, using the alphabetical order of their first names. Each child was interviewed by a trained tester in order to ensure that the children understood the questions. Separate trained testers read the scenarios to each child during their home interview. The tester changed the wording if the primary caregiver was not the mother (e.g., How sure are you that your father will take you swimming?). Children used cards with "very sure," "a bit sure," "don't know," "a bit unsure," and "very unsure" to indicate their responses. The child could either tell the tester their answer or hold up the card if confidentiality was an issue. Testers marked the answer in the booklet using the 1 (very sure) to 5 (very unsure) Likert scale.

Measures

Each child was interviewed about their trust beliefs regarding two specific familiar targets: their primary caregiver (which were mothers for 99 percent of the families) and the other sibling in the study (i.e., target sibling). The scales were based on the Children's Generalized Trust Belief Scale (CGTB) created by Rotenberg, Fox, Green, Ruderman, Slater, Stevens, and Carlo (2005). The CGTB measures children's trust beliefs in others, using scenarios based on realistic situations, and uses a Likert scale to capture variability. Our measures were created for the TAPS study in consultation with Ken Rotenberg and Lucy Betts, and were based on Rotenberg's (1994) theory. The same method was used and included scenarios concerning all three bases of trust outlined in Rotenberg's theory: reliability, emotional trust, and honesty.

Trust beliefs: Mother Both children (i.e., Child 1 and Child 2) were given eleven scenarios regarding trust beliefs concerning their mothers. The interview included questions about their mothers' promise-keeping, secret-keeping, and honesty. Two questions in the interview were excluded in the final scale because their intercorrelations were lower than .20 for both reporters. The first excluded item asked if the mother would keep a secret from the sibling. It was the only item concerning the sibling and may represent a form of collusion. The second excluded item asked if the mother would keep a secret from a gym teacher about activities the child cannot perform. It seems likely that it would be inappropriate for the mother to keep this information secret. Consequently, the scales were created using the remaining nine items (see Appendix A for the nine interview questions). Cronbach alphas for children's trust beliefs in the mother using the nine-item scale were .82 and .80 for Child 1 and Child 2 reports, respectively.

Trust beliefs: Sibling Both children (i.e., Child 1 and Child 2) were given twelve scenarios regarding trust beliefs concerning the target sibling in the study. The scale included items about their siblings' promise-keeping, secret-keeping, and honesty. Two questions in the interview were excluded from the scale because their intercorrelations were lower than .20 for both reporters. The two excluded items asked about the siblings' ability to keep a secret about a fight with a friend from the child's other friend, and to honor an agreement to give a friend a note at school. These items may require the sibling to have access to the other child's peer group that the sibling may not have. Consequently, the scales were created using the remaining ten items (see Appendix B for the ten interview questions). Cronbach alphas for children's trust beliefs in the sibling were .84 and .85 for Child 1 and Child 2 reports, respectively.

Sibling intimacy and conflict Each child completed a thirteen-item questionnaire scale about the quality of the relationship with the target sibling. Eight of the items were from a scale created by Blyth and colleagues (Blyth and Foster-Clark, 1987; Blyth, Hill, and Thiel, 1982) to measure intimacy in adolescents' relationships with significant others. Children used a Likert scale (1 = Not at all to 5 = Very much/A lot) to report the degree of support and satisfaction in the relationship. The measure has shown high internal consistency reliabilities in other studies of children's sibling relationships (e.g., McGuire, McHale, and Updegraff, 1996). Cronbach alphas for children's reports of sibling intimacy dyad were .81 and .83 for Child 1 and for Child 2 reports, respectively.

The other five items used to assess sibling conflict were from Stocker and McHale's (1992) Sibling Relationship Inventory; the subscale has also demonstrated high internal consistency reliabilities in other studies of children's sibling relationships (e.g., McGuire, McHale, and Updegraff, 1996). Children used a Likert scale (1 = Not at all to 5 = Very much/A lot) to report the degree of fighting, annoyance, and anger in the

Table 7.3 *Correlations between children's trust beliefs in sibling and other family relationship measures for Child 1 and Child 2 reports*

Measure	Child 1	Child 2
Trust beliefs: Mother	.39**	.36**
Sibling intimacy	.51**	.46**
Sibling conflict	−.39**	−.43**

Notes: *n*=252 for Child 1 reports and for Child 2 reports
**$p<.01$

relationship with their siblings. Cronbach alphas for children's reports of sibling conflict were .92 for both Child 1 and Child 2 reports.

Results

Preliminary analyses Links between age and sex differences and the two trust measures were examined first to see if the data needed to be examined separately for boys and girls, and older and younger children. Correlations were conducted between children's age in months and both trust measures, and between the age difference for the sibling pair and sibling trust. None of the associations was significant. Independent t-tests were conducted to explore sex differences for both trust measures and to examine sex composition of the dyad differences (i.e., same-sex versus different-sex) for sibling trust. There were no significant sex differences for any of the measures.

Correlations between trust beliefs in mother and in sibling To test the first hypothesis, the association between children's trust beliefs about the mother and about the sibling was examined. The prediction based on attachment theory was supported. Children's trust beliefs in the mother and their trust beliefs in the sibling were significant and positive (see Table 7.3).

Correlations between trust beliefs in sibling and sibling intimacy and conflict To test the second hypothesis, associations between children's trust beliefs about the sibling and children's reports of sibling intimacy and conflict were examined. The prediction based on attachment theory and previous studies of children's interpersonal trust and self-disclosure was supported. The correlation between children's trust beliefs

Table 7.4 *Mean differences and standard deviations for children's trust beliefs in sibling: By dyad type and reporter*

	MZ	DZ	FS	VT
Reporter	(n=54 pairs)[a]	(n=86 pairs)	(n=69 pairs)	(n=43 pairs)
Child 1	37.0$_a$ (8.6)	33.1$_b$ (9.6)	32.8$_b$ (9.1)	29.4$_b$ (8.5)
Child 2	39.1$_a$ (8.0)	33.0$_b$ (10.2)	34.2$_b$ (8.8)	30.8$_b$ (9.3)

Note: Means in the same row that do not share subscripts differ at p<.05 in the Tukey honesty significant difference comparison.

concerning the sibling and children's reports of sibling intimacy was significant and positive for both Child 1 and Child 2 reports (see Table 7.4). In addition, the correlation between children's trust beliefs concerning the sibling and children's reports of sibling conflict was significant and negative for both Child 1 and Child 2 reports.

Mean differences by genetic relatedness A 2 (reporter) x 4 (dyad type) mixed ANOVA was conducted to test the evolutionary hypotheses concerning mean differences in children's trust beliefs in the sibling. Child 1 and Child 2 reports were included in the means analysis as a repeated measure variable. Dyad type consisted of: MZ twins (MZ), DZ twins (DZ), full sibling pairs (FS), and virtual twins (VT).

Based on evolutionary theory, it was predicted that the means for children's trust beliefs in the sibling would show the following pattern: MZ twins > DZ twins = FS pairs > VT pairs. Results showed a significant effect for dyad type, F (3,248)=9.94, p<.001. There was no reporter effect, F (1,248)=2.93, *n.s.*, or reporter-by-dyad type interaction, F (3,248)=.52, *n.s.* Follow-up Tukey tests revealed that children in MZ twins reported significantly higher trust beliefs in their sibling (at least p<.05) compared to those in DZ twins, full sibling pairs, and virtual twins. Although the means were in the predicted direction, DZ twins, full siblings, and virtual twins did not differ from each other significantly.

Discussion

This chapter explored the nature of sibling trust in twin and sibling relationships during middle childhood. Several of our hypotheses concerning correlates of children's trust beliefs in their siblings were supported. Trust beliefs in the sibling were positively related with trust beliefs in the mother and sibling intimacy. Trust beliefs in the sibling were also negatively related to sibling conflict. These results are consistent with attachment theory: children may learn how to trust each other from their relationship with their caregivers. A warm, close sibling relationship may also provide children with the support they need to trust their siblings with their secrets (Howe, Aquan-Assee, Bukowski, Lehoux, and Rinaldi, 2001).

Future research should examine the role of sibling trust in adjustment. There is evidence that siblings can serve as buffers in single-parent families (e.g., East, Weisner, and Reyes, 2006), in divorced families (e.g., Hetherington and Clingempeel, 1992; Hetherington, Henderson, and Reiss, 1999), and in non-divorced families with high marital conflict (e.g., Gass, Jenkins, and Dunn, 2007). Sibling trust may be a key component. Being able to count on and confide in one's sibling may be a protective factor for children and teenagers in stressful circumstances.

Our hypotheses concerning genetic differences in children's trust beliefs in the sibling and the mother were only partially supported. As predicted, MZ twins did report higher trust beliefs concerning their siblings compared to the other sibling pairs. This finding is also consistent with Tancredy and Fraley's (2006) study of attachment in adult twins. Furthermore, DZ twins and FS pairs were not significantly different from each other. Contrary to our predictions, VT pairs did not differ significantly from the DZ twins and FS pairs in trust beliefs concerning the sibling, although the means were in the hypothesized direction. MZ twins may be the only sibling type that experiences the levels of closeness, cooperation, and support necessary to develop high levels of sibling trust. However, it may be that our sample size was not large enough to find a subtle difference between VT pairs and DZ and FS pairs.

This study had several limitations. The measures focused on the cognitive/affective dimension of sibling trust (i.e., children's trust beliefs concerning their sibling). Studies are needed to examine trust-related behavior. Future TAPS analyses are planned, examining children's behavior in joint decision-making games from the marital literature, and cooperation and coordination tasks based on the behavioral economic literature (Hardin, 2002). In addition, relying on only one reporter prevented us from assessing trustworthiness, which would require multiple informants of each person's behavior (Rotenberg, McDougall, Boulton, Vaillancourt, Fox, and Hymel, 2004). Of course, longitudinal studies of sibling trust would also allow antecedents and consequences of sibling trust to be examined.

It is also important to note that TAPS is a community-based study. Trust between brothers and sisters may develop differently in abusive or neglectful family contexts. Sibling trust could work to hinder, rather than help, healthy development. Keeping secrets, a form of emotional trust, may be the basis of sibling collusion that is found in coercive families (Bullock and Dishion, 2002). It may be self-interested trust, and not sibling warmth, that is the foundation of delinquency training found in some sibling pairs (Fagan and Najman, 2003; Slomkowski, Rende, Conger, Simons, and Conger, 2001). In order to participate in crime together, siblings would have to agree not to tell others about their illegal activities. Family systems, social exchange, and conflict theories all predict the development of family alliances, including between siblings, based on the self-interest of those family members (White and Klein, 2008). On the other hand, warm, supportive family interaction may cultivate family-level trust that could serve as a source of social capital (Delsing, van Aken, Oud, De Bruyn, and Scholte, 2005). Work is needed in both the research and the clinical areas to help us understand the positive and negative aspects of keeping secrets and promises in the family.

Acknowledgments

Funding was provided by NIMH grant R01 MH63351 (Shirley McGuire, principal investigator, and Nancy L. Segal, co-principal investigator) and by Faculty Development awards to the first author from the University of San Francisco. The authors would like to thank the families who participated in the study and the research assistants who assisted with data collection.

References

Ainsworth, M. D. S. (1989). Attachments beyond infancy. *American Psychologist*, **44**, 709–716.
Bank, S. P. and Kahn, M. D. (1997). *The sibling bond* (2nd edn.). New York: Basic Books.
Blyth, D. A. and Foster-Clark, F. (1987). Gender differences in perceived intimacy with different members of adolescents' social networks. *Sex Roles*, **17**, 689–718.
Blyth, D. A., Hill, J. P., and Thiel, K. S. (1982). Early adolescents' significant others: Grade and gender differences in perceived relationships with familial and nonfamilial adults and young people. *Journal of Youth and Adolescence*, **11**, 425–450.
Bowlby, J. (1969). *Attachment and loss: Vol. 1. Attachment*. New York: Basic Books.
Brazelton, T. B. and Sparrow, J. D. (2005). *Understanding sibling rivalry: The Brazelton way*. Cambridge, MA: Da Capo Lifelong Books.

Brody, G. H. (1998). Sibling relationship: Its causes and consequences. *Annual Review of Psychology*, **49**, 1–24.

Buhrmester, D. and Furman, W. (1987). The development of companionship and intimacy. *Child Development*, **58**, 1101–1113.

(1990). Perceptions of sibling relationships in childhood and adolescence. *Child Development*, **61**, 1387–1398.

Bullock, B. M. and Dishion, T. J. (2002). Sibling collusion and problem behavior in early adolescence: Toward a process model for family mutuality. *Journal of Abnormal Child Psychology*, **30**, 143–153.

Buss, D. M. (2004). *Evolutionary psychology: The new science of the mind* (2nd edn.). Boston, MA: Allyn & Bacon.

Cicirelli, V. G. (1995). *Sibling relationships across the life span*. New York: Plenum Press.

Deater-Deckard, K., Dunn, J., O'Connor, T. G., and Golding, J. (2002). Sibling relationships and social-emotional adjustment in different family contexts. *Social Development*, **11**, 571–590.

Delsing, M. J. M. H., van Aken, M. A. G., Oud, J. H. L., De Bruyn, E. E. J., and Scholte, R. H. J. (2005). Family loyalty and adolescent problem behavior: The validity of the family group effect. *Journal of Research on Adolescence*, **15**, 127–150.

Doherty, N. A. and Feeney, J. A. (2004). The composition of attachment networks throughout the adult years. *Personal Relationships*, **11**, 469–488.

Dunn, J. (1996). Siblings: The first society. In N. Vanzetti and S. Duck (eds.), *A lifetime of relationships* (pp. 105–124). Belmont, CA: Thomson Brooks/Cole.

Dunn, J. and McGuire, S. (1992). Sibling and peer relationships in childhood. *Journal of Child Psychology and Psychiatry*, **33**, 67–105.

East, P. L. and Rook, K. S. (1992) Compensatory support among children's peer relationships: A test using friends, nonschool friends and siblings. *Developmental Psychology*, **28**, 163–172.

East, P. L., Weisner, T. S., and Reyes, B. T. (2006). Youths' caretaking of their adolescent sisters' children: Its costs and benefits for youths' development. *Applied Developmental Science*, **10** (2), 86–95.

Erikson, E. H. (1964). *Childhood and society* (2nd edn.). Oxford: W. W. Norton & Company.

Faber, A. and Mazlish, E. (2004). *Siblings without rivalry: How to help your children live together so you can live too*. New York: Collins.

Fagan, A. A. and Najman, J. M. (2003). Sibling influences on adolescent behavior: An Australian longitudinal study. *Journal of Adolescence*, **26**, 547–559.

Gass, K., Jenkins, J., and Dunn, J. (2007). Are sibling relationships protective? A longitudinal study. *Journal of Child Psychology and Psychiatry*, **48**, 167–175.

Guiaux, M., van Tilburg, T., and van Groenou, M. B. (2007). Changes in contact and support exchange in personal networks after widowhood. *Personal Relationships*, **14**, 457–473.

Hamilton, W. D. (1964). The genetical evolution of social behavior. I and II. *Journal of Theoretical Biology*, 7, 1–52.

Hardin, R. (2002). *Trust and trustworthiness*. New York: Russell Sage Foundation.

Hetherington, E. M. and Clingempeel, W. G. (1992). Coping with marital transitions: A family systems perspective. *Monographs for the Society for Research in Child Development*, **57** (Serial No. 227), 1–242.

Hetherington, E. M., Henderson, S. H., and Reiss, D. (1999). Adolescent siblings in stepfamilies: Family functioning and the adolescent adjustment. *Monographs for the Society for Research in Child Development*, **64** (Serial No. 259), 1–222.

Howe, N., Aquan-Assee, J., Bukowski, W. M., Lehoux, P. M., and Rinaldi, C. M. (2001). Siblings as confidants: Emotional understanding, relationship warmth, and sibling self-disclosure. *Social Development*, **10**, 439–454.

Howe, N., Aquan-Assee, J., Bukowski, W. M., Rinaldi, C. M., and Lehoux, P. M. (2000). Sibling self-disclosure in early adolescence. *Merrill Palmer Quarterly*, **46**, 653–671.

McGuire, S., McHale, S., and Updegraff, K. A. (1996). Children's perceptions of the sibling relationship during middle childhood: Connections within and between family relationships. *Personal Relationships*, **3**, 229–239.

McHale, S. M. and Crouter, A. C. (1996). The family contexts of children's sibling relationships. In G. H. Brody (ed.), *Sibling relationships: Their causes and consequences* (pp. 173–195). Westport, CT: Ablex Publishing.

Michalski, R. L., Euler, H. A. (2008). Evolutionary perspectives on sibling relationships. In C. A. Salmon and T. K. Shackelford (eds.), *Family relationships: An evolutionary perspective* (pp. 185–204). New York: Oxford University Press.

Milevsky, A. and Levitt, M. J. (2005). Sibling support in early adolescence: Buffering and compensation across relationships. *European Journal of Developmental Psychology*, **2**, 299–320.

Noller, P. (2005). Sibling relationships in adolescence: Learning and growing together. *Personal Relationships*, **12**, 1–22.

Plomin, R. (1994). *Genetics and experience: The interplay between nature and nurture*. Thousand Oaks, CA: Sage.

Reiss, D., Neiderhiser, J. M., Hetherington, E. M., and Plomin, R. (2000). *The relationship code*. Cambridge, MA: Harvard University Press.

Rotenberg, K. J. (1991). *Children's interpersonal trust: Sensitivity to lying, deception, and promise violations*. New York: Springer-Verlag.

   (1994). Loneliness and interpersonal trust. *Journal of Social and Clinical Psychology*, **13**, 152–173.

Rotenberg, K. J., Boulton, M. J., and Fox, C. L. (2005). Cross-sectional and longitudinal relations among children's trust beliefs, psychological maladjustment, and social relationships, during childhood: Are very high as well as very low trusting children at risk? *Journal of Abnormal Child Psychology*, **33**, 595–610.

Rotenberg, K. J., Fox, C., Green, S., Ruderman, L., Slater, K., Stevens, K., and Carlo, G. (2005). Construction and validation of a children's interpersonal trust belief scale. *British Journal of Developmental Psychology*, **23**, 271–292.

Rotenberg, K.J., MacDonald, K.J., and King, E.V. (2004). The relationship between loneliness and interpersonal trust during middle childhood. *Journal of Genetic Psychology*, **165**, 233–249.

Rotenberg, K.J., McDougall, P., Boulton, M.J., Vaillancourt, T., Fox, C., and Hymel, S. (2004). Cross-sectional and longitudinal relations among relational trustworthiness, social relationships, and psychological adjustment during childhood and adolescence in the UK and Canada. *Journal of Experimental Child Psychology*, **88**, 46–67.

Salmon, C.A. and Shackelford, T.K. (2008). *Family relationships: An evolutionary perspective*. New York: Oxford University Press.

Segal, N.L. (1997). Same-age unrelated siblings: A unique test of within family environment influences on IQ similarity. *Journal of Educational Psychology*, **89**, 381–390.

(2000). *Entwined lives: Twins and what they tell us about human behavior*. New York: Plume.

Segal, N.L., McGuire, S.A., Havlena, J., Gill, P., and Hershberger, S.L. (2007). Intellectual similarity of virtual twin pairs: Developmental trends. *Personality and Individual Differences*, **42**, 1209–1219.

Segal, N.L., Seghers, J.P., Marelich, W.D., Mechanic, M., and Castillo, R. (2007). Social closeness of monozygotic and dizygotic twin parents toward their nieces and nephews. *European Journal of Personality*, **21**, 487–506.

Simpson, J.A. (2007). Psychological foundations of trust. *Current Directions in Psychological Science*, **16**, 264–268.

Slomkowski, C., Rende, R., Conger, K.J., Simons, R.L., and Conger, R. (2001). Sisters, brothers, and delinquency: Evaluating social influence during early and middle adolescence. *Child Development*, **72**, 271–283.

Stewart, R.B. (1983). Sibling attachment relationship: Child–infant interactions in the strange situation. *Developmental Psychology*, **19**, 192–199.

Stewart, R.B. and Marvin, R.S. (1984). Sibling relations: The role of conceptual perspective-taking in the ontogeny of sibling caregiving. *Child Development*, **55**, 1322–1332.

Stocker, C. and McHale, S.M. (1992). The nature and family correlates of preadolescents' perceptions of their sibling relationship. *Journal of Personal and Social Relationships*, **9**, 179–195.

Tancredy, C.M. and Fraley, R.C. (2006). The nature of adult twin relationships: An attachment-theoretical perspective. *Journal of Personality and Social Psychology*, **90**, 78–93.

Teti, D.M. and Ablard, K.E. (1989). Security of attachment and infant-sibling relationships: A laboratory study. *Child Development*, **60**, 1519–1528.

White, J.M. and Klein, D.M. (2008). *Family theories* (3rd edn.). Los Angeles, CA: Sage.

Appendix A

You and your mom

Think about you and your mom during the last year. For each question, circle the best answer about your feelings about your mother.

1. Your mom promised that she would buy you a special treat. How sure are you that your mom will buy you some candy?

VERY SURE	A BIT SURE	DON'T KNOW	A BIT UNSURE	VERY UNSURE

2. Your mom said that if you cleaned your room, you could watch your favorite video. You cleaned your room. How sure are you that your mom will let you watch your favorite video?

VERY SURE	A BIT SURE	DON'T KNOW	A BIT UNSURE	VERY UNSURE

3. You tell your mom that you held hands with a boy/girl at school, but you ask your mom not to tell anyone. How sure are you that your mom will not tell anyone?

VERY SURE	A BIT SURE	DON'T KNOW	A BIT UNSURE	VERY UNSURE

4. You ask your mom to help you with your homework. Your mom says that she cannot help you because she has a headache. How sure are you that your mom has a headache?

VERY SURE	A BIT SURE	DON'T KNOW	A BIT UNSURE	VERY UNSURE

5. One day your mom was doing some cleaning. While cleaning, your mom accidentally misplaced one of your CDs or video games. You wonder what happened to your CD or game. How sure are you that your mom will tell you what happened?

VERY SURE	A BIT SURE	DON'T KNOW	A BIT UNSURE	VERY UNSURE

6. Your mom said that she would take you swimming on Sunday. How sure are you that your mom will take you swimming?

VERY SURE	A BIT SURE	DON'T KNOW	A BIT UNSURE	VERY UNSURE

7. You tell your mom that you do not like one of your classes at school. You ask your mom not to tell anyone. How sure are you that your mom will not tell anyone about it?

| VERY SURE | A BIT SURE | DON'T KNOW | A BIT UNSURE | VERY UNSURE |

8. You really want something new to wear. Your mom says that she will buy you something new to wear on Wednesday. Will your mom buy you something on Wednesday?

| VERY SURE | A BIT SURE | DON'T KNOW | A BIT UNSURE | VERY UNSURE |

9. You ask your mom if you can borrow her special pen. Your mom says that you cannot borrow the pen because it has run out of ink. How sure are you that the pen has run out of ink?

| VERY SURE | A BIT SURE | DON'T KNOW | A BIT UNSURE | VERY UNSURE |

Appendix B

You and your sibling

Think about your relationship with your sibling, _____ (insert sibling name), during the last year. For each question, circle the best answer about your feelings about your sibling.

1. Pretend your sibling has a new bike and he or she promised that you could ride it this weekend. How sure are you that _____ will let you ride it?

| VERY SURE | A BIT SURE | DON'T KNOW | A BIT UNSURE | VERY UNSURE |

2. You lend your sibling your CD or book or video for the day. At the end of day, you see your sibling put the CD/book/video in his/her backpack. How sure are you that _____ will give the CD/book/video back?

| VERY SURE | A BIT SURE | DON'T KNOW | A BIT UNSURE | VERY UNSURE |

3. You tell your sibling that you like a boy or girl at school, but you ask your sibling not to tell your best friend. How sure are you that _____ will not tell your best friend?

VERY SURE	A BIT SURE	DON'T KNOW	A BIT UNSURE	VERY UNSURE

4. You buy a present for your mom's birthday. Your sibling promised to help you pay for it. How sure are you that _____ will help you pay for it?

VERY SURE	A BIT SURE	DON'T KNOW	A BIT UNSURE	VERY UNSURE

5. You lend your sibling your new video game. How sure are you that _____ will take good care of your new game?

VERY SURE	A BIT SURE	DON'T KNOW	A BIT UNSURE	VERY UNSURE

6. You buy your best friend a present. You ask your sibling not to tell your friend about the present. How sure are you that _____ will not tell your friend about the present?

VERY SURE	A BIT SURE	DON'T KNOW	A BIT UNSURE	VERY UNSURE

7. Your sibling promised to share his or her chips or fruit with you at lunchtime. How sure are you that _____ will share the chips or fruit with you?

VERY SURE	A BIT SURE	DON'T KNOW	A BIT UNSURE	VERY UNSURE

8. One day your sibling was walking through your room and accidentally broke one of your favorite things. You wonder what happened to it. How sure are you that _____ will tell you what happened?

VERY SURE	A BIT SURE	DON'T KNOW	A BIT UNSURE	VERY UNSURE

9. You tell your sibling that you are scared of spiders. You ask your sibling not to tell your friend. How sure are you that _____ will not tell your best friend?

VERY SURE	A BIT SURE	DON'T KNOW	A BIT UNSURE	VERY UNSURE

10. Your sibling promised to play a game with you later. How sure are you that _____ will keep the promise and play the game with you?

VERY SURE	A BIT SURE	DON'T KNOW	A BIT UNSURE	VERY UNSURE

8 The role of promises for children's trustworthiness and honesty

Kay Bussey (Macquarie University)

The ability to keep promises is often considered a major hallmark of trustworthiness (Rotenberg, McDougall, Boulton, Vaillancourt, Fox, and Hymel, 2004; Talwar, Lee, Bala, and Lindsay, 2002). But what are promises? Why do we keep and break them, and what purpose do they serve? It is surprising that so little is known about such an everyday concept. Apart from their colloquial use, promises serve a vital role in the legal system. In criminal proceedings, witnesses are required to take a sworn oath which entails promising to tell the truth. In this context, it is believed that promises have an honesty-promoting effect. On the other hand, promises are not always used to promote honesty. At times, they are used to inhibit it. For example, perpetrators of child sexual abuse sometimes ask their victims to promise to keep the abuse secret. Adults ask children to keep secrets within the family, and children swear each other to secrecy. Children may witness a school friend damage property and be sworn to secrecy by their friend; they may swear each other to secrecy over a less serious matter, such as who they like best in their class; or they may swear the victims of bullying to secrecy.

It is apparent, therefore, that promises can serve different purposes in different situations. In some circumstances they can promote truth-telling and in others they can undermine it. How can promises serve such different purposes? How can they both inhibit (promise to keep a secret) and promote (promise to tell the truth) honesty? This chapter begins with a consideration of the philosophical definition of promising and the developmental course of children's conceptions of promises. This is followed by an examination of the extent to which children actually keep promises. The role of promises in the model of trustworthiness developed by Rotenberg and his colleagues is presented (Rotenberg, McDougall, Boulton, Vaillancourt, Fox, and Hymel, 2004). In this model, the focus is on trustworthiness in interpersonal relationships, with keeping promises, keeping secrets, and telling the truth forming part of a conceptual model of trustworthiness. The remainder of the chapter is devoted to an examination of the role of promises within a social cognitive model of disclosure and secrecy (Bandura, 1986; Bussey and Grimbeek, 1995), which focuses on motivational factors. Finally, this model is applied in a context that is relevant to child sexual abuse victims who serve as witnesses in the prosecution of their cases in the legal system.

Promises: What are they?

There has been considerable philosophical discussion about the nature of promises. In his writings, Searle (1969) drew on Austin's (1962) speech act theory to devise a set of rules governing a range of utterances, including asserting, requesting, and promising. A promise is defined as a commitment on the part of the speaker to accomplish a future action (Searle, 1969). The rules governing promising state that "the utterance ... predicates some future act A of the speaker S ... counts as the undertaking of an obligation to do A" (Searle, 1969, p. 63). It is regarded as the commonest form of the category of commissives whose goal "is to commit the speaker to a certain course of action" (Austin, 1962, p. 156). It is argued that although such a commitment could be made without using the word "promise," by saying, "I will do it," the use of the word "promise" enables commitment to be distinguished from intention. A commitment places a person under an obligation to do what they said they will do, and makes explicit to others the person's commitment to performing what they say they will do.

Despite the importance of promises in philosophical discourses and their frequent everyday use, they have been the subject of little psychological research. In a systematic series of studies, Astington (1988a, 1988b, 1988c) investigated the developmental course of children's and adults' understanding of promises, to establish when children understand promises, and whether children's and adults' understanding was similar to the philosophical conception of promises.

At what age do children produce commissive speech acts that commit them to a particular future action? Astington (1988a) assessed the spontaneous use of the word "promise" by children from four age levels (4, 6, 8, and 10 years), when they were engaged in an interactive task with an interviewer. The interviewer asked each child to perform a task and the interviewer sought reassurance from the child that they would do it. The majority of the 8- and 10-year-olds spontaneously used the word "promise" ("I promise," "I'll do it, I promise,") to explicitly reassure the interviewer that they would carry out the task they said they would do. The majority of the 4- and 6-year-olds, however, did not use the word "promise," although they did use commissive speech acts, such as "I will do it," "I will, don't worry." Astington argued that all age groups demonstrated an understanding of the future personal commitment involved in making commissive speech acts. Only the older children, however, spontaneously used the word "promise" to provide explicit reassurance to the listener of their commitment to carry out what they said they would do.

Although younger children did not use the word "promise" in an interview situation to reassure the interviewer that they would keep their word (Astington, 1988a), even 4- and 5-year-olds sometimes used the word "promise" with parents as they attempted to get their own way: "But you promised!" (Astington, 1988b). Are they using the word in the same manner as older children, and are their definitions consistent with philosophical definitions? To address this issue, Astington (1988b) conducted a further study to assess the extent to which children's definitions conformed to philosophical definitions rather than the colloquial use of the word "promise." In Searle's view, making a promise about a past action does not qualify as a promise because there is no commitment about future action. In addition, promising about an event outside one's control is not considered a promise either. In Astington's study, the former example was considered asserting, and the latter predicting, and these were differentiated from promising, which involved a future commitment within one's control. Children from four age levels (5, 7, 9, and 11 years) were provided with examples relating to predicting (John is sick and Lisa says he will feel better tomorrow. John says he won't and Lisa says, "Yes you will, I promise"), asserting (John is supposed to empty the garbage. John says he has done it, but his mum said he forgot yesterday. John says, "Well I did it today, I promise"), and promising (John is going swimming with a friend and doesn't want to take Lisa. He says, "I will take you next week, I promise"). Children were required to judge if the story character had really made a promise. Surprisingly, there was little difference in children's correct responses across age for the promising stories. The majority of children correctly identified that promising stories involved promising. As children aged they were less likely to regard predictions involving actions beyond the speaker's control as promises. There were no age differences, however, in children's identification of assertions as promises. Children were not able to distinguish an assertion from a promise. An adult sample was included in this study. The adults' responses were similar to those of the children in that they accurately identified promises in the promising story. Adults' performances were superior to those of children for the asserting and predicting stories; however, even their performance on these tasks was not completely accurate. A sizable proportion of adults believed that a promise could be made about future events over which one had no control (predicting) and that a promise could be made about past actions (asserting). These findings challenge the restrictive nature of Searle's definition of the speech act of promising to the obligation to perform future actions. The extent to which a promise is simply a reassurance or an obligation that refers to a future or past event remains controversial in philosophical circles (Harrison, 1979).

Even within the more restrictive definition of a promise as being only a future obligation to perform an action, there are significant developmental changes in children's conceptual understanding of promises. Numerous studies have revealed that for young children a promise only qualifies as a promise if it is fulfilled (Astington, 1988a, b; Maas and Abbeduto, 2001) – that is, children use the word "promise" to refer to the performance of the promise rather than to the speech act. If the promise is not fulfilled, then a promise is not believed to have been made. However, if the performance is fulfilled, then a promise has occurred. Even if the speaker's intention was to keep the promise, the fact that it was not fulfilled is the basis on which children, up until about 7 to 9 years (depending on the assessment procedures), judge whether a promise has been made (Maas and Abbeduto, 2001). Similarly, Astington (1988c) has shown that 5-year-olds have little conception of promises and intentions. They did not differentiate between story characters promising to engage in an action or saying they will engage in an action and the actual action. The speech act was not considered separately from the action and *promise* was not differentiated from *will*. Eight- and 10-year olds believed that a story character was performing an action because they had previously promised to perform the action. The younger children explained the story character's performance of the action based on the intrinsic features of the activity rather than on keeping the promise. In addition, Astington (1988b) showed that younger children believed that an unfulfilled promise negated the promise being made in the first place. As a consequence, Astington concluded that young children have difficulty in differentiating word and deed – that is, they do not distinguish between the promise and carrying out the action associated with the promise. As children develop, promising is established as a speech act separate from performance and is increasingly differentiated from intentions, predictions, and assertions. However, as stated earlier, whether these differentiations are made as strongly even by adults as they are made by philosophers remains controversial.

The focus on children's understanding of promises has advanced knowledge on the cognitive underpinnings of promises. However, this line of research does not address the social and motivational bases for keeping and breaking promises. Once children understand that a promise is a commitment on the part of the speaker, how do they evaluate the morality of keeping or breaking promises? Further, what are the psychological factors associated with keeping or breaking promises? Before addressing these issues, the extent to which children actually keep promises is addressed.

Children's promise-keeping

There has been a small body of recent research examining whether children keep promises. This research has been driven mainly by a significant applied concern emanating from doubts raised in the legal system about children's ability to understand and keep promises. This understanding is crucial for children to be deemed competent to take an oath or an affirmation so that they can testify in court as witnesses. It has been assumed that if a witness testifies under oath, their testimony is more likely to be truthful than if they testify without taking the oath (Lyon and Saywitz, 1999).

The necessity for testifying under oath came under scrutiny in the early 1980s, when an increasing number of children were required to testify as witnesses in adult criminal courts. In most jurisdictions it had been deemed that children below the age of 12 years did not have the capacity to understand the oath and were therefore ineligible to testify in courts. Consequently, as the number of children below this age who reported sexual abuse increased during the 1980s, the prosecution of many of these cases could not proceed, as there was no evidence about the alleged abuse other than that provided by the child victim. To accommodate the reception of children's evidence, the rules relating to sworn testimony were relaxed and continue to be the subject of ongoing reform in many jurisdictions. One of the first changes was to allow children to testify without taking the oath. However, there was a mandatory requirement that judges were to warn the jury about the dangers of convicting the accused on the uncorroborated and unsworn testimony of the child. Because of the difficulty of gaining convictions under such conditions, the mandatory warning was changed to a discretionary one in some jurisdictions and abolished completely in others. In these latter jurisdictions, children were simply required to undertake a competency test to show that they understood the difference between lying and truth-telling and that they would promise to tell the truth. In other jurisdictions, because there was concern that children do not understand the word "promise," children were simply asked to tell the truth or to tell no lies. There has been a recent call for abolishing any form of inquiry into children's knowledge of lying and truth-telling and simply asking them to tell the truth, with or without a promise to do so, thereby leaving it up to the jury to decide the reliability and credibility of the information reported by children (Bala, Lee, Lindsay, and Talwar, 2001). Many countries have followed these recommendations and abolished competence testing as a prerequisite for children's eligibility to testify as witnesses in court (Hoyano and Keenan, 2007).

Due to the serious nature of these reforms, psychologists began to investigate the extent to which children keep promises in contexts relevant to the legal situation, and the extent to which such promising promotes truth-telling. In a recent series of laboratory-based studies, Talwar and her colleagues have shown that children between 3 and 7 years who have been asked to tell the truth, when questioned about a transgression, were more likely to do so after promising to tell the truth than if they had not made such a promise (Talwar, Lee, Bala, and Lindsay, 2002). In a further study, children between 3 and 11 years, whose parents committed a transgression and asked their child not to tell anyone, were more likely to tell the truth about their parents' transgression if they had discussed issues concerning lying and truth-telling prior to questioning and they had promised to tell the truth (Talwar, Lee, Bala, and Lindsay, 2004).

The research reviewed thus far has shown that children are able to keep promises from as early as 3 years of age. Although their definition of promises may not be as sophisticated and complex as that of older children, adults, and philosophers, they do seem to have developed a rudimentary understanding of promises that enables them to regulate their behavior in accord with promises they have made. Why do promises carry such value for children from such an early age?

Why are promises important and what purpose do they serve?

One way in which promises attain their value is through their linkage with trust. Rotenberg has conducted a broad range of research on children's promises, with the uniting theme being their link to interpersonal trust (Rotenberg, 1991). Promises are considered integral to trust. Drawing on Rotter's (1967, p. 65) definition of interpersonal trust as "the expectancy held by an individual or group that the word, promise or written statement of another individual or group can be relied upon" (p. 65), Rotenberg (1980) investigated the age when children begin to base their judgments of trust on the basis of a person keeping their promise. Children from three grades – kindergarten, second, and fourth grades – provided higher trust ratings for story characters who kept their promise and thereby engaged in helpful behavior than for those characters who broke their promise and did not help. Analysis of children's explanations for their trust ratings, however, showed that only the second- and fourth-graders explained their trust ratings with reference to the protagonist keeping their promise. Kindergarten children explained their ratings on the basis of the helpful behavior performed by the protagonist rather than on the basis of their promise-keeping. In addition, second- and fourth-graders trusted a protagonist who behaved consistently with their promise, regardless of their level of helpfulness. The kindergarten children's rating of trust was unaffected by whether the protagonist acted in accord with their promise. Indeed, the protagonist who engaged in the most helpful behavior was judged the most trustworthy – that is, kindergarten children judged trustworthiness on the basis of the person's deeds, not whether their words matched their deeds. Further, all the fourth-grade children preferred to share with the protagonist who kept their promise, whereas only 50 percent of kindergarten children chose to share with this protagonist. Therefore, as with Astington's (1988c) findings where children judged promises on the basis of actions rather than intentions, kindergarten children in Rotenberg's study focused only on deeds in determining who they liked and who they trusted, not on whether their actions matched their word.

As children age, trustworthy judgments are increasingly determined by the extent to which others keep their word. In Rotenberg's model of interpersonal trust, keeping promises, keeping secrets, and telling the truth contribute to the three bases of trust. These bases constitute a broader model that has been conceptualized as a 3 (bases) × 3 (domains) × 2 (targets) model of trustworthiness (Rotenberg, Boulton, and Fox, 2005; Rotenberg, Fox, and Boulton, 2005; Rotenberg, McDougall, Boulton, Vaillancourt, Fox, and Hymel, 2004). The three bases of trust include reliability, emotional trust, and honesty. The reliability component refers to keeping one's word or promise. Emotional trust is the reliance on others not to cause emotional harm – this can be achieved by being receptive to disclosure, keeping disclosures secret, not being critical, and not embarrassing others. Finally, honesty covers not only telling the truth, but engaging in behaviors that are well-intentioned and not of malicious or manipulative intent. The other two components of Rotenberg's model of interpersonal trust include domains and target dimensions. The domains of trust cover the cognitive/affective and behavioral domains. The cognitive/affective domain relates to people's beliefs and the accompanying emotional states associated with those beliefs. The behavioral domains (behavior-dependent and behavior-enacting) refer to the engagement in the various bases of trust. The dimensions of trust can vary in their specificity, ranging from a specific person to a generalized category of person, and familiarity, ranging from somewhat unfamiliar to very familiar.

Rotenberg and his colleagues (Rotenberg, Fox, Green, Ruderman, Slater, Stevens, and Carlo, 2005) have developed a Children's Generalized Trust Belief (CGTB) Scale, with children from the fifth and sixth grades, that covers each of the three bases of trust for four person categories: mother, father, teacher, and peer. Children's generalized trust beliefs were stronger for mother, father, and peer than they were for teacher. Moreover, children who were more trusting of peers were rated as more trustworthy by their peers, and children who scored more highly on the interpersonal trust belief scale were more helpful towards their classmates.

Although trustworthiness is considered a personality characteristic, the model adopts an interactive perspective in which an individual's basic trustworthiness is expected to be moderated in different situations (Rotenberg, 2001; Rotenberg, McDougall, Boulton, Vaillancourt, Fox, and Hymel, 2004). Consistent with this proposal, Rotenberg, Fox, and Boulton (2005) showed that children who were rated as more trustworthy, as measured by the peer group, experienced more positive peer group relationships than children who were rated as less trustworthy by the peer group. Further, it was found that children's peer ratings of secret-keeping were more predictive of children's maintenance of friendships, whereas keeping promises was more characteristic of trustworthiness in the peer group. Keeping promises, therefore, serves as an important marker of trustworthiness in the peer group. Furthermore, perceptions of trustworthiness in the peer group were related to psychological adjustment (Betts and Rotenberg, 2007), friendship (Rotenberg, 1986), social competence (Buzzelli, 1988; Wentzel, 1991), and academic performance (Imber, 1973; Wentzel, 1991).

Self-regulatory control has been considered a major facet of trustworthiness (Wentzel, 1991, 1996). Although trustworthiness involves more than keeping secrets and keeping promises, these aspects of trustworthiness have been the major components of trustworthiness measured in many studies. Self-regulatory control is implicated in keeping both secrets and promises. Secret-keeping involves inhibiting a response when instructed to do so or when information is requested, and promise-keeping typically requires children to comply with a commitment to do or say something they may not otherwise have said or done. Evidence for the early developmental links between trustworthiness and aspects of self-regulatory control has been provided by Rotenberg, Michalik, Eisenberg, and Betts (2008) with preschoolers. They showed that inhibitory control was related to peer-reported trustworthiness, as measured by secret- and promise-keeping; and, further, that peer-reported trustworthiness partially mediated the relationship between inhibitory control and children's social behavior related to school adjustment. These findings provide support for Wentzel's (1991) proposal that trustworthiness involves self-regulatory control and that it is associated with better school adjustment.

It is surprising that in Rotenberg, Michalik, Eisenberg, and Betts's (2008) study, preschoolers' trustworthiness, as indexed by their secret- and promise-keeping, was related to their school adjustment. As shown earlier, previous research has found that children of this age have limited understanding of promises. It is noteworthy that these results obtained when children were provided with a definition of secret- and promise-keeping. Children were asked whether they agreed with the provided definitions of "promise" and "secret." Young children's acquiescence tendencies may have inflated their actual level of understanding. However, counter to this interpretation was the finding that there was a modest positive correlation between child- and teacher-reported trustworthiness. This is also consistent with the findings of Talwar, Lee, Bala, and Lindsay (2002), showing that children in the age range of 3 to 7 years who promised to tell the truth increased their truth-telling as a result of promising to do so. It is therefore important for future researchers to use more child appropriate measures than those used by Astington (1988c) and Rotenberg (1980) to establish children's knowledge of promises. Children's understanding of promises may be greater than has been previously shown, or only a rudimentary knowledge of promises may be required for children to engage in trustworthy behavior.

Many of Rotenberg, Michalik, Eisenberg, and Betts's (2008) findings have been replicated with slightly older children from the first and second grades (Betts and Rotenberg, 2007). Children from the latter study were all able to define keeping a secret and keeping a promise, and they were able to provide examples of each. This study provided further evidence obtained longitudinally over 12 months that peer-reported trustworthiness was associated with school adjustment, and that peer acceptance contributed in part to the relationship between trustworthiness and school adjustment. In a further longitudinal study involving pre-adolescents and adolescents, Rotenberg, McDougall, Boulton, Vaillancourt, Fox, and Hymel, (2004) established the linkage between trustworthiness and peer relations. Peer-reported promise- and secret-keeping were positively related to a greater number of friendships and predictive of increased friendships over time (Study 1), and positively related to peer acceptance (Studies 1 and 2).

Apart from promise-keeping being an index of trustworthiness, promises are used in a variety of contexts to promote consistency between words and deeds. They are used in everyday contexts by parents to seek reassurance from their children that they will obey rules such as returning home directly from school or cleaning their bedroom on the weekend. They are also used in more formal settings, such as professional organizations who require members of a profession to take an oath to indicate that they will follow certain standards of conduct. They are used in courts of law to promote truth-telling by witnesses. Apart from these positive usages of promises, however, promises can be used in negative ways too. People can be sworn to secrecy by someone who has engaged in transgressive conduct or has committed a serious crime. Is a person who is requested by such a transgressor to promise to keep the transgression secret, and complies with the request, trustworthy or not? On the one hand, they are keeping a promise, which is one of the indices of trustworthiness, and yet if they do not tell the truth about the transgressive event, they are not being honest and thereby not acting in a trustworthy manner, as indexed by another component of trustworthiness. Bok (1978) argues that there is no obligation to keep a promise that involves a criminal or immoral activity. However, if the person broke the promise and told the truth about an antisocial event, they would lose their status as a trustworthy person in the eyes of the person or group of persons who elicited the promise. This gives meaning to the phrase "honor among thieves." People who keep promises involving immoral activities may be regarded as trustworthy by their peer group, but may not be considered trustworthy by society at large. Therefore, in some situations, promises may promote honesty and in others they may undermine it. To begin to examine how promises can serve such divergent purposes, contextual influences on promises are considered.

Contextual influences on promises

Rotenberg and his colleagues have convincingly established the importance of keeping promises in the interpersonal domain. In this context, keeping promises and keeping secrets have been positively associated with each other. It would not be expected, however, that each of the three bases of Rotenberg's trustworthiness model would be positively correlated in all situations. As already indicated, promises can be used both to promote truth-telling and to attenuate it. Therefore, it could be expected that the relationship between promises, secrecy, and truth-telling would be positive in some situations, but not in others. These three aspects of trust may be related differently, depending on the context in which they are used. In the interpersonal context, one of the main purposes of keeping promises and secrets is to establish and to maintain interpersonal relationships (Rotenberg, McDougall, Boulton, Vaillancourt, Fox, and Hymel, 2004). When peers share secrets, for example, about innocuous events, such secret-keeping can build trust between peers and help develop their friendship. However, when children are sworn to secrecy by an adult they have witnessed committing a transgression, such promising may gain the children's compliance, but it is unlikely to build trust between the child and adult. Therefore, promises serve different purposes in different situations, depending on how they are used. Their use can vary from being volitional or coerced; made between equals or in relationships in which there is a power differential; made to develop friendships, to establish the truth, or to maintain secrecy. It is beyond the scope of this chapter to examine the wide array of situations in which promise-keeping occurs. Therefore, the remainder of the chapter is devoted to an examination of promises in the legal system, particularly in relation to child witnesses who may have been victims of sexual abuse. This example is selected because of its applied significance and recent research prominence. To establish the context in which promises occur in the legal system relevant to child sexual abuse cases, background material relevant to such cases is presented.

Child sexual abuse and the legal system

Children have been victims of child sexual abuse for centuries. It is only since the mid-1970s, when many Western countries introduced mandatory reporting of crimes against children, that community awareness of the prevalence of child sexual abuse was awakened. Mandatory reporting requirements, coupled with community outrage about this crime, led to increasing reports of child sexual abuse. It soon became apparent that the legal system was ill-equipped to deal with child witnesses. Most cases of child sexual abuse are dealt with in the criminal court and, because there is usually no other evidence apart from that provided by the victim, the child is generally required to testify in court. However, because children, and young children in particular, often provide too little information to enable the prosecution of the case, children were frequently asked leading and suggestive questions, in order to increase the amount of detailed information children reported or to disclose the abuse.

A number of high-profile cases highlighted the poor quality of these interviewing practices used to obtain children's evidence. Laboratory research has shown consistently that leading and suggestive questions render children's evidence unreliable (Goodman and Melinder, 2007). Consequently, since the turn of the century, in response to concerns about poor-quality interviewing practices, there has been considerable research attention to developing better interview protocols that do not rely on leading and suggestive questions. Through the use of better questioning strategies, and memory enhancement practices such as context reinstatement and supportive interview practices that help the child to scaffold their narrative, children are enabled to increase their accurate and detailed reporting of information (Sternberg, Lamb, Orbach, Esplin, and Mitchell, 2001). There has also been considerable legal reform, allowing a child's initial interview to be videotaped and tendered as evidence-in-chief in the court case. Although these reforms have not solved all of the issues related to children providing their evidence in court, they have gone partway towards doing so (Malloy, Mitchell, Block, Quas, and Goodman, 2007).

Apart from children being able to retrieve information about the event and being able to report it accurately, there has been concern about the veracity of children's reports. Although much of the research has focused on children's unintentional reporting of false information in response to leading and suggestive questions, there has also been concern about children's intentional false allegations and the extent to which children can be trusted to present a true account of the alleged event. To address this issue, children are usually asked to promise to tell the truth both before a forensic interview and before providing evidence in court. As reviewed earlier, the efficacy of such procedures has been shown in laboratory-based studies in which children's truth-telling increases in response to promising to do so. It is instructive to note that in Talwar, Lee, Bala, and Lindsay's (2002) study, even 3-year-olds were shown to increase their truth-telling when they promised to do so. However, the research reviewed in the earlier part of this chapter revealed that children up until about 7 years have a less sophisticated understanding of promises than do older children and adults. In view of this limitation, it has been recommended that young children still be required to state that they will promise to tell the truth, because even if they do not understand promising, they do understand the intention associated with saying that they will tell the truth. However, this raises the concern that if young children do not appreciate that promises entail an additional obligation beyond the intention of telling the truth, they will be less concerned about carrying out their obligation than a person who understands the importance of carrying it out. This is a particularly important issue, since jurors are more likely to believe a child who has promised to tell the truth than a child who has not made a promise to do so (Leach, Talwar, Lee, Bala, and Lindsay, 2004).

Even if children do understand the concept of promising, making a promise to tell the truth does not guarantee that they will do so. Among older children in Talwar, Lee, Bala, and Lindsay's (2002) study, although more children told the truth after promising to do so, not all children complied with this request. Therefore, it is necessary to understand the psychological processes associated with keeping promises that promote greater truth-telling when a promise has been made. Before examining the psychological processes underpinning promising to tell the truth, a further role of promises in sexual abuse is considered.

Child sexual abuse usually occurs in private and perpetrators often use a variety of strategies to silence their victims. For example, perpetrators of child sexual abuse sometimes ask their victims to promise to keep the abuse secret (Burns, Finkelhor, and Williams, 1988; Palmer, Brown, Rae-Grant, and Loughlin, 1999; Sauzier, 1989). This creates a dilemma for children, who may promise to tell the truth and therefore have an obligation to tell the truth about the abuse, but who have also promised the perpetrators that they would keep the abuse secret. In such situations, truth-telling and secrecy are in conflict with each other. Therefore, to understand how promises can serve these diverse purposes, in the following section the psychological processes underpinning promises when they are used to promote children's secrecy and disclosure are also examined. This examination occurs within a model of disclosure and secrecy that draws on the social cognitive theory model of disclosure developed by Bussey and Grimbeek (1995). The aim is to explicate the psychological processes that influence children's reporting of information – either its disclosure or its secrecy – and how promising attenuates or strengthens these processes.

The influence of promises on disclosure and secrecy

Bussey and Grimbeek's (1995) model of disclosure was developed in response to the increasing recognition of the difficulty that many children encounter when they have been sexually victimized and need to disclose abuse. The goals of disclosure in this context mainly involve stopping the abuse and gaining support for dealing with its effects. Despite wanting to achieve these goals, many children find the disclosure process problematic. Therefore, the disclosure model aimed to establish factors that facilitate disclosure and those that inhibit it. The model was based on principles of social cognitive theory (Bandura, 1986). From this theoretical perspective, Bussey and Grimbeek (1995) considered not only the cognitive processes associated with disclosure, but also the social and motivational processes that may come into play. For children to disclose sexual abuse, it was posited that they need to have an adequate memory of the events that took place and the necessary skills to communicate details of those events. The capacity to disclose abuse is more of an issue with younger children and this has been the focus of a considerable amount of child witness research, because often young children do not report sufficient details about the events for prosecutions to proceed. As indicated earlier, children have frequently been subjected to flawed interviewing practices, involving leading and suggestive questioning procedures, which have contributed to inaccurate testimony by these children (Ceci and Bruck, 1995). Even if children are interviewed in a forensically defensible manner and are capable of articulating their abusive experiences, there is no guarantee that they will do so. Children may be reluctant to report the abuse because of their concerns about what may happen as a result of their disclosure. Therefore, abuse may not be disclosed because: (1) the child is not capable of disclosing, either because of a memory deficit or a lack of verbal skills to report it adequately; or (2) the child elects not to disclose it, actively or by omission.

If children have the capability to report abuse, whether or not they do disclose is expected to be under the influence of external and self-directed influences. Socio-cognitive theory distinguishes three major motivational determinants of disclosure: external influences, which range from positive (support from a trusted adult) to negative (fear of punishment from the perpetrator, fear of disbelief); internal influences, which range from positive (proud of oneself for reporting) to negative (embarrassment, self-blame); and self-efficacy, which also ranges across the spectrum from positive (belief in one's ability to convey the details of the abuse) to negative (lack of belief in one's ability to effectively disclose the abuse). During the early years of development, children's behavior is mainly regulated by the external outcomes they expect to receive from others. By abstracting how others have responded to their disclosures of positive and negative events, children formulate outcome expectancies about how they believe others will respond to different types of disclosure. As children age, they become more aware that people react differently to their disclosures. Over time, children synthesize these diverse reactions to formulate their own standards of conduct. Consequently, with increasing cognitive maturity and social experience, children's conduct is regulated not only by the reactions expected of others, but by their own self-generated reactions. Children learn to evaluate their own conduct, and react with self-praise when they live up to their standards and with self-criticism when they do not. For children who have developed internal standards, behavior is regulated by an interplay of internal and external factors. It is expected that while younger children's conduct is regulated primarily by external factors, with increasing cognitive competence and social experience, conduct is increasingly regulated by self-generated ones (Bussey, 1992; Bussey and Bandura, 1999a).

The third socio-cognitive process that influences conduct is self-efficacy. Self-efficacy refers to an individual's beliefs in his or her ability to use a skill (Bandura, 1986). With increasing development, individuals self-reflect on their own capabilities. The concept of self-efficacy recognizes a distinction between possessing a particular skill and being able to use that skill effectively. Debilitating thoughts, for example, can undermine the use of a skill to maximum capability. Self-doubts serve to inhibit optimal performance. In this context, self-doubts about being able to disclose distressing and embarrassing information could serve to inhibit disclosure, whereas self-belief in one's capacities for disclosure may enable it.

The more children anticipate negative reactions from others, self-censure for disclosure, or believe they are incapable of disclosing the abuse, the more likely that disclosure will be inhibited. In contrast, the more positive reactions children anticipate from others, the more self-pride they anticipate for disclosure, and the more they believe they are capable of making the disclosure, the more likely it is that disclosure will occur.

As stated earlier, this model lends itself to understanding not only children's disclosure processes, but also secrecy processes. Disclosure and secrecy are not necessarily the inverse of each other. Children who do not spontaneously disclose information may not necessarily be actively withholding information, as is the case when keeping information secret. Rather, omission may result from not being directly asked about the relevant information or not deeming its disclosure relevant. Therefore, in this model, both disclosure and secrecy are considered. In considering the secrecy process, the same elements associated with the disclosure process are involved. These include children's conceptual understanding of secrecy and their knowledge of the secret event. The same socio-cognitive regulators that were posited for disclosure are posited for secrecy: others and self outcome expectations and self-efficacy beliefs linked to secrecy.

The differentiation between disclosure and secrecy enables an assessment of the separate impact of promises on disclosure and secrecy. Promises will either promote or attenuate truth-telling, depending on situational factors, such as the requirement to disclose information or to keep it secret. In some situations, promises will serve to increase truth-telling as disclosure is facilitated, and in others they will reduce it as secrecy is facilitated. A model based on principles of social cognitive theory involving self-regulatory processes is eminently suited to investigate the influence of promises on disclosure and secrecy. Despite there usually being a public or externally induced commitment to promise, ultimately, the person keeping or breaking the promise needs to exercise their own agency through the engagement of self-regulatory processes that either facilitate or attenuate keeping the promise. It is proposed that promises will promote disclosure and secrecy to the extent that the various social cognitive processes of disclosure and secrecy posited above are heightened. That is, on the basis of the model proposed above, it would be expected that promising to tell the truth would promote disclosure as other-outcome expectations, self-expectations, and self-efficacy are increased. Similarly, the extent to which promising to keep a secret impacts the socio-cognitive regulators of secret-keeping, the greater the possibility that truth-telling would be attenuated. The role of promises in the socio-cognitive model of disclosure and secrecy is illustrated next with an example relevant to child sexual abuse.

The role of promises on disclosure and secrecy involving adult transgressive conduct

The influence of promises on children's disclosure and secrecy has been investigated using a vignette study (Fitzpatrick and Bussey, 2008). Vignettes were constructed in which an adult male committed a transgression, either of a serious (stealing TVs from a warehouse) or minor (taking flowers from the park) nature, and then asked a child not to reveal the transgression, with or without a promise. Although the crimes depicted in the vignettes differed from child sexual abuse in many dimensions, they did involve an adult committing a transgression that was witnessed by a child who was requested by the transgressor to keep the transgression secret, with or without a promise. Later, another adult asked the child to tell the truth about what happened, with or without a promise. This combination of vignettes enabled the investigation of the socio-cognitive regulatory processes associated with two types of promises – promising to keep a secret (secrecy promise) and promising to tell the truth (disclosure promise) – with children from two age groups, 8 and 11 years. The socio-cognitive regulators associated with children's disclosure and secrecy were assessed based on the model proposed above. That is, children's beliefs about vignette characters' ability to disclose the transgression or keep it secret (self-efficacy beliefs), their beliefs about others' reactions to their disclosure and secrecy (others outcome expectations), and their self-reactions to their disclosure and secrecy (self outcome expectations) were measured.

The results from this study revealed that, regardless of age or gender, children believed that vignette characters would be better able to disclose and less able to keep secret serious transgressions. They also believed that the characters would be better able to disclose transgressions than keep them secret if they had promised to tell the truth than if no promise had been made. In contrast, children reported that the characters would be less able to disclose the transgression and more able to keep it secret if the transgressor had requested them to promise not to tell about the transgression. Therefore, promises served to promote or inhibit truth-telling about the transgression depending on the context in which they were embedded. Children believed that the vignette character would be better able to tell the truth about the transgression if they promised an interviewer they would tell the truth. However, if they promised the transgressor that they would keep the transgression secret, their ability to tell the truth was attenuated. These findings underscore the dual func-tion of promises. They can both promote honesty and undermine it. It is of interest to note that each of the promises acted independently. A promise to tell the truth about the transgression did not override a prom-ise to the transgressor to keep the transgression secret.

Apart from children's disclosure and secrecy self-efficacy, the other socio-cognitive factors expected to influence children's disclosure and secrecy were their beliefs about how the vignette character and others would react to disclosure and secrecy. Only the 11-year-old girls believed that others would judge the vignette character less harshly for keeping the transgression secret if the transgressor had requested that they prom-ise to do so. This may reflect the more intimate nature of friendships among pre-adolescent girls than among boys and younger girls, whereby their peer acceptance may be contingent on keeping secrets, especially when they have promised to do so (Rotenberg, 1986).

Although all children believed that the vignette character would feel less pleased with themselves about disclosing the transgression if they had promised to keep it secret, only the girls believed that the vignette char-acter would feel pleased about keeping the transgression secret. Although both boys and girls were uncomfortable about disclosure in such circum-stances, only the girls believed that the vignette character would feel little remorse for keeping the secret when they promised to keep it.

There were fewer disclosure-promise effects than secret-promise effects in this study. Children did not believe that the vignette characters would anticipate that they or others would respond any more favorably if they told the truth after promising to do so than if they had not made such a promise. Possibly, because telling the truth involved telling on someone else, children did not believe that the vignette character would have felt more virtuous by keeping their promise. The 11-year-old children, how-ever, believed that the vignette character would anticipate more remorse if they kept the transgression secret if they had promised to tell the truth about it than if they had not promised to do so. Older children, who have more strongly developed moral standards than younger children, anticipated more displeasure for not keeping the promise to tell the truth, even though they did not anticipate feeling virtuous for telling it. The disclosure promise only influenced children's self-reactions for secrecy and not for disclosure. This is consistent with other research showing that children are more likely to anticipate remorse for lying than virtuousness for telling the truth (Bussey, 1992, 1999). Consequently, undertaking the added commitment of promising to tell the truth increased children's anticipated self-censure for not telling the truth, rather than heightening their positive self-reactions for telling it.

The findings from this study showed that disclosure and secrecy were not necessarily the inverse of each other. Although promises did not influence truth-telling, they did have an impact on children's secret-keeping. This highlights the importance of distinguishing between disclosure and secret-keeping. Although promises may not affect children's spontaneous disclosure, if children are asked specifically about an event they are less likely to keep the event secret. However, if they are not asked about it, children can withhold information by omitting to report it. Therefore, on the basis of these findings, requiring the reporting of sexual abuse through promising to report it may inhibit secrecy self-efficacy beliefs, but may not promote disclosure-enabling beliefs. These findings mirror research on lying and truth-telling which show that lying and truth-telling are not the inverse of each other (Bussey, 1999).

Conclusion

The analysis of promises provided in this chapter has shown that promises can both increase and decrease truth-telling. Therefore, they are sometimes linked to honesty and other times not. The goal of promises, however, is universal. It is to promote individuals keeping their word, through word or deed. In the interpersonal domain, where promises are used to signal and maintain trust, children's promise-keeping was shown to be related positively to their secret-keeping and overall trustworthiness. Most notably, it was also linked with peer acceptance and positively with school adjustment. It was shown, however, that in other situations, where promises are used to promote secrecy and truth-telling involving reporting an adult's transgression, for example, they are not always linked to honesty. Telling the truth about an adult's transgression after having promised to do so was related to honesty. However, keeping the adult's promise of secrecy was not related to it. This suggests that promises, although they may form part of the basis of trust, are not intrinsically honest or moral. They can be used to promote honesty and dishonesty. Whether they promote honesty depends on what is being promised rather than the promise itself. Similarly, trust can involve but does not have to involve morality. In Rotenberg's model of trust, the honesty basis has clear links with morality, but, as already discussed, this is not always the case for promises and secrecy. This lack of relationship with morality is consistent with other models of trust. In Harris's model of trust (Harris and Koenig, 2006), it is the predictability of people's responses that is linked to trust, and presumably it is this predictability that is the forerunner of keeping promises. In that conceptualization of trust, morality is not integral to its definition.

The extent to which morality is central to trustworthiness is a vexed issue which requires further consideration. Not all promises are equal. Promises acquire their value not only from what is being promised, but from the context in which they occur. Not keeping a promise to tell the truth in court carries more severe consequences, for example, than not keeping a promise to tell the truth to a friend. The promise could be about the same event. Breaking a promise in court constitutes perjury, which is a criminal offense. Not keeping a promise made to a friend can lead to negative inter-personal consequences, such as losing friendships and lack of acceptance by the peer group, but it is not a criminal offense. Further, breaking a promise made to a perpetrator about keeping his immoral conduct secret is not illegal, and some would argue that there is no moral requirement to keep a promise involving such activity (Bok, 1978). Therefore, the morality of promises needs to be considered not only in light of what is being prom-ised, but in view of the situation in which it is kept and broken.

Although the psychological benefits of keeping promises has been established by Rotenberg and his colleagues in the interpersonal domain, their benefit and cost have not been assessed in other domains. The psy-chological impact would be expected to vary depending on the context in which they are embedded. If telling the truth entails telling on someone and this is distressing for a child, the psychological impact of disclosure may be negative. However, it is also possible that by promising to tell the truth, the child takes less responsibility for telling on the other person. This may attenuate their psychological distress. Further research needs to assess the conditions under which promises are more likely to be hon-ored and the psychological benefits and costs of keeping them.

References

Astington, J. W. (1988a) Children's production of commissive speech acts. *Journal of Child Language*, **15**, 411–423.

(1988b). Children's understanding of the speech act of promising. *Journal of Child Language*, **15**, 157–173.

(1988c). Promises: Words or deeds? *First Language*, **8**, 259–270.

Austin, J. L. (1962). *How to do things with words*. Cambridge, MA: Harvard University Press.

Bala, N., Lee, K., Lindsay, R., and Talwar, V. (2001). A legal approach to the assessment of the competence of child witnesses. *Osgoode Hall Law Journal*, **38**, 409–451.

Bandura, A. (1986). *Social foundations of thought and action: A social cognitive theory*. Englewood Cliffs, NJ: Prentice Hall.

Betts, L. R. and Rotenberg, K. J. (2007). Trustworthiness, friendships and self-control: Factors that contribute to young children's school adjustment. *Infant and Child Development*, **16**, 491–508.

Bok, S. (1978). *Lying: Moral choice in public and private life*. New York: Pantheon.

Burns, N., Finkelhor, D., and Williams, L. M. (1988). Disclosure and detection. In D. Finkelhor and L. M. Williams (eds.), *Nursery crimes: Sexual abuse in day care* (pp. 99–113). Newbury Park, CA: Sage.

Bussey, K. (1992). Lying and truthfulness: Children's definitions, standards, and evaluative reactions. *Child Development*, **63**, 129–137.

  (1999). Children's categorization and evaluation of different types of lies and truths. *Child Development*, **70**, 1338–1347.

Bussey, K. and Bandura, A. (1999). Social cognitive theory of gender development and differentiation. *Psychological Review*, **106**, 676–713.

Bussey, K. and Grimbeek, E. J. (1995). Disclosure process: Issues for child sexual abuse victims. In K. J. Rotenberg (ed.), *Disclosure processes in children and adolescents* (pp. 166–203). New York: Cambridge University Press.

Buzzelli, C. A. (1988). The development of trust in children's relations with peers. *Child Study Journal*, **18**, 33–46.

Ceci, S. J. and Bruck, M. (1995). *Jeopardy in the courtroom: A scientific analysis of children's testimony*. Washington, DC: American Psychological Association.

Fitzpatrick, S. and Bussey, K. (2008). *The influence of promises on children's truth telling*. Manuscript submitted for publication.

Goodman, G. S. and Melinder, A. (2007). Child witness research and forensic interviews of young children: A review. *Legal and Criminological Psychology*, **12**, 1–19.

Harris, P. L. and Koenig, M. A. (2006). Trust in testimony: How children learn about science and religion. *Child Development*, **77**, 505–524.

Harrison, B. (1979). *An introduction to the philosophy of language*. London: Macmillan.

Hoyano, L. and Keenan, C. (2007). *Child abuse: Law and policy across boundaries*. Oxford University Press.

Imber, S. (1973). Relationship of trust to academic performance. *Journal of Personality and Social Psychology*, **28**, 145–150.

Leach, A., Talwar, V., Lee, K., Bala, N., and Lindsay, R. C. L. (2004). "Intuitive" lie detection of children's deception by law enforcement officials and university students. *Law and Human Behavior*, **28**, 661–685.

Lyon, T. D. and Saywitz, K. J. (1999). Young maltreated children's competence to take the oath. *Applied Developmental Science*, **3**, 16–27.

Maas, F. K. and Abbeduto, L. (2001). Children's judgements about intentionally and unintentionally broken promises. *Journal of Child Language*, **28**, 517–529.

Malloy, L. C., Mitchell, E., Block, S., Quas, J. A., and Goodman, G. S. (2007). Children's eyewitness memory: Balancing children's needs and defendants' rights when seeking the truth. In M. P. Toglia, J. D. Read, D. F. Ross, and R. C. L. Lindsay (eds.), *Handbook of eyewitness psychology: Vol. 1. Memory for events* (pp. 545–574). Mahwah, NJ: Lawrence Erlbaum Associates.

Palmer, S. E., Brown, R. A., Rae-Grant, N. I., and Loughlin, M. J. (1999). Responding to children's disclosure of familial abuse: What survivors tell us. *Child Welfare*, **78**, 259–282.

Rotenberg, K. J. (1980). "A promise kept, a promise broken": Developmental bases of trust. *Child Development*, **51**, 614–617.

  (1986). Same-sex patterns and sex differences in the trust-value basis of children's friendship. *Sex Roles*, **15**, 613–626.

  (1991). Children's interpersonal trust: An introduction. In K. J. Rotenberg (ed.), *Children's interpersonal trust: Sensitivity to lying, deception, and promise violations* (pp. 1–4). New York: Springer.

  (2001). Trust across the life-span. In N. J. Smelser and P. B. Baltes (eds.), *International encyclopedia of the social and behavioral sciences* (pp. 7866–7868). New York: Pergamon.

Rotenberg, K. J., Boulton, M. J., and Fox, C. L. (2005). Cross-sectional and longitudinal relations among children's trust beliefs, psychological maladjustment and social relationships: Are very high as well as very low trusting children at risk? *Journal of Abnormal Child Psychology*, **33**, 595–610.

Rotenberg, K. J., Fox, C., and Boulton, M. (2005). *Conceptual model for the investigation of trustworthiness in children*. Paper presented at the Society for Research in Child Development Conference, Atlanta, GA.

Rotenberg, K. J., Fox, C., Green, S., Ruderman, L., Slater, K., Stevens, K., and Carlo, G. (2005). Construction and validation of a children's interpersonal trust belief scale. *British Journal of Developmental Psychology*, **23**, 271–292.

Rotenberg, K. J., McDougall, P., Boulton, M. J., Vaillancourt, T., Fox, C., and Hymel, S. (2004). Cross-sectional and longitudinal relations among peer-reported trustworthiness, social relationships, and psychological adjustment in children and early adolescents from the United Kingdom and Canada. *Journal of Experimental Child Psychology*, **88**, 46–67.

Rotenberg, K. J., Michalik, N., Eisenberg, N., and Betts, L. R. (2008). The relations among young children's peer-reported trustworthiness, inhibitory control, and preschool adjustment. *Early Childhood Research Quarterly*, **23**, 288–298.

Rotter, J. B. (1967). A new scale for the measurement of interpersonal trust. *Journal of Personality*, **35**, 651–665.

Sauzier, M. (1989). Disclosure of child sexual abuse: For better or for worse. *Psychiatric Clinics of North America*, **12**, 455–469.

Searle, J. R. (1969). *Speech acts: An essay in the philosophy of language*. Cambridge University Press.

176   Kay Bussey

Sternberg, K. J., Lamb, M. E., Orbach, Y., Esplin, P. W., and Mitchell, S. (2001). Use of a structured investigative protocol enhances young children's responses to free recall prompts in the course of forensic interviews. *Journal of Applied Psychology*, **86**, 997–1005.

9   Liar liar! Pants on fire: Detecting the trustworthiness of children's statements

Victoria Talwar (McGill University) and
Sarah-Jane Renaud (McGill University)

Interpersonal trust is essential to our social relations and is vital for maintaining positive interpersonal relations, both in terms of friendship formation and maintenance and in terms of conventions of day-to-day communications (Grice, 1980; Rotenberg, 1991; Rotter, 1980). Honesty is an integral part of trustworthiness. According to Rotenberg and colleagues' conceptualization of trustworthiness, honesty is one of three bases of trust (Rotenberg, Boulton, and Fox, 2005; Rotenberg, Fox, Green, Ruderman, Slater, Stevens, and Carlo, 2005; Rotenberg, MacDonald, and King, 2004). According to this framework, there are three fundamental bases of trustworthiness that include honesty (which is the focus of this chapter), reliability, and emotional trust (see Chapter 2 for further details). Others' perceptions of one's honesty are also an important aspect of trustworthiness, as they can affect the assessment of one's trustworthiness and have social consequences. Individuals hold cognitive representations of the extent to which they trust another (i.e., belief that another is telling the truth). Thus, an adult may *believe* that a child is honest. However, there is also the actual behavior of the child, which is their *dispositional trustworthiness*. A child's dispositional trustworthiness is reflected in their behavior to tell the truth and keep promises. Thus, there is a dyadic relationship between both trust beliefs and the trustworthiness revealed by the child's behavior. A dyadic partner holds trust beliefs that may match (or mismatch) the trustworthiness of another. So someone can believe that a person is lying (and as a result mistrust them), but the person may or may not be engaging in such behavior. There are consequences for both parties. The perceiver's beliefs regarding the other's trustworthiness guides how they will feel and act towards the other person. There are also consequences for the other individual, whose behavior may be interpreted in different ways, thus affecting their perceived trustworthiness. These consequences can lead to positive and negative outcomes, depending on the individual's perceived trustworthiness. For instance, children's trustworthiness has been related to their school adjustment and to the number of friends they have (e.g., Rotenberg, Michalik, Eisenberg, and Betts, 2008). Thus, a child who frequently lies and is perceived as being dishonest may suffer grave consequences in their social relations and development.

To perceive another as trustworthy, we must have confidence that their verbal and nonverbal communication accurately represents reality (Rotenberg, 1991). In other words, the other person must appear truthful and we must be able to believe their statements as being the truth. This is one of the most fundamental conventions governing interpersonal communication – the maxim of quality. This maxim states that one should be truthful and inform, not misinform, communicative partners (Grice, 1980). Telling a lie is a major violation of this cardinal rule of communication, and getting caught in that lie could result in a loss of trust and a negative image of the liar. This could jeopardize social relationships, create an image of the liar as someone who lacks integrity or credibility, and lead to social isolation, thus further perpetuating an individual's antisocial behaviors. Studies examining the prevalence of behavior problems in children have suggested that lying is related to aggression, delinquency and conduct problems (Achenbach and Edelbrock, 1979, 1981; Gervais, Tremblay, Desmarais-Gervais, and Vitaro, 2000; Rutter, 1967; Stouthamer-Loeber and Loeber, 1986).

While it is clear that dishonesty can have a negative impact on one's perceived trustworthiness, nevertheless lying is not an infrequent day-to-day behavior. Research with adults shows that adults tell lies daily (DePaulo and Kashy, 1998; DePaulo, Kashy, Kirkendol, Wyer, and Epstein, 1996). People tell lies not only for self-gain and to avoid negative repercussions, but also to smooth interpersonal relationships and present a positive image of themselves to others. Telling the occasional lie to ease an awkward moment with an acquaintance (e.g., telling them a fib about why you didn't turn up to their party) can sometimes be a successful social strategy, as it can lead to positive feelings and maintenance of the interpersonal relation (e.g., you say that you were ill and the other person feels better not thinking you were rejecting their company). Nevertheless, we generally perceive others' lies as being bad and give a negative evaluation of individuals who lie (Lindskold and Walters, 1983; Seiter, Brushke, and Bai, 2002). As a result, both the telling of lies *and* the detection of lies can have serious interpersonal consequences.

Detection of a lie may lead to the detector suffering from feelings of skepticism and betrayal, resulting in negative feelings about the lie-teller; while the lie-teller may suffer a loss of credibility and trust with others.

The costs associated with lie-telling generally come when one is unsuccessful in deception, usually resulting from the hidden information being discovered. There is also the social cost of losing credibility. That is, one whose opinion was valued and was frequently sought may no longer be consulted once it is revealed that the individual never offered an honest opinion. Similarly, one who lies frequently to get out of trouble may not be believed when denying later wrongdoing. Thus, lie-telling of any type can lose its strategic social advantages, once the lie-teller loses credibility.

From a very young age, children are taught about the consequences of lying. Through the use of stories such as "Pinocchio" and "The boy who cried wolf," children are shown the social and emotional consequences of lying (Arruda, Brunet, Poplinger, Ross, McCarthy, and Talwar, 2007; Biskin and Hoskisson, 1977). Despite the popularity of moral stories of deception, less is known about deception by children and perceptions of children's lies compared to adults', especially under circumstances where there are consequences to both the deceived and the liar. Yet children's abilities to deceive others successfully and be perceived by others as being trustworthy have important consequences for their social relations and social competence (DePaulo and Jordan, 1982; Feldamn and Philippot, 1991; Talwar, Murphy, and Lee, 2007). Lying successfully requires an understanding not only of the perspective of the person you are deceiving, but also of the need to regulate one's verbal expressive behaviors accordingly (Talwar, Gordon, and Lee, 2007; Talwar and Lee, 2008).

Detection also brings children into more conflict with their environment, can create negative perceptions among others that they are insincere and untrustworthy, and can seriously undermine their interpersonal relations with parents, peers, and others. However, like adults, children's occasional use of deception to smooth and maintain positive social relations may actually increase others' positive feelings towards them. For instance, Saarni (1988), in her study on children's understanding of dissembled nonverbal expressiveness, found that a majority of children reported that children who always showed their real feelings, and rarely inhibited their nonverbal behavior cues to emotion, would be rejected by peers. Thus, occasionally, strategic dissemblance can increase one's attractiveness as an associate. But it is a fine line in terms of maintaining others' trust, as Saarni also reported that children who are described as never showing true emotions are perceived as disliked, emotionally maladjusted, and difficult to know. Therefore, a child needs to lie strategically and effectively in order to avoid both detection and negative evaluations by others.

Thus, the aim of this chapter is to cover children's trustworthiness in terms of children's lie-telling behavior (i.e., dispositional trustworthiness) and how others perceive children's deceptive behavior (i.e., trust beliefs in the child). Specifically, we will describe the results of several of our recent and ongoing studies on perceptions of children's honesty. We will also discuss the implications of the perceived trustworthiness and veracity of children, both for close interpersonal relations, and in more applied settings, such as forensic and legal cases.

Development of lying behavior

Research on the development of children's lie-telling behavior has examined both children's conceptual moral understanding of lies and their actual lie-telling behavior. Until recently, research has concentrated on how children understand lies. Research on children's understanding of deception has found that children as young as 4 years of age have a rudimentary understanding of lies. Even young children are able to recognize the intention of the speaker as a crucial component for determining whether a statement is true, and also as a cue to identify lies involving misdeeds (Bussey, 1992, 1999; Peterson, Peterson, and Seeto, 1983). While younger children tend to evaluate all lies negatively and focus on the factuality of the statement (e.g., Strichartz and Burton, 1990), with increased age, children gradually take into consideration the social context in which lies are told and the intention of the lie-teller when evaluating lies (Bussey, 1992, 1999). In addition, theory-of-mind research suggests that preschool children are able to understand that another may hold a false belief about reality and that one can use this ability to deceive another (Chandler, Fritz, and Hala, 1989; Polak and Harris, 1999; Talwar, Gordon, and Lee, 2007).

Recently, research has focused on why and when children begin to lie. Anecdotal evidence and observational studies suggest that children begin telling lies in the preschool years, with some lies appearing as early as 2 years of age (Newton, Reddy, and Bull, 2000; Wilson, Smith, and Ross, 2003). DePaulo and Jordan (1982) suggest the earliest lies children tell are those that allow them to escape imminent punishment. Also among the early lies that children tell are lies to obtain a reward. This may first be motivated by a desire for material benefits (e.g., a cookie from a forbidden cookie jar), and later by a desire for social rewards (e.g., self-presentation lies). The most frequent lies that children tell tend to be antisocial lies to conceal misdeeds (Newton, Reddy, and Bull, 2000; Stouthamer-Loeber, 1986; Wilson, Smith, and Ross, 2003).

Until recently, research had mainly focused on reports of children's lie-telling behavior from parents or teachers. These studies found that, like adults, children tell lies on a frequent basis, and that children who lie chronically are more likely to be maladjusted and perceived negatively by others (e.g., Gervais, Tremblay, Desmarais-Gervais, and Vitaro, 2000; Stouthamer-Loeber and Loeber, 1986). In recent years, experimental studies have focused on examining children's actual lie-telling behavior. Many of these studies have typically relied on a temptation-resistance paradigm (Lewis, Stanger, and Sullivan, 1989; Polak and Harris, 1999; Talwar and Lee, 2002a; Talwar, Lee, Bala, and Lindsay, 2002).

Originally pioneered by Sears, Rau, and Alpert (1965), children participating in the temptation-resistance paradigm are typically told by a researcher not to peek at or play with a toy when left alone. Due to children's curiosity and difficulty resisting temptation, most children disobey the researcher's instructions and peek or play when left alone. Upon returning, the researcher asks children whether they peeked at or played with the toy. Thus, the temptation-resistance paradigm creates a situation where children who have transgressed by disobeying an adult's instruction can make a decision either to lie or to tell the truth about that transgression. The advantage of this paradigm is that it elicits spontaneous lies from children attempting to conceal their transgression, resulting in children who are self-motivated to lie. More importantly, the temptation-resistance paradigm mimics the naturalistic conditions in which children tend to lie (DePaulo and Jordan, 1982; Newton, Reddy, and Bull, 2000; Stouthamer-Loeber, 1986; Wilson, Smith, and Ross, 2003).

Using a temptation-resistance paradigm, Lewis, Stanger, and Sullivan, (1989) found that 38 percent of 3-year-olds who peeked at the forbidden toy denied peeking, while 38 percent confessed to peeking at the toy, and the remaining children gave no answer. Similarly, Talwar and Lee (2002a) found that most children between 4 and 7 years of age lied about peeking at the toy, while 64 percent of 3-year-olds confessed to their transgression. Thus, some children as young as 3 years of age, and most children by 4 years of age, can and will tell lies to conceal transgressions and escape potential punishment. Similar results have been observed among American, Canadian, British, and Chinese children (Lewis, Stanger, and Sullivan, 1989; Polak and Harris, 1999; Talwar and Lee, 2002a; Talwar, Lee, Bala, and Lindsay, 2002; Xu and Lee, 2007). Hence, there is convergent evidence to suggest that this age pattern is a common developmental phenomenon and is related to children's abilities to understand the mental states of others (Chandler, Fritz, and Hala, 1989; Talwar and Lee, 2008; Talwar, Gordon, and Lee, 2007).

Research has found, however, that despite children's tendency to lie, young children are not skilled lie-tellers (Polak and Harris, 1999; Talwar and Lee, 2002a). To successfully deceive another and avoid detection, a liar must be able not only to produce a false statement, but also to ensure consistency between their initial lie and subsequent statements. The ability to maintain consistency between statements when deceiving is known as semantic leakage control (Talwar and Lee, 2002a). In several studies of children's abilities to maintain their lies, Talwar and colleagues have found differences between preschool children and older children (Talwar and Lee, 2002a; Talwar, Gordon, and Lee, 2007; Talwar, Murphy, and Lee, 2007). In one study, after falsely denying a transgression, the majority of preschoolers revealed incriminating information in their subsequent statements. For example, after denying peeking at the toy, many preschoolers justified their guess by describing what the mystery toy looked like, whereas approximately half of 6- and 7-year-olds who committed the transgression were able to conceal and maintain their lies when answering follow-up questions (Talwar and Lee, 2002a). This age trend continued in another study with children between 7 and 11 years of age (Talwar, Gordon, and Lee, 2007). Thus, it appears that preschool-aged children are limited in their semantic leakage control abilities and consequently are not skilled, elaborate lie-tellers. As they get older, however, children become more sophisticated at concealing their lies verbally, and are therefore more successful at maintaining their lies over time.

Detection and perceptions of children's lie-telling

Are individuals able to differentiate between lying and truth-telling? After all, lies are created with the intention to deceive the listener. Detecting the intentionally false statement of another is one of the challenging tasks of interpersonal perception. In order to avoid giving any cues to their deceit, a skilled liar will attempt to conceal their deception in their nonverbal and verbal expressive behaviors. However, research on children's lie-telling behavior suggests that young children are not skilled lie-tellers. This immature ability to control semantic leakage may result in children telling lies that are more likely to be detected. However, while there has been considerable research on adults' detection of other adults' lies (e.g., Bond and DePaulo, 2005; Bond, Omar, Pitre, Lashley, Skaggs, and Kirk, 1992; Ekman, 1985; Ekman and O'Sullivan, 1991; O'Sullivan, 2005; Vrij and Mann, 2005), there have been relatively few studies examining the detection and perceptions of children's lies.

Research examining adults' ability to detect children's intentional lies or false testimony has obtained mixed findings. Studies have found that adults may have difficulty detecting younger children's deceit when children are motivated to lie to conceal their own transgressions (e.g., Leach, Talwar, Lee, Bala, and Lindsay, 2004; Talwar and Lee, 2002a).

Such motivation has been found to result in adult detection rates of children's lies at a level no greater than chance. Other research has suggested detection accuracy can improve when the detector views the same child under different interview conditions, and when children are asked follow-up questions. Such results are likely due to the fact that children's control of their verbal expressive behaviors (i.e., their semantic leakage control) is often lagging behind their control of their nonverbal behaviors (e.g., Crossman and Lewis, 2006; Feldman, Jenkins, and Popoola, 1979; Leach, Talwar, Lee, Bala, and Lindsay, 2004; Orcutt, Goodman, Tobey, Batterman-Faunce, and Thomas, 2001; Talwar and Lee, 2002a; Talwar, Gordon, and Lee, 2007).

Indeed, as mentioned above, several studies of children's abilities to maintain their lies have found age differences between preschool children and older children (Talwar and Lee, 2002a; Talwar, Gordon, and Lee, 2007; Talwar, Murphy, and Lee, 2007). For instance, in their study examining children's lies to conceal a transgression, Talwar and Lee (2002a) found that younger children who had poor semantic leakage control were more likely to be detected by adults than older children who had good semantic leakage control. These older children were able to maintain their lies during follow-up questioning and were indistinguishable from children who were telling the truth. However, despite this distinction between the lies of younger and older children, overall, adults were still just above chance levels at distinguishing lie-tellers from truth-tellers (although this detection rate was elevated for younger children). This may reflect adults' beliefs about the trustworthiness of children. Indeed, Talwar and Lee (2002a) reported that there was a general bias among adults to rate boys as lie-tellers and girls as truth-tellers.

It has also been suggested that expertise or familiarity with children may aid detection and increase sensitivity to the cues of children's deceit. Individuals such as parents, teachers, or other professionals, who have extensive experience working with many children over a range of contexts, may have an advantage when detecting children's lies (O'Sullivan, 2005). However, only a few studies have examined this question. Westcott, Davies, and Clifford (1991), for instance, found that professionals who interact with children as part of their work (e.g., educational psychologists, occupational psychologists) were more accurate in detecting children's deception than others. Crossman and Lewis (2006) also found that adults who had professional experience with children were better at detection than those without experience. Thus, having experience with children may aid in detection, although it is not clear if these differences are due to individual differences in ability to detect deception or experience.

Parents' abilities to detect their own child's honesty

The detection of children's lies and the development and socialization of children's trustworthiness is of particular concern for parents. Besides research that has found that lying is related to children's adjustment (e.g., Gervais, Tremblay, Desmarais-Gervais, and Vitaro, 2000; Stouthamer-Loeber and Loeber, 1986), research has also found that parents, teachers, and clinicians all perceive lying as a serious behavioral problem (Stouthamer-Loeber, 1986). For this reason, parents directly socialize children about the inappropriateness of lying (DePaulo and Jordan, 1982), and these discussions often occur when a fib has been discovered (Wilson, Smith, and Ross, 2003). Thus, detecting children's lies is a critical opportunity for parents to teach their children about the importance of honesty (Crossman and Lewis, 2006). Parents who have close interpersonal relationships with their own children, and presumably are more familiar with their children's behavior than others, may have a particular expertise at detecting children's deception. For example, observational data suggest that very young children's lies are frequently detected by their parents, perhaps due to the somewhat immature nature of their lies and evident cues to their deception (Newton, Reddy, and Bull, 2000; Wilson, Smith, and Ross, 2003). One possible explanation for such frequent detection is the anxiety and remorse that children often display when telling lies to parents. Oldershaw and Bagby (1997) suggest that, given the importance of the parent–child relationship, it is possible that such lies are experienced as high stakes by children. Thus, lies told to parents may elicit greater anxiety and remorse than lies told in other situations. Perhaps also related to greater anxiety and remorse, Leach, Talwar, Lee, Bala, and Lindsay (2004) found that children who engaged in a moral discussion about lying, or who promised to be honest, were more readily detected by adults when later telling lies.

A few studies that have examined parents' abilities to detect children's lies have been inconsistent (Chahal and Cassidy, 1995; Leach, Talwar, Lee, Bala, and Lindsay, 2004; Oldershaw and Bagby, 1997; Talwar and Lee, 2002a). In a study by Chahal and Cassidy (1995), children were instructed to lie about the major events in a film. Results indicated that parents were no better at detecting children's honesty than other adults. Furthermore, in another study that used a more naturalistic situation, where children spontaneously chose to lie to conceal a transgression, Talwar and Lee (2002a) also found that parents were poor at detecting children's lies. In similar research, others have also reported the poor detection abilities of parents (e.g., Crossman and Lewis, 2006; Leach, Talwar, Lee, Bala, and Lindsay, 2004). Thus, it appears that parents may not actually be good at detection. However, it is important to note that in all these studies, parents were detecting *other* children's lies, and it may be that parents have a specialized ability to detect the lies of their own children.

The present study investigated parents' ability to detect the lies of their children. Since it is more ecologically relevant to examine children's spontaneous and self-motivated lies (i.e., children are not asked to lie by the experimenter), we report a study in which children were self-motivated to lie about their own transgression. In such cases, the motivation to lie is high for the child and the motivation to detect is high for the parent. The child wishes to get away with their transgression and avoid any negative punishment or repercussions, and the parent wishes to accurately assess the veracity of their child's statements.

Method

Participants

The present study was part of a wider study examining the development of children's lie-telling behavior in relation to their cognitive development (for details, see Talwar and Lee, 2008). Participants were 250 mother–child dyads. The children were divided into three age groups for the analyses: the preschool group consisted of children aged 3 and 5 years (N = 97, 59 males); the early elementary school group consisted of children aged 6 and 8 years (N = 79, 43 males); and the older elementary school group consisted of children aged between 9 and 11 years (N = 74, 32 males).

Design and procedure

Temptation-resistance paradigm Children participated in a modified temptation-resistance paradigm where children were told not to look at a forbidden toy while the experimenter was out of the room. The toy was located directly behind the children and they were told explicitly that they should not turn around and peek at the toy. The toy made a noise, and children were told to listen to the noise to see if they could guess the identity of the toy. A hidden video camera captured the children's movements while they were alone in the room. Upon returning, the experimenter asked the child to promise to tell the truth, then interviewed the child about their behavior while alone in the room. Children were asked, "Did you peek at the toy? Did you turn around in your chair? Who do you think it is [the toy]?" Children's lie-telling behavior is reported in detail in Talwar and Lee (2008) and is not the focus of the current investigation.

Parents did not see their children participate in the temptation-resistance paradigm. They were in a separate room and the temptation-resistance situation was explained to them. Thus, parents were blind to their children's actual behavior. Each parent was asked two questions. First, they were asked, "Do you think your child peeked?" Parents then viewed the video clip of their child being interviewed about their behavior. Subsequently, parents were asked, "Do you think your child is telling the truth?"

Results and discussion

There were three groups of children: non-peeking truth-tellers, liars, and confessors. Non-peeking truth-tellers did not peek at the toy and truthfully denied peeking when asked about their behavior. All children who did not peek, truthfully denied having peeked. There were 93 children who did not peek (37 percent) and hence were labeled as non-peeking truth-tellers. There were 157 children who did peek at the toy when the experimenter left the room. These children were divided into two groups: liars and confessors. The 115 children who were labeled liars (46 percent of the entire sample) peeked at the toy and then falsely denied peeking when later asked. The 42 children who were labeled confessors (17 percent of the entire sample) peeked at the toy and then truthfully confessed their peeking behavior when later asked. We examined parents' perceptions of each of these three groups of children.

Children's peeking behavior

When parents' predictions about whether their child would peek or not were examined, 54 percent of parents thought their child would not peek. To further investigate parents' abilities to accurately predict whether their child would peek or not, we calculated parents' accuracy scores. Overall, 64 percent of parents accurately predicted their child's peeking behavior, a rate that is significantly above the chance rate of accuracy, $t(249) = 4.60, p < 0.001$. Thus, it appears that the majority of parents were accurate at predicting whether their child would peek or not. Parents' accuracy at predicting the peeking behavior of the three groups of children was examined using a logistic regression analysis. The variables of age of child, sex of child, and type of child (non-peeking truth-teller, liar, or confessor) were entered as predictors, with interactions between the variables entered second. The best fitting model included age, sex,

Table 9.1 *Parents' accuracy rates (standard deviations) predicting children's peeking behavior*

	Preschool	Early elementary	Older elementary
Non-peekers	.47 (.52)	.76 (.44)	.83 (.38)
Liars	.68 (.47)	.50 (.51)	.19 (.40)
Confessors	.82 (.37)	.64 (.50)	.00 (.00)

and type of child, as well as an age by type of child interaction, χ^2 (4, $N = 250$) = 33.76, $p < .01$, Nagelkerke R squared = .17. Parents were more accurate at predicting younger children's peeking behavior than older children's ($\beta = 0.78$, *Wald* = 7.98, $p < .05$); see Table 9.1. There was also a significant difference for type of child ($\beta = 2.46$, *Wald* = 6.93, $p < .001$). Parents were more accurate in predicting non-peeking truth-tellers' ($M = .75$, $SD = .44$) and confessors' ($M = .74$, $SD = .45$) behavior than liars' behavior ($M = .52$, $SD = .50$). Thus, parents whose children told the truth (either by truthfully claiming they did not peek or by confessing truthfully to having peeked) appeared to have more realistic ideas of their children's transgressive behavior. The lower accuracy for liars may reflect a bias by some parents to think their children innocent of committing a minor transgression. There was a mismatch between their trust beliefs regarding their child's behavior and the child's actual trustworthiness, as reflected by their behavior in the temptation-resistance paradigm. However, interestingly, parents whose children confessed appeared not to have this bias. Perhaps, as their children are more likely to confess and tell the truth about their transgressions than to lie, these parents had a more accurate knowledge of their children's likely behavior in such a situation.

However, these effects were qualified by an interaction between age of child and type of child ($\beta = -1.56$, *Wald* = 25.51, $p < .001$). As shown in Table 9.1, adults were better at predicting the preschool-age confessors' behavior, but this reversed with age, as adults were more accurate when predicting the non-peeking behavior of the older elementary age group. For the older children, most parents seemed to rate their children as not peeking. This suggests that parents' bias towards thinking their child can resist temptation, and not commit a minor transgression, appears to be strongest for children of late elementary school age. Perhaps parents are more realistic about their children's transgressive behavior when children are younger, but with age, their standards and expectations for their children increase, thus making them less willing to believe that their child would commit such a transgression.

Table 9.2 *Parents' accuracy rates (standard deviations) in identifying their children's honest and dishonest statements*

	Preschool	Early elementary	Older elementary
Non-liars	.71 (.47)	.89 (.32)	.83 (.38)
Liars	.53 (.50)	.33 (.36)	.27 (.46)
Confessors	.68 (.47)	1 (.0)	1 (.0)

Children's lie-telling behavior

After seeing their child answer questions about their peeking behavior, parents' perceptions of whether they thought their child was telling the truth or lying were measured. Overall, 74 percent of parents thought their children were telling the truth. To further investigate parents' abilities to accurately assess whether their children were lying or telling the truth, parents' accuracy scores at detecting their child's lie- or truth-telling was calculated (i.e., correctly saying their child was the telling the truth or lying). Overall, 66 percent of parents accurately identified their child's lie-telling behavior, a rate that is again significantly above the chance rate of accuracy, $t(249) = 5.33$, $p < 0.001$. A logistic regression analysis was conducted with parents' accuracy scores (correct versus incorrect) as the predicted variable. The variables of age of child, sex of child, and type of child (non-peeking truth-teller, confessors, liars) were entered as predictors, with interactions between the variables entered second. The best-fitting model included age, sex, and type of child, as well as an age by type of child interaction, $\chi^2(4, N=250)=21.83$, $p<.001$. There was a significant difference for age ($\beta=0.75$, $Wald = 7.50$, $p<.05$) and type of child ($\beta = 2.09$, $Wald = 12.82, p<.001$), as well as significant age by type of child interaction ($\beta = -1.24$, $Wald = 17.439$, $p<.001$). Parents were more accurate at labeling confessors and non-peeking truth-tellers than labeling lie-tellers. While all but two confessors were rated as truth-tellers by their parents, and the accuracy rate for non-peeking truth-tellers ($M=.81$, $SD=.39$) was also high, parents' accuracy rate for lie-tellers was significantly lower ($M=.42$, $SD=.49$). As seen in Table 9.2, adults were less accurate at detecting preschool children's true statements compared to those of older children. However, the reverse pattern is seen for children's lies. Parents' accuracy at detecting liars decreased as children increased in age. These results suggest that parents had a strong bias to rate their child as a truth-teller, but were much poorer at detecting if their child was lying.

Thus, while parents have an overall higher detection rate than is usually found in adult detection literature, this ability seems to be fueled by parents' belief in the honesty of their children. It may be that since children's dishonesty is a form of interpersonal betrayal, as it is a serious violation of the norms and expectations of communication in interpersonal relationships, parents develop Nelsonian blindness to their children's lie-telling behaviors. In fact, of the parents who initially thought their child did peek at the toy, 35 percent of them changed their minds and believed their child when they heard their child lie and state that he/she "did not peek." However, most parents who initially thought their child did not peek continued to believe their child was being honest when they heard the child's dishonest denial of peeking.

This Nelsonian blindness can have positive as well as negative consequences for parents and their children. It is important for parents to perceive their children as having high trustworthiness. There may be serious consequences to a parent–child relationship if the parent does not trust the child and does not take their verbal statements at face value (DePaulo and Jordan, 1982). Stouthamer-Loeber (1991) reported that mothers get along less well with those children who they see as lying more frequently. On the other hand, if a parent does not detect a child's dishonest behaviors, they are not able to correct these behaviors or teach children the value of honesty (Crossman and Lewis, 2006). Thus, it may be that these findings reflect a parental coping strategy to deal with children's dishonesty. For many parents, their response to children's lies is to ignore the act of lying and focus instead on the child's actions about which they are lying (Lewis, 1993). Hence, parents may be practiced in overlooking children's cues to deception. Nevertheless, of the parents who accurately predicted that their child would peek, 65 percent of them accurately detected their children's dishonest statement. Therefore, some parents may be more realistic about their children's cheating and lying behaviors. On the other hand, when actually detecting deception related to these behaviors (i.e., the actual lie), many parents are no longer as realistic. Further research is needed to see how parents' perceptions of their children's honesty impacts on the parent–child relationship. Furthermore, it may be that if parents had seen children answer additional follow-up questions, parents' detection performance may have been even better.

Adults' detection of children's dishonesty: Implications for applied settings

Children's ability to appear honest is not only important in terms of the interpersonal consequences it has for their significant close social relations, but can also affect their perceived credibility in the eyes of relative strangers. A critical example of this takes place in courtroom settings, where children's testimony may play a vital role. Children who witness a crime, such as murder or sexual assault, may be called upon to give testimony in court. In some cases, the child will provide key testimony and the case may rest largely on whether the child is believed to be honest (Goodman, Golding, Helegen, Haith, and Michelli, 1987). If the trial takes place before a jury, the jury members must assess the veracity of the child's statements. In such a setting, the trustworthiness of children's verbal reports will be assessed in terms of their veracity and credibility. Lie detection might be important in such cases, for the protection of children as well as those around them. Hence, it is necessary to determine whether adults can detect children's honesty, and whether they are able to assess the credibility of children's reports (Oldershaw and Bagby, 1997; Orcutt, Goodman, Tobey, Batterman-Faunce, and Thomas, 2001).

As a result, research on children's lie-telling behaviors and others' perceptions of the trustworthiness of their reports has not only been of interest in terms of children's development, but also has important implications for applied contexts such as the credibility of child witness testimony. The question of credibility addresses the issue of what factors lead to others believing a child's testimony. Factors that may affect adults' perceptions of child witness veracity and/or credibility may include a child's perceived general competence, suggestibility, trustworthiness, nonverbal demeanor, age, gender, and other personal characteristics (e.g., Bottoms and Goodman, 1994; Goodman, Bottoms, Herscovici, and Shaver, 1989; Haugaard and Reppucci, 1992; Ross, Dunning, Toglia, and Ceci, 1990). Compared to adults, child witnesses are perceived as less cognitively competent and more susceptible to suggestion, but also as more trustworthy and sincere (Brigham and Spier, 1992; Goodman, Bottoms, Herscovici, and Shaver, 1989; Ross, Dunning, Toglia, and Ceci, 1990; Yarmey and Jones, 1983).

In terms of adults' ability to accurately assess the veracity of a child's statement, there has been little ecologically relevant research. The majority of research on children's lie-telling and others' assessment of their lies has been from a developmental perspective. In most published studies on adults' detection of children's lies, children were only required to give brief responses to questions, and they were lying to conceal their own transgressions (e.g., Lewis, Stanger, and Sullivan, 1989). When children testify in court, they are often required to provide many details about an alleged criminal act involving others. Thus, a more ecologically relevant study is one in which children are reporting about a true or fabricated event in their lives that involves others.

Few studies have examined adults' assessments of the veracity of children's testimony (Haugaard and Reppucci, 1992; Honts, 1994), and none has examined the relationship between adults' veracity assessments and their judgments of child witness credibility. In fact, some findings suggest that adults may have a bias towards disbelieving children's statements, which is in contrast with the typical truth bias found with adult statements (Masip, Garrido, and Herrero, 2004; Vrij and Baxter, 1999). This suggests that children who are telling the truth about an experience or event are more likely to be perceived as liars, rather than being given the "benefit of the doubt." Such findings also stress the importance of research on the perceptions and interpretations of children's testimony.

In a recent study, we examined adults' abilities to detect children's true and false testimony (Talwar, Lee, Bala, and Lindsay, 2006). In this study, adults watched video clips of children testifying about an event in a court simulation. A total of forty-eight children between 4 and 7 years of age participated in the court simulation procedure (twenty-four boys and twenty-four girls). Children either gave a true or a fabricated false report about an event that happened in their lives involving others (e.g., a trip to the zoo). Children's true reports included details of a truly experienced event, whereas children's fabricated false reports were about an event that the child had never experienced. Children were brought into a simulated courtroom, where law and psychology graduate students played the roles of lawyers (i.e., prosecutor and defense) and judge. All children were asked to testify about the assigned event by the "prosecutor," who prompted them with open-ended questions. After children had told their story, children were "cross-examined" by the "defense attorney" about the truthfulness of their story. A video camera was placed to obtain an upper torso and head shot of the child in the witness box. The researchers and the participants in the court simulation were blind to whether or not each child was telling the truth. The entire session lasted approximately 15 minutes.

Adults ($N = 193$) were then shown video clips of children's "court appearance," and were asked a series of questions based on their observations of the child's testimony. First, they were asked whether they believed that the events described by the witness really happened. They were also asked to fill out a child witness credibility questionnaire, which included a range of questions concerning the child's perceived credibility. The questions covered aspects of the child's testimony such as perceived abilities to accurately report events, truthfulness, resistance to suggestion, consistency of the testimony, reliability of memory, and the child's demeanor. After answering all of these questions, all adults saw a final video clip in which the "defense attorney" asked children about the truthfulness of their story. Participants were asked to make a final verdict of whether they believed that the events described by the child really happened.

In examining adults' assessments of children's testimony, the results of the study found that adults were more accurate at detecting truth-tellers (74 percent) than lie-tellers (26 percent), but their overall accuracy was at chance level (50 percent). Adults tended to rate the majority of children as giving truthful testimony (73 percent), regardless of whether the children were actually telling true or false stories. This is in keeping with previous research which has found that adults (who are not familiar with children) are unable to discriminate accurately between the true and false reports of children by merely observing children testifying (e.g., Crossman and Lewis, 2006; Leach, Talwar, Lee, Bala, and Lindsay, 2004). In fact, signal detection analyses revealed that adults tended to have a "truth" bias. They believed the children's testimony regardless of children's actual veracity. However, after seeing a short cross-examination, the truth bias disappeared. Yet adults' detection accuracy of veracity remained unimproved (52 percent).

In terms of adults' perceptions of children's testimony, an exploratory factor analysis was performed on adults' ratings on the items of the child witness credibility questionnaire. This analysis yielded six factors that accounted for 51 percent of the variance. The first factor, labeled integrity, contained items that described the perceptions of the witnesses' perceived truthfulness, intention, and motivation to be truthful or deceptive. The second factor, labeled maturity, contained items describing children's age-related abilities. The third factor, labeled testimony quality, contained items describing the perceived reliability and amount of detail in the child's testimony. The fourth factor, labeled conceptual knowledge, contained items describing children's understanding of truths, lies, and promises). The fifth factor contained items describing testimony consistency. The sixth factor, labeled suggestibility, contained items describing the degree to which the testimony was perceived to be spontaneous or rehearsed.

Adults' judgments of children's credibility were significantly predicted by their perceptions of the child and the child's perceived trustworthiness. Specifically, adults' initial perceptions of children's maturity, suggestibility, and integrity predicted their judgments of the veracity and credibility of children's testimony. However, adults' final verdict scores, given after seeing children answering cross-examination questions, were only related to their perception of the child's integrity. Thus, when the "trustworthiness" of the children's reports was called into question, adults' perceptions of the children as being truthful and credible changed. These findings are consistent with previous research showing that children's perceived honesty and cognitive abilities predict adult assessment of children's credibility. Similar to Ross, Jurden, Lindsay, and Keeney

(2003), this study found that adults' perceptions of children's honesty had the biggest predictive value of adults' credibility assessment of child witnesses. Thus, while adults are unable to reliably distinguish true from false testimony, their perceptions of children's integrity influenced their overall credibility ratings and the likelihood of believing a child's report as being true.

Summary and future directions

Undoubtedly, lying is considered a negative social behavior and we expect others to be honest with us. It is a fundamental assumption of human communication that we expect our communicative partners to give us accurate information and not to mislead us (Grice, 1980; Sweetser, 1987). Honesty is a fundamental aspect of trustworthiness, and dishonesty can have an impact on individuals' relations with others (Rotenberg, 1991). Nevertheless, research suggests that deception is a normative part of typical development, and that adults and children tell lies on a daily basis (e.g., DePaulo, Kashy, Kirkendol, Wyer, and Epstein, 1996; Newton, Reddy, and Bull, 2000). However, the degree to which one is successful at telling lies determines the negative or positive impact this behavior may have on one's relationships. The current chapter reviewed the research on children's lie-telling behavior and their ability to tell lies successfully to avoid detection. Although children's lie-telling emerges in the preschool years, children are not skilled lie-tellers until the later elementary school years (e.g., Talwar, Gordon, and Lee, 2007). However, as seen in the second study described in this chapter, and in previous research, adults are equally unskilled at detecting deception in others, including children. Adults' perceptions of a child as being trustworthy may influence whether they believe children to be truthful or not. This can have an impact on children's perceived trustworthiness when recounting the details of important events, whether it is in a courtroom or on the playground. Children whose integrity and truthfulness appears unassailed may be more likely to be believed than others.

The findings described in this chapter suggest that parents may have some advantage when detecting children's lies. Overall, parents were fairly accurate at predicting their children's transgressive behavior and were able to detect the veracity of children's assertions about their behavior. They were particularly adept at detecting truthful statements. However, parents may have a truth bias which acts as a protective strategy to avoid negative feelings towards their child and the quality of the parent–child relationship. Nevertheless, parents achieved higher detection rates than is commonly found with adults, as seen in the second study. Parents were

making judgments of someone they had a close interpersonal relationship with (i.e., their own child), whereas the adults in the second study
were making judgments of children they did not know and had no relationship with. The degree of the relationship between the detector and
the deceiver is an important factor to examine further in future studies.
Given the interpersonal consequences of detecting another's lie or being
detected by someone with whom one is in a close relationship, the familiarity of the individuals involved could either aid or hamper accurate
assessments of trustworthiness.

Other factors that have remained largely unexplored are the different
types of lies and motivations for lying. Most studies that have examined
children's lies have focused on children's lies of trickery or about their
own transgressions. While many lies are antisocial in nature, told for personal gain or to escape punishment, lies can also be told for prosocial
reasons. These are lies told without malicious or malignant intent (Bok,
1978), and in order to benefit another person or be polite. The little
research that has examined the development of prosocial lies in children
suggests that children are socialized to tell these lies from a young age,
as a strategy to smooth social relations and maintain social conventions
of politeness (Talwar and Lee, 2002b; Talwar, Murphy, and Lee, 2007).
Given the benign intentions behind prosocial lies, it would be interesting
to investigate others' perceptions of these lies when told by children. As
these lies develop later than lies told for antisocial purposes, these lies
may be easier to detect. On the other hand, detectors may be more willing to ignore the signs of deception when they are being told a prosocial
lie. If a friend gives a birthday gift that the child does not like, the child
may lie about liking the gift in order to preserve the other's feelings and
also to maintain positive social relations (Saarni, 1979; Talwar, Murphy,
and Lee, 2007). Similarly, the gift-giver may detect signs of disappoint-
ment in the child's demeanor, but may ignore these signs and believe the
child's assertions of liking the gift in order to preserve positive feelings of
closeness in the relationship. Thus, a future direction is to examine children's prosocial lie-telling, others' detection of these lies, and the impact
of detection on children's interpersonal relations.

Another interesting area to investigate further in terms of children's
perceived trustworthiness and deceptive behavior, is the flip side of the
coin: children who are blunt truth-tellers or "tattletales." While lie-telling
is considered a negative social behavior and children are exhorted to tell
the truth at all times, children are also counselled against "carrying tales"
and being a "tell-tale tit." Telling on others is seen as a reproachable
behavior by peers and even adults. This can be a confusing contradiction
for children: they are urged to be honest at all times, while at the same

time encouraged to omit information about others' behaviors (Ekman, 1989). Furthermore, our society paints individuals who snitch on others in a very negative light, and may even consider them to be less trustworthy. Indeed, Rotenberg and colleagues have found that children who are too high in trust beliefs (e.g., high on honesty and reliability) may be at risk for psychosocial problems such as peer rejection and social exclusion (Rotenberg, Boulton, and Fox, 2005). Little research has examined tattling in children and the impact it has on other's perceptions of the child or their social relations. Future research should examine the impact of children's blunt honesty and reporting of others' transgressions on peers' acceptance and perceptions of the child's trustworthiness.

References

Achenbach, T. M. and Edelbrock, C. S. (1979). The child behavior profile: Boys aged 12 to 16 and girls aged 6 to 11 and 12 to 16. *Journal of Consulting and Clinical Psychology*, 47, 223–233.
    (1981). Behavioral problems and competencies reported by parents of normal and disturbed children aged 4 through 16. *Monographs of the Society for Research in Child Development*, 46, 1–82.
Arruda, C., Brunet, M., Popliger, M., Ross, I., McCarthy, A., and Talwar, V. (2007). *"I cannot tell a lie": Enhancing truth-telling in children through the use of traditional stories.* Poster session presented at the biennial meeting of the Society for Research in Child Development, Boston, MA, March.
Biskin, D. and Hoskisson, K. (1977). An experimental test of the effects of structured discussions of moral dilemmas found in children's literature on moral reasoning. *Elementary School Journal*, 77, 407–416.
Bok, S. (1978). *Lying: Moral choices in public and private life.* New York: Pantheon.
Bond, C. F. and DePaulo, B. M. (2005). Accuracy of deception judgments. *Personality and Social Psychology Review*, 10, 214–234.
Bond, C. F., Jr., Omar, A., Pitre, U., Lashley, B. R., Skaggs, L. M., and Kirk, C. T. (1992). Fishy-looking liars: Deception judgment from expectancy violation. *Journal of Personality and Social Psychology*, 63, 969–977.
Bottoms, B. L. and Goodman, G. (1994). Perception of children's credibility in sexual assault cases. *Journal of Applied Social Psychology*, 24, 702–732.
Brigham, J. C. and Spier, S. A. (1992). Opinions held by professionals who work with child witnesses. In H. Dent and R. Flin (eds.), *Children as witnesses* (pp. 93–111). Chichester: John Wiley & Sons, Ltd.
Bussey, K. (1992). Lying and truthfulness: Children's definitions, standards, and evaluative reactions. *Child Development*, 63, 129–137.
    (1999). Children's categorization and evaluation of different types of lies and truths. *Child Development*, 70, 1338–1347.
Chahal, K. and Cassidy, T. (1995). Deception and its detection in children: A study of adult accuracy. *Psychology, Crime and Law*, 1, 237–245.

Chandler, M., Fritz., A. S., and Hala, S. (1989). Small-scale deceit: Deception as a marker for two-, three-, and four-year olds' early theories of mind. *Child Development*, **60**, 1263–1277.

Crossman, A. M. and Lewis, M. (2006). Adults' ability to detect children's lying. *Behavioral Sciences & the Law*, **24**, 703–715.

DePaulo, B. M. and Jordan, A. (1982). Age changes in deceiving and detecting deceit. In R. S. Feldman (ed.), *Development of non-verbal behavior in children* (pp. 151–179). New York: Springer-Verlag.

DePaulo, B. M. and Kashy, D. A. (1998). Who lies? *Journal of Personality and Social Psychology*, **70** (5), 1037–1051.

DePaulo, B. M., Kashy, D. A., Kirkendol, S. E., Wyer, M. M., and Epstein, J. A. (1996). Lying in everyday life. *Journal of Personality and Social Psychology*, **70** (5), 979–995.

Ekman, P. (1985). *Telling lies: Clues to deceit in the marketplace, politics, and marriage*. New York: W. W. Norton & Company.

   (1989). *Why kids lie: How parents can encourage truthfulness*. New York: Scribner.

Ekman, P. and O'Sullivan, M. (1991). Who can catch a liar? *American Psychologist*, **46**, 913–920.

Feldman, R. S. and Philippot, P. (1991). Children's deception skills and social competence. In K. Rotenberg (ed.), *Children's interpersonal trust: Sensitivity to lying, deception, and promise violations* (pp. 43–57). New York: Springer-Verlag.

Feldman, R. S., Jenkins, L., and Popoola, O. (1979). Detection of deception in adults and children via facial expressions. *Child Development*, **50**, 350–355.

Gervais, J., Tremblay, R. E., Desmarais-Gervais, L., and Vitaro, F. (2000). Children's persistent lying, gender differences, and disruptive behaviors: A longitudinal perspective. *International Journal of Behavioral Development*, **24**, 213–221.

Goodman, G. S., Bottoms, B. L., Herscovici, B. B., and Shaver, P. (1989). Determinants of the child victim's perceived credibility. In S. J. Ceci, D. F. Ross, and M. P. Toglia (eds.), *Perspectives on children's testimony* (pp. 1–22). New York: Springer-Verlag.

Goodman, G. S., Golding, J. M., Helegen, V. S., Haith, M. M., and Michelli, J. (1987). When a child takes the stand. *Law and Human Behavior*, **11**, 27–40.

Grice, H. P. (1980). *Studies in the way of words*. Cambridge, MA: Harvard University Press.

Haugaard, J. J. and Reppucci, N. D. (1992). Children and the truth. In S. J. Ceci, M. D. Leichtman, and M. Putnick (eds.), *Cognitive and social factors in early deception* (pp. 29–45). Hillsdale, NJ: Lawrence Erlbaum Associates.

Honts, C. R. (1994). Assessing children's credibility: Scientific and legal issues in 1994. *North Dakota Law Review*, **70**, 879–899.

Leach, A., Talwar, V., Lee, K., Bala, N., and Lindsay, R. C. L. (2004). Intuitive lie detection of children's deception by law enforcement officials and university students. *Law and Human Behavior*, **28**, 661–685.

Lewis, M. (1993). The development of deception. In M. Lewis and C. Saarni (eds.), *Lying and deception in everyday life* (pp. 90–105). New York: Guilford Press.

Lewis, M., Stanger, C., and Sullivan, M. W. (1989). Deception in 3-year-olds. *Developmental Psychology*, **25**, 439–443.

Lindskold, S. and Walters, P. S. (1983). Categories for acceptability of lies. *Journal of Social Psychology*, **120**, 129–136.

Masip, J., Garrido, E., and Herrero, C. (2004). Facial appearance and impressions of credibility: The effects of facial babyishness and age on person perception. *International Journal of Psychology*, **39** (4), 276–289.

Newton, P., Reddy, V., and Bull, R. (2000). Children's everyday deception and performance on false-belief tasks. *British Journal of Developmental Psychology*, **18**, 297–317.

Oldershaw, L. and Bagby, R. M. (1997). Children and deception. In R. Rogers (ed.), *Clinical assessment of malingering and deception* (2nd edn.) (pp. 153–166). New York: Guilford Press.

Orcutt, H. K., Goodman, G. S., Tobey, A. E., Batterman-Faunce, J. M., and Thomas, S. (2001). Detecting deception in children's testimony: Factfinders' abilities to reach the truth in open court and closed-circuit trials. *Law and Human Behavior*, **25**, 339–372.

O'Sullivan, M. (2005). Emotional intelligence and deception detection: Why most people can't "read" others, but a few can. In R. E. Riggio and R. S. Feldman (eds.), *Applications of nonverbal communication* (pp. 215–253). Mahwah, NJ: Lawrence Erlbaum Associates.

Peterson, C. C., Peterson, J. L., and Seeto, D. (1983). Developmental changes in ideas about lying. *Child Development*, **54**, 1529–1535.

Polak, A. and Harris, P. L. (1999). Deception by young children following noncompliance. *Developmental Psychology*, **35**, 561–568.

Ross, D. F., Dunning, D., Toglia, M., and Ceci, S. J. (1990). The child in the eyes of the jury: Assessing mock jurors' perceptions of the child witness. *Law and Human Behavior*, **14**, 5–23.

Ross, D. F., Jurden, F. H., Lindsay, R. C. L., and Keeney, J. M. (2003). Replications and limitations of a two-factor model of child witness credibility. *Journal of Applied Social Psychology*, **33**, 418–431.

Rotenberg, K. J. (1991). Children's cue use and strategies for detecting deception. In K. J. Rotenberg (ed.), *Children's interpersonal trust: Sensitivity to lying, deception and promise violations* (pp. 43–57). New York: Springer-Verlag.

Rotenberg, K. J., Boulton, M. J., and Fox, C. L. (2005). Cross-sectional and longitudinal relations among trust beliefs, psychological maladjustment, and social relationships during childhood: Are very high as well as very low trusting children at risk? *Journal of Abnormal Child Psychology*, **33**, 595–610.

Rotenberg, K. J., Fox, C. L., Green, S., Ruderman, L., Slater, K., Stevens, K., and Carlo, G. (2005). Construction and validation of a children's interpersonal trust belief scale. *British Journal of Developmental Psychology*, **23**, 271–292.

Rotenberg, K. J., MacDonald, K. J., and King, E. V. (2004). The relation-ship between loneliness and interpersonal trust during middle childhood. *Journal of Genetic Psychology*, **165**, 233–249.

Rotenberg, K. J., Michalik, N., Eisenberg, N., and Betts, L. R. (2008). The relations among young children's peer-reported trustworthiness, inhibitory control, and preschool adjustment. *Early Childhood Research Quarterly*, **23**, 288–298.

Rotter, J. B. (1980). Interpersonal trust, trustworthiness and gullibility. *American Psychologist*, **35**, 1–7.

Rutter, M. (1967). A children's behaviour questionnaire for completion by teachers: Preliminary findings. *Journal of Child Psychology and Psychiatry*, **8**, 1–11.

Saarni, C. (1979). Children's understanding of display rules for expressive behavior. *Developmental Psychology*, **15**, 424–429.

(1988). Children's understanding of the interpersonal consequences of dissemblance on nonverbal emotional-expressive behavior. *Journal of Nonverbal Behavior*, **12**, 275–294.

Sears, R., Rau, L., and Alpert, R. (1965). *Identification and child rearing*. New York: Wiley.

Seiter, J. S., Bruschke, J., and Bai, C. (2002). The acceptability of deception as a function of perceivers' culture, deceivers' intention, and deceiver-deceived relationship. *Western Journal of Communication*, **66** (2), 158–180.

Stouthamer-Loeber, M. (1986). Lying as a problem behavior in children: A review. *Clinical Psychology Review*, **6**, 267–289.

(1991). Young children's verbal misrepresentations of reality. In K. Rotenberg (ed.), *Children's interpersonal trust: Sensitivity to lying, deception and promise violations* (pp. 20–42). New York: Springer-Verlag.

Stouthamer-Loeber, M. and Loeber, R. (1986). Boys who lie. *Journal of Abnormal Child Psychology*, **14**, 551–564.

Strichartz, A. F. and Burton, R. V. (1990). Lies and truth: A study of the development of the concept. *Child Development*, **61**, 211–220.

Sweetser, E. (1987). The definition of "lie". An examination of the folk models underlying a semantic prototype. In D. Hollard and N. Quinn (eds.), *Cultural models in language and thought*. New York: Cambridge University Press.

Talwar, V. and Lee, K. (2002a). Development of lying to conceal a transgression: Children's control of expressive behavior during verbal deception. *International Journal of Behavioral Development*, **26**, 436–444.

(2002b). Emergence of white-lie telling in children between 3 and 7 years of age. *Merrill-Palmer Quarterly*, **48**, 160–181.

(2008). Socio-cognitive correlates of children's lying behaviour: Conceptual understanding of lying, executive functioning, and false beliefs. *Child Development*, **79**, 866–881.

Talwar, V., Gordon, H., and Lee, K. (2007). Lying in the elementary school: Verbal deception and its relation to second-order belief understanding. *Developmental Psychology*, **43**, 804–810.

Talwar, V., Lee, K., Bala, N., and Lindsay, R. C. L. (2002). Children's conceptual knowledge of lie-telling and its relation to their actual behaviors: Implications for court competence examination. *Law and Human Behavior*, **26**, 395–415.

(2006). Adults' judgments of children's coached reports. *Law and Human Behavior*, **30**, 561–570.

Talwar, V., Murphy, S., and Lee, K. (2007). White lie-telling in children for politeness purposes. *International Journal of Behavioral Development*, **31**, 1–11.

Vrij, A. and Baxter, M. (1999). Accuracy and confidence in detecting truth and lies in elaborations and denials: Truth bias, lie bias, and individual differences. *Expert Evidence*, 7 (1), 25–36.

Vrij, A. and Mann, S. (2005). Police use of nonverbal behaviour as indicators of deception. In R. E. Riggio and R. S. Feldman (eds.), *Applications of nonverbal communication* (pp. 63–94). Mahwah, NJ: Lawrence Erlbaum Associates.

Westcott, H., Davies, G., and Clifford, B. (1991). Adults' perceptions of children's videotaped truthful and deceptive statements. *Children and Society*, 5, 123–135.

Wilson, A. E., Smith, M. D., and Ross, H. S. (2003). The nature and effects of young children's lies. *Social Development*, **12**, 21–45.

Xu, F. and Lee, K. (2007). Promoting honesty in young children. In V. Talwar (Chair), *Honesty in children: Social-cognitive factors and its promotion.* Symposium conducted at the biennial meeting of the Society for Research in Child Development, Boston, MA, March.

Yarmey, A. D. and Jones, H. P. T. (1983). Is the psychology of eyewitness identification a matter of common sense? In S. M. A. Lloyd-Bostock and B. R. Clifford (eds.), *Evaluating witness evidence: Recent psychological research and new perspectives* (pp. 13–40). Chichester: Wiley.

Section III

Adolescence and early adulthood

10 Trust, but verify: Knowledge, disclosure, and mothers' beliefs about adolescents' trustworthiness

Nancy Darling (Oberlin College) and
Bonnie Dowdy (Boaz and Ruth, Inc.)

The literature on parental monitoring has undergone a radical reconceptualization since the turn of the century (Smetana, 2008). Parental monitoring is a parenting practice that captures the extent to which parents actively attend to and gather information about their children's activities, intentions, and emotions (Dishion and McMahon, 1998). Like many parenting practices, parental monitoring is expressed differently and is associated with different outcomes at different developmental stages. For example, in early childhood, monitoring may include eyes-on awareness of where toddlers are and exactly what they are doing. At this age, it is associated with lower rates of accidental injury. In childhood, parental monitoring may be expressed by tracking school progress, going through backpacks to look at schoolwork, discouraging particular peer associations, or watching children out the back window. In addition to lower rates of accidental injury, parental monitoring begins to be associated with school performance and a range of problem behaviors (Dishion, Burraston, and Li, 2003). As children enter adolescence, they spend more time outside the family and the direct supervision of adults, and become more sensitive to issues of privacy and autonomy. Parental monitoring changes as well, becoming less dependent upon direct access to information (going through school papers) and increasingly dependent upon shared network information, direct inquiry, and adolescents' voluntary disclosure of information (Crouter and Head, 2002; Crouter, Bumpus, Davis, and McHale, 2005). During late childhood and early adolescence, children increasingly resist parents' direct efforts to gain information about their lives, defining more issues as "personal" and outside the legitimate domain of parental authority, resulting in a concomitant decline in parental knowledge (Smetana, Metzger, Gettman, and Campione-Barr, 2006).

Although conceptualized as a parenting practice, researchers interested in parental monitoring of adolescents had often measured parental knowledge instead (for an extended discussion of this argument, see Kerr and Stattin, 2000; Stattin and Kerr, 2000). For example, adolescents were asked how much their parents knew about where they were after school, who their friends were, how they spent their money, and so on (e.g., Fletcher, Darling, and Steinberg, 1995). Because parents can know about their adolescents' lives either through their own efforts and activities (parenting practices) or because their adolescents share information about their lives (adolescent disclosure), the causal processes relating high parental monitoring, greater parental knowledge, and positive adolescent outcomes were unclear. Since the publication of the seminal critiques by Kerr and Stattin, research in this area has maintained a clearer distinction between parent practices (including monitoring) and the outcome of parental practices (parental knowledge) (e.g., Laird, Pettit, Dodge, and Bates, 2003; Pettit, Laird, Dodge, Bates, and Criss, 2001). Major research efforts have been invested in understanding the relationship between different sources of parental knowledge and parental knowledge (Brody, 2003; Capaldi, 2003; Crouter, Bumpus, Davis, and McHale, 2005; Kerr and Stattin, 2000, 2003; Stattin and Kerr, 2000). In addition, researchers have begun to investigate adolescents' decisions to disclose information to parents, rather than to hide information or lie, when they and their parents disagree (Darling, Cumsille, Caldwell, and Dowdy, 2006; Darling, Cumsille, Peña-Alampay, and Coatsworth, in press; Smetana, Metzger, Gettman, and Campione-Barr, 2006). When adolescents disagree with their parents, it is common for them not to disclose their true beliefs or their own disobedience to their parents (Darling, Cumsille, Caldwell, and Dowdy, 2006; Darling, Cumsille, Peña-Alampay, and Coatsworth, in press). Darling, Cumsille, Caldwell, and Dowdy (2006) reported that all adolescents in their study who reported disagreement with their mothers reported at least some use of deception. If honesty is one of the fundamental bases of trust (Rotenberg, McDougall, Boulton, Vaillancourt, Fox, and Hymel, 2004), and trust is one important foundation of positive relations among dyadic partners (Kerr, Stattin, and Trost, 1999), what is the association between adolescents' deception (one aspect of their trustworthiness), their parents' trust beliefs, and the adolescents' perceptions of their parents' trust beliefs?

Parental knowledge and parents' trust beliefs in their adolescents

Several researchers have investigated the association of adolescents' voluntary disclosure of information and their use of deception with parental trust beliefs about their adolescents. In one of the first such investigations, Kerr, Stattin, and Trost (1999) proposed that parents' trust beliefs would be founded upon their knowledge of their adolescents' feelings, daily activities, and past behavior. Based upon earlier work, they hypothesized that trust beliefs were founded upon previous experience that the partner's behavior is predictable and dependable (Rempel, Holmes, and Zanna, 1985), and that the partner is honest and acting out of benevolent intent (e.g., Bernath and Feshbach, 1995; Rotter, 1971). In this context, the researchers defined parental trust of the adolescent as the parents' belief that the adolescent would act in a mature and trustworthy manner (e.g., he or she will not lie about whereabouts, will act in accordance with parental standards, and will be able to make good decisions). Consistent with this hypothesis, Kerr, Stattin, and Trost (1999) found that adolescents' spontaneous disclosure of information about their daily activities was the single most important factor predicting both parents' and adolescents' reports of parents' trust beliefs in the adolescent, controlling for adolescent delinquency. Both parents' and adolescents' reports of low parental trust beliefs in the adolescent were associated with a wide range of negative family outcomes, including a lack of family activities, and poor mother–child and father–child relations. The authors argued that low parental trust beliefs in the adolescent mediated the association between adolescent delinquency and family dysfunction. Building upon this work, Finkenauer, Frijns, Rutger, Engels, and Kerkhof (2005) found that when parents believed that their adolescents were not sharing information with them, they were less responsive to and less accepting of their adolescents, controlling for adolescents' reports of their overall tendency to conceal information from them. In addition, these researchers further distinguished between adolescents' concealing information, lying, and disclosure. Both lying and concealment were associated with negative parental reactions, controlling for adolescent disclosure. Importantly, parents' perceptions of lying and concealment were as important as adolescents' reports of their own lying and concealment in predicting parents' trust beliefs.

The goal of the current paper was to further understand the association between adolescents' reports of their own trustworthiness and mothers' trust beliefs in their adolescents, as reported by (1) the mothers themselves and (2) the adolescents. The current research is situated within the literature on parental monitoring and knowledge, and the line of research focusing on adolescents' decisions to share information with their parents (see Crouter and Head, 2002, for reviews of this area; Smetana, 2008). Two important differences exist between the conceptualization of what has been called "trust" within this literature (e.g., Frijns, Finkenauer, Vermulst, and Engels, 2005; Kerr, Stattin, and Trost, 1999) and that in the literature on interpersonal trust represented in this volume (Chapter 2 of this volume). First, within the literature on parental monitoring and knowledge, parents' "trust" of their adolescents has been measured as a global construct assessing parents' beliefs that the adolescent generally follows rules, makes good decisions, and conforms to social norms (see Kerr, Stattin, and Trost, 1999).

Second, Kerr, Stattin, and Trost (1999) embed their measurement of "parental trust" (what we will refer to as "parents' global trust beliefs in their adolescents") in the context of the parent–adolescent social role. Specifically, the parental social role is partly defined by parents' obligation to protect and socialize their adolescents, and includes the right and obligation to set rules (Smetana, 2006). The adolescent's social role within the parent–adolescent relationship includes acknowledgment of their parents' right to set rules and their own obligation to obey parental rules (Darling, Cumsille, and Martinez, 2007). Age-related changes in these obligations and beliefs have been the focus of research on social domain theory and the development of moral decision-making, and are embedded in an understanding of the development of adolescent autonomy (Darling, Cumsille, and Martinez, 2008; Smetana, 2006). Kerr, Stattin, and Trost's (1999) operationalization of parents' global trust beliefs in their adolescents includes asking whether the parent can "trust" that their child "will not hang out with bad people," "will be careful with his/her money," will "take responsibility for his/her life," will "try his or her best in school," will " not do anything dumb during his/her free time," and that what the child "says that he/she is going to do on a Saturday night is true."

By contrast, the conceptualization by Rotenberg and his colleagues (Chapter 2 of this volume) highlights that, in this social context, trust beliefs correspond to adolescents' belief that a parent will show reliability, emotional trustworthiness, and honesty. These beliefs are not bound to a given role per se. Consequently, trust beliefs are fundamentally universal, but apply to a given social relationship: in this case, parent–adolescent (i.e., unique targets). Also, this conceptualization highlights the importance of emotional trust beliefs which entail the confidence that others maintain confidence of disclosure and are acceptant/uncritical of disclosure. Disclosure is an example of an emotional trusting behavior and is linked to emotional trust beliefs. Consequently, the framework directly accounts for the relation between adolescents' willingness to disclose their activities to their parents and the adolescents' trust beliefs – presumably emotionally based – in their parents. In addition, the framework highlights the dyadic nature of trust within relationships. As such, there are links between adolescents' and parents' trust beliefs in each other which emerge from a social interaction history. Finally, trust beliefs are differentiated from trustworthiness, which is behavior-enacting. For example, adolescents may hold high trust beliefs in their parents (i.e., believe that they show reliability, emotional trustworthiness, and honesty), but the parents may not engage in such behavior, instead showing a lack of reliability and emotional trustworthiness, and dishonesty. When trustworthiness is assessed only by a given observer's reports (e.g., a parent) then the distinction between trust beliefs and trustworthiness becomes blurred because those are essentially trust beliefs. Trustworthiness – as behavior-enacting – is more clearly identified by the convergence of reports of behavior by others or by direct observations (see Betts and Rotenberg, 2008). There is some overlap between Rotenberg's conceptualization of interpersonal trust and those arising from the conceptualization and measurement by Kerr, Stattin, and Trost (1999), as shown by a common consideration of reliability and honesty as trust beliefs/trustworthiness. In other ways, the two approaches are not compatible and provide divergent views of the interpersonal trust in adolescent–parent relationships. The distinction between trustworthiness and trust beliefs was not followed in the current research project.

In the first phase of the project we address the question: Are mothers' beliefs about their adolescents' trustworthiness consistent with adolescents' reports of their own trustworthiness? Like Kerr, Stattin, and Trost (1999), we frame mothers' trust beliefs about their adolescents within the context of the implicit obligation of adolescents to obey parents and agree with socialization norms. In this first phase of the project, two aspects of adolescent trustworthiness were assessed: the extent to which the adolescent agreed with their mother and the extent to which the adolescent deceived their mother or told the truth when the adolescent perceived mother–adolescent disagreement. Differences between adolescents' reports of their own trustworthiness (agreement and deception) and mothers' beliefs about these two aspects of the adolescents' trustworthiness were examined at the dyadic level, both globally and in terms of individual behaviors. The former addresses the extent of overall agreement between mothers' beliefs about their adolescents' trustworthiness and adolescents' reports of their behavior (e.g., Are adolescents who report deceiving their mothers about more issues than their peers perceived by mothers to use more deception?). The latter addresses the concordance between adolescents' reports of their behavior and mothers' beliefs about their adolescents' behaviors (When adolescents report deceiving their mothers about a particular issue, do mothers believe that their adolescents are acting deceptively?). Prior research in this area (e.g., Finkenauer, Engels, and Meeus, 2002;

Finkenauer, Frijns, Engels, and Kerkhof, 2005; Kerr, Stattin, and Trost, 1999) was based upon global reports of adolescents' concealment and disclosure, as well as parents' global beliefs about their own adolescents' trustworthiness.

In the second phase of the study, mothers' global beliefs about adolescents' trustworthiness were predicted from mothers' beliefs about adolescents' shared information (those issues adolescents did not deceive their parents about), and from adolescents' own reports of their trustworthy behavior. Adolescents reported on three specific aspects of their own trustworthy behavior: involvement in problem behavior, adolescents' belief in the right of their parents to set rules (legitimacy of parental authority), and shared information. In this second phase of the study, mothers' global trust beliefs about their adolescents were assessed similarly to prior research by Kerr, Stattin, and Trost (1999), by asking mothers to rate how much they trusted their adolescents to use good judgment, independently conform to parental standards, and tell the truth. A mother's global trust beliefs in her adolescent's trustworthiness was assessed by self-report (what she herself says she believes) and through the reports of her adolescent child (what the adolescent thinks she believes). Prior research (Kerr, Stattin, and Trost, 1999) had suggested that greater parental knowledge was associated with higher parental trust beliefs and more positive parental attitudes towards adolescent children (Finkenauer, Frijns, Engels, and Kerkhof, 2005). In the second phase of this study, mothers' beliefs about adolescents' shared information and adolescents' self-reports of trustworthy behaviors were first used to predict maternal knowledge. Maternal knowledge was then entered as a covariate in the prediction of mothers' global trust beliefs in her adolescent.

Method

Participants

The data used in these analyses were collected as part of the Home:School Linkages Project, a study of social influences on the development of adolescents' academic and psychosocial competence during the transition from middle to high school (see Darling, Dowdy, Van Horn, and Caldwell, 1999 for a more complete description of the study.) All data used in this paper are from year three of the project, with all participants having participated in data collection in at least one prior phase of the study and currently enrolled in the ninth grade (freshman year in high school). This study relies on data provided by the sixty-seven mother–adolescent dyads, in which both mothers and adolescents were interviewed and which included thirty-four mother–daughter and thirty-three mother–son dyads. Forty-nine families included both biological parents, ten were currently single mothers, nine were divorced and remarried, and one adolescent was adopted and living with two parents. Sixty-five adolescents self-identified as White, two as African American, and two as "Other" than African American, Asian American, Hispanic, or White.

Procedure

After recruitment, questionnaires were mailed separately to adolescents and their mothers. Participants were asked to bring the completed questionnaires to the interview with them. Adolescents and their mothers were interviewed separately by pairs of trained undergraduate interviewers. Completing the interview took between 90 and 150 minutes. Those who did not bring completed questionnaires with them were asked to complete them before leaving. All interviews were taped and checked for accuracy of protocol.

Areas of potential conflict A set of thirty-eight issues of potential conflict between parents and adolescents was derived from work by Smetana (Smetana, 1988, 1989; Smetana, Yau, Restrepo, and Braeges, 1991) and interviews with middle school and college students. Issues were selected that were frequently named by adolescents as sources of conflict with parents, and areas where adolescents frequently kept information from parents that they felt parents would like to know (Darling, Cumsille, Caldwell, and Dowdy, 2006; Darling, Cumsille, and Martinez, 2007; Darling, Cumsille, Peña-Alampay, and Coatsworth, in press). Selected issues included duties and chores (e.g., "doing homework," "what chores you do"), leisure activities (e.g., "the type of TV shows or videos you watch," "what you do after dinner"), social activities (e.g., "who your friends are," "going to a friend's house when their parents aren't home"), dating (e.g., "how much time you spend with your boyfriend/girlfriend," "inviting a boyfriend or girlfriend over when your parents are away"), and substance use ("using drugs," "drinking," "smoking cigarettes").

Adolescents answered twelve questions about each issue, eight on the questionnaire, and four during the strategic disclosure card sort (Darling, Cumsille, Caldwell, and Dowdy, 2006, see below). Mothers answered eight questions about each issue, four on the questionnaire and four during the strategic disclosure card sort.

The strategic disclosure card sort Because of the length of the protocol, the age of the participants, and the number of questions participants were required to answer about each question, it was difficult for participants to sustain attention in a purely paper-and-pencil format. The strategic disclosure card sort was designed to provide an alternative way of collecting data about participants' behaviors and beliefs about each of the thirty-eight issues. Each issue was printed on a card and participants answered questions about each issue by sorting cards into piles indicating their responses.

First, participants sorted cards into four piles indicating how easy or hard it was for them to discuss the issue with each other (mothers with their adolescents, adolescents with their mothers). Responses included "Easy," "Not bad," "Hard," and "Very hard." Issues that were not relevant to the dyad (e.g., a question about a boyfriend/girlfriend when the adolescent had never engaged in a romantic relationship) were removed from the issue set at this time.

Second, participants re-sorted cards into three piles indicating agreement with each other. Responses included "Basically agree," "Basically disagree," or "Sometimes agree and sometimes disagree." Because the focus of the study was on understanding how adolescents and mothers behaved during conflict, issues that the participants felt they agreed about were removed from the issue set at this time. Importantly, please note that the issue set will now differ for mothers and adolescents.

Third, for each item the informant believed to be an area of parent–adolescent disagreement, the adolescent indicated their disclosure strategy or the mother indicated their perception of the adolescent's disclosure strategy by sorting the cards into four piles according to what the adolescent usually did when he or she disagreed with the parent about that issue. Strategy choices included "Tell parents all the important details," "Leave out important details parents would want to know," "Make up a story or lie," and "Avoid discussing the issue."

Finally, informants indicated the adolescents' primary motivation for "telling parents all the important details" about issues of perceived disagreement or for not fully disclosing into two separate sorts (for full description, see Darling, Cumsille, Caldwell, and Dowdy, 2006).

Measures

Correlations between variables are reported in Table 10.1. Descriptive information about each measure is reported with its respective scale.

Table 10.1 *Correlation of adolescent and mother reports of adolescent characteristics, mothers' assessment of adolescent trustworthiness, and maternal knowledge*

	2	3	4	5	6	7	8
Adolescent reports:							
1. Problem behavior	−.44*	−.40*	−.56*	−.52*	−.44*	−.39*	−.25*
2. Legitimacy	—	.20	.32*	.44*	.42*	.12	.20
3. Shared information		—	.49*	.32*	.21	.08	.14
4. Maternal knowledge			—	.50*	.37*	.35*	.03
5. Mothers' global trust beliefs in adolescents				—	.38*	.38*	.12
Mother reports:							
6. Maternal knowledge					—	.41*	.29*
7. Mothers' global trust beliefs in adolescents						—	.09
8. Shared information							—

Notes: N = 77
*p < .05

Trustworthy behavior Five aspects of adolescents' trustworthy behavior were assessed: (1) parent–adolescent agreement, (2) adolescents' deception, (3) adolescents' shared information (a composite variable that includes areas of agreement and disclosed disagreement), (4) adolescents' beliefs about the legitimacy of parental authority, and (5) problem behavior.

Ratings of *agreement* for each issue were coded dichotomously as Agree (1) or Disagree and Sometimes disagree (0). On average, mothers reported adolescents agreed with them about 19.60 issues of 38 issues (*SD* = 9.18) and adolescents reported agreeing with their mothers about 21.30 issues of 38 issues (*SD* = 6.88).

Issues were coded as areas of *shared information* if informants reported it to be an area of parent–adolescent *agreement* or one in which they typically "tell parents all the important details" (*disclosed disagreement*). On average, areas of shared information included 24.16 of 38 issues for mothers (*SD* = 9.78) and 26.93 of 38 issues for adolescents (*SD* = 6.90). Issues were coded as areas of *deception* if the participant reported that they typically "leave out important details parents would want to know," "make up a story or lie," or "avoid discussing the issue."

During the questionnaire component of the study, for each issue in the strategic disclosure card sort, adolescents and mothers indicated whether it was okay for parents to set rules about this issue ("yes" = 1, "no" = 0).

A global measure of perceived *parental legitimacy* was created by summing the number of issues adolescents endorsed as "okay" (students' m = 23.6, SD = 10.2, and mothers' m = 32.4, SD = 7.6).

Involvement in *problem behavior* was measured using composites from two scales. Students rated three items on a scale from 1 (strongly disagree) to 5 (strongly agree) (sample item: "My parents would be unhappy if they knew how I spent my free time"). They also reported on frequency of substance use in the last 30 days on a four-point scale from 1 (never) to 4 (three or more times). Z scores were calculated for each item and a mean calculated (α = .84).

Maternal knowledge In the questionnaire component of the study, adolescents were asked to respond to four questions asking "How much do your parents REALLY know ... ": "where you go at night?" "how you spend your money?" "what you do with your free time?" "where you are most afternoons after school?" Identical questions were reworded so that mothers could report on their own knowledge and monitoring. Mothers and adolescents responded on a three-point scale, with 1 representing "Don't know" and 3 representing "Know a lot." Means were calculated (student α = .79; α mother = .78).

Mother's global trust beliefs in adolescent In the questionnaire component of the study, adolescents and mothers were asked to rate "How much does your mother/do you trust you/your adolescent to ... ": "use good judgment?" "not do anything really dumb?" "follow rules when they're/you're not around?" "act the way they/you want when they're/you're not around?" "tell them/you the truth?" Mothers and adolescents responded on a three-point scale, with 1 representing "Almost never" and 3 representing "Most of the time," and means were calculated (α student = .90, mean = 2.67, SD = .48; α mother = .83, mean = 2.75, SD = .35).

Results

Phase 1: Are mothers' beliefs about their adolescents' trustworthiness consistent with adolescents' reports of their own trustworthiness?

Two aspects of adolescents' trustworthy behavior and mothers' beliefs about their adolescents' trustworthy behavior were assessed: parent–adolescent agreement and deception. The concordance between mothers' trust beliefs and adolescents' trustworthy behaviors was approached at two levels: globally and at the level of specific issue. Normatively, mothers and adolescents reported fairly similar levels of mother–adolescent agreement, although mothers were more pessimistic. On average, mothers reported that they and their adolescents agreed on about seventeen of thirty-eight issues, while adolescents reported agreement on twenty-one. At the dyadic level, however, the correlation between mothers' global beliefs about their adolescents' agreement with them and their adolescents' reports of overall agreement was significant, but low (r = .25, df = .65, p = .03), and they disagreed about their disagreement on an average of 3.6 issues, with a startlingly high standard deviation of 11.6 (paired sample t = 2.7, df = 65, p = .008). For 37.9 percent of issues, both mothers and adolescents agreed that they agreed. In 22.8 percent of cases, both mothers and adolescents agreed that they disagreed. In almost 40 percent of cases, however, mothers and adolescents disagreed about their agreement. These errors occurred in both directions. Mothers sometimes assumed agreement when it did not exist, but also saw disagreement where it did not exist. For example, in 35.9 percent of instances where mothers thought their adolescents agreed with them, adolescents reported that they did not. On the other hand, in 32.3 percent of instances where mothers reported that their adolescents disagreed with them, adolescents reported agreeing.

A similar misperception existed between mothers' trust beliefs about adolescents' deception and adolescents' self-reports of their deception. In this sample, adolescents and mothers reported on whether adolescents disclosed disagreement or whether they used deception for the 533 issues that both members of the dyad reported disagreeing about. Consistent with other studies, non-disclosure was fairly common. Adolescents reported disclosing disagreement to parents for only 36 percent of issues where they perceived disagreement with their mothers, while using deception for the rest. Although deception was common, results indicate that mothers were markedly inaccurate in their trust beliefs with regard to adolescent non-disclosure. Mothers correctly reported that adolescents disclosed disagreement in only 38 percent of instances (74 of 193 issues where adolescents reported that they disclosed). In the other 62 percent of instances where adolescents reported disclosing, mothers falsely believed that their adolescents were using deception. Mothers were better at spotting lies. Mothers correctly reported that adolescents had used deception for 71 percent of the 340 issues that adolescents reported using deception. In 29 percent of instances, mothers believed that adolescents were disclosing disagreement when their adolescents reported using deception. Taken together, these results indicate that adolescents use deception fairly regularly (in 64 percent of instances where they disagree with mothers). Mothers were rightly suspicious of their adolescents and believed that their adolescents use deception 68 percent of the time. However, mothers were not notably accurate in their assessment of when adolescents were using deception and when they were not.

Although mothers accurately detected 71 percent of deception, they also believed that adolescents were using deception in 62 percent of instances where adolescents reported that they were not. Looked at another way, 57 percent of the time, mothers believed that adolescents were not using deception, while the adolescents reported that they were. Thirty-three percent of the time, mothers believed that the adolescents were using deception, while the adolescents reported that they were not. Overall, there appears to be a large gap between mothers' trust beliefs with regard to adolescents' trustworthy behaviors and adolescents' self-reports of their trustworthy behavior, when trustworthiness is assessed by parent–adolescent agreement and adolescent deception.

Phase 2: Predicting mothers' global beliefs about adolescents' trustworthiness from mothers' trust beliefs and adolescents' trustworthy behavior

Two series of multiple regression analyses were carried out, predicting (1) maternal knowledge of the adolescent from adolescent trustworthiness (shared information, adolescent legitimacy beliefs, and adolescent problem behavior) and (2) a mother's global trust beliefs about her adolescent from adolescent trustworthiness and maternal knowledge. Adolescent legitimacy beliefs and problem behavior were measured using adolescent reports. Shared information was measured from both adolescent and mother reports. First, mothers' self-reports of their own knowledge of the adolescents and global trust beliefs were predicted. Next, adolescents' perceptions of maternal knowledge and global trust beliefs were predicted. The results are reported in Table 10.2.

Mothers whose adolescents reported lower levels of problem behaviors and higher levels of legitimacy beliefs reported themselves to be more knowledgeable about their adolescents' activities than their peers. Shared information, as reported by both mothers and adolescents, was not associated with mothers' perceptions of their own knowledge. Mothers who reported high global beliefs about their adolescents' trustworthiness also believed themselves to be high in knowledge of their adolescent and had adolescents who reported low problem behavior. Neither adolescents' legitimacy beliefs nor mother- or adolescent-reported shared knowledge predicted mothers' global trust beliefs. Taken together, these findings suggest that of the three aspects of adolescent trustworthy behavior

Table 10.2 *Results of regression analyses predicting mothers' knowledge of their adolescents and mothers' global trust beliefs about their adolescents (reported values are standardized regression coefficients)*

Adolescent trustworthiness	Mother reports		Adolescent reports	
	Knowledge	Trust beliefs	Knowledge	Trust beliefs
Adolescent-reported problem behavior	−0.27*	−0.36**	−0.42**	−0.25#
Adolescent-reported legitimacy beliefs	0.27*	−0.15	0.10	0.25*
Adolescent-reported shared information	0.03	−0.10	0.32**	0.05
Mother-reported shared information	0.16	−0.05	−0.14	0.00
Mother-reported knowledge		0.35**		
Adolescent-reported knowledge				0.26#
Model R	.53	.50	.66	.61

Notes: # $p \le .10$; *$p \le .05$; **$p \le .01$

considered, only adolescent problem behavior and legitimacy beliefs were associated with mothers' perceptions of their knowledge of their adolescents. Only adolescents' self-reported problem behavior was associated with mothers' global trust beliefs about their adolescents once mothers' self-perceived knowledge was controlled.

Adolescents who reported that their mothers were more knowledgeable reported themselves to be less involved in problem behavior and higher in shared information. Neither mothers' beliefs about shared information nor adolescents' legitimacy beliefs were associated with adolescents' reports of mothers' knowledge. Adolescents who reported that their mothers had higher global trust beliefs in them also reported themselves to have higher legitimacy beliefs, and showed a trend such that they were less involved in problem in behavior (p = .08) and reported their mothers to be more knowledgeable about their behaviors (p = .06). Neither mothers' nor adolescents' reports of shared information were associated with adolescents' reports of mothers' global trust beliefs (p > .67). Together, these findings suggest that adolescents' perception of their mothers' knowledge was based upon their knowledge of two aspects of their perceptions of their own trustworthy behavior: involvement in problem behavior and shared information. Adolescents' perceptions of the extent to which their mothers trust them (i.e., of mothers' global trust beliefs) was associated only with their beliefs in parental legitimacy.

Discussion

The current chapter examined the association between adolescents' reports of their own trustworthy behaviors and mothers' beliefs about their adolescents' trustworthiness. Analyses were conducted at three levels: (1) mothers' beliefs about adolescents' honesty and agreement were assessed at the issue level as well as globally; (2) mothers' global trust beliefs about their adolescents were also predicted from a broader suite of adolescents' trustworthy behaviors, including honesty, problem behavior, and legitimacy beliefs; (3) the extent to which trustworthy behaviors were associated with mothers' knowledge about their adolescents' behavior and the extent to which knowledge was associated with mothers' global trust beliefs were examined as well. Because the current research is situated within the literature on parenting, parental knowledge and monitoring, and adolescent disclosure, rather than within the literature on interpersonal trust, the differences between our conceptualization of trust and that of other researchers (e.g., Rotenberg, Boulton, and Fox, 2005; Chapter 2 of this volume) should be recognized. Specifically, this research, and that of other researchers within the parenting field (e.g., Finkenauer, Frijns, Engels, and Kerkhof, 2005; Kerr, Stattin, and Trost, 1999), focuses on parents' trust beliefs about their adolescents within the parent–adolescent role. Parents' trust beliefs therefore include beliefs about the extent to which the adolescent will act autonomously in a manner consistent with social norms and parents' presumed socialization efforts.

In the first phase of this study, we examined the congruence between mothers' beliefs about adolescents' agreement and deception and adolescents' reported agreement with parents and their deception of parents when they perceived themselves to be in disagreement with mothers. Results indicated that there was only a very modest association between adolescents' reports of their trustworthy behavior and mothers' trust beliefs. This was true both when agreement and deception were examined on an issue-by-issue basis, and when behaviors and beliefs were aggregated across issues. Mothers and adolescents disagreed about whether or not they agreed with one another. Consistent with other studies (Darling, Cumsille, Caldwell, and Dowdy, 2006; Darling, Cumsille, Peña-Alampay, and Coatsworth, in press), adolescents reported that they frequently used deception when they disagreed with their parents. Nonetheless, mothers were notably inaccurate at identifying which adolescents were relatively more or less deceptive than their peers, and which issues adolescents tried to deceive them about.

Honesty, the converse of deception, is one of the bases of interpersonal trust (see Chapter 2 of this volume), and thus the frequent use of deception by adolescents in the mother–adolescent relationship is notable. Deception is a common tactic used by individuals in relatively powerless positions to assert control and autonomy in the face of control attempts by powerful others (Finkenauer, Engels, and Meeus, 2002). Adolescents judge deception of parents to be morally defensible, as well as pragmatically useful, when parental directives are perceived by the adolescent to be illegitimate (Perkins and Turiel, 2007). Adolescents' use of deception and concealment in the parent–adolescent relationship is not without its cost, however, in that, over time, it tends to undermine positive parenting (Finkenauer, Frijns, Engels, and Kerkhof, 2005) and parental trust beliefs in the adolescent (Kerr, Stattin, and Trost, 1999). Cross-sectional research also suggests that positive parenting fosters adolescents' honesty and open discussion of disagreement (Darling, Cumsille, Caldwell, and Dowdy, 2006; Darling, Cumsille, Peña-Alampay, and Coatsworth, in press; Smetana, Metzger, Gettman, and Campione-Barr, 2006). Given the centrality of honesty to both the construct of interpersonal trust and trust within the parent–adolescent role, this makes sense. These data also suggest another negative correlate of deception: distrust or suspicion. Research on romantic relationships has documented the extent to which distrust evokes hurt feelings and undermines relationships (Feeney, 2005). Given the lack of congruence between mothers' beliefs about adolescents' deception and adolescents' reports of deception, it is likely that false accusations of deception are relatively frequent within many parent–adolescent dyads. Normatively, mothers and adolescents report quite similar (and high) levels of deception. Thus the lack of congruence between mothers' beliefs and adolescents' reported behaviors at the dyad level suggests that factors other than adolescents' underreporting of deception are at play. The factors underlying mothers' beliefs about adolescents' deception, the consequences of false accusations of deception, and the relationship of the use of deception in the parent–adolescent relationship to the construct of interpersonal trust merit further research.

In the second phase of this project, we examined the association between different aspects of adolescents' trustworthy behaviors – sharing information, legitimacy beliefs, and involvement with problem behaviors – with mothers' knowledge and with their global trust beliefs about their adolescents. Both mothers' trust beliefs and the aspects of trustworthy behaviors chosen as predictors were framed within the context of mothers' trust beliefs about adolescents' fulfillment of their role within the parent–adolescent relationship. Mothers believed they were more knowledgeable when their adolescents were less involved in problem behavior and held higher legitimacy beliefs. They held higher global trust beliefs towards the adolescents when they were more knowledgeable and also when their adolescents were less involved in problem behavior. Adolescents' legitimacy beliefs, which reflect a global positive attitude of the adolescent towards the parent role, were indirectly associated with maternal trust beliefs through mothers' greater perceived knowledge. Honesty, which was assessed through both mother and adolescent reports, was not associated with mothers' global trust beliefs in the adolescent either directly or indirectly.

Interestingly, adolescents' perception of their mothers' knowledge of their behavior, and their perception of their mothers' trust beliefs towards them, showed a very different set of correlates. Adolescents' perception of mothers' knowledge was predicted by both their problem behavior and their own reports of shared information. In other words, adolescents believe their mothers to be more knowledgeable about their lives when they are uninvolved in problem behaviors and when they share more information with their mothers. Shared information was not, however, directly associated with adolescents' perception that their mothers trusted them (maternal global trust beliefs), once knowledge was controlled. Rather, adolescents, like their mothers, reported that mothers had lower global trust beliefs in them when they were involved in problem behavior. Adolescents' reports that they believed their parents had the right to set rules – their legitimacy beliefs – were directly associated with their perception that their mothers' trusted them. Taken together, these findings suggest that a mother's perception of her knowledge is based on the adolescent's problem behavior and the adolescent's general attitude towards her authority (adolescent legitimacy beliefs). In contrast, adolescents' perception of maternal knowledge is based upon what they do that is most likely to directly shape parental knowledge – their involvement in problem behaviors and sharing information. As reported by both mothers and their adolescents, mothers' global trust beliefs are associated with a key element of trustworthy behavior in the context of parent–adolescent relationships – adolescent involvement in problem behavior – and on parental knowledge. For adolescents, it is also predicted by the extent to which they believe their mothers have a right to set rules.

In trying to understand the relationship between adolescents' trustworthy behaviors, parental trust beliefs, and parental knowledge, it may be useful, perhaps, to go back to the literature on trust in other intimate relationships that are not characterized by differences in power. We expect our friends and romantic partners to tell us about their lives and their feelings (Feeney, 2005). We experience rejection when our partners avoid sharing information and we may see avoidance as a signal that something is wrong. It may, in fact, make us distrustful. Similarly, parents who perceive that their adolescents do not share information with them report themselves to be less involved and less positive (Finkenauer, Frijns, Engels, and Kerkhof, 2005). Although adolescents' increasing desire for privacy and lack of disclosure about their daily activities may be a necessary step towards maturity (Finkenauer, Frijns, Engels, and Kerkhof, 2005) and has been associated with greater autonomy (Finkenauer, Engels, and Meeus, 2002), it is also associated with lower relationship satisfaction (Finkenauer, Engels, Branje, and Meeus, 2004). Normative and individual differences in the line between the legitimate assertion of privacy and behaviors that evoke the parental response "What are they trying to hide?" may be important. A similar tension may exist between parental expression of interest in their adolescents' lives (an aspect of support expected in intimate relationships) and more intrusive inquiry (which communicates distrust and is seen as hurtful). These distinctions are quite nuanced and not easily addressed in the kinds of questionnaire-based research that has been conducted to date. Observational research, focusing on individual differences in each participant's interpretation of their partner's behavior may be one fruitful area of future research. Further exploration of adolescents' and parents' understanding of the limits of parental authority and adolescents' obligation to disclose (e.g., Smetana, Metzger, Gettman, and Campione-Barr, 2006) may also provide complementary insights.

Effective parenting requires many skills. The study of parental trust beliefs brings out some of the contradictory nature of the parenting task. Parents need to communicate support and trust in order to foster positive relationships with their adolescents that evoke openness. Parents need to be vigilant and effectively gather information when signs indicate that their children may be in danger or are straying from prescribed behavior. Parents need to see when their children step over the line so that they can effectively discipline them. Yet they need to do that without appearing to be waiting for their children to make a mistake. In other words, effective parenting may involve communicating support and trust, while remaining constantly vigilant to see whether the trust is deserved. Discovering how parents find that balance may well provide insight into the core elements of our understanding of effective parent socialization.

References

Bernath, M. S. and Feshbach, N. D. (1995). Children's trust: Theory, assessment, development, and research directions. *Applied & Preventive Psychology*, **4** (1), 1–19.

Betts, L. R. and Rotenberg, K. J. (2008). A social relations analysis of young children's trust in their peers across the early years of school. *Social Development*, **17**, 1039–1055.

Brody, G. H. (2003). Parental monitoring: Action and reaction. In A. C. Crouter and A. Booth (eds.), *Children's influence on family dynamics: The neglected side of family relationships* (pp. 163–169). Mahwah, NJ: Lawrence Erlbaum Associates.

Capaldi, D. M. (2003). Parental monitoring: A person–environment interaction perspective on this key parenting skill. In A. C. Crouter and A. Booth (eds.), *Children's influence on family dynamics: The neglected side of family relationships* (pp. 171–179). Mahwah, NJ: Lawrence Erlbaum Associates.

Crouter, A. C. and Head, M. R. (2002). Parental monitoring and knowledge of children. In M. H. Bornstein (ed.), *Handbook of parenting: Vol. 3* (pp. 461–484). Mahwah, NJ: Lawrence Erlbaum Associates.

Crouter, A. C., Bumpus, M. F., Davis, K. D., and McHale, S. M. (2005). How do parents learn about adolescents' experiences? Implications for parental knowledge and adolescent risky behavior. *Child Development*, **76** (4), 869–882.

Darling, N., Cumsille, P., Caldwell, L. L., and Dowdy, B. (2006). Predictors of adolescents' disclosure strategies and perceptions of parental knowledge. *Journal of Youth and Adolescence*, **35** (4), 667–678.

Darling, N., Cumsille, P., and Martinez, M. L. (2007). Adolescents as active agents in the socialization process: Legitimacy of parental authority and obligation to obey as predictors of obedience. *Journal of Adolescence*, **30** (2), 297–311.

    (2008). Individual differences in adolescents' beliefs about the legitimacy of parental authority and their own obligation to obey: A longitudinal investigation. *Child Development*, **79** (4), 1103–1118.

Darling, N., Cumsille, P., Peña-Alampay, L., and Coatsworth, J. D. (in press). Individual and issue-specific differences in parental knowledge and adolescent disclosure in Chile, the Philippines, and the United States. *Journal of Research on Adolescence*.

Darling, N., Dowdy, B. B., Van Horn, M. L., and Caldwell, L. L. (1999). Mixed-sex settings and the perception of competence. *Journal of Youth and Adolescence*, **28** (4), 461–480.

Dishion, T. J. and McMahon, R. J. (1998). Parental monitoring and the prevention of child and adolescent problem behavior: A conceptual and empirical formulation. *Clinical Child and Family Psychology Review*, **1**, 61–75.

Dishion, T. J., Burraston, B., and Li, F. (2003). Family management practices: Research design and measurement issues. In Z. Sloboda and W. J. Bukoski (eds.), *Handbook for drug abuse prevention theory, science, and practice* (pp. 587–607). New York: Plenum Press.

Feeney, J. A. (2005). Hurt feelings in couple relationships: Exploring the role of attachment and perceptions of personal injury. *Personal Relationships,* **12** (2), 253–271.

Finkenauer, C., Engels, R. C. M. E., Branje, S. J. T., and Meeus, W. (2004). Disclosure and relationship satisfaction in families. *Journal of Marriage and Family,* **66** (1), 195–209.

Finkenauer, C., Engels, R. C. M. E., and Meeus, W. (2002). Keeping secrets from parents: Advantages and disadvantages of secrecy in adolescence. *Journal of Youth and Adolescence,* **31**, 123–136.

Finkenauer, C., Frijns, T., Engels, R. C. M. E., and Kerkhof, P. (2005). Perceiving concealment in relationships between parents and adolescents: Links with parental behavior. *Personal Relationships,* **12**, 387–406.

Fletcher, A. C., Darling, N., and Steinberg, L. (1995). Parental monitoring and peer influences on adolescent substance use. In J. McCord (ed.), *Coercion and punishment in long-term perspective* (pp. 259–271). New York: Cambridge University Press.

Frijns, T., Finkenauer, C., Vermulst, A. A., and Engels, R. C. M. E. (2005). Keeping secrets from parents: Longitudinal associations of secrecy in adolescence. *Journal of Youth and Adolescence,* **34** (2), 137–148.

Kerr, M. and Stattin, H. (2000). What parents know, how they know it, and several forms of adolescent adjustment: Further support for a reinterpretation of monitoring. *Developmental Psychology,* **36** (3), 366–380.

  (2003). Parenting of adolescents: Action or reaction? In A. C. Crouter and A. Booth (eds.), *Children's influence on family dynamics: The neglected side of family relationships* (pp. 121–151). Mahwah, NJ: Lawrence Erlbaum Associates.

Kerr, M., Stattin, H., and Trost, K. (1999). To know you is to trust you: Parents' trust is rooted in child disclosure of information. *Journal of Adolescence,* **22** (6), 737–752.

Laird, R. D., Pettit, G. S., Dodge, K. A., and Bates, J. E. (2003). Change in parents' monitoring knowledge: Links with parenting, relationship quality, adolescent beliefs, and antisocial behavior. *Social Development,* **12** (3), 401–419.

Perkins, S. A. and Turiel, E. (2007). To lie or not to lie: To whom and under what circumstances. *Child Development,* **78** (2), 609–621.

Pettit, G. S., Laird, R. D., Dodge, K. A., Bates, J. E., and Criss, M. M. (2001). Antecedents and behavior-problem outcomes of parental monitoring and psychological control in early adolescence. *Child Development,* **72** (2), 583–598.

Rempel, J. K., Holmes, J. G., and Zanna, M. P. (1985). Trust in close relationships. *Journal of Personality and Social Psychology,* **49**, 95–112.

Rotenberg, K. J., Boulton, M. J., and Fox, C. L. (2005). Cross-sectional and longitudinal relations among children's trust beliefs, psychological maladjustment and social relationships: Are very high as well as very low trusting children at risk? *Journal of Abnormal Child Psychology,* **33**, 595–610.

Rotenberg, K. J., McDougall, P., Boulton, M. J., Vaillancourt, T., Fox, C., and Hymel, S. (2004). Cross-sectional and longitudinal relations among relational trustworthiness, social relationships, and psychological adjustment during childhood and adolescence in the UK and Canada. *Journal of Experimental Child Psychology*, **88** (1), 46–67.

Rotter, J. B. (1971). Generalized expectancies for interpersonal trust. *Journal of Personality*, **35**, 651–665.

Smetana, J. G. (1988). Adolescents' and parents' conceptions of parental authority. *Child Development*, **59** (2), 321–335.

(1989). Adolescents' and parents' reasoning about actual family conflict. *Child Development*, **60** (5), 1052–1067.

(2006). Social-cognitive domain theory: Consistencies and variations in children's moral and social judgments. In M. Killen and J. G. Smetana (eds.), *Handbook of moral development* (pp. 119–153). Mahwah, NJ: Lawrence Erlbaum Associates.

(2008). "It's 10 o'clock: Do you know where your children are?": Recent advances in understanding parental monitoring and adolescent disclosure. *Child Development Perspectives*, **2** (1), 19–25.

Smetana, J. G., Metzger, A., Gettman, D. C., and Campione-Barr, N. (2006). Disclosure and secrecy in adolescent–parent relationships. *Child Development*, **77** (1), 201–217.

Smetana, J. G., Yau, J., Restrepo, A., and Braeges, J. L. (1991). Adolescent–parent conflict in married and divorced families. *Developmental Psychology*, **27** (6), 1000–1010.

Stattin, H. and Kerr, M. (2000). Parental monitoring: A reinterpretation. *Child Development*, **71** (4), 1072–1085.

11 The role of trust in adolescent–parent relationships: To trust you is to tell you

Judith G. Smetana (University of Rochester)

> Trust is a fragile plant, which may not endure inspection of its roots, even when they were, before the inspection, quite healthy
> Baier, 1986, p. 260

Trust has been a central construct in psychological theorizing about healthy psychosocial development, particularly from ethological and psychodynamic perspectives. For instance, in Erikson's (1950) developmental theory, developing an appropriate balance of trust versus mistrust in early childhood is one of the normative crises that must be resolved during the lifespan and is central to how later developmental crises, especially the development of identity in adolescence, is resolved. As Bernath and Feshbach (1995) have noted, for Erikson, "basic trust is ... sensory, prelogical, and pervasive or fundamental" (p. 2).

Trust is also a core construct in Bowlby's and Ainsworth's attachment theory (Ainsworth, Blehar, Waters, and Wall, 1978; Bowlby, 1969/1982). Sensitive caregiving, including the caretaker's availability and responsiveness to the child's needs, is seen as facilitating the development of secure attachment relationships in infancy, leading to stable internal working models of relationships. Thus, in early childhood, trust in attachment figures' availability, dependability, and responsiveness is an integral element of attachment and relatedness (Bridges, 2003). Attachment relationships are also seen as influencing positive adjustment in childhood and beyond, and as extending to more positive peer and romantic relationships as well. In adolescence, maintaining a "goal-corrected partnership" with parents means that adolescents must maintain trust and warmth in their relationships with parents (Allen and Land, 1999).

Several studies have shown that children's interpersonal trust is associated with higher social status (Buzzelli, 1988), more socially responsible behavior (Wentzel, 1991), less loneliness (Rotenberg, MacDonald, and King, 2004), better peer relationships, including more friendships and prosocial behavior (Rotenberg, McDougall, Boulton, Vaillancourt, Fox, and Hymel, 2004), and better psychosocial adjustment (Lester and Gatto, 1990; Rotenberg, McDougall, Boulton, Vaillancourt, Fox, and

223

Hymel, 2004). In addition, Rotenberg, Boulton, and Fox (2005) have shown that both very high and very low trust, but especially very low trust beliefs, are associated with poorer adjustment. To date, however, most of the empirical research on interpersonal trust has focused on trust in the context of children's peer or friendship relationships (Rotenberg, Boulton, and Fox, 2005; Rotenberg, McDougall, Boulton, Vaillancourt, Fox, and Hymel, 2004; Selman, 1980), or in adult intimate relationships (Larzelere and Huston, 1980). Although Rotenberg (1995) has studied trust in parent–child relationships, few empirical studies have examined interpersonal trust in the context of adolescent–parent relationships or in samples other than White, middle-class children (Bernath and Feshbach, 1995; but see Rotenberg and Cerda, 1994 for a comparison of Native American and non-Native American children).

The present chapter extends prior theorizing to consider why trust may be centrally important for healthy adolescent psychosocial development, and, in particular, adolescents' disclosure to parents about their activities, whereabouts, and friendships. The results from recent research are used to consider associations among trust in adolescent–parent relationships, parental knowledge of adolescents' activities, and adolescents' disclosure about those activities to parents. Associations between adolescents' disclosure to parents about different types of activities and perceptions of trust, as experienced in different interpersonal relationships in the family, are examined. Finally, variations in these associations among adolescents of different ethnicities are considered.

Development during adolescence

The development of autonomy, or the process of becoming a self-governing person, has been considered one of the central developmental tasks of adolescence (Collins, Gleason, and Sesma, 1997; Steinberg, 1990; Steinberg and Silk, 2002; Zimmer-Gembeck and Collins, 2003). Research has shown that autonomy develops in the context of the family, as parent–adolescent relationships are transformed from more hierarchical to more mutual relationships (Smetana, Campione-Barr, and Daddis, 2004; Youniss and Smollar, 1985). Although parents believe that it is important to facilitate teens' independence, they are also concerned with protecting their adolescents and keeping them safe. Thus, parents must balance adolescents' desires for greater autonomy with judgments about whether they are mature enough to make their own decisions (Smetana and Chuang, 2001). With age, adolescents spend more time away from home and in the company of peers (Csikszentmihalyi and Larson, 1984; Larson, Richards, Moneta, Holmbeck, and Duckett, 1996). Accordingly, more proximal forms of supervision and control must give way to more distal methods, and parental monitoring, including knowing where children are, whom they are with, and what they are doing when they are away from home, becomes increasingly important. By carefully supervising their teens from a distance, parents can attempt to keep their adolescents safe while facilitating their developing autonomy. Effective monitoring, however, is built on a foundation of trust and, particularly, parents' beliefs in the trustworthiness of their teen (Kerr, Stattin, and Trost, 1999). Parents must trust their adolescents to be responsible, follow their rules, and share information about their plans, activities, and companions. When parents do not trust their teens, they are likely to surveil them more closely and ask more questions about their whereabouts (Kerr and Stattin, 2000; Stattin and Kerr, 2000).

Although parental monitoring has been defined in terms of parents' active tracking and surveillance, several researchers have noted recently that in most of the available research, monitoring has been assessed primarily in terms of parents' *knowledge* of adolescents' activities rather than their monitoring behavior (Crouter and Head, 2002; Kerr and Stattin, 2000; Stattin and Kerr, 2000), and parents' knowledge can be obtained in different ways. Parents can seek information by talking to the adolescent's siblings, friends, or to other parents, by asking informed others, such as the adolescent's teachers or one's spouse, or by listening in on conversations – for instance, while in the car or when the teen is on the phone (Waizenhofer, Buchanan, and Jackson-Newsom, 2004). Parents can also control or restrict their adolescents' behavior (Kerr and Stattin, 2000; Stattin and Kerr, 2000) or obtain information from their adolescent, either directly, by asking the child about their activities, or through adolescents' willingness to disclose information about where they are going and who they are with.

In their groundbreaking research, Kerr and Stattin (2000; Kerr, Stattin, and Trost, 1999; Stattin and Kerr, 2000) compared the influence of adolescents' willingness to disclose to parents about their activities (without being asked), parental behavioral control, and parental solicitation of information on juvenile delinquency. They found that, contrary to the conventional wisdom, and controlling for the influence of parents' reports of trust in their adolescent, only adolescents' voluntary disclosure about their activities influenced adjustment. Subsequent studies have confirmed that adolescents who willingly tell their parents about their activities (without parents asking) demonstrate better adjustment, including less externalizing behavior and less internalizing distress. As adolescents spend more time away from home, they have more opportunities to decide whether to disclose their activities or keep them secret. Thus, it is important to understand the characteristics of parent–adolescent relationships that facilitate adolescents' willingness to disclose their activities to their parents. (This recent research on disclosure of activities differs from earlier research, prominent in the 1980s, examining adolescents' self-disclosure of private thoughts and feelings; see reviews by Berndt and Hanna, 1995, and Buhrmester and Prager, 1995.)

The available research has shown consistently that adolescents' willingness to tell parents about their activities is associated with adolescents' perceptions of better relationships with parents (Finkenauer, Engels, and Meeus, 2002; Smetana, Metzger, Gettman, and Campione-Barr, 2006; Soenens, Vansteenkiste, Luyckx, and Goossens, 2006) and parents' greater responsiveness to their teens (Soenens, Vansteenkiste, Luyckx, and Goossens, 2006). Several studies have examined parents' perceptions of more trust in their adolescents (Kerr and Stattin, 2000; Kerr, Stattin, and Trost, 1999; Stattin and Kerr, 2000), but few studies have specifically examined adolescents' perceptions of trust in parents or compared parents' versus adolescents' trust perceptions.

Based on characteristics that children ascribed to hypothetical friends, Rotenberg (1994, 2001) has proposed a model of interpersonal trust with peers that stresses the importance of mutuality, or the tendency for dyadic partners to match each other's trusting behaviors. However, mutuality may be easier to achieve in the context of more horizontal relationships, such as peer, friendship, and adult romantic relationships, than in parent–child relationships, where the power balance is unequal. Kerr, Stattin, and Trost (1999) have suggested that parents' trust in their adolescents is much closer to partner (e.g., equal) relationships than is adolescents' trust in parents. For parents, Kerr et al. suggest, trust is based on knowledge of the adolescents' past and present behavior (for instance, whether they have conformed to parental rules in the past), and their values and attitudes. In their large, cross-sectional study of middle adolescents and their parents, they found that adolescents who shared more of their feelings and concerns with their parents were more likely to believe that their parents trusted them. Teenagers' feelings and concerns did not influence parents' trust, however. Rather, parents reported being more trusting of their adolescents when they had more knowledge of their teens' daily activities (except when that knowledge included awareness of teenagers' past delinquency), especially when knowledge was obtained through the adolescent's voluntary disclosure. The authors posited that parents may be more trusting of teens who voluntarily share more information about their activities. They acknowledged, however, that parental trust and teen disclosure are likely to be complexly intertwined.

Baier (1986), a moral philosopher, has noted that in hierarchical relationships, the lower-status individuals (who also have less power) are much more restricted than are higher-status individuals in their ability to enter freely into voluntary agreements and to trust that others will keep their agreements. Because of adolescents' dependent relationship with parents, parental availability and responsiveness (Ainsworth, Blehar, Waters, and Wall, 1978) may be especially salient to trust; children need to be able to rely on their caregivers for protection and support (Bernath and Feshbach, 1995). Baier (1986), however, has noted that trust goes beyond merely relying on others' dependability; rather, it entails a reliance on others' goodwill. For instance, adolescents' belief that parents are emotionally trustworthy, and their expectations that parents will act accordingly, are likely to facilitate adolescents' disclosure. Honesty is a crucial dimension of trust in interpersonal relationships (Rotenberg, 1994, 2001), but because their power is restricted, lower-status partners in unequal relationships may resort to dishonesty or concealment to get their way. Both psychological and anthropological research have shown that individuals in subordinate positions often resort to subversion and resistance as a means of dealing with the perceived injustices that may occur in relationships that are unequal in power and status. For instance, several recent ethnographic accounts have described the covert processes that women in traditional societies, including women in Moroccan harems (Mernissi, 1994) and in polygenous Bedouin societies (Abu-Lughod, 1993), have used to subvert their subordinate positions and attain desired goals. Although these examples are far removed from parent–adolescent relationships in Western societies, they provide vivid examples of the lengths individuals in subordinate positions will go to get their way.

Empirical psychological research has shown that parent–adolescent and peer relationships differ when it comes to issues like honesty, lying, and secrecy. A recent study by Perkins and Turiel (2007) demonstrated that children evaluate honesty and lying differently in the context of peer versus parent–child relationships. These researchers examined early and middle adolescents' evaluations of hypothetical scenarios that depicted either parents or friends asking teens to violate a moral precept (e.g., not to see a friend of another race or to fight back against a teasing peer), a personal choice (e.g., not to date a person they do not like or join a club that is seen as a waste of time), or a prudential concern (e.g., not completing homework or riding a motorcycle). The authors found that early and middle adolescents were more accepting of lying to parents than to friends about moral and personal issues, while adolescents were more accepting of lying to friends than to parents about prudential issues. Moreover, when justifying whether it was acceptable to lie to friends, adolescents rejected lying based primarily on concerns with the importance of openness and trust in relationships, and condoned lying based on concerns with personal choice and relationship maintenance. In contrast, when justifying whether it is acceptable to lie about personal issues with parents, adolescents' justifications focused primarily on concerns with personal choices. When asked whether lying in general was acceptable, however, all participants evaluated it as wrong. Thus, although honesty is integral to trust in interpersonal relationships (Rotenberg, 1994, 2001), this study suggests that teenagers view it as acceptable to lie to parents in some circumstances. Likewise, several studies have shown that late adolescents and college students lie fairly frequently to parents (DePaulo and Kashy, 1998; Jensen, Arnett, Feldman, and Cauffman, 2004), with high school students lying to parents more than college students (Jensen, Arnett, Feldman, and Cauffman, 2004), even when they report close relationships (DePaulo and Kashy, 1998).

But what do adolescents lie about? In my program of research, and as described in the following section, social domain theory (for overviews, see Helwig and Turiel, 2003; Nucci, 1996, 2001; Smetana, 1995, 2006; Turiel, 1983, 2002, 2006) has provided a theoretical lens for understanding transformations in adolescent–parent relationships (Smetana, 1988b, 2002), and, more recently, for illuminating the types of issues that adolescents disclose and keep secret from parents.

Social domain theory and adolescent–parent relationships

Numerous studies in the United States, and other cultures in Asia, South America, Europe, and Africa, have shown that both adolescents and parents consistently agree that parents have the legitimate authority to regulate *moral issues* (pertaining to others' welfare, rights, or fairness), *conventional issues* (which pertain to the arbitrary and consensually agreed-on norms or expectations, like etiquette and manners, for appropriate behavior), and *prudential issues* (pertaining to safety, harm to the self, comfort, and health). Parents and adolescents also agree (although somewhat less consistently) that adolescents should be granted some autonomy over *personal issues*, which pertain to privacy, the state of one's body, and preferences and choice regarding appearances, recreational activities, and friends. However, adolescents and parents often disagree about where the boundaries of adolescents' personal jurisdiction should be drawn; adolescents typically want more control than parents are willing to grant (Fuligni, 1998; Lins-Dyer, 2003, described in Nucci, Hasebe, and Lins-Dyer, 2005; Nucci, Camino, and Milnitsky-Sapiro, 1996; Smetana, 1988a, b, 2000; Smetana and Asquith, 1994; Smetana, Crean, and Campione-Barr, 2005). For instance, parents may view keeping the bedroom clean as a conventional issue of custom, authority, or social coordination, while adolescents may view it as a personal issue of identity, autonomy, or control. We have referred to such issues, which entail overlaps between the domains, as *multifaceted.*

A number of studies, both cross-sectional and longitudinal, have shown that these differences in parents' and adolescents' interpretations of issues (especially multifaceted issues) lead to conflict in parent–adolescent relationships. In the context of warm, supportive relationships, adolescents' and parents' negotiations over these divergent perspectives can result in changes in the boundaries of parental authority and increases in adolescents' autonomy (Smetana, 1989; Smetana and Asquith, 1994; Smetana and Gaines, 1999). Much research has shown that the boundaries and the content of the personal domain vary cross-culturally. Cultures differ in how much personal freedom individuals are granted and, to some extent, the issues that are treated as personal (Turiel, 2002, 2006; Wainryb, 2006). Furthermore, individuals' concepts of personal jurisdiction increase with age (Nucci, 2001; Smetana, 2002). Nevertheless, children and adolescents in all cultures claim personal jurisdiction over some issues; Nucci (1996) has asserted that claims to personal choice are part of our universal human needs for agency, autonomy, and effectance. Therefore, disagreements over the boundaries of the personal domain appear to be a normative aspect of adolescent development (see Nucci, 2001; Smetana, 2002 for a discussion).

Content analyses have shown that adolescent–parent conflicts, particularly in early adolescence, typically occur over issues like doing the chores and helping around the house, keeping the bedroom clean, doing homework, fighting with siblings, and choice of activities (Montemayor, 1986; Smetana, 1989) – issues that are relatively "out in the open" and directly or easily observable by parents. As adolescents spend more time away from home and in the company of peers, they have increased opportunities to conceal their activities from their parents and keep them secret, perhaps because they fear parental disapproval or punishment, because they worry that parents would not understand their behavior, or because they view their behavior as private or as not harmful (Darling, Cumsille, Caldwell, and Dowdy; 2006; Smetana, Villalobos, Tasopoulos-Chan, Gettman, and Campione-Barr, 2009). Thus, rather than openly confront their parents to get their way, they may choose to selectively manage information in situations of disagreement, as Darling, Cumsille, Caldwell, and Dowdy (2006) have found. For instance, these authors found that when adolescents disagreed with parents about an issue, they typically did not tell parents about their behavior vis-à-vis that issue. Thus, managing information, and choosing when to disclose and when to conceal information from parents, provide another route to autonomy.

In a recent program of research, we have examined adolescents' willingness to disclose to parents about their activities as a function of both the domain of the activity as well as the quality of parent–adolescent relationships. In studies using different samples and methods, we have examined adolescents' willingness to disclose to parents (without parents asking) about activities in different conceptual domains (moral, conventional, prudential, and personal) and their overlap in multifaceted activities. In these studies, we have examined associations between adolescents' disclosure to parents about different activities and levels of trust in their relationships.

We have assessed trust using the ten-item trust subscale (sometimes shortened to eight items) of the Inventory of Parent and Peer Attachment (IPPA; Armsden and Greenberg, 1987). The IPPA draws on attachment theory to assess (in a global way) adolescents' perceptions of how much they trust and feel accepted by their parents and how much they perceive their parents as respecting their feelings. We have also used a reworded version to assess parents' trust in their teens. Thus, in contrast to Rotenberg (1994, 2001), who has viewed honesty as one of three fundamental dimensions of trust (along with reliability and emotional reliance), our assessment has focused on the reliable and emotional aspects of trust, and, in turn, our assessment has focused on associations with honesty, as reflected by assessments of adolescents' reports of their willingness to disclose to parents (and the extent to which they keep secrets) about their activities in different domains.

Adolescent trust and disclosure to parents regarding activities in different domains

Interpersonal trust has typically been viewed as a personality characteristic –that is, as a stable dimension that varies among individuals. In our analyses, we hypothesized that adolescents' trust in their parents may vary as a function of the type of situations or activities that adolescents disclose or conceal. In one study (Smetana, Metzger, Gettman, and Campione-Barr, 2006), 276 ethnically diverse lower-middle-class ninth- and twelfth-graders (averaging 14.62 and 17.40 years of age, respectively) and one of their parents ($n = 249$ parents) rated their beliefs about adolescents' obligations to disclose to parents about different types of activities (assessed by asking adolescents whether they "*should* tell parents what they are doing, that is whether they have a duty or obligation to tell parents about their behavior"), as well as their actual disclosure of those activities to mothers and fathers. Both adolescents and parents viewed adolescents as most obligated to disclose to parents about their prudential activities (like smoking cigarettes, drinking alcohol, and going to a party where alcohol is served), and least obligated to disclose to parents about their personal activities (like how teens spend their free time, spend their own money, or what they talk about on the phone with friends). Indeed, both parents and adolescents viewed disclosure over prudential activities as obligatory, but they viewed disclosure over personal activities as discretionary (Smetana, Metzger, Gettman, and Campione-Barr, 2006). Obligations to disclose moral, conventional, and multifaceted activities fell in between. We hypothesized that adolescents who reported more trusting relationships with their parents may disclose more to parents, particularly about personal issues.

Adolescents and parents each rated their trust in the other on the IPPA (with teens rating parental trust perceptions separately for their mothers and fathers) and completed a questionnaire assessing adolescents' disclosure to parents (or, for parents, their perceptions of adolescents' disclosure). Consistent with Kerr, Stattin, and Trost's (1999) assertion, adolescents' perceptions of their trust in their parents and parents' perceptions of their trust in their teens were significantly, but only moderately, associated, $rs = .29, .25, ps < .01$. Using r to z transformations, we compared the strength of the associations between trust and adolescents' disclosure regarding different types of activities. As reported elsewhere (Smetana and Metzger, 2008), and consistent with our hypothesis, statistical tests of the differences between the correlations indicated that adolescents' perceived trust in each parent was more strongly associated with teens' reports of their disclosure to that parent regarding their personal activities (and for fathers, peer activities) than (combined) moral and conventional activities. Similar results were obtained for parents' perceptions of trust in their teens. Parent-rated trust was more strongly associated with parents' perceptions of their teens' disclosure regarding personal activities than (combined) moral and conventional activities, $rs(248) = .35, .24$. This finding is interesting, as it highlights the reciprocal nature of trust. Parents who are more trusting of their teenagers have teens who are more likely to share the personal details of their lives with their parents, suggesting that teenagers feel secure that their confidences will not be betrayed.

In this study, we did not ask adolescents to rate their actual disclosure to parents about prudential activities. This was because the assessment of disclosure did not distinguish between adolescents who reported not disclosing to parents (because they did not engage in certain activities and thus they had nothing to disclose) and adolescents who engaged in the behavior but were not willing to disclose to parents (because they did not want parents to know). Yet prudential behaviors such as going to parties where alcohol is served or drinking alcohol are exactly the types of behaviors that more vigilant parental monitoring is intended to prevent.

In our more recent research, we overcame this methodological limitation. Smetana, Villalobos, Tasopoulos-Chan, Gettman, and Campione-Barr (2009) used a novel sorting task, with 118 predominantly European American, lower-middle-class seventh- and tenth-graders, one parent, and, as described below, a sibling. Families were recruited from a suburban middle school and high school and seen in a university lab. In an individual interview, the teens were given a set of cards that described various prudential, multifaceted, and personal behaviors. First, they sorted the cards to distinguish the behaviors in which they had engaged at least once. If they had engaged in the behavior, they then rated on a five-point scale how willingly they had disclosed that behavior to their parents without the parents asking. As noted previously, both adolescents and parents rated their trust in the other on the IPPA.

Statistical comparisons of the correlations (again, using r to z transformations) indicated that adolescents' perceived trust in parents was more strongly associated with disclosure about prudential activities, $r(118) = .40, p < .001$, than peer activities, $r(118) = .19, p < .01$. The association between trust and personal issues, $r(118) = .33, p < .01$, did not differ significantly from the association between trust and either peer or prudential issues, however. Interestingly, and similar to the results just described, parents' trust in their adolescent was more strongly associated with teens' disclosure over personal issues than disclosure regarding either prudential or peer activities, $rs(118) = .25$ versus $.12, .18, ps < .01$.

Why would adolescents' perceptions of more trusting relationships with parents be associated with greater reported voluntary disclosure of prudential than of peer activities? Because most of the prudential activities in this study were ones that are likely to garner parental disapproval, adolescents may be more likely to risk disclosure if they feel confident that disclosure will not damage their relationships. Our analysis of justifications helps to better understand these findings.

In the sorting task, adolescents also sorted the different items into categories representing different reasons for not disclosing the activities (see Smetana, Villalobos, Tasopoulos-Chan, Gettman, and Campione-Barr, 2009 for more details): 51 percent of the justifications for not disclosing prudential activities pertained to concerns with getting in trouble or parental disapproval; 21 percent pertained to claims that the acts do not harm anyone; 12 percent were that the acts are private and not their parents' business; 10 percent pertained to assertions that they would feel bad, embarrassed or ashamed; and 6 percent felt their parents would think less of them. Greater trust in their parents was not significantly associated with adolescents' use of these different justifications, except that adolescents' greater trust in their parents was associated with the belief that their parents would think less of them for engaging in the prudential behaviors, $r = -.48$, $p < .001$. Parents' trust was also not significantly associated with adolescents' justifications for not disclosing their prudential behavior, but teenagers whose parents reported trusting them more were more likely to feel bad, embarrassed, or ashamed for not disclosing about their peer behavior, $r = .20$, $p < .05$. Thus, both adolescents' trust in parents and parents' trust in their teens were related to psychological qualities of their relationship (embarrassment, shame), pointing to the emotional aspects of trust.

This study also offered a unique opportunity to gain insight into within-family variations in trust, as the sample for this study also included an older or younger sibling within 1 to 4 years of age of the target teens. Siblings completed many of the same measures as the target adolescents, including trust in their parents as assessed on the IPPA. Previous research has shown that behavioral control is significantly associated with adolescents' disclosure of their activities to their parents (Soenens, Vansteenkiste, Luyckx, and Goossens, 2006). Thus, behavioral control was assessed using Steinberg's (1987; Brown, Mounts, Lamborn, and Steinberg, 1993) eight-item measure of behavioral control, which assesses how much teens viewed their parents as restricting or setting limits on activities like the amount of time spent watching TV, on the phone or computer, or checking to see if homework is done.

Regression analyses were conducted to examine the unique associations among the three different reports of trust in the family (teens' and siblings' trust in parents and parents' trust in the target teen), behavioral control, and disclosure regarding different types of activities. (For both target teens and siblings, ratings of mothers and fathers were combined for these analyses, as ratings were moderately but significantly associated, $r = .35$, $p < .01$, and differences between ratings of fathers and mothers were not of interest here.) As might be expected, siblings' and target teens' ratings of their trust in parents were also moderately but significantly associated, $r = .44$, $p < .001$, but these ratings were not combined, given our interest in examining their unique associations with adolescents' disclosure to parents.

Preliminary correlations showed that adolescents' age and sex and other family demographic variables such as parental marital status or education were not significantly associated with disclosure; thus, these variables were not included in subsequent analyses. Teens' ordinal position in the family was also not associated with disclosure about different types of activities, but it was controlled in the first step of the analysis, as interactions between siblings' ordinal position and trust were of interest in these analyses. The second step of the analyses included the three trust variables, as well as the measure of behavioral control. Finally, the third step of the analysis examined interactions between adolescents' ordinal position in the family and trust in their parents. These analyses were run separately on adolescents' disclosure to parents regarding prudential, multifaceted, and personal activities.

In each analysis, behavioral control was uniquely associated with adolescents' reports of voluntary disclosure to parents regarding multifaceted, personal, and prudential activities, βs $=.34, .23, .20$, ps $< .05$, respectively. These findings indicated that, consistent with previous research (Soenens, Vansteenkiste, Luyckx, and Goossens, 2006), adolescents reported willingly disclosing more to their parents when they perceived their parents as setting more limits on their behavior. Only behavioral control (and none of the measures of trust) was uniquely associated with disclosure regarding multifaceted activities, total $R^2 = .19$.

In addition to behavioral control, siblings' trust in parents was significantly associated with adolescents' reports of voluntary disclosure to parents regarding their prudential behavior, $\beta = .26$, $p < .05$, total $R^2 = .27$. Adolescents' trust in parents (either alone or in interaction with ordinal position) or parents' trust in their teens was not significant in the analyses. Thus, regardless of ordinal position in the family, the more siblings trusted their parents, the more the adolescents reported willingly disclosing their prudential behavior to their parents. Of course, it is possible that this is because parents are perceived as trustworthy by both offspring, and trust is associated with disclosure of prudential matters. But these findings are intriguing, as several studies have shown that siblings influence other siblings' dating, sexual, and problem behavior. For instance, siblings are more alike than would be expected by chance in their levels of deviant behavior and sexual intimacy (Rowe, Rodgers, Meseck-Bushey, and St. John, 1989). In addition, compared to girls whose older sisters have not borne children, younger sisters of childbearing adolescents have been found to be at higher risk and more accepting of nonmarital adolescent childbearing (Cox, Emans, and Bithoney, 1993; East, 1996). They also expect to marry and have a child at a younger age, engage in more problem behavior, and are more pessimistic about school and future career goals. Thus, these findings suggest that when deciding whether to disclose about prudential behaviors that might potentially get them in trouble, teens are influenced by whether their siblings perceive that their relationships with parents are trustworthy. These findings are also consistent with research on sibling relationships during adolescence. This research shows that although the quality of their relationships declines across adolescence, siblings are still seen as important sources of support (Buhrmester and Furman, 1990; Furman and Buhrmester, 1992).

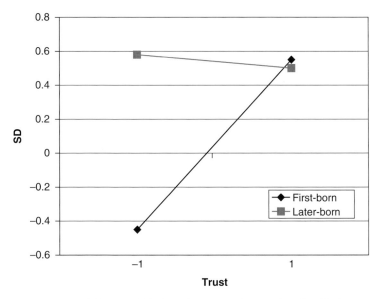

Figure 11.1 Adolescents' birth order × trust interaction for disclosure regarding personal activities

Adolescents' trust in parents, $\beta=.30$, $p<.05$, and, marginally, parents' trust in their teens, $\beta=.16$, $p=.07$, had unique influences on adolescents' voluntary disclosure to parents about their personal activities; siblings' trust in parents was not significant. In this analysis, the interaction between trust and ordinal position in the family approached significance, $\beta=-.21$, $p<.07$. It was interpreted by plotting the regression lines for the predicted high ($+1$ SD) versus low (-1 SD) values of the moderator, as recommended by Aiken and West (1991). The statistical significance of the regression slopes was then examined to determine whether each slope differed significantly from zero. As shown in Figure 11.1, adolescents' disclosure to parents about their personal activities increased as trust increased, but only among first-born teens. Thus, the findings suggest that first-born teens who are more trusting of their parents are more likely to tell their parents about their personal activities. One possible interpretation of the findings for older siblings is that while older siblings use trustworthy parents as targets of disclosure, younger siblings have their older siblings as confidants. This seems somewhat unlikely, however, as Figure 11.1 suggests that disclosure to parents about personal activities is relatively high among later-born siblings as well. Another possibility is that closely spaced, later-born siblings have the opportunity to observe their older siblings' relationships with parents (and, perhaps, the effects of their disclosure about personal activities to parents) and then decide whether they want to divulge or conceal personal information to them.

We did not obtain information on disclosure from the younger siblings of seventh-graders, as some of the items might have been inappropriate for children as young as 7 or 8 years of age. But both younger and older siblings of the tenth-graders rated their disclosure about their activities. Thus, we were able to examine this hypothesis. The sibling dyad was the unit of analysis in these analyses. We examined the gender constellation of the dyad (same-sex or mixed-sex siblings) and whether the target tenth-grader was first-born or later-born. (Given constraints on the sample size, male–male and female–female sibling dyads were not distinguished.) The results added some complexity. A gender constellation × ordinal status × sibling (older versus younger) analysis of variance (ANOVA) revealed a significant three-way interaction, $F(1, 66) = 3.80$, $p < .05$, for disclosure regarding personal activities. This was found to be due to a significant sibling dyad × sex constellation interaction among older sibling dyads (e.g., among tenth-graders with older siblings), $F(1, 26) = 4.59$, $p < .05$. The interaction is depicted graphically in Figure 11.2.

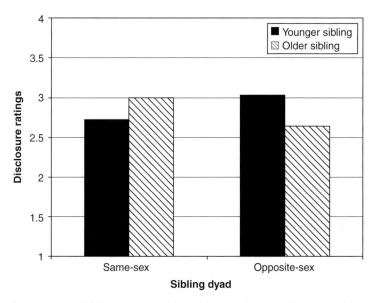

Figure 11.2 Middle (tenth grade) and late adolescent sibling dyads' disclosure to parents about personal activities

As can be seen, target tenth-graders with an older, opposite-sex sibling disclosed more about personal issues to parents than did same-age teens (tenth-graders) with an older, same-sex sibling, but same- or opposite-sex older siblings in the dyads (the late adolescents) did not differ in their disclosure. Same-sex siblings have closer and warmer relationships than do opposite-sex siblings (Buhrmester and Furman, 1990) and thus may serve as targets for disclosure, particularly for the younger sibling in the dyad. Because sibling relationships are less close and warm in opposite-sex dyads, tenth-graders may rely on their mothers rather than their older sibling to disclose about personal activities.

Ethnic and cultural differences in adolescents' trust and disclosure to parents

Finally, as noted elsewhere (Smetana, 2008), the studies of disclosure regarding adolescents' activities that we have discussed thus far have focused primarily on European and European American adolescents, and research on ethnic minorities has been lacking. However, the social domain framework structuring the previously discussed studies has been applied and shown to be valid for children and adolescents of different ethnicities and cultures (see reviews by Nucci, 2001; Smetana, 2006; Turiel, 2002, 2006; Wainryb, 2006).

Tasopoulos-Chan and Smetana (2009) examined disclosure in nearly 500 teens – 175 Chinese American (primarily first and second generation), 204 Mexican American (primarily second and third generation), and 91 European American adolescents (primarily third generation) – who ranged from 14 to 18 years of age. They were recruited from several high schools in the Los Angeles area. Consistent with the patterns of immigration in this geographical area, generational status differed among teens from the three ethnic groups, as did level of parental education, and these differences were controlled in subsequent analyses.

Using questionnaires, adolescents' trust in parents was assessed globally using the IPPA, as was done in the previous studies. In addition, their willingness to disclose to parents (without being asked) regarding prudential activities (including whether the teens use marijuana or other drugs, drink beer or wine, have unprotected sex, or cut classes), multi-faceted activities (like whether they stay out late, watch movies with explicit sex or violence, and what they "instant message" to friends), and personal activities (like how they spend their free time or their allowance money, and what they talk about with friends) was also assessed. Chinese American, Mexican American, and European American adolescents'

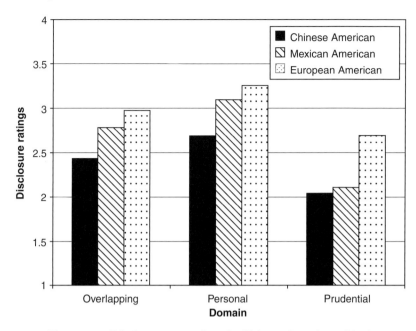

Figure 11.3 Disclosure to mothers in Chinese American, Mexican American, and European American adolescents

ratings of their voluntary disclosure to parents about different types of activities are shown in Figure 11.3.

With generational status and parents' educational background controlled in covariate analyses, European American youth reported disclosing more to their mothers about their prudential activities than did Mexican American teens, and more to their mothers about personal and multifaceted activities than did Chinese American teens (see Figure 11.3). However, Chinese American adolescents also reported less trust in their mothers than did either Mexican American or European American teens, $F(2, 461) = 4.87, p < .01$. When trust was added as a covariate in the analyses (along with the other covariates), the differences between Chinese American and European American adolescents in disclosure regarding personal and multifaceted activities was no longer statistically significant. This finding suggests that ethnic differences in disclosure may reflect differences in perceptions of trust in parents. This is consistent with findings from a qualitative study of African American, Latino, and Asian adolescent boys in low-income families (Jeffries, 2004). Jeffries found that in contrast to Latino and African American boys, Asian American boys reported very little communication with either of their parents about

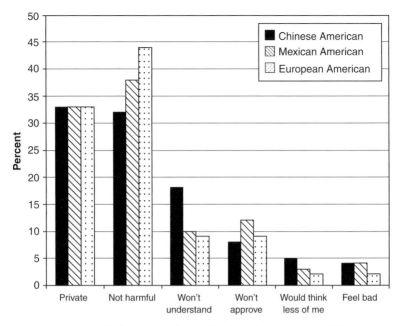

Figure 11.4 Chinese American, Mexican American, and European American adolescents' reasons for not disclosing to parents about personal activities

private topics, because they believed that parents would not approve, understand, or care. The findings are also consistent with discussions of Chinese parents' childrearing orientations as entailing strict discipline and frequent use of shaming, scolding, and physical punishment (Chao, 1994). Although this style of discipline is child-focused and conducted to further the child's development, it may have negative implications for the development of close, trusting relationships that encourage adolescents' disclosure about their activities.

Yau, Tasopoulos-Chan, and Smetana (2009) also examined adolescents' endorsement of various reasons for not disclosing about the different types of activities. Across ethnic groups, adolescents indicated that they did not disclose about personal activities primarily because they viewed the acts as personal matters (36 percent) or as not harmful (37 percent), and, less frequently, because parents would not listen or understand (11 percent), because parents would not approve or the teen would get in trouble (10 percent), because parents might think less of them (3 percent), and because they might feel bad, embarrassed, or ashamed (3 percent). As shown in Figure 11.4, endorsement of these reasons differed significantly by ethnicity. While youth from the three ethnic groups did not differ significantly in viewing personal activities as private matters, European American adolescents were somewhat more likely than Chinese American adolescents to report that they were not harmful. Consistent with Jeffries' (2004) qualitative findings and the ethnic/cultural differences in adolescents' trust just discussed, Chinese American teens were more likely to report not disclosing about personal activities because their parents would not listen or understand than were either Mexican American or White adolescents.

Conclusions

Recent research has challenged long-standing conclusions about the importance of parental monitoring for adolescent adjustment. This research has shown that even with the quality of parent–adolescent relationships controlled, adolescents' willingness to disclose to their parents about their activities is a primary source of parents' knowledge of their adolescents' behavior. Adolescent disclosure accounts for more of the variance in parental knowledge than parents' surveillance or control, or parents' solicitation of information (Kerr and Stattin, 2000; Stattin and Kerr, 2000), and, in turn, has been associated with reductions in juvenile delinquency and conduct problems. These findings highlight the importance of understanding the conditions that facilitate adolescents' willingness to disclose to parents about their activities.

Previous research on trust in childhood and adolescence has focused primarily on peer or friendship relationships. Yet because of the power imbalance, parent–adolescent relationships pose particular challenges to the establishment of trusting relationships (Baier, 1986), particularly for children, who are lower in status and have less power than parents. The results of the research discussed in this chapter indicate that adolescents' perceived trust in their parents, and, to a lesser extent, parents' perceived trust in their teens, is central to adolescents' willingness to disclose information about their activities to their parents. The studies discussed here further indicate that the strength of the association between trust and adolescents' disclosure depends on the type (domain) of the activity to be disclosed and whose perceptions of trust (parents' or teenagers') are assessed. In a lower-middle-class sample of primarily European American families, teenagers' perceptions of trust in parents were more strongly associated with their disclosure regarding their prudential activities than their peer or personal activities, while parents' perceived trust in their teens was more strongly associated with adolescents' disclosure over personal than other activities. Moreover, the findings suggested that ordinal position in the family was also associated with levels of disclosure.

Although the analyses reported here were narrowly focused on associations between perceptions of trust and disclosure, it is important to note that adolescents who have better relationships with their parents and view their parents as more trustworthy may also be less likely to engage in problem behaviors, like drinking alcohol, hanging around with undesirable peers, and engaging in drug use. Thus, while the focus here was on associations between trust and types of disclosure, these need to be considered within a broader model of the factors that contribute to adolescent adjustment. Moreover, the cross-ethnic study discussed here (Yau, Tasopoulos-Chan, and Smetana, 2009) shows that adolescents' trust in parents may vary as a function of ethnicity or culture; in different groups, childrearing orientations may differ in the extent to which they discourage or encourage emotionally close and trusting parent–child relationships.

Finally, in the studies discussed here, trust was defined within an attachment theory framework and assessed using a global measure of perceptions that focused on teens' trust in parents and perceptions that parents reciprocate with availability and responsiveness. It would be worthwhile in future research to distinguish between different dimensions of trust, as Rotenberg (1994, 2001) has done, and to further specify the different aspects of trust that are important for parents versus adolescents, as Kerr, Stattin, and Trost (1999) have suggested. Future research should determine how different dimensions of trust influence adolescents' disclosure to parents and adolescent–parent relationships more generally. Additional research is also needed to examine how trust develops and is maintained (or undermined) in family contexts.

References

Abu-Lughod, L. (1993). *Writing women's worlds: Bedouin stories*. Berkeley: University of California Press.

Aiken, L. S. and West, S. G. (1991). *Multiple regression: Testing and interpreting interactions*. Newbury Park, CA: Sage.

Ainsworth, M. D. S., Blehar, M. C., Waters, E., and Wall, S. (1978). *Patterns of attachment: A psychological study of the Strange situation*. Hillsdale, NJ: Lawrence Erlbaum Associates.

Allen, J. P. and Land, D. (1999). Attachment in adolescence. In J. Cassidy and P. R. Shaver (eds.), *Handbook of attachment: Theory, research, and clinical applications* (pp. 319–335). New York: Guilford Press.

Armsden, G. C. and Greenberg, M. T. (1987). The Inventory of Parent and Peer Attachment: Individual differences and their relationship to psychological well being in adolescence. *Journal of Youth and Adolescence*, 16, 427–454.

Baier, A. C. (1986). Trust and antitrust. *Ethics*, 96, 231–260.

Bernath, M. S. and Feshbach, N. D. (1995). Children's trust: Theory, assessment, development, and research directions. *Applied and Preventive Psychology*, **4**, 1–19.

Berndt, T. J. and Hanna, N. A. (1995). Intimacy and self-disclosure in friendships. In K. Rotenberg (ed.), *Disclosure processes in children and adolescents* (pp. 57–77). Cambridge University Press.

Bowlby, J. (1969/1982). *Attachment and loss: Vol. 1. Attachment*. New York: Basic Books.

Bridges, L. J. (2003). Trust, attachment, and relatedness. In M. H. Bornstein and L. Davidson (eds.), *Well-being: Positive development across the life course. Crosscurrents in contemporary psychology* (pp. 177–189). Mahwah, NJ: Lawrence Erlbaum Associates.

Brown, B. B., Mounts, N., Lamborn, S. D., and Steinberg, L. (1993). Parenting practices and peer group affiliations in adolescence. *Child Development*, **64**, 467–482.

Buhrmester, D. and Furman, W. (1990). Perceptions of sibling relationships during middle childhood and adolescence. *Child Development*, **61**, 1387–1398.

Buhrmester, D. and Prager, K. (1995). Patterns and functions of self-disclosure during childhood and adolescence. In K. Rotenberg (ed.), *Disclosure processes in children and adolescents* (pp. 10–56). Cambridge University Press.

Buzzelli, C. A. (1988). The development of trust in children's relations with peers. *Child Study Journal*, **18**, 33–46.

Chao, R. K. (1994). Beyond parental control and authoritarian parenting style: Understanding Chinese parenting through the cultural notion of training. *Child Development*, **65**, 1111–1119.

Collins, W. A., Gleason, T., and Sesma A., Jr. (1997). Internalization, autonomy, and relationships: Development during adolescence. In J. E Grusec and L. Kuczynski (eds.), *Parenting and the internalization of values* (pp. 78–99). New York: Wiley.

Cox, J., Emans, S. J., and Bithoney, W. (1993). Sisters of teen mothers: Increased risk for adolescent parenthood. *Adolescent and Pediatric Gynecology*, **6**, 138–142.

Crouter, A. C. and Head, M. R. (2002). Parental monitoring and knowledge of children. In M. Bornstein (ed.), *Handbook of parenting: Vol. 3. Becoming and being a parent* (2nd edn.) (pp. 461–483). Mahwah, NJ: Lawrence Erlbaum Associates.

Csikszentmihalyi, M. and Larson, R. (1984). *Being adolescent*. New York: Basic Books.

Darling, N., Cumsille, P., Caldwell, L. L., and Dowdy, B. (2006). Predictors of adolescents' disclosure to parents and perceived parental knowledge: Between- and within-person differences. *Journal of Youth and Adolescence*, **35**, 667–678.

DePaulo, B. M. and Kashy, D. A. (1998). Everyday lies in close and casual relationships. *Journal of Personality and Social Psychology*, **74**, 63–79.

East, P. L. (1996). The younger sisters of childbearing adolescents: Their attitudes, expectations and behaviors. *Child Development*, **67**, 267–282.

Erikson, E. H. (1950/1963). *Childhood and society.* New York: W. W. Norton & Company.

Finkenauer, C., Engels, R. C. M. E., and Meeus, W. (2002). Keeping secrets from parents: Advantages and disadvantages of secrecy in adolescence. *Journal of Youth and Adolescence,* **2**, 123–136.

Fuligni, A. J. (1998). Authority, autonomy, and parent–adolescent conflict and cohesion: A study of adolescents from Mexican, Chinese, Filipino, and European backgrounds. *Developmental Psychology,* **34**, 782–792.

Furman, W. and Buhrmester, D. (1992). Age and sex in perceptions of networks of personal relationships. *Child Development,* **63**, 103–115.

Helwig, C. C. and Turiel, E. (2003). Children's social and moral reasoning. In P. K. Smith and C. H. Hart (eds.), *Blackwell handbook of childhood social development* (pp. 475–490). Oxford: Blackwell.

Jeffries, E. D. (2004). Experiences of trust with parents: A qualitative investigation of African American, Latino, and Asian American boys from low-income families. In N. Way and J. Y. Chu (eds.), *Adolescent boys: Exploring diverse cultures of boyhood* (pp. 107–128). New York University Press.

Jensen, L. A., Arnett, J. J., Feldman, S. S., and Cauffman, E. (2004). *Journal of Youth and Adolescence,* **33**, 101–112.

Kerr, M. and Stattin, H. (2000). What parents know, how they know it, and several forms of adolescent adjustment: Further support for a reinterpretation of monitoring. *Developmental Psychology,* **36**, 366–380.

Kerr, M., Stattin, H., and Trost, K. (1999). To know you is to trust you: Parents' trust is rooted in child disclosure of information. *Journal of Adolescence,* **22**, 737–752.

Larson, R., Richards, M., Moneta, G., Holmbeck, G., and Duckett, E. (1996). Changes in adolescents' daily interactions with their families from ages 10–18: Disengagement and transformation. *Developmental Psychology,* **32**, 744–754.

Larzelere, R. E. and Huston, T. L. (1980). The dyadic trust scale: Toward understanding inter-personal trust in close relationships. *Journal of Marriage and the Family,* **42**, 595–604.

Lester, D. and Gatto, J. (1990). Interpersonal trust, depression, and suicidal ideation in teenagers. *Psychological Reports,* **67**, 786.

Mernissi, F. (1994). *Dreams of trespass: Tales of a harem girlhood.* Reading, MA: Addison-Wesley.

Montemayor, R. (1986). Family variation in storm and stress. *Journal of Adolescent Research,* **1**, 15–31.

Nucci, L. P. (1996). Morality and personal freedom. In E. S. Reed, E. Turiel, and T. Brown (eds.), *Values and knowledge* (pp. 41–60). Mahwah, NJ: Lawrence Erlbaum Associates.

(2001). *Education in the moral domain.* Cambridge University Press.

Nucci, L., Camino, C., and Milnitsky-Sapiro, C. (1996). Social class effects on Northeastern Brazilian children's conceptions of areas of personal choice and social regulation. *Child Development,* **67**, 1223–1242.

Nucci, L., Hasebe, Y., and Lins-Dyer, M. T. (2005). Adolescent psychological well-being and parental control of the personal. In J. G. Smetana (ed.),

Changing boundaries of parental authority during adolescence (pp. 17–30). San Francisco: Jossey-Bass.

Perkins, S.A. and Turiel, E. (2007). To lie or not to lie: To whom and under what circumstances. *Child Development*, **78**, 609–621.

Rotenberg, K.J. (1994). Loneliness and interpersonal trust. *Journal of Social and Clinical Psychology*, **13**, 152–173.

(1995). The socialization of trust: Parents' and their children's interpersonal trust. *International Journal of Behavioral Development*, **18**, 713–726.

(2001). Trust across the life-span. In N.J. Smelser and P.B. Baltes (eds.), *International encyclopedia of the social and behavioral sciences* (pp. 7866–7868). New York: Pergamon.

Rotenberg, K.J., Boulton, M.J., and Fox, C.L. (2005). Cross-sectional and longitudinal relations among children's trust beliefs, psychological maladjustment and social relationships: Are very high as well as very low trusting children at risk? *Journal of Abnormal Child Psychology*, **33**, 595–610.

Rotenberg, K.J. and Cerda, C. (1994). Racially based trust expectancies of Native American and Caucasian children. *Journal of Social Psychology*, **134**, 621–631.

Rotenberg, K.J., MacDonald, K.J., and King, E.V. (2004). The relationship between loneliness and interpersonal trust during middle childhood. *Journal of Genetic Psychology*, **165**, 233–249.

Rotenberg, K.J., McDougall, P., Boulton, M.J., Vaillancourt, T., Fox, C., and Hymel, S. (2004). Cross-sectional and longitudinal relations among relational trustworthiness, social relationships, and psychological adjustment during childhood and adolescence in the UK and Canada. *Journal of Experimental Child Psychology*, **88**, 46–67.

Rowe, D. C., Rodgers, J.L., Meseck-Bushey, S., and St. John, C. (1989). Sexual behavior and nonsexual deviance: A sibling study of their relationship. *Developmental Psychology*, **25**, 61–69.

Selman, R.L. (1980). *The growth of interpersonal understanding: Developmental and clinical analyses.* New York: Academic Press.

Smetana, J.G. (1988a). Adolescents' and parents' conceptions of parental authority. *Child Development*, **59**, 321–335.

(1988b). Concepts of self and social convention: Adolescents' and parents' reasoning about hypothetical and actual family conflicts. In M.R. Gunnar and W.A. Collins (eds.), *21st Minnesota Symposium on child psychology: Development during the transition to adolescence* (pp. 77–122). Hillsdale, NJ: Lawrence Erlbaum Associates.

(1989). Adolescents' and parents' reasoning about actual family conflict. *Child Development*, **60**, 1052–1067.

(1995). Morality in context: Abstractions, ambiguities, and applications. In R. Vasta (ed.), *Annals of child development: Vol. 10* (pp. 83–130). London: Jessica Kingsley.

(2000). Middle-class African American adolescents' and parents' conceptions of parental authority and parenting practices: A longitudinal investigation. *Child Development*, **71**, 1672–1686.

(2002). Culture, autonomy, and personal jurisdiction in adolescent–parent relationships. In H.W. Reese and R. Kail (eds.), *Advances in child development and behavior: Vol. 29* (pp. 51–87). New York: Academic Press.

(2006). Social domain theory: Consistencies and variations in children's moral and social judgments. In M. Killen and J.G. Smetana (eds.), *Handbook of moral development* (pp. 119–154). Mahwah, NJ: Lawrence Erlbaum Associates.

(2008). "It's 10 o'clock: Do you know where your children are?": Recent advances in understanding parental monitoring and child disclosure. *Child Development Perspectives*, **2**, 19–25.

Smetana, J.G. and Asquith, P. (1994). Adolescents' and parents' conceptions of parental authority and adolescent autonomy. *Child Development*, **65**, 1147–1162.

Smetana, J.G. and Chuang, S. (2001). Middle-class African American parents' conceptions of parenting in the transition to adolescence. *Journal of Research on Adolescence*, **11**, 177–198.

Smetana, J.G. and Gaines, C. (1999). Adolescent–parent conflict in middle-class African American families. *Child Development*, **70**, 1447–1463.

Smetana, J.G. and Metzger, A. (2008). Don't ask, don't tell (your mother or father): Disclosure and nondisclosure in parent–adolescent relationships. In M. Kerr, H. Stattin, and R. Engels (eds.), *What can parents do?: New insights into the role of parents in adolescent problem behavior* (pp. 65–87). New York: Wiley.

Smetana, J.G., Campione-Barr, N., and Daddis, C. (2004). Developmental and longitudinal antecedents of family decision-making: Defining health behavioral autonomy for African American adolescents. *Child Development*, **75**, 1418–1434.

Smetana, J.G., Crean, H., and Campione-Barr, N. (2005). Adolescents' and parents' conceptions of parental authority. In J.G. Smetana (ed.), *New directions for child and adolescent development: Changing boundaries of parental authority during adolescence: No. 108* (pp. 31–46). San Francisco: Jossey-Bass.

Smetana, J.G., Metzger, A., Gettman, D.C., and Campione-Barr, N. (2006). Disclosure and secrecy in adolescent–parent relationships. *Child Development*, **77**, 201–217.

Smetana, J.G., Villalobos, M., Tasopoulos-Chan, M., Gettman, D.C., and Campione-Barr, N. (2009). Early and middle adolescents' disclosure to parents about their activities in different domains. *Journal of Adolescence*, **32**, 693–713.

Soenens, B., Vansteenkiste, M., Luyckx, K., and Goossens, L. (2006). Parenting and adolescent problem behavior: An integrated model with adolescent self-disclosure and perceived parental knowledge as intervening variables. *Developmental Psychology*, **42**, 305–318.

Stattin, H. and Kerr, M. (2000). Parental monitoring: A reinterpretation. *Child Development*, **71**, 1072–1085.

Steinberg, L. (1987). Single parents, stepparents, and the susceptibility of adolescents to antisocial peer pressure. *Child Development*, **58**, 269–275.

(1990). Interdependency in the family: Autonomy, conflict, and harmony in the parent–adolescent relationship. In S.S. Feldman and G.R. Elliot (eds.), *At the threshold: The developing adolescent* (pp. 255–276). Cambridge, MA: Harvard University Press.

Steinberg, L. and Silk, J. (2002). Parenting adolescents. In M.H. Bornstein (ed.), *Handbook of parenting: Vol. 1.* (2nd edn.) (pp 103–133). Mahwah, NJ: Lawrence Erlbaum Associates.

Tasopoulos-Chan, M., Smetana, J.G. and Yau, J.Y. (2009). How much do I tell thee? Strategic management of information among American adolescents from Mexican, Chinese, and European backgrounds. *Journal of Family Psychology*, **23**, 364–374.

Turiel, E. (1983). *The development of social knowledge: Morality and convention.* Cambridge University Press.

  (2002). *The culture of morality: Social development, context, and conflict.* Cambridge University Press.

  (2006). The development of morality. In W. Damon, R.M. Lerner (series eds.), and N. Eisenberg (vol. ed.), *Handbook of child psychology: Vol. 3. Social, emotional, and personality development* (6th edn.) (pp. 789–857). New York: Wiley.

Wainryb, C. (2006). Moral development in culture: Diversity, tolerance, and justice. In M. Killen and J.G. Smetana (eds.), *Handbook of moral development* (pp. 211–240). Mahwah, NJ: Lawrence Erlbaum Associates.

Waizenhofer, R.N., Buchanan, and C.M., Jackson-Newsom, J. (2004). Mothers' and fathers' knowledge of adolescents' daily activities: Its sources and its links with adolescent adjustment. *Journal of Marriage and the Family*, **18**, 348–360.

Wentzel, K.R. (1991). Relationships between social competence and academic achievement in early adolescence. *Child Development*, **62**, 1066–1078.

Yau, J.Y., Tasopoulos-Chan, M., and Smetana, J.G. (2009). Disclosure to parents about everyday activities among American adolescents from Mexican, Chinese, and European backgrounds. *Child Development*, **80**, 1481–1498.

Youniss, J. and Smollar, J. (1985). *Adolescents' relations with mothers, fathers, and friends.* University of Chicago Press.

Zimmer-Gembeck, M.J. and Collins, W.A. (2003). Autonomy development during adolescence. In G.R. Adams and M. Berzonsky (eds.), *Blackwell handbook of adolescence* (pp. 175–204). Oxford: Blackwell.

12   A new scale for the assessment of adolescents' trust beliefs

Brandy A. Randall (North Dakota State University),
Ken J. Rotenberg (Keele University),
Casey J. Totenhagen (University of Arizona),
Monica Rock (North Dakota State University), and
Christina Harmon (North Dakota State University)

> *You may be deceived if you trust too much, but you will live in torment*
> *if you do not trust enough.*   Frank Crane

Trust is a key ingredient in the formation and maintenance of healthy interpersonal relationships. According to Rotter (1967), trust is "an expectancy held by an individual or group that the word, promise, or written statement of another individual or group can be relied upon" (p. 651). Interpersonal trust holds a prominent place in theoretical models of development. Erikson described the key developmental task of infancy as that of learning to see others as trustworthy (Erikson, 1963). The infant's trust in the caregiver is believed to be one of the primary bases in the formation of the attachment bond (Bowlby, 1979). Trust remains important across the life-span. Building a new relationship rests, in part, upon the partners' joint ability to trust the other as they engage in a process of reciprocal disclosure of thoughts, feelings, and life experiences (Rempel, Holmes, and Zanna, 1985). Maintenance of relationships also rests upon trust; relationship disintegration frequently results from either a lack of trust (e.g., romantic jealousy) or an outright betrayal of trust (e.g., infidelity) (Collins and Read, 1990; Feeney, 2005; Mikulincer, 1998). Given the significance of trust in the life-course of the individual, continued empirical research charting the developmental progression of interpersonal trust is necessary.

The research presented in this chapter was guided by Rotenberg and his colleagues' interpersonal trust framework (see Rotenberg, 1994, 2001; Rotenberg, Boulton, and Fox, 2005; Rotenberg, Fox, Green, Ruderman, Slater, Stevens, and Carlo, 2005; Rotenberg, MacDonald, and King, 2004; Rotenberg, McDougall, Boulton, Vaillancourt, Fox, and Hymel, 2004), which is described in detail in Chapter 2 of this volume. Briefly, the framework is a 3 bases (reliability, emotional, and honesty) × 2 domains (cognitive and behavior) × 2 target dimensions (specificity and familiarity). The three bases of trust are: (a) reliability, which refers to a person fulfilling his or her word and promise; (b) emotional trust, which refers to a person refraining from causing emotional harm, such as being receptive to disclosures, maintaining confidentiality of disclosures, refraining from criticism, and avoiding acts that elicit embarrassment; and (c) honesty, which refers to a person telling the truth and engaging in behaviors that are guided by benign rather than malicious intent, and by genuine rather than manipulative strategies.

Adolescents hold trust beliefs in relationship partners comprised of cognitive representations (and accompanying affect) of the extent to which the partner maintains confidentiality (emotional), keeps promises (reliability), and tells the truth (honesty). These cognitive representations manifest in trusting behavior such as depending on others to keep promises. A person's trustworthiness is an attribute or disposition that is demonstrated by his/her behaviors, including maintaining confidentiality (e.g., emotionally trustworthy), keeping promises (e.g., reliability trustworthy), and telling the truth (e.g., honesty trustworthy). There is potential dyadic trust for both trust beliefs and trustworthiness, whereby dyadic partners hold trust beliefs that match and their trustworthiness matches, respectively (Betts and Rotenberg, in press). The frameworks for understanding trust beliefs and trustworthiness are similar. Furthermore, an individual's beliefs regarding the trustworthiness of others and his/her own trustworthiness are likely associated (Rotenberg, Fox, and Boulton, 2009). Nevertheless, they are distinct phenomena.

Given the nature of the relationship changes that adolescents experience, trust becomes an increasingly important aspect of relationships across the adolescent period. The function of friends goes through a developmental progression characterized by increasing levels of intimacy and a greater reliance upon friends for emotional support during adolescence (Furman and Buhrmester, 1992). A survey of over a thousand adolescents aged 12 to 19 showed that the majority agreed with statements such as "I'm more myself with my close friends than with my parents" (Youniss and Smollar, 1985). Intimacy-building in the form of self-disclosure, which requires emotional trust, appears to increase by the time adolescents are in the tenth grade (McNelles and Connolly, 1999). Furthermore, the role of intimacy is not limited to friendships. A study of early adolescents showed an increase with age in describing both friendships and romantic relationships as partially characterized by intimacy (including both trust and self-disclosure) (Connolly, Craig, Goldberg, and Pepler, 1999). Thus, by late adolescence, trust is an integral component in the development of intimacy.

Trust also holds a prominent place in forming and maintaining adult relationships, an important feature of emerging adulthood (Collins and van Dulmen, 2006; Tanner, 2006). These relationships are laying the foundations for adult social networks, and for some emerging adults may evolve into more committed relationships, such as marriage. Trust beliefs, which may be fairly consolidated and of long-standing duration by emerging adulthood, should have a key influence on young adults' expectations and behaviors in these more adult-like relationships.

The trust framework does bear on attachment theory, which posits that individuals develop internal working models (IWM) of what relationships in general are like based upon their experiences within specific relationships, and that these IWMs guide behavior (Berlin and Cassidy, 1999). The IWMs together constitute the individual's attachment style, which varies in security. Beliefs about the extent to which others are trustworthy are a critical component of IWMs. Prior research has shown that individuals with a secure attachment style were more likely to hold high trust beliefs in others (Collins and Read, 1990; Feeney, 2005; Mikulincer, 1998). Furthermore, attachment security affects the behaviors individuals use to deal with relationship-related concerns, such as talking with a partner rather than worrying (Mikulincer, 1998). Thus, as one dimension of IWMs, an individual's trust beliefs should be linked to his/her relationship-relevant behaviors, such as communication and conflict patterns, and use of the relationship partner as a source of support, and can be expected to ultimately influence overall relationship quality.

While IWMs are seen as a global construct and individuals do develop a general attachment style, the quality of the attachment with distinct relationship partners may vary. As Thompson (2006) points out, within the domain of attachment research, there is evidence that attachment security is both a general characteristic of the person and a feature of specific relationships in both childhood and adolescence. Thus, while globalized IWMs may guide some behaviors, attachment to a specific individual can have a differential impact on the behavior within that relationship. This is consistent with Rotenberg and his colleagues' framework, which posits that interpersonal trust varies as a function of the target dimensions of specificity and familiarity. Furthermore, the framework permits examination of trust in targets who would not be considered attachment figures (e.g., teachers). The framework is not prescriptive, but does provide a conceptual basis for suggesting that adolescents' trust beliefs are different when they pertain to mothers (a highly familiar and specific target) as compared to adolescents' general peer group (a comparatively less familiar and less specific target). According to the framework, different social histories of reciprocal patterns on trust beliefs, trusting behavior, and trustworthiness account for the difference in adolescents' trust beliefs in those different targets. Related research on intimacy has found little association between young adults' intimacy with parents and with friends, with the exception of a positive correlation between intimacy with mothers and with friends for girls only (Rice and Mulkeen, 1995). Given that trust beliefs pertaining to specific partners arise from differentiated experiences with those partners, it is predicted that target-specific trust beliefs will be differentially correlated with other variables of interest. Specifically, trust beliefs for particular partners (e.g., mothers) are expected to be more closely associated with dimensions of functioning within that relationship than with variables assessing other relationships.

Furthermore, theoretical models emphasize different developmental functions of parents and peers over the course of childhood (e.g., Bowlby, 1979; Sullivan, 1953), and empirical research supports this notion (e.g., Markiewicz, Lawford, Doyle, and Haggart, 2006). Several studies have shown that the quality of particular relationships is differentially linked to specific developmental outcomes (e.g., Carlo, Crockett, Randall, and Roesch, 2007; Crockett and Randall, 2006). Within the arena of trust, Couch and Jones (1997) examined the associations of different types of outcomes with romantic partner trust, friends/family trust, and general trust among college students. They found that general trust linked most closely with measures of personality and emotions, while relationship trust was most strongly associated with relationship outcomes. Examining links between partner-specific trust beliefs and multiple adjustment outcomes will provide a clearer understanding of the role that different relationships play in development.

Trust has been associated with psychosocial adjustment across both childhood and adolescence. For example, researchers have found that children's or adolescents' trust beliefs are positively and linearly associated with honesty (Wright and Kirmani, 1977), low depression (Lester and Gatto, 1990), social status (Buzzelli, 1988), helping (Rotenberg, Fox, Green, Ruderman, Slater, Stevens, and Carlo, 2005), and low loneliness (Hamid and Lok, 2000; Rotenberg, 1994; Rotenberg, MacDonald, and King, 2004). Trust in teachers contributes to adolescents' school adjustment (Lee, 2007). Adolescent trust beliefs for mothers have been linked with lower levels of sexual intercourse and cigarette use (Guilamo-Ramos, Jaccard, Dittus, and Bouris, 2006). The effects on sexual intercourse were primarily through the mechanism of mother–adolescent communication about sexual activity; however, the effects on smoking appeared both through the communication mechanism and independently. Thus, trust beliefs have been implicated in multiple indices of adjustment, contributing to a greater likelihood of positive behaviors and reduced likelihood of negative behaviors.

Given the research findings thus far, it is expected that relationship variables such as loneliness will be most closely associated with trust in peers and romantic partners. Trust in mothers and fathers might also be associated with loneliness, though by emerging adulthood, parents do not fill the same companionship role that similar-age companions fill. In contrast, it is expected that greater trust in mothers, and perhaps fathers, will be associated with reduced levels of deviance and substance use, given the regulatory role that parents have played regarding such behaviors. Finally, it is expected that self-esteem and the tendency to feel positive emotions will be significantly associated with trust in relationship partners, who are more likely to be attachment figures (i.e., parents, peers, romantic partners) than with non-attachment figures (i.e., professors), as the nature of attachment relationships likely lead these individuals to have a more substantial impact on an individual's emotional well-being.

Although the different bases of trust are interrelated, they are not identical. One can believe that a partner is trustworthy on one dimension, but not on others (Rotenberg, Fox, and Boulton, 2009). Beliefs about a partner's trustworthiness with respect to a specific dimension of trust can be expected to predict other variables that are most closely related conceptually to that dimension of trust. For example, an adolescent's beliefs about his/her mother's emotional trustworthiness (i.e., maintaining confidentiality of disclosures) should be more closely tied than the other bases of trust to whether the adolescent discloses intimate details to his/her mother. Similarly, emotional trust should be related to parental monitoring, as there is increasing evidence that monitoring is a function of how much adolescents choose to disclose to their parents (Kerr, Stattin, and Trost, 1999). Kerr *et al.* found that adolescents' spontaneous disclosures to their parents were linked to parents' trust in their adolescent. Feelings of closeness to a parent logically seem to be the most closely associated with a sense that the parent can be trusted emotionally and be trusted to be honest, and reliability might not be related to closeness. Parental reliability and honesty do, however, seem logically linked to a sense that the parent is supportive of the adolescent. These predictions are tentative, given the limited amount of empirical evidence addressing these relations in such a fine-grained manner. Overall, however, a differential pattern of associations between the bases of trust and particular relationship dimensions is to be expected.

In sum, given the significance of trust for interpersonal relationships and the importance of interpersonal relationships during the late adolescent and emerging adult periods, it is critical that researchers have the ability to empirically examine trust during this developmental period. Prior measures of trust suitable for use with late adolescent and emerging adult populations are somewhat limited in that they permit either the examinations of generalized trust beliefs about others in general (e.g., Interpersonal Trust Scale; Rotter, 1967) or are limited to a particular relationship (e.g., Dyadic Trust Scale; Larzelere and Huston, 1980). Furthermore, the three bases of trust described by Rotenberg are not simultaneously assessed in any existing measure for this age group. Other measures are tapping the broader construct of intimacy, limiting the extent to which investigators can assess the specific role trust plays in development (e.g., Blyth and Foster-Clark, 1987). While useful, these measures do not permit more fine-grained analyses, such as comparisons of trust beliefs across distinct targets, particularly as they relate to outcomes of interest. Furthermore, existing measures do not allow for investigation into the correlates of the different bases of trust.

Rotenberg and his colleagues developed the Children's Generalized Trust Beliefs (CGTB) measure, which is a multidimensional self-report measure intended for elementary school children (Rotenberg, Fox, Green, Ruderman, Slater, Stevens, and Carlo, 2005). Items on the CGTB assess the three bases of trust: reliability, honesty, and secret-keeping. Rotenberg et al. have shown the utility of distinguishing between different relationship partners for children's trust beliefs. While global trust beliefs were important, they found that for some behaviors, trust beliefs towards specific types of relationship partners were the most predictive. Empirical investigations into the correlates and consequences of children's trust have been aided by the availability of the CGTB Scale; however, there is still a dearth of measures suitable for adolescents and young adults.

The present study was designed to test the reliability and validity of the Generalized Trust Beliefs-Late Adolescence (GTB-LA) Scale, for use with late adolescents and emerging adults. The measure included the four targets included in the Rotenberg et al. measure for children (i.e., mothers, fathers, peers, and teachers). In addition, a fifth target, romantic partners, was added, due to the increasing importance of romantic relationships in adolescence and emerging adulthood (Furman and Buhrmester, 1992). Psychometric properties of the scale were first examined. Second, relations between trust in specific targets, and several indices of social, emotional, and behavioral functioning were examined. Finally, the unique associations between the three bases of trust and adolescent family processes were examined separately for mothers and fathers.

Method

Participants

Participants were 162 undergraduate college students (137 women, M age = 20.52 years, SD = 2.79, range 18–45 years) at an upper Midwestern state university in the United States. Participants were recruited through class announcements and signs posted on campus. Students could receive extra credit in a participating class or receive $5.

Measures

Generalized Trust Beliefs-Late Adolescence Based on Rotenberg, Fox, Green, Ruderman, Slater, Stevens' and Carlo's (2005) measure of generalized trust beliefs for children, ninety items were written by the primary author and a research team of undergraduate and graduate students. Items were revised until they were judged by the research team to clearly reflect one of the three bases of trust: reliability, emotional, or honesty. Items for the reliability basis assessed beliefs that the target kept promises. Items for the emotional basis assessed beliefs that the target did not disclose a secret. Items for the honesty basis assessed beliefs that the target was truthful. Each item assessed trust beliefs about one of five targets: mother, father, professors, peers, or romantic partners. Six items were included for each base × target, resulting in eighteen items per target.

Each item consisted of a brief description of a situation involving a protagonist and the target of the trust belief. Participants were instructed to imagine that they were the person whose name was underlined for each item and to mark the number that shows what they would believe about how likely it was that the target was trustworthy. Responses were on a five-point scale, ranging from 1 (very unlikely) to 5 (very likely). The story protagonists and the target peers were the same sex as the participant. However, the target romantic partners were the opposite sex to the participant. The items with professors as targets included both men and women.

Family and parenting processes The fifty-item Adolescent Family Process (AFP) measure was used to assess respondents' perceptions of their family and parenting processes when they were seniors in high school (Vazsonyi, Hibbert, and Snider, 2003). Twenty-five items assessed seven subscales separately for mothers and fathers; item wording was identical except for the target. The AFP comprises seven subscales that are designed to tap into three broad domains of family processes: harmony, autonomy, and conflict. Harmony is captured through the closeness, intimate communication, and instrumental communication subscales. Autonomy is captured through the support, monitoring, and peer approval subscales. Conflict is captured by the conflict subscale.

Three subscales (closeness, support, monitoring) were rated on a five-point scale, ranging from 1 (strongly disagree) to 5 (strongly agree). Closeness was assessed by six items (e.g., "My mother gives me the right amount of affection"). Support was assessed by four items (reverse-scored) (e.g., "My mother seems to wish I were a different type of person"). Monitoring was assessed by four items (e.g., "My mother wants to know who I am with when I go out with friends or on a date"). Four subscales (intimate communication, instrumental communication, conflict, and peer approval) were rated on a five-point scale, ranging from 1 (never) to 5 (very often). Intimate communication was assessed by two items (e.g., "How often do you talk to your mother about things that are important to you?"). Instrumental communication was assessed by three items (e.g., "How often do you talk with your mother about problems you have at school?"). Conflict was assessed by three items (e.g., "How often do you have disagreements or arguments with your mother?"). Peer approval was assessed by three items (e.g., "How often does your mother approve of your friends?"). Participants received a subscale score if they answered at least 75 percent of the items.

Loneliness Nine items adapted from the UCLA Loneliness Scale (Russell, Peplau, and Cutrona, 1980) were used to assess loneliness. Participants responded on a five-point scale, ranging from 1 (never) to 5 (always) (e.g., "There is no one I can turn to"). Participants received a scale score if they answered at least 75 percent of the items.

Emotional tone Eleven items from the Self-Image Questionnaire for Young Adolescents (SIQYA; Petersen, Schulenberg, Abramowitz, Offer, and Jarcho, 1984) were used to assess the extent to which respondents experienced positive emotion. Participants responded on a six-point scale, ranging from 1 (very strongly disagree) to 6 (very strongly agree) (e.g., "Most of the time I am happy"). Participants received a scale score if they answered at least 75 percent of the items.

Self-esteem Ten items from the Rosenberg Self-Esteem Scale were used to assess the extent to which respondents had a positive global sense of self (Rosenberg, 1965). Participants responded on a four-point scale, ranging from 1 (strongly disagree) to 4 (strongly agree) (e.g., "I feel that I am a person of worth, at least on an equal plane with others"). Participants received a scale score if they answered at least 75 percent of the items.

Deviance Nine items from the Primary Prevention Awareness, Attitudes, and Usage Scale were used to measure the extent to which participants engaged in deviant behavior (Swisher, Shute, and Bibeau, 1985). Participants responded on a six-point scale, ranging from 1 (never happened) to 6 (happens almost every day or more) (e.g., "Taken things from a store"). Participants received a scale score if they answered at least 75 percent of the items.

Substance use Three items from the Primary Prevention Awareness, Attitudes, and Usage Scale were used to measure the frequency with which participants used tobacco products, alcohol, and drugs (Swisher, Shute, and Bibeau, 1985). Participants responded on a six-point scale, ranging from 1 (never happened) to 6 (happens almost every day or more) (e.g., "been drunk"). Participants received a scale score if they responded to at least two of the three items.

Social desirability A twenty-five-item measure was used to assess the tendency to respond in a socially desirable manner (Crowne and Marlowe, 1964). Participants responded 1 (true) or 2 (false) (e.g., "I have never intensely disliked anyone"). Higher scores indicated a greater tendency to respond in a manner consistent with social expectations. Participants received a scale score if they answered at least 75 percent of the items.

Procedure

Participants completed the self-report survey packet during an experimental session that lasted approximately one hour. Some participants completed the survey during their regular class time. Others signed up for a time to complete the survey individually or in small groups. All sessions were held in university buildings and were conducted by a trained research assistant. Participants were informed that they were participating in a study to examine late adolescents' relationships and behaviors,

assured of anonymity and confidentiality, and their consent to participate was obtained. Participants completed the survey packet with all
measures presented in the same order. Upon completion, participants
were given a letter providing additional details about the study and were
thanked for their participation.

Results

Creation of the final version of the GTB-LA

Initially, ninety items were included on the GTB-LA. Principal components analyses with varimax rotation were computed separately for each
target to eliminate problematic items. A three-factor solution corresponding to the three bases of trust emerged for all targets except romantic partners. Final items were chosen for the mother, father, peers, and
professors subscales by identifying the two items per factor with the highest factor loadings (minimum loading of .30), resulting in six items per
target. The factor analyses were recalculated for each target using only
the six items that were retained for that target. Each factor accounted
for at least 20 percent of the systematic variance, with the overall factor
solutions accounting for at least 65 percent of the systematic variance for
each target.

For the romantic partner subscale, a clear factor solution did not
emerge. Thus, to identify items for the aggregate measure, a reliability
analysis was calculated for each of the bases of trust. The two items with
the highest item-total correlations were chosen to create the aggregate
measure for each of the bases. Thus, the final version of the GTB-LA
contained thirty items (two items per basis for each target, six items per
target, and ten items per basis).

Interrelations among the GTB-LA subscales

The correlations among the subscales of the GTB-LA are presented
in Table 12.1. As can be seen, there were modest positive correlations
among many of the subscales. An examination of the correlations for
each target shows that, with three exceptions, there were significant
positive correlations among the bases for a given target. The subscales
that did not show significant correlations with a target were the professor emotional subscale, which was not significantly correlated with the
professor honesty subscale; and the father emotional subscale, which
was not significantly correlated with either the father reliability or the
father honesty subscale. An examination of the correlations among the

Table 12.1 Intercorrelations among the GTB-LA subscales

	2.	3.	4.	5.	6.	7.	8.	9.	10.	11.	12.	13.	14.	15.
1. M[a] Reli	.35***	.24**	.38***	.44***	.10	.27***	.21**	.06	.36***	.24**	.33***	.22**	.16*	.36***
2. M Hon		.21**	.31***	.53***	.09	.50***	.21**	.05	.25***	.21**	.19*	.38***	.33***	.32***
3. M Emo			.06	.18*	.16*	.09	.20*	.08	.32***	.17*	.19*	.24**	.26***	.28***
4. F[b] Reli				.27***	.11	.33***	.16*	.12	.24**	.19*	.06	.33***	.14	.24**
5. F Hon					.11	.27***	.17*	-.03	.40***	.18*	.38***	.31***	.23**	.26***
6. F Emo						.15	.03	.17*	.02	.03	.09	.10	.06	.20*
7. Peer Reli							.27***	.23**	.14	.18*	.02	.52***	.36***	.30***
8. Peer Hon								.24**	.15	.37***	.05	.30***	.37***	.35***
9. Peer Emo									.10	.26***	.01	.24**	.18*	.32***
10. Prof[c] Rel										.25***	.34***	.27***	.20*	.17*
11. Prof Hon											.13	.16*	.26***	.23**
12. Prof Emo												.16*	.10	.38***
13. RP[d] Rel													.43***	.36***
14. RP Hon														.37***
15. RP Emo														

[a]Mother [b]Father [c]Professor [d]Romantic partner

*p < .05; **p < .01; ***p < .001

Table 12.2 *Correlations between the GTB-LA scale and social, emotional, and behavioral functioning*

	Social desirability	Loneliness	Emotional tone	Deviance	Substance use	Self-esteem
Mother trust	−.20*	−.16	.17*	−.06	−.20*	.16
Father trust	−.01	−.18*	.30***	−.11	−.11	.24**
Peers trust	.07	−.14	.18*	.05	−.20*	.09
Prof trust	−.05	−.18*	.19*	.02	−.08	.11
RP trust	−.06	−.21*	.30***	−.02	−.20*	.20*
Trust total score	−.06	−.23**	.31***	−.03	−.22**	.21*

Notes: *p<.05; **p<.01; ***p<.001

same bases across targets shows that, with four exceptions, there were significant positive correlations between subscales that were designed to tap into the same bases of trust. The exceptions to this were the peer and mother emotional subscales, the father and professor emotional subscales, the peer and professor reliability subscales, and the peer and professor emotional subscales.

Relations of GTB-LA target scores and total score to social, emotional, and behavioral functioning: Evidence for discriminant and convergent validity

Correlations were calculated for each target score and for the trust total score, with measures of socially desirable responding, loneliness, positive emotional tone, deviant behavior, substance use, and self-esteem (see Table 12.2). The GTB-LA does not appear to be tapping into socially desirable response tendencies. Only the mother subscale showed a significant correlation to social desirability, and that correlation was negative as opposed to positive, which would be indicative of a social desirability bias. All the other correlations were non-significant.

Examination of the correlations between trust in different relationship partners and emotions reveals several patterns. Trust in fathers, professors, and romantic partners was significantly negatively related to loneliness, as was the total trust score. Self-esteem was significantly positively correlated with trust in fathers and in romantic partners, as well as with the total trust score. Thus, the pattern of correlations between trust beliefs and both loneliness and self-esteem appeared to vary across partners. In contrast, there were positive correlations between positive emotional tone and trust for all the scores by target, as well as the total trust score.

Two variables that assess the individual's problem behaviors were included: deviance and substance use. Interestingly, there were no significant relationships between deviant behavior and any aspect of trust. In contrast, substance use was significantly negatively correlated with trust in mothers, peers, romantic partners, and the total trust score.

Finally, correlations were calculated for each target score and for the trust total score, with separate dimensions of maternal and paternal parenting (see Table 12.3). Trust in mothers was positively significantly associated with maternal closeness, support, intimate communication, instrumental communication, and peer approval. There was not a significant association between trust in mothers and either maternal monitoring or conflict. Trust in mothers was also significantly positively correlated with paternal peer approval. Trust in fathers was significantly positively associated with paternal closeness, support, intimate communication, instrumental communication, and peer approval, while it was significantly negatively correlated with paternal conflict. Trust in fathers also had a significant positive correlation with maternal closeness and maternal instrumental communication. Interestingly, trust in peers was not significantly correlated with any dimension of either maternal or paternal parenting. However, trust in professors had a significant positive correlation with maternal closeness, maternal support, maternal instrumental communication, maternal peer approval, and paternal peer approval. Trust in romantic partners had a significant positive correlation with maternal closeness, maternal peer approval, and paternal peer approval. The trust total score was significantly positively associated with maternal closeness, maternal support, maternal intimate communication, maternal instrumental communication, maternal peer approval, paternal closeness, paternal support, paternal intimate communication, paternal instrumental communication, and paternal peer approval, while it was negatively associated with paternal conflict.

Relations between the bases of trust and dimensions of family processes

A series of multiple regression analyses were conducted to explore the links between the non-shared variance of three bases of trust for a particular target (either mothers or fathers) and emerging adults' perceptions of that target's behaviors and the relationship. For each regression model, one dimension from the AFP served as the criterion variable and

Table 12.3 Correlations between trust for different targets and dimensions of mother– and father–child relationships

	M Close	M Supp	M Mon	M Int Comm	M Inst Comm	M Conf	M Peer Appr	P Close	P Supp	P Mon	P Int Comm	P Inst Comm	P Conf	P Peer Appr
M[a] Trust	.35***	.26***	.14	.26***	.29***	−.10	.24**	.13	.14	−.01	.12	.11	−.01	.22**
F[b] Trust	.31***	.15	.15	.14	.23**	−.03	.23**	.35***	.28***	.08	.30***	.29***	−.21**	.28***
P[c] Trust	.12	.02	.01	.03	.08	.01	.14	.06	.15	−.09	.11	.09	−.07	.07
Prof[d] Trust	.21**	.21**	.14	.15	.18*	−.03	.27***	.08	.13	.04	.09	.07	−.07	.24**
RP[e] Trust	.21**	.14	.04	.12	.12	−.09	.26***	.14	.10	−.07	.10	.11	−.12	.28***
Trust total	.32***	.21**	.12	.19*	.24**	−.06	.31***	.20*	.21**	−.02	.19*	.18*	−.13	.29***

Notes: [a]Mother [b]Father [c]Peer [d]Professor [e]Romantic partner

M = maternal; P = paternal; Close = closeness; Supp = support; Mon = monitoring; Int Comm = intimate communication;

Inst Comm = instrumental communication; Conf = conflict; Appr = approval

*p < .05; **p < .01; ***p < .001

the three bases of trust for that target were the predictor variables (see Tables 12.4 and 12.5).

Reliability trust in mothers and honesty trust in mothers were significant positive predictors of maternal closeness; a similar pattern emerged for reliability trust in fathers and honesty trust in fathers with paternal closeness. Reliability trust in mothers and reliability trust in fathers were significant positive predictors of maternal and paternal support respectively; honesty trust in fathers was an additional significant positive predictor of paternal support. Reliability trust in mothers was a significant positive predictor of maternal monitoring. In contrast, honesty trust in fathers was a significant positive predictor and emotional trust in fathers was a significant negative predictor of paternal monitoring. Emotional trust in mothers was a significant positive predictor of maternal intimate communication. Reliability trust in fathers was a significant positive predictor of paternal intimate communication. Reliability trust in mothers and reliability trust in fathers were significant positive predictors of maternal and paternal instrumental communication respectively. Emotional trust in mothers was significantly negatively associated with maternal conflict; none of the three bases significantly predicted paternal conflict. Reliability trust in mothers was a significant positive predictor of maternal peer approval, while honesty trust in fathers was a significant positive predictor of paternal peer approval.

Discussion

The present findings provide evidence that the GTB-LA can serve as a tool for assessing generalized trust beliefs in late adolescence. While further refinement of the scale is needed, the measure has adequate psychometric properties to allow researchers to begin exploring the correlates of trust beliefs across five targets and three bases of trust. The results also build upon the prior work of Rotenberg and his colleagues that demonstrated the usefulness of examining children's trust beliefs in a more differentiated way, and extend this to the late adolescence/emerging adulthood period.

Trust for some partners was associated with specific indices of well-being, as evidenced by the positive correlations between trust in some (but not all) partners and loneliness and self-esteem. However, trust in all partners was significantly associated with having a positive emotional tone, suggesting that trusting others with whom one is in relationship, regardless of the particular type of relationship, may contribute to a general sense of well-being. However, it is also possible that the reverse is true, namely, that positive emotional states contribute to a greater feeling

Table 12.4 *Regression analyses predicting dimensions of mother–child relationships using the three bases of trust*

	Maternal closeness b SE	Maternal support b SE	Maternal monitoring b SE	Maternal intimate communication b SE	Maternal instrumental communication b SE	Maternal conflict b SE	Maternal peer approval b SE
Reliability (mother)	.13** .05	.13* .06	.21** .07	.11 .07	.16* .07	−.01 .06	.12* .05
Honesty (mother)	.07* .03	−.02 .04	.03 .04	.03 .05	.05 .05	.03 .04	.03 .03
Emotional (mother)	.04 .03	.13** .04	−.07 .05	.11* .05	.08+ .05	−.09* .04	.04 .03
R squared	.13***	.10***	.08**	.08**	.09**	.04+	.07**

Notes: $*p < .05$; $**p < .01$; $***p < .001$

Table 12.5 *Regression analyses predicting dimensions of father–child relationships using the three bases of trust*

	Paternal closeness b SE	Paternal support b SE	Paternal monitoring b SE	Paternal intimate communication b SE	Paternal instrumental communication b SE	Paternal conflict b SE	Paternal peer approval b SE
Reliability (father)	.16*** .05	.14** .05	.08 .07	.20** .06	.25*** .06	-.09+ .05	.09+ .05
Honesty (father)	.12** .04	.09* .04	.12* .05	.09+ .05	.09+ .05	-.08+ .04	.10* .04
Emotional (father)	.02 .04	.01 .04	-.10* .05	.04 .05	-.01 .05	-.01 .04	.05 .04
R squared	.16***	.10***	.07*	.11***	.14***	.06*	.09**

Notes: $*p < .05$; $**p < .01$; $***p < .001$

of trust. Dunn and Schweitzer (2005) demonstrated that experimentally induced positive emotional states increase trust. Whether a similar process plays out in ongoing relationships remains to be seen.

Trust does appear to contribute to several aspects of adjustment, though trust in all relationship targets was not associated significantly with all outcomes. Trust beliefs for mothers, romantic partners, and peers were negatively associated with substance use. The extensive literature on substance use indicates that some substance use takes the form of "self-medication" for negative emotional states (e.g., Bolton, Cox, Clara, and Sareen, 2006). As noted, trust in fathers, professors, and romantic partners was negatively associated with loneliness. The associations found in the present study suggest the intriguing possibility that diminished or nonexistent trust in one's relationship partners may be a contributing factor to the kinds of negative emotional states that may precipitate substance use. Interestingly, however, trust was unrelated to deviance. Further research to disentangle the processes via which trust may be associated with some problem behaviors, but not others, is clearly warranted.

Target-specific trust beliefs are developed primarily through experience with that relationship partner; thus, it was predicted that target-specific trust beliefs would be associated with particular aspects of relationship functioning for that partner. Additional evidence for the utility of the GTB-LA is provided by examination of the correlations between specific targets (e.g., mother) and indices of family functioning. Notably, trust beliefs for mothers were mostly closely related to indices of maternal behavior and of the quality of the maternal relationship, with a similar pattern seen for fathers. There were few significant associations between trust beliefs and indices of functioning across partners. It is not wholly unexpected that a few such cross-partner associations with functioning would appear, given the potential for rater bias. However, the majority of the significant associations were between the trust beliefs and aspects of family functioning for the same target. Furthermore, all significant correlations were in the expected direction, with trust beliefs positively related to indices of healthy parental functioning and negatively related to indices of problematic parental functioning.

The bulk of the research literature examines trust as a unidimensional construct. However, as Rotenberg, Fox, Green, Ruderman, Slater, Stevens, and Carlo (2005) have argued, trust beliefs are, in fact, a composite of beliefs across different aspects of trust. Thus, examining links between the three bases of trust measured by the GTB-LA (i.e., reliability, honesty, and emotional) and other constructs of interest can provide insight into the role that particular types of experiences may play in forming specific types of trust beliefs, as well as the contribution that each of the three bases of trust may make to development. An interesting pattern emerged when examining the links between the three bases of trust beliefs towards parents and emerging adults' perceptions of particular features of their relationship with their parents. For both mothers and fathers, reliability emerged as the trust basis most frequently associated with parenting. The association was significant for five of the seven maternal variables and four of the paternal variables. Conceptually, reliability trust rests upon an individual matching his/her words and actions, and is the most overt of the three bases of trust. Reliability trust may also, to a greater extent than the other bases of trust, be built upon reciprocity between the partners. Thus, the association between maternal monitoring and reliability trust for the mother may result, in part, from the mother's trust in the adolescent. Regardless, reliability trust is important across a range of parent–late adolescent relationship variables for both mothers and fathers.

The pattern for the other two bases of trust – emotional and honesty – though not consistent across parents, was informative. Emotional trust for mothers was associated with three of the mother relationship variables, and honesty was only significantly associated with one. This pattern was reversed for fathers, with emotional trust associated with a single father relationship variable, and honesty associated with four. This pattern is not surprising when one considers the rich literature demonstrating that the line of emotional communication is stronger with mothers than it is with fathers (e.g., Holmbeck, Paikoff, and Brooks-Gunn, 1995). Moreover, the sample for the present study was drawn from a region of the United States with a strong Scandinavian tradition emphasizing stoicism, particularly for men. This may discourage the sorts of exchanges that would build emotional trust for fathers. Adolescents who are lacking such exchanges are likely more dependent on observing the overt behaviors of parents, especially fathers, to build a sense over time of their parents as trustworthy in specific ways, leading some bases of trust to carry greater weight overall. Exploring issues such as this can shed light upon the dynamic processes through which trust beliefs develop over time.

Thus, the present study demonstrated the usefulness of the GTB-LA for examining trust beliefs across five targets. This research also highlighted a number of distinctive associations between trust beliefs for particular targets and indices of adjustment and well-being. Finally, it was shown that examining the links between specific bases of trust and aspects of relationship functioning revealed interesting patterns that can inform future research. Although the measure is in need of further refinement, continuing to explore these associations with additional samples will show whether trust beliefs are consistently linked with adjustment in the ways found here. Furthermore, utilizing samples from other geographical areas can clarify whether the associations observed for mothers and fathers derived from the relatively strong gender role norms of the region. Research is also needed that examines the links between the quality of the attachment relationship and trust beliefs for specific partners. Finally, longitudinal investigations are needed that track change and stability in trust beliefs over time, utilizing measures that assess the multifaceted aspects of trust in an age-appropriate way. Such lines of research will allow us to chart the developmental course for trust beliefs as they emerge in particular relationships in a dynamic and changing process.

References

Berlin, L. J. and Cassidy J. (1999). Relations among relationships: Contributions from attachment theory and research. In J. Cassidy and P. R. Shaver (eds.), *Handbook of attachment: Theory, research, and clinical applications* (pp. 688–712). New York: Guilford Press.

Betts, L. R. and Rotenberg, K. J. (in press). A social relations analysis of children's trust in their peers across the early years. *Social Development*.

Blyth, D. A. and Foster-Clark, F. S. (1987). Gender differences in perceived intimacy with different members of adolescents' social networks. *Sex Roles*, **17**, 689–718.

Bolton, J., Cox, B, Clara, I., and Sareen, J. (2006). Use of alcohol and drugs to self-medicate anxiety disorders in a nationally representative sample. *Journal of Nervous and Mental Disease*, **194**, 818–825.

Bowlby, J. (1979). *The making and breaking of affectional bonds*. London: Tavistock Publications.

Buzzelli, C. A. (1988). The development of trust in children's relations with peers. *Child Study Journal*, **18**, 33–46.

Carlo, G., Crockett, L. J., Randall, B. A., and Roesch, S. C. (2007). Parent and peer correlates of prosocial development in rural adolescents: A longitudinal study. *Journal of Research on Adolescence*, **17**, 301–324.

Collins, N. L. and Read, S. J. (1990). Adult attachment, working models, and relationship quality in dating couples. *Journal of Personality and Social Psychology*, **58**, 644–663.

Collins, W. A. and van Dulmen, M. (2006). Friendships and romance in emerging adulthood: Assessing distinctiveness in close relationships. In J. J. Arnett and J. L. Tanner (eds.), *Emerging adults in America: Coming of age in the 21st century* (pp. 219–234). Washington, DC: American Psychological Association.

Connolly, J., Craig, W., Goldberg, A., and Pepler, D. (1999). Conceptions of cross-sex friendships and romantic relationships in early adolescence. *Journal of Youth and Adolescence*, **28**, 481–494.

Couch, L.L. and Jones, W.H. (1997). Measuring levels of trust. *Journal of Research in Personality*, **31**, 319–336.

Crockett, L.J. and Randall, B.A. (2006). Linking adolescent family and peer relationships to the quality of young adult romantic relationships: The mediating role of relationship behaviors. *Journal of Social and Personal Relationships*, **23**, 761–780.

Crowne, D.P. and Marlowe, D. (1964). *The approval motive*. New York: Wiley.

Dunn, J.R. and Schweitzer, M.E. (2005). Feeling and believing: The influence of emotion on trust. *Journal of Personality and Social Psychology*, **88**, 736–748.

Erikson, E.H. (1963). *Childhood and society*. New York: W.W. Norton & Company.

Feeney, J.A. (2005). Hurt feelings in couple relationships: Exploring the role of attachment and perceptions of personal injury. *Personal Relationships*, **12**, 253–271.

Furman, W. and Buhrmester, D. (1992). Age and sex differences in perceptions of networks of personal relationships. *Child Development*, **63**, 103–115.

Guilamo-Ramos, V., Jaccard, J., Dittus, P., and Bouris, A.M. (2006). Parental expertise, trustworthiness, and accessibility: Parent–adolescent communication and adolescent risk behavior. *Journal of Marriage and Family*, **68**, 1229–1246.

Hamid, P.N. and Lok, D.P.P. (2000). Loneliness in Chinese adolescents: A comparison of social support and interpersonal trust in 13- to 19-year-olds. *International Journal of Adolescence and Youth*, **8**, 45–63.

Holmbeck, G., Paikoff, R.L., and Brooks-Gunn, J. (1995). Parenting adolescents. In M.H. Bornstein (ed.), *Handbook of parenting: Vol. 1* (pp. 91–118). Mahwah, NJ: Lawrence Erlbaum Associates.

Kerr, M., Stattin, H., and Trost, K. (1999). To know you is to trust you: Parents' trust is rooted in child disclosure of information. *Journal of Adolescence*, **22**, 737–752.

Larzelere, R.E. and Huston, T.L. (1980). The Dyadic Trust Scale: Toward understanding interpersonal trust in close relationships. *Journal of Marriage and the Family*, **42**, 595–604.

Lee, S. (2007). The relations between the student–teacher trust relationship and school success in the case of Korean middle schools. *Educational Studies*, **33** (2), 209–216.

Lester, D. and Gatto, J. (1990). Interpersonal trust, depression, and suicidal ideation in teenagers. *Psychological Reports*, **67**, 786.

Markiewicz, D., Lawford, H., Doyle, A.B., and Haggart, N. (2006). Developmental differences in adolescents' and young adults' use of mothers, fathers, best friends, and romantic partners to fulfill attachment needs. *Journal of Youth and Adolescence*, **35**, 127–140.

McNelles, L.R. and Connolly, J.A. (1999). Intimacy between adolescent friends: Age and gender differences in intimate affect and intimate behaviors. *Journal of Research on Adolescence*, **9**, 143–159.

Mikulincer, M. (1998). Attachment working models and the sense of trust: An exploration of interaction goals and affect regulation. *Journal of Personality and Social Psychology*, **74**, 1209–1224.

Petersen, A.C., Schulenberg, J., Abramowitz, R., Offer, D., and Jarcho, H. (1984). A Self-Image Questionnaire for Young Adolescents (SIQYA): Reliability and validity studies. *Journal of Youth and Adolescence*, **13**, 93–110.

Rempel, J.K., Holmes, J.G. and Zanna, M.P. (1985). Trust in close relationships. *Journal of Personality and Social Psychology*, **49**, 95–112.

Rice, K.G. and Mulkeen, P. (1995). Relationships with parents and peers: A longitudinal study of adolescent intimacy. *Journal of Adolescent Research*, **10**, 338–357.

Rosenberg, M. (1965). *Society and the adolescent self-image*. Princeton University Press.

Rotenberg, K.J. (1994). Loneliness and interpersonal trust. *Journal of Social and Clinical Psychology*, **13**, 152–173.

(2001). Trust across the life-span. In Neil J. Smelser and Paul B. Baltes (eds.), *International encyclopedia of the social and behavioral sciences* (pp. 7866–7868). New York: Pergamon.

Rotenberg, K.J., Boulton, M.J., and Fox, C.L. (2005). Cross-sectional and longitudinal relations among children's trust beliefs, psychological maladjustment and social relationships: Are very high as well as very low trusting children at risk? *Journal of Abnormal Child Psychology*, **33**, 595–610.

Rotenberg, K.J., Fox, C., and Boulton, M. (2009). The cross-sectional and longitudinal relations between the coherence of interpersonal trust and psychosocial functioning during childhood. Manuscript submitted for publication.

Rotenberg, K.J., Fox, C., Green, S., Ruderman, L., Slater, K., Stevens, K., and Carlo, G. (2005). Construction and validation of a children's interpersonal trust belief scale. *British Journal of Developmental Psychology*, **23**, 271–292.

Rotenberg, K.J., MacDonald, K.J., and King, E.V. (2004). The relationship between loneliness and interpersonal trust during middle childhood. *Journal of Genetic Psychology*, **165**, 233–249.

Rotenberg, K.J., McDougall, P., Boulton, M.J., Vaillancourt, T., Fox, C., and Hymel, S. (2004). Cross-sectional and longitudinal relations among peer-reported trustworthiness, social relationships, and psychological adjustment in children and early adolescents from the United Kingdom and Canada. *Journal of Experimental Child Psychology*, **88**, 46–67.

Rotter, J.B. (1967). A new scale for the measurement of interpersonal trust. *Journal of Personality*, **35**, 651–665.

Russell, D., Peplau, L.A., and Cutrona, C.E. (1980). The revised UCLA Loneliness Scale: Concurrent and discriminant validity evidence. *Journal of Personality and Social Psychology*, **39**, 472–480.

Sullivan, H.S. (1953). *The interpersonal theory of psychiatry*. New York: W.W. Norton & Company.

Swisher, J.D., Shute, R.E., and Bibeau, D. (1984). Assessing drug and alcohol abuse: An instrument for planning and evaluation. *Measurement and Evaluation in Counseling and Development*, **17**, 91–97.

Tanner, J.L. (2006). Recentering during emerging adulthood: A critical turning point in life span human development. In J.J. Arnett and J.L. Tanner (eds.), *Emerging adults in America: Coming of age in the 21st century* (pp. 21–55). Washington, DC: American Psychological Association.

Thompson, R.A. (2006). The development of the person: Social understanding, relationships, self, conscience. In W. Damon, R.M. Lerner (series eds.), and N. Eisenberg (vol. ed.), *Handbook of child psychology: Vol. 3. Social, emotional, and personality development* (6th edn.) (pp. 24–98). New York: Wiley.

Vazsonyi, A.T., Hibbert, J.R., and Snider, J.B. (2003). Exotic enterprise no more? Adolescent reports of family and parenting processes from youth in four countries. *Journal of Research on Adolescence*, **13**, 129–160.

Wright, T.L. and Kirmani, A. (1977). Interpersonal trust, trustworthiness, and shoplifting in high school. *Psychological Reports*, **41**, 1165–1166.

Youniss, J. and Smollar, J. (1985). *Adolescent relations with mothers, fathers, and friends*. University of Chicago Press.

13 A friend in need is a friend indeed: Exploring the relations among trust beliefs, prosocial tendencies, and friendships

*Gustavo Carlo (University of Nebraska-Lincoln),
Brandy A. Randall (North Dakota State University),
Ken J. Rotenberg (Keele University), and
Brian E. Armenta (University of Nebraska-Lincoln)*

> *Caring, as helping another grow and actualize himself, is a process, a way of relating to someone that involves development, in the same way that friendship can only emerge in time through mutual trust and a deepening and qualitative transformation of the relationship.*
>
> (Mayeroff, 1971, p. 1)

The recent movement in positive psychology has beckoned a call for more attention to the strengths and positive aspects of human functioning (Seligman and Csikszentmihalyi, 2000). Much of the intellectual basis for this recent movement in psychology stems from a reemergence of an interest in philosophical perspectives on what constitutes a good and moral life. Not surprisingly, scholars have long noted that prosocial tendencies (e.g., kindness, caring, helping) and trust are basic elements of persons with strong moral and good character (e.g., Aristotle, 1980; Blum, 1980; Mayeroff, 1971; Noddings, 2003; Rotter, 1980). The belief that trust and prosocial tendencies are basic elements of moral character also extends the notion that these are markers of close, interpersonal relationships. As Bukowski and Sippola (1996) noted, "particular qualities are essential for 'morally excellent' friendships. These qualities include: (a) a deep concern for the other for his or her own sake ... (c) high levels of trust and commitment to the relationship" (p. 245). These authors further assert that there are conceptual reasons to expect ties between trust and prosocial tendencies – that, indeed, friendship requires goodness.

In his classic essay, *On caring*, Milton Mayeroff (1971) eloquently introduces to us the intricate links between caring, helping, trust, and interpersonal relationships. Mayeroff further asserts that when people grow through caring, they must trust others so that they may open themselves to positive change. As many other scholars have noted, caring, trust, and helping are core aspects of human functioning that serve to promote and maintain individual and social well-being (Bernath and Feshbach, 1995; Carlo and Randall, 2001; DeNeve and Cooper, 1998; Maslow, 1973; Rotenberg, 1991, 1995; Rotenberg and Cerda, 1995; Rotter, 1967). Moreover, attachment and psychosocial theorists noted the central importance of trust relationships in early childhood in establishing precedence for children's social functioning throughout the course of development (Ainsworth, 1973; Erikson, 1963; Thompson, 2006). As Bernath and Feshbach (1995) asserted, responsive caregivers provide a sense of trust for children that establishes a basis for future positive social interactions, including benevolence and cooperation with peers. From these various philosophical and psychological perspectives, there is a growing recognition of the role of trust and prosocial tendencies to positive human functioning and well-being (Carlo, 2006). However, our understanding of the links between trust and prosocial tendencies is limited by the relative lack of empirical research on this topic. The present chapter aims to critically examine the relations between trust and prosocial tendencies.

In the first section of the chapter, we will briefly present two recently developed frameworks of trust and prosocial behaviors. In the second section, we will explore the conceptual and empirical bases of the relations between trust and prosocial behaviors and present preliminary findings from an ongoing investigation designed to examine those links. Finally, in the third and final section of the chapter, we will summarize and discuss future directions in this area of study.

Trust framework and measurement

Although there are several conceptual frameworks on trust, the current chapter and investigation described within was guided by Rotenberg's trust model (outlined in detail in Chapter 2 of this volume). Briefly, the model prescribes that there are three bases of trust (reliability, emotionality, and honesty), three domains of trust (cognitive/affective, behavior-dependent and behavior-enacting) and two dimensions of the target of trust (familiarity and generality). This framework guided the development of the Children's Generalized Trust Belief scale (CGTB; Rotenberg, Fox, Green, Ruderman, Slater, Stevens, and Carlo, 2005) that assesses the three bases of trust across and for four modestly familiar and general target groups (i.e., mother, father, teachers, and peers). Rotenberg, Fox, Green, Ruderman, Slater, Stevens, and Carlo (2005) presented evidence for the reliability and validity of the CGTB. More recently, Randall and her colleagues have developed the Generalized Trust Beliefs-Late Adolescence (GTB-LA) Scale, which is described in more detail in Chapter 12. In the present investigation, the GTB-LA Scale is used to examine the relations between trust and prosocial behaviors.

Models and measurement of prosocial behaviors

Interest in understanding the development and correlates of prosocial behaviors (i.e., behaviors primarily intended to benefit others) continues to flourish. In recent years, the emphasis on positive human characteristics and strengths has served to enliven the scrutiny of such behaviors (see Carlo, 2006). Scholars have often noted the importance of understanding behaviors that benefit society, but surprisingly few measures are currently available for studying prosocial behaviors. While some measures do exist, these have typically been characterized by a conceptualization of prosocial behavior as a global construct. However, investigators have shown that there are different types of prosocial behaviors and that these types are related differently to theoretically related constructs (see Batson, 1998; Eisenberg and Fabes, 1998; Staub, 1978).

Most measures of prosocial behavior can be classified into one of at least two categories – those that assess global prosocial behaviors or those that assess prosocial behavior in a specific situation. The most common measures of prosocial behaviors are those that were designed to assess global prosocial behavioral tendencies. Global prosocial behavior measures are defined as measures that assess personal tendencies to exhibit a number of prosocial behaviors across contexts and motives (e.g., Green, Shirk, Hanze, and Wanstrath, 1994; Johnson, Danko, Darvill, Bochner, Bowers, Huang, Park, Pecjack, Rahim, and Pennington, 1989; Rushton, Chrisjohn, and Fekken, 1981; Weir and Duveen, 1981). Related to these global measures of prosocial behaviors are measures used to assess the broader construct of social competence or aspects of social competence (e.g., Ladd and Profilet, 1996; Rydell, Hagekull, and Bohlin, 1997). The second type of prosocial behavior measure is an assessment of prosocial behaviors in specific contexts. These assessments are often behavioral observations of helping opportunities (e.g., picking up dropped items, donating money) designed for specific studies – often experimental in nature. Although evidence for the reliability and validity of global and situation-specific measures of prosocial behaviors has been presented, there are reasons to believe that there is limited utility to both assessment approaches.

Global prosocial behavior measures are limited because prior researchers have shown that there are different types of prosocial behaviors and that each of these types has different personal and situational correlates (Eisenberg, Fabes, and Spinrad, 2006). The use of global, rather than situation-specific, assessments of prosocial behaviors has been presented as one possible explanation for prior weak and inconsistent relations between socio-cognitive and socio-emotional variables and prosocial behaviors (Eisenberg, 1986). Thus, global measures of prosocial behavior might limit investigators' ability to address specific conceptual questions regarding the correlates of prosocial behaviors.

In contrast, situation-specific prosocial behavior measures are useful in addressing specific conceptual questions about the development and correlates of different types of prosocial behaviors. Furthermore, observational and behavioral assessments of these behaviors might be considered more ecologically valid than paper-and-pencil measures. However, there are potential limitations to the use of these measures. First, as is true for all observational techniques, these measures are susceptible to observer and coding biases. Second, behavioral and observational approaches might be costly in time and sometimes preclude the assessment of prosocial behaviors in applied settings and of data collection from large samples. And third, evidence of the psychometric qualities of these types of measures is sometimes limited to the evidence presented in the particular study for which it was designed. Researchers have pointed out that standardization of measures is necessary to enable researchers to compare and integrate findings across studies. Therefore, a paper-and-pencil measure of prosocial behavior was constructed and designed to assess different types of prosocial behaviors in a standardized format.

Development of a Prosocial Tendencies Measure (PTM)

Based on prior theory and research, Carlo and Randall (2001) developed a typology of prosocial behaviors that guided the development of a measure designed to assess six types of prosocial behaviors: altruistic, dire, compliant, emotional, anonymous, and public. One set of prosocial behaviors that has stirred much interest in the philosophical and social science literature is altruism (Batson, 1991; Bierhoff, 2002; Dovidio, Piliavin, Schroeder, and Penner, 2006). Altruistic prosocial behavior refers to voluntary helping behavior motivated primarily by concern for the needs and welfare of another, often induced by sympathy responding and internalized norms/principles consistent with helping others (Carlo, 2006; Eisenberg and Fabes, 1998; Staub, 2005). These behaviors often incur a cost to the helper and the helper usually does not anticipate self-reward.

Although scholars have debated whether altruism exists (see Batson, 1991), there are several lines of research that support this notion. First, scholars have presented evidence on the personality characteristics of moral and care exemplars (individuals who have been identified as exhibiting strong moral character and action) (Colby and Damon, 1992; Hart and Fegley, 1995; Oliner and Oliner, 1988). Second, investigators have reported that personality variables (e.g., sympathy, perspective-taking, social responsibility, moral reasoning) predict prosocial behaviors across contexts and under selflessly motivated conditions (Carlo and Randall, 2002; Carlo, Eisenberg, Troyer, Switzer, and Speer, 1991; Carlo, Hausmann, Christiansen, and Randall, 2003; Dovidio, Piliavin, Schroeder, and Penner, 2006; Eisenberg, Miller, Schaller, Fabes, Fultz, Shell, and Shea, 1989; Laible, Eye, and Carlo, in press; Staub, 2005). Third, animal behavior researchers have presented evidence for the existence of altruism across several species of social animals (de Waal, 1996). And fourth, in humans, evidence on the genetic heritability, biological basis, and longitudinal stability of empathy and prosocial behaviors has been reported (Carlo, Crockett, Randall, and Roesch, 2007; Davis and Franzoi, 1991; Lamm, Batson, and Decety, 2007; see also Eisenberg and Fabes, 1998) – although altruism per se has been not been examined in these studies. Taken together, however, these studies are consistent with ethological perspectives that altruism is an evolutionarily adaptive behavior necessary for the survival of the human genetic pool (de Waal, 1996; Wilson, 1978).

A second common form of prosocial behavior is compliant prosocial behavior, or helping when asked to help (Eisenberg, Cameron, Tryon, and Dodez, 1981). Children and adolescents are often asked to help by parents and teachers, as well as by peers. Although there is some evidence that compliant helping behaviors occur relatively frequently (Carlo, Hausmann, Christiansen, and Randall, 2003), research on compliant prosocial behaviors is sparse. One might expect that children who exhibit defiant and oppositional behaviors would be less likely to engage in helping when asked to help, and there is recent evidence to support this notion (Carlo, Knight, McGinley, Zamboanga, and Jarvis, in press). Furthermore, investigators have shown that elementary school children who frequently engage in compliant prosocial behavior are relatively nonassertive (Eisenberg, 1986). In early adolescence, investigators have shown that compliant helpers are less hedonistic and score relatively high on perspective-taking, social responsibility, and sympathy (Carlo, Hausmann, Christiansen, and Randall, 2003). Other researchers have yielded evidence that compliant helping is associated with high levels of moral reasoning, sympathy, perspective-taking, and social responsibility in late adolescents (Carlo and Randall, 2002).

A third form of helping involves opportunities that present themselves when the situation is emotionally charged. For example, a child who has hurt his or her arm, is crying, and is bleeding, is more emotionally evocative than a child who has hurt his or her arm but shows little or no distress or injury. Under those circumstances, some individuals respond benevolently, whereas others might become overwhelmed by the situation and exhibit personal distress (Eisenberg, Shea, Carlo, and Knight, 1991). Such circumstances define emotional prosocial behaviors. A number of other factors (e.g., relationship to the needy other, perceived similarity) might influence the level of emotional evocativeness, and, in turn, perceived emotional evocativeness might influence the observer's emotional responses. These emotional evocative tendencies have been linked to emotion regulation skills (Eisenberg, Fabes, Carlo, and Karbon, 1992) and to selfless and egoistic modes of helping. In general, however, helping in highly emotionally evocative situations would be expected to be strongly associated with sympathy responding and other-oriented personal tendencies (e.g., perspective-taking and higher-level, empathic modes of moral reasoning) (Carlo and Randall, 2002; Carlo, Allen, and Buhman, 1999; Carlo, Hausmann, Christiansen, and Randall, 2003).

Carlo and his colleagues identified a fourth form of helping: public prosocial behaviors. Prosocial behaviors exhibited in front of others are likely to be motivated, at least in part, by a desire to gain the approval and respect of others (e.g., parents, peers) and enhance one's self-worth. This set of prosocial behaviors, although motivated by egoistic desires, might result in benefits for others, and is referred to as public prosocial behaviors (Carlo and Randall, 2001). Previous studies have shown that helping is more likely to occur when one's actions are conducted in front of an audience (but see the research on bystander intervention in emergency situations for exceptions; Latané and Darley, 1970). Thus, unlike altruism, one might expect a different pattern of relations regarding public, as compared to other types, of prosocial behaviors. Carlo and Randall (2002) reported that public prosocial behaviors were associated with lower levels of perspective-taking, sympathy, moral reasoning, and personal responsibility. Interestingly, such relations were not found when examined in early and middle adolescents (Carlo, Hausmann, Christiansen, and Randall, 2003), suggesting that there might be relevant age-graded mechanisms. That is, perhaps public prosocial behaviors might not require higher levels of socio-cognitive skills, as compared to other forms of helping. This notion requires further research.

Two other sets of prosocial behaviors were identified: dire and anonymous prosocial behaviors (Carlo and Randall, 2001). There is a substantial literature on prosocial behaviors in emergency bystander situations

(Latané and Darley, 1970). These scholars convincingly demonstrated the role of situational factors in determining prosocial behaviors in crisis and potentially dire circumstances. However, although the bulk of the studies have examined situational factors associated with dire helping, studies examining socio-cognitive and socio-emotive correlates of dire helping are needed to account for individual differences in responding to situational factors. Finally, one of the most common occurrences of prosocial action is when individuals donate money or gifts anonymously for charity. Frequent occurrences of anonymous helping are when there are local, national, or international disasters or other tragedies (such as hurricanes, tsunamis, earthquakes). In these situations, individuals assist others without revealing their identity. Although such behaviors are very common, the personal variables and environmental conditions for predicting such behaviors are little understood.

Thus, six different forms of prosocial behaviors have been identified: altruistic, compliant, emotional, public, dire, and anonymous. Although some overlap might exist between different forms of prosocial behaviors, the overlap is expected to be modest. Furthermore, under specific circumstances, one might expect that a tendency to behave in one set of prosocial actions does not necessarily predict other forms of prosocial behavior. In a recent study, Carlo, Knight, McGinley, Zamboanga, and Jarvis (in press) showed that a six-factor solution of the PTM-R (the version for early adolescents) showed adequate fit in European and Mexican American early adolescents. Additional evidence on the validity of the six types of prosocial behaviors, as assessed in the PTM, has been demonstrated in several studies of adolescents (e.g., Carlo and Randall, 2002; Carlo, Hausmann, Christiansen, and Randall, 2003; Carlo, McGinley, Hayes, Batenhorst, and Wilkinson, 2007).

Relations between trust and the types of prosocial behaviors

Conceptually, there are at least two mechanisms that can help explain why trust ought to be associated with prosocial behaviors: cognitive schema and social interaction processes. These processes stem from social information-processing and social interaction models of behavior and have been used to explain a wide range of actions.

Cognitive schema mechanism

Trust beliefs serve as a cognitive schema comprising an individual's representation of social relationships that affects their interpretation of social interactions (Rotenberg, MacDonald, and King, 2004). Individuals who hold low trust beliefs represent others as unreliable, emotionally untrust-worthy, and dishonest – a "malevolent" cognitive schema. By contrast, individuals who hold high trust beliefs represent others as reliable, emo-tionally trustworthy, and honest – a "benevolent" cognitive schema (see Rotenberg, Michalik, Eisenberg, and Betts, 2007). According to the framework, cognitive honesty basis is belief that a person is telling the truth and engaging in behaviors that are guided by benign rather than malicious intent, and by genuine rather than manipulative strategies. Children's cognitive schema of trust is developed from interactions with significant social relationships, notably their mothers (see Rotenberg, 1995), consistent with attachment theory (see Armsden and Greenberg, 1987; Waters, Vaughn, Posada, and Kondo-Ikemura, 1995).

The honesty basis of trust beliefs may be the most critical basis of trust for prosocial behavior according to the cognitive mechanism. When confronted by a person who is in need and suffering, individuals need to infer the sincerity or genuineness of that suffering if they are to engage in prosocial behavior. Based on the cognitive schema mechanism, children who hold high as opposed to low honesty-based trust beliefs would be inclined to infer that the neediness and suffering of others are sincere or genuine, and thus be inclined to engage in prosocial behavior. Moreover, that relation would hold for altruistic prosocial behavior because the act of inferring the sincerity or genuineness of the needy/suffering person leads to an inference of his or her internal emotional state and provides the potential for empathy. By contrast, the relation should not hold for public prosocial behavior, which does not require the inference of the sincerity or genuineness and the internal emotional state of the needy/suffering person. Because of mothers' influential role in children's trust (Rotenberg, 1995), children's trust in mothers may be the principal cor-relate of prosocial behavior. However, expectations regarding the rela-tions between trust and anonymous, dire, emotional, and compliant forms of prosocial behaviors are necessarily difficult to develop a priori, based on the lack of prior research.

Social interaction mechanism

According to Rotenberg's interpersonal trust framework, trusting behav-iors involve depending on others to act in a reliably, emotionally trust-worthy, and honest fashion. According to the framework, there is a link between trust beliefs and trusting behavior. For example, a child who is low in behavioral trust (and thus holds low trust beliefs) would be unlikely to depend on a person to fulfill his or her promises, maintain confiden-tiality of information, and be honest. By contrast, a child who is high in behavioral trust (who likely holds high trust beliefs) would be likely to depend on a person to fulfill his or her promises, maintain confidentiality of information, and be honest. As a result, the children will establish different styles of social interaction. Compared to low-trusting counterparts (spanning both beliefs and behavior), high-trusting children will be likely to reciprocate promised cooperation, disclose personal information, and initiate interactions (i.e., make social overtures) because of the perceived sincerity of others.

Consistent with the social interaction mechanisms, Rotenberg (1994) found that adults who held low generalized trust beliefs were less likely to show reciprocated cooperation across trials in the Prisoner's Dilemma game than their high-trusting counterparts. Also, Rotenberg, MacDonald, and King, (2004) found a similar relation between elementary school children's trust beliefs in peers and reciprocal cooperation with peers in a simplified Prisoner's Dilemma game. Consistent with the social interaction mechanism, Rotenberg, Michalik, Eisenberg, and Betts (2007) found a concurrent positive association between elementary school children's trust beliefs in peers and the number of peer friendships they have. Finally, a substantial number of studies have revealed positive associations between trust beliefs and the willingness to disclose personal information to others (Kerr, Stattin, and Trost, 1999; Steel, 1991).

There are various processes by which the social interaction mechanism of trusting may promote prosocial behavior. For example, peers often promise to engage in sharing as a prosocial activity with other children (i.e., an example of promised cooperation). Because high-trusting children are inclined to depend on peers to fulfill their promises as a reliability basis, they would be likely to engage in sharing – in contrast to low-trusting children (see Rotenberg, Fox, Green, Ruderman, Slater, Stevens, and Carlo, 2005 for similar arguments). As another example, high-trusting children would be more likely to disclose person information to peers than would low-trusting children, as evidence of emotional trust. Because disclosure tends to be reciprocal among children during later elementary school (Rotenberg and Mann, 1986), they would be likely to receive disclosures of personal information from peers that, in turn, would foster a degree of perspective-taking and even empathy. Based on these arguments, it would be expected that: (1) children's reliability trust beliefs, notably in peers, would be associated with compliant prosocial behavior and perhaps altruism; (2) children's emotional-based trust beliefs, notably in peers, would be associated with empathic concerns; and (3) children's reliability and emotional trust beliefs, notably in peers, would be associated with children's perceptions of their friends as prosocial. As general support for these hypotheses, Rotenberg and his colleagues (Rotenberg, Fox, Green, Ruderman, Slater, Stevens, and Carlo, 2005) found positive associations between elementary school children's trust beliefs in peers and measures of generosity and helpfulness towards peers. To date, however, no studies on the relations between trust and specific forms of prosocial behaviors exist. Thus, we present an exploratory study of these relations.

An exploratory study

Based on the conceptual links between trust and prosocial behaviors, and given the relatively sparse empirical literature on this topic, we designed a study to further investigate these relations in a sample of women college students. In contrast to previous studies, we included multidimensional measures of trust (honesty, keeping secrets, keeping promises) and prosocial behaviors (dire, emotional, altruistic, public, anonymous, and compliant), rather than relying solely on global measures of these constructs. The present investigation utilized a newly modified measure of the Generalized Trust Belief Scale to use with late adolescents (GTB-LA; see Chapter 12 in this book). The items were adapted from the original version that was developed to use with children to assess trust beliefs across a number of targets, including parents, peers, teachers, and romantic partners.

Based on multidimensional models of trust and prosocial behaviors, are there aspects of trust that are more strongly related to prosocial behaviors? Similarly, are there specific forms of prosocial behaviors that are more strongly linked to specific aspects of trust? Given the dearth of research on the relations between specific dimensions of trust and specific types of prosocial behaviors, no a priori hypotheses were developed. Furthermore, because trust and prosocial behaviors might be expected to be particularly relevant in close, interpersonal relationships, we focused on trust beliefs in parents and romantic partners (rather than professors and peers). In addition, to assess whether trust is associated with other prosocial traits, we assessed the number of prosocial friends and sympathy tendencies in late adolescents. These variables allowed us to examine whether trust beliefs are related to having friends with prosocial tendencies and with individuals' sympathy.

Finally, as alluded to earlier, it is possible that the relations between trust beliefs and prosocial behaviors are explained by individual differences in sympathy (caring for others). Individuals who develop close, trusting relationships with others might be more susceptible to emotional sensitivity, and this, in turn, might predict prosocial outcomes. That is, trust is the basis for attachment relationships which foster sensitivity towards others, and, in turn, more prosocial behaviors and more prosocial friends. Therefore, we further examined whether sympathy mediated the relations between trust and both prosocial behaviors and prosocial friends.

Method

Participants

Participants were 102 female undergraduate college students (M age = 20.29 years, SD = 3.02) at an upper Midwestern state university. The majority of this sample was White (95 percent), but also included Asian Americans (3 percent), Latinos (1 percent), and Native Americans (1 percent). Participants were recruited through class announcements and signs posted on campus. Students could receive extra credit in a participating class or receive $5.

Measures

Generalized Trust Beliefs-Late Adolescence The Generalized Trust Beliefs-Late Adolescence (GTB-LA) Scale is a thirty-item self-report measure for late adolescents, designed to tap into three bases of trust beliefs across five targets (mother, father, professors, peers, romantic partners). Because we were interested in close interpersonal relationships, only the mother, father, and romantic partner trust subscales were used in the present study. Participants were instructed to imagine that they were the person whose name was underlined for each item and to mark the number that showed what they would believe. Responses were on a five-point scale, ranging from 1 (very unlikely) to 5 (very likely). Two items per basis were included for each target, for a total of six items per target and ten items per basis. Items for the reliability basis assess beliefs that the target keeps promises (e.g., "Luke's mother told Luke she would pay for all of his textbooks for the next semester if he helped clean out their garage for the winter. Luke helped his mom clean out their garage. How likely is it that Luke's mother will pay for all of his textbooks?"). Items for the emotional basis assess beliefs that the targets do not disclose secrets (e.g., "Curt won two tickets to a concert. He really wants to take a friend, but knows that if his brother finds out he will have to take his brother instead. Curt discusses this dilemma with his mother and asks her not to mention the tickets to his brother. How likely is it that Curt's mother won't tell his brother about the concert tickets?"). Items for the honesty basis assess beliefs that the target is truthful (e.g., "Nate asked Justin to help him with his homework after class. Justin said he does not have the time. How likely is it that Justin does not have time?"). Cronbach's alpha coefficients for the short sub-scales on this measure ranged from .43 (mother-honesty) to .70 (father-honesty). Factor scores were created for each subscale and used in the primary analyses.

Prosocial Tendencies Measure Twenty-two self-report items from the Prosocial Tendencies Measure (PTM) were used to assess prosocial behavior (i.e., behavior intended to benefit another) on a five-point scale, ranging from 1 (does not describe me at all) to 5 (describes me greatly) (Carlo and Randall, 2002). Six dimensions of prosocial behavior were assessed. Public prosocial behavior is performed in front of others (four items, e.g., "Helping others when I am in the spotlight is when I work best"; Cronbach's alpha coefficient = .72). Anonymous prosocial behavior is performed without others' knowledge (five items, e.g., "Most of the time, I help others when they do not know who helped them"; alpha = .86). Dire prosocial behavior is performed in emergency or crisis situations (three items, e.g., "I tend to help people who are in a real crisis or need"; alpha = .66). Emotional prosocial behavior is performed in emotionally evocative situations (three items, e.g., "I tend to help others particularly when they are emotionally distressed"; alpha = .70). Compliant prosocial behavior is performed in response to a request (two items, e.g., "When people ask me to help them, I don't hesitate"; alpha = .81). Altruistic prosocial behavior is performed with expectation of reward to the self (five items, e.g., "I believe I should receive more recognition for the time and energy I spend on charity work"; reverse-scored; alpha = .71). Participants received a subscale score if they answered at least 75 percent of the items. Factor scores were created for each subscale and used in the primary analyses.

Prosocial friends Four items were used to assess the extent to which participants believed their close friends are prosocial (Tilton-Weaver and Galambos, 2003). Participants responded on a four-point scale, ranging from 1 (strongly disagree) to 4 (strongly agree) (e.g., "Most of my friends would jump in and help a stranger in trouble"; alpha = .82).

Global prosocial behaviors The prosocial behavior subscale from the Primary Prevention Awareness, Attitudes, and Usage Scale (PPAAUS; Swisher, Shute, and Bibeau, 1984) was used to assess helping. This is a six-item scale that includes items tapping into volunteering in a charitable organization, helping a friend with a problem, raising or donating money, sharing in household tasks, and doing favors or lending money to others. Responses could range from 1 (never happened) to 6 (happens almost every day) (alpha = .46).

Sympathy To assess the emotional sensitivity component of sympathy, the empathic concern (i.e., feelings of concern for a needy other) scale was administered. The five-point scale, ranging from 1 (does not describe me well) to 5 (describes me very well), consisted of seven items (sample item: "I often have tender, concerned feelings for people less fortunate than me"). The scale is from the Interpersonal Reactivity Questionnaire (Davis, 1983; alpha = .67).

Procedure

Participants completed the survey packet during an experimental session that lasted approximately one hour. Some participants completed the survey during their regular class time. Others signed up for a time to complete the survey individually or in small groups. All sessions were held in university buildings and were conducted by a trained research assistant. Participants were informed that they were participating in a study to examine late adolescents' relationships and behaviors, assured of anonymity and confidentiality, and their consent to participate was obtained. Participants completed the survey packet with all measures presented in the same order. Upon completion, participants were given a letter providing additional details about the study and were thanked for their participation.

Results

Descriptive and correlational analyses were conducted to examine the means, standard deviations, and relations among trust, prosocial behaviors, sympathy, and number of prosocial friends (see Tables 13.1 and 13.2). Because we expected positive relations between trust and prosocial behaviors and traits, we discuss the significant results at the $p < .05$ level (one-tailed).

As can be seen in Table 13.2, students who frequently reported public prosocial behaviors were less likely to report that their mothers keep secrets, and less likely to report that their father and romantic partner were honest. In contrast, those who frequently reported altruism were more likely to report that their mothers kept secrets, and that their fathers and romantic partner were honest. Those students who frequently reported helping in emergency (i.e., dire) situations were more likely to report

Table 13.1 *Descriptive statistics*

Variable	Mean	Standard deviation
Empathic concern	4.14	.50
Interpersonal trust		
Mother		
Promise	4.40	.61
Honest	3.79	.86
Secret	3.75	.87
Father		
Promise	4.11	.73
Honest	3.97	.83
Secret	2.38	.89
Romantic partner		
Promise	3.17	.93
Honest	3.13	1.03
Secret	4.08	.69
Prosocial tendencies		
Public	2.08	.70
Altruistic	4.18	.68
Dire	3.23	.77
Compliant	3.88	.83
Anonymous	2.79	.88
Emotional	3.02	.78
Prosocial friends	4.51	.73
Prosocial behaviors	3.90	.48

Note: All statistics are based on raw scale scores.

that their mothers kept promises and secrets. Students who frequently reported helping in emotional situations were more likely to report that their mothers were honest. Compliant and anonymous helping behaviors were not significantly associated with interpersonal trust.

In general, those who reported having a number of prosocial friends were more likely to report trust across the targets, with the exception of father keeping promises and father and romantic partner keeping secrets. Furthermore, honesty was associated with more sympathy across all three targets. Global prosocial behaviors were associated with keeping promises with mothers and honesty with mothers and fathers.

Interestingly, those who reported high levels of compliant, anonymous, dire, and emotional prosocial behaviors also reported many prosocial friends and high scores on sympathy. Moreover, sympathy was positively related to altruism, and negatively related to public prosocial behaviors. Furthermore, helping in dire, emotional, and anonymous conditions was associated with more prosocial behavior, as assessed by the global

Table 13.2 *Zero-order correlations among the main study variables*

		Prosocial tendencies						Prosocial	
	Sympathy	Public	Altruistic	Dire	Compliant	Anonymous	Emotional	Friends	Behavior
Interpersonal trust									
Mother									
Promise	.10	-.14	.05	.25**	.11	.14	.14	.29**	.24**
Honest	.18*	-.05	.12	.14	-.01	-.07	.23**	.22*	.18*
Secret	.10	-.27**	.24**	.18*	.14	.12	.14	.18*	.06
Father									
Promise	.10	.04	.01	-.04	.01	-.05	.05	.13	.13
Honest	.27**	-.25*	.25**	.12	.12	.07	.10	.27**	.21*
Secret	-.03	-.15	.03	-.04	-.11	-.07	-.05	-.10	.10
Romantic partner									
Promise	.06	-.10	.14	-.10	.01	-.06	.07	.21*	.08
Honest	.22**	-.25**	.20*	.01	.05	-.01	.10	.35**	.08
Secret	-.01	-.09	.07	-.07	-.04	-.04	.10	.15	.01
Sympathy	—	-.27**	.20*	.22**	.34**	.28**	.45**	.35**	.26**
Prosocial friends	.35**	-.09	.07	.25**	.28**	.22**	.25**	—	.12
Prosocial behavior	.26**	-.01	.01	.25**	.13	.27**	.21*	.12	—

Notes: *p ≤ .05; **p ≤ .01;
All tests were one-tailed.

measure of prosocial behavior. Importantly, altruism, compliant helping, and helping in public situations were not significantly associated
with this measure of global prosocial behaviors. Finally, sympathy was
positively associated with both global prosocial behaviors and number of
prosocial friends.

To test whether sympathy accounted for the relations between trust
and prosocial behaviors, and between trust and prosocial friends, a series of regression analyses were conducted using Baron and Kenny's
(1986; Kenny, Kashy, and Bolger, 1998) procedures. The indirect (i.e.,
mediated) effects were tested using MacKinnon's Z-test (MacKinnon,
Lockwood, Hoffman, West, and Sheets, 2002). The significant models are reported in Tables 13.3 and 13.4. These results showed that
the relationship between honesty with mothers and emotional prosocial tendencies was partially mediated by sympathy. Trust in the
honesty with mothers was associated with more sympathy, which in
turn was associated with higher reports of emotional prosocial behaviors. Moreover, the relationships for honesty with fathers and romantic
partners with altruism were partially mediated by sympathy. Trust in
fathers and romantic partners to be honest were associated with more
sympathy, which, in turn, was associated with greater altruism. In addition, the relationships of honesty in fathers and romantic partners with
public prosocial tendencies were partially mediated by sympathy. Trust
in fathers and romantic partners to be honest was associated with more
sympathy. However, sympathy was negatively related to reports of public prosocial behaviors.

Results for the mediation of trust and prosocial friends by sympathy are
shown in Table 13.4. These results showed that the relationships between
honesty for all three targets and prosocial friends were partially mediated
by sympathy. Trust in the honesty of mothers, fathers, and romantic partners was associated with more sympathy, which, in turn, was associated
with more prosocial friends.

Discussion of findings

The present findings suggest that honesty is deemed the dimension of
trust (across fathers, mothers, and romantic relationships) most relevant
to altruism, and public and emotional prosocial behaviors. Furthermore,
the study yielded evidence that the relations between trust and those
forms of prosocial behaviors are partially accounted for by individual
differences in sympathy. Overall, then, support for the need to examine
specific dimensions of trust and specific types of prosocial behaviors was
provided.

Table 13.3 *Tests of mediation of trust and prosocial tendencies by sympathy*

	β	b	SE	Z
Mother honest → Emotional prosocial behaviors				
Step 1				
Trust → Prosocial behavior	.23**	.23	.10	2.30
Step 2				
Trust → Sympathy	.18*	.10	.05	1.97
Step 3				
Sympathy → Prosocial behavior	.43**	.86	.18	4.73
Trust → Prosocial behavior	.15†	.15	.09	1.68
Indirect effect	.08*			9.32
Father honest → Public prosocial behaviors				
Step 1				
Trust → Prosocial behavior	−.23*	−.23	.10	− 2.38
Step 2				
Trust → Sympathy	.27**	.13	.05	2.79
Step 3				
Sympathy → Prosocial behavior	−.22*	−.44	.20	− 2.19
Trust → Prosocial behavior	−.18†	−.17	.10	− 1.75
Indirect effect	−.06*			− 6.11
Father honest → Altruism				
Step 1				
Trust → Prosocial behavior	.23*	.23	.10	2.33
Step 2				
Trust → Sympathy	.27**	.13	.05	2.79
Step 3				
Sympathy → Prosocial behavior	.15	.30	.15	1.45
Trust → Prosocial behavior	.19†	.19	.10	1.87
Indirect effect	.04*			4.05
Romantic partner honest → Public prosocial behaviors				
Step 1				
Trust → Prosocial behavior	−.22*	−.22	.10	− 2.26
Step 2				
Trust → Sympathy	.22*	.11	.05	2.25
Step 3				
Sympathy → Prosocial behavior	−.23*	−.47	.20	− 2.31
Trust → Prosocial behavior	−.17†	−.17	.10	− 1.75
Indirect effect	−.05*			5.20
Romantic partner honest → Altruism				
Step 1				
Trust → Prosocial behavior	.16†	.16	.10	1.65
Step 2				
Trust → Sympathy	.22*	.11	.05	2.25
Step 3				
Sympathy → Prosocial behavior	.17†	.34	.20	1.67
Trust → Prosocial behavior	.13	.13	.10	1.25
Indirect effect	.04*			3.76

Notes: *p ≤.05; **p≤.01; †p≤.10
For indirect effect, Z> 2.18 is significant at a .05 level (MacKinnon, Lockwood, Hoffman, West, and Sheets, 2002).

Table 13.4 *Tests of mediation of trust and prosocial friends by sympathy*

	β	b	SE	Z
Mother honest → Prosocial friends				
Step 1				
Trust → Prosocial friends	.22*	.16	.07	2.17
Step 2				
Trust → Sympathy	.18*	.10	.15	1.97
Step 3				
Sympathy → Prosocial friends	.32**	.47	.14	3.33
Trust → Prosocial friends	.16†	.12	.07	1.65
Indirect effect	.06*			6.56
Father honest → Prosocial friends				
Step 1				
Trust → Prosocial friends	.27**	.20	.07	2.80
Step 2				
Trust → Sympathy	.27**	.13	.05	2.77
Step 3				
Sympathy → Prosocial friends	.30**	.43	.14	3.03
Trust → Prosocial friends	.19*	.14	.07	1.99
Indirect effect	.08*			8.39
Romantic partner honest → Prosocial friends				
Step 1				
Trust → Prosocial friends	.35**	.26	.07	3.66
Step 2				
Trust → Sympathy	.22*	.11	.05	2.26
Step 3				
Sympathy → Prosocial friends	.28**	.42	.14	3.03
Trust → Prosocial friends	.29**	.21	.07	3.04
Indirect effect	.06*			6.87

Notes: $*p \leq .05$; $**p \leq .01$; $†p \leq .10$
For indirect effect, $Z > 2.18$ is significant at a .05 level (MacKinnon, Lockwood, Hoffman, West, and Sheets, 2002).

Honesty, rather than keeping promises and secrets, was reported as most relevant to understanding the relations between specific forms of prosocial behaviors and trust beliefs in close, interpersonal relationships. Honesty was particularly relevant in predicting altruism and public and emotional prosocial behaviors. As mentioned previously, altruism is an extreme form of prosocial behavior that often incurs a direct cost to one's self and emphasizes the well-being of another, and is associated with higher moral functioning (Carlo, 2006). Interestingly, of the three dimensions of trust in Rotenberg's framework, honesty is the most relevant to morality – it is considered an aspect of fairness, equity, and justice. Being honest and sincere, and not cheating or lying to others, are central aspects of morality. In contrast, keeping promises and secrets might be more central aspects to interpersonal relationships, but not necessarily central to moral issues. So perhaps it is not too surprising that individuals with altruistic tendencies, and who assist in emotionally evocative situations, were more likely to emphasize the importance of honesty in trusting relationships. Conversely, individuals who deemed honesty as important were less likely to engage in public prosocial behaviors, which reflect a selfish mode of helping (which might reflect a desire to gain others' approval or to enhance one's social status). These results suggest that it is important to distinguish between specific aspects of trust and specific types of prosocial behaviors.

Of additional importance were the findings that showed that sympathy partially accounted for the relations between trust beliefs and those forms of prosocial behaviors. The findings suggest that honesty (in parent–adolescent and romantic relationships) might facilitate sympathy, which, in turn, facilitates specific types of prosocial behaviors. Perhaps the reported honesty in those close interpersonal relationships reflects secure attachment relationships (and positive internal working models) that foster and nurture sympathy and prosocial behaviors in late adolescence. Clearly, there is a need for longitudinal studies to better examine whether these relations are established early in life and to determine direction of causality.

Consistent with the findings on prosocial behaviors, we also found that sympathy mediated the relations between trust (honesty and keeping promises or secrets) and number of prosocial friends. This set of findings extends prior research on the association between trust and prosocial behaviors by suggesting that honesty is deemed important to care-based, interpersonal relationships. One might speculate on the basis of these findings that trust (especially honesty) and prosocial behaviors form the basis for close, interpersonal relationships and friends. Furthermore, sympathy appears to play a central mediating role in facilitating these relations. Indeed, the present findings are consistent with prior research that suggests that an important characteristic of friendship is the ability to provide emotional support and comfort, and that friends are expected to be honest with one another (Bukowski and Sippola, 1996).

The results also showed evidence for significant relations between the global measure of prosocial behavior and trust dimensions, sympathy, and number of prosocial friends. However, the pattern of relations does not allow one to disentangle what specific types of prosocial behaviors are most strongly associated with these correlates. Furthermore, there were no significant relations between the global index of prosocial behavior and trust in romantic partners – quite possibly because the global measure of prosocial behavior does not tap into types of prosocial behavior (altruism and public) that might be most relevant to understanding the links between trust and prosocial behaviors in romantic relationships. Consistent with this notion, the global index of prosocial behavior was not significantly related to altruism and public prosocial behaviors; both of these latter behaviors were significantly related to trust (honesty).

There are a number of important limitations to the present findings. First, given prior reported gender differences in prosocial traits and behaviors, studies on the relations between trust and prosocial behaviors in men are needed. Given prior reported gender differences in prosocial behaviors and in the quality of interpersonal relationships, it is likely that the associations might differ as a function of other dimensions of trust or other types of prosocial behaviors. Second, studies that examine these relations using a measure of prosocial behavior that assesses the recipient or target of helping might be useful. According to cognitive schema theory, one would expect that the associations between trust and prosocial behaviors would be stronger when the characteristics of the target protagonist of measures (and the underlying schema) are more similar. Furthermore, one might expect that trustworthiness among friends might be predictive of prosocial behaviors towards friends and, in turn, predictive of more prosocial friends. Unfortunately, the lack of target specificity in the prosocial behavior measure and specificity in the status of the peer (e.g., close friend, acquaintance) in the peer trust scale precluded a close examination of this possibility. Third, it will be important to investigate other potential mediators (e.g., moral reasoning, guilt) of the relations between trust and prosocial behaviors. And fourth, experimental and longitudinal studies need to be conducted to discern possible bidirectional effects and direction of causality in these relations.

Despite the study limitations, the present findings showed evidence of the links among trust, prosocial behaviors, and friendships. The results yielded evidence on the usefulness of investigating specific dimensions of trust and specific types of prosocial behaviors, and on the central importance of sympathy in understanding the relations between trust and prosocial behaviors. Moreover, we extended the previous literature by showing that the honesty dimension of trust and sympathy is also relevant in understanding prosocial friendships. Taken together, the evidence points to the usefulness of multifaceted models of trust and prosocial behaviors, and to the role of sympathy as a mediating process that helps explain the links between trust and prosocial behaviors.

Conclusions

The recent calls for more attention to the positive aspects of human functioning require different conceptual approaches to understanding human behavior. Models of positive functioning necessitate the identification of positive behavioral mechanisms and outcomes. The present chapter focused on several positive functioning variables: trust, prosocial behaviors, sympathy, and prosocial relationships. Although research on such variables is not new, conceptual models and empirical work on the links among these important positive functioning variables are relatively sparse. The present chapter presented recent frameworks of trust and prosocial behaviors, which might prove useful in spurring studies on these topics. We then presented exploratory research using these frameworks that confirmed a number of connections between trust, sympathy, and prosocial behaviors. Perhaps more importantly, the tantalizing evidence that trust, prosocial behaviors, and sympathy are key mechanisms in understanding interpersonal relationships should encourage future researchers to build on this promising area of research in positive psychology.

Acknowledgments

The authors would like to acknowledge the suggestions and feedback from Lisa Crockett on the writing of this chapter. Funding support to Gustavo Carlo was provided by a grant from the National Science Foundation (BNS 0132302).

References

Ainsworth, M. D. S. (1973). The development of infant–mother attachment. In B. M. Caldwell and H. N. Ricciuti (eds.), *Review of child development research: Vol. 3* (pp. 1–91). University of Chicago Press.

Aristotle (1980). *The Nicomachean ethics* (trans. D. Ross). Oxford University Press.

Armsden, G. and Greenberg, M. (1987). The Inventory of Parent and Peer Attachment: Individual differences and their relationship to psychological well-being in adolescence. *Journal of Youth and Adolescence*, **16** (5), 427–454.

Baron, R. M. and Kenny, D. A. (1986). The moderator–mediator variable distinction in social psychological research: Conceptual, strategic and statistical considerations. *Journal of Personality and Social Psychology*, **51**, 1173–1182.

Batson, C. D. (1991). *The altruism question: Toward a social psychological answer.* Hillsdale, NJ: Lawrence Erlbaum Associates.

(1998). Altruism and prosocial behavior. In D.T. Gilbert, S.T. Fiske, and G. Lindzey (eds.), *The handbook of social psychology: Vol.* **2** (4th edn.) (pp. 282–316). Boston, MA: McGraw-Hill.

Bernath, M. and Feshbach, N. (1995). Children's trust: Theory, assessment, development, and research directions. *Applied & Preventive Psychology,* **4** (1), 1–19.

Bierhoff, H. (2002). *Prosocial behaviour.* New York: Psychology Press.

Blum, L.A. (1980). *Friendship, altruism, and morality.* London: Routledge and Kegan Paul.

Bukowski, W.M. and Sippola, L.K. (1996). Friendship and morality. In W.M. Bukowski and A.F. Newcomb (eds.), *The company they keep: Friendship in childhood and adolescence* (pp. 238–261). Cambridge University Press.

Carlo, G. (2006). Care-based and altruistically-based morality. In M. Killen and J.G. Smetana (eds.), *Handbook of moral development* (pp. 551–579). Mahwah, NJ: Lawrence Erlbaum Associates.

Carlo, G. and Randall, B. (2001). Are all prosocial behaviors equal? A socioecological developmental conception of prosocial behavior. In F. Columbus (ed.), *Advances in psychology research: Vol. 2* (pp. 151–170). Huntington, NY: Nova Science Publishers.

(2002). The development of a measure of prosocial behaviors for late adolescents. *Journal of Youth and Adolescence,* **31,** 31–44.

Carlo, G., Allen, J.B., and Buhman, D.C. (1999). Facilitating and disinhibiting prosocial behaviors: The nonlinear interaction of trait perspective taking and trait personal distress on volunteering. *Basic and Applied Social Psychology,* **21,** 189–197.

Carlo, G., Crockett, L.J., Randall, B.A., and Roesch, S.C. (2007). Parent and peer correlates of prosocial development in rural adolescents: A longitudinal study. *Journal of Research on Adolescence,* **17,** 301–324.

Carlo, G., Eisenberg, N., Troyer, D., Switzer, G., and Speer, A.L. (1991). The altruistic personality: In what contexts is it apparent? *Journal of Personality and Social Psychology,* **61,** 450–458.

Carlo, G., Hausmann, A., Christiansen, S., and Randall, B.A. (2003). Sociocognitive and behavioral correlates of a measure of prosocial tendencies for adolescents. *Journal of Early Adolescence,* **23,** 107–134.

Carlo, G., Knight, G.P., McGinley, M., Zamboanga, B.L., and Jarvis, L. (in press). The multidimensionality of prosocial behaviors: Evidence of measurement invariance in early Mexican American and European American adolescents. *Journal of Research on Adolescence.*

Carlo, G., McGinley, M., Hayes, R., Batenhorst, C., and Wilkinson, J. (2007). Parenting styles or practices? Parenting, sympathy, and prosocial behaviors among adolescents. *Journal of Genetic Psychology,* **168,** 147–176.

Colby, A. and Damon, W. (1992). *Some do care: Contemporary lives of moral commitment.* New York: Free Press.

Davis, M.H. (1983). Measuring individual differences in empathy: Evidence for a multidimensional approach. *Journal of Personality and Social Psychology,* **44,** 113–126.

Davis, M.H. and Franzoi, S. (1991). Stability and change in adolescent self-consciousness and empathy. *Journal of Research in Personality,* **25,** 70–87.

DeNeve, K. and Cooper, H. (1998). The happy personality: A meta-analysis of 137 personality traits and subjective well-being. *Psychological Bulletin*, **124**, 197–229.

de Waal, F. (1996). *Good natured: The origins of right and wrong in humans and other animals.* Cambridge, MA: Harvard University Press.

Dovidio, J. F., Piliavin, J. A., Schroeder, D. A., and Penner, L. A. (2006). *The social psychology of prosocial behavior.* Mahwah, NJ: Lawrence Erlbaum Associates.

Eisenberg, N. (1986). *Altruistic emotion, cognition and behavior.* Hillsdale, NJ: Lawrence Erlbaum Associates.

Eisenberg, N. and Fabes, R. A. (1998). Prosocial development. In W. Damon, R. M. Lerner (series eds.), and N. Eisenberg (vol. ed.), *Handbook of child psychology: Vol. 3. Social, emotional, and personality development* (5th edn.) (pp. 701–778). New York: Wiley.

Eisenberg, N., Cameron, E., Tryon, K., and Dodez, R. (1981). Socialization of prosocial behavior in the preschool classroom. *Developmental Psychology*, **71**, 773–782.

Eisenberg, N., Fabes, R. A., Carlo, G., and Karbon, M. (1992). Emotional responsivity to others: Behavioral correlates and socialization antecedents. In N. Eisenberg and R. A. Fabes (eds.), *Emotion and its regulation in early development* (pp. 57–73). San Francisco: Jossey-Bass.

Eisenberg, N., Fabes, R. A., and Spinrad, T. L. (2006). Prosocial development. In W. Damon, R. M. Lerner (series eds.), and N. Eisenberg (vol. ed.), *Handbook of child psychology: Vol. 3. Social, emotional, and personality development* (6th edn.) (pp. 646–718). New York: Wiley.

Eisenberg, N., Miller, P. A., Schaller, M., Fabes, R. A., Fultz, J., Shell, R., and Shea, C. L. (1989). The role of sympathy and altruistic personality traits in helping: A reexamination. *Journal of Personality*, **57**, 41–67.

Eisenberg, N., Shea, C. L., Carlo, G., and Knight, G. P. (1991). Empathy-related responding and cognition: A "chicken and the egg" dilemma. In W. M. Kurtines and J. L. Gewirtz (eds.), *Handbook of moral behavior and development: Vol. 2. Research* (pp. 63–88). New York: Lawrence Erlbaum Associates.

Erikson, E. H. (1963). *Childhood and society* (2nd edn.). New York: W. W. Norton & Company.

Green, B., Shirk, S., Hanze, D., and Wanstrath, J. (1994). The Children's Global Assessment Scale in clinical practice: An empirical evaluation. *Journal of American Academy of Child and Adolescent Psychiatry*, **33**, 1158–1164.

Hart, D. and Fegley, S. (1995). Altruism and caring in adolescence: Relations to self understanding and social judgment. *Child Development*, **66**, 1346–1359.

Johnson, R. C., Danko, G. P., Darvill, T. J., Bochner, S., Bowers, J. K., Huang, Y.-H., Park, J. Y., Pecjak, V., Rahim, A. R. A., and Pennington, D. (1989). Cross-cultural assessment of altruism and its correlates. *Personality and Individual Differences*, **10**, 855–868.

Kenny, D. A., Kashy, D. A., and Bolger, N. (1998). Data analysis in social psychology. In D. T. Gilbert, S. T. Fiske, and G. Lindzey (eds.), *The handbook of social psychology: Vol. 1* (4th edn.) (pp. 233–265). Boston, MA: McGraw-Hill.

Kerr, M., Stattin, H., and Trost, K. (1999). To know you is to trust you: Parents' trust is rooted in child disclosure of information. *Journal of Adolescence*, **22**, 737–752.

Ladd, G.W. and Profilet, S.M. (1996). The Child Behavior Scale: A teacher-report measure of young children's aggressive, withdrawn, and prosocial behaviors. *Developmental Psychology*, **32**, 1008–1024.

Laible, D., Eye, J., and Carlo, G. (in press). Dimensions of conscience in mid-adolescence: Links with social behavior, parenting, and temperament. *Journal of Youth and Adolescence*.

Lamm, C., Batson, C.D., and Decety, J. (2007). The neural substrate of human empathy: Effects of perspective-taking and cognitive appraisal. *Journal of Cognitive Neuroscience*, **19**, 42–58.

Latané, B. and Darley, J.M. (1970). *The unresponsive bystander: Why doesn't he help?* New York: Appleton-Century-Crofts.

MacKinnon, D.P., Lockwood, C.M., Hoffman, J.M., West, S.G., and Sheets, V. (2002). A comparison of methods to test the significance of the mediated effect. *Psychological Methods*, 7, 83–104.

Maslow, A. (1973). *The farther reaches of human nature.* New York: McGraw-Hill.

Mayeroff, M. (1971). *On caring.* New York: Harper & Row.

Noddings, N. (2003). *Caring: A feminine approach to ethics and moral education* (2nd edn.). Berkeley: University of California Press.

Oliner, S.P. and Oliner, P.M. (1988). *The altruistic personality: Rescuers of Jews in Nazi Europe.* New York: Free Press.

Rotenberg, K.J. (ed.) (1991). *Children's interpersonal trust: Sensitivity to lying, deception, and promise violations.* New York: Springer-Verlag.

(1994). Loneliness and interpersonal trust. *Journal of Social and Clinical Psychology*, **13**, 152–173.

(1995). The socialization of trust: Parents' and their children's interpersonal trust. *International Journal of Behavioral Development*, **18**, 713–726.

Rotenberg, K.J. and Cerda, C. (1994). Racially based trust expectancies of Native American and Caucasian children. *Journal of Social Psychology*, **134**, 621–631.

Rotenberg, K. and Mann, L. (1986). The development of the norm of the reciprocity of self-disclosure and its function in children's attraction to peers. *Child Development*, **57**, 1349–1357.

Rotenberg, K.J., Fox, C., Green, S., Ruderman, L., Slater, K., Stevens, K., and Carlo, G. (2005). Construction and validation of a children's interpersonal trust belief scale. *British Journal of Developmental Psychology*, **23**, 271–292.

Rotenberg, K.J., MacDonald, K.J., and King, E.V. (2004). The relationship between loneliness and interpersonal trust during middle childhood. *Journal of Genetic Psychology*, **165**, 233–249.

Rotenberg, K.J., Michalik, N., Eisenberg, N., and Betts, L.R. (2008). The relations among young children's peer-reported trustworthiness, inhibitory control, and preschool adjustment. *Early Childhood Research Quarterly*, **23**, 288–298.

Rotter, J. B. (1967). A new scale for the measurement of interpersonal trust. *Journal of Personality*, **35**, 651–665.

  (1980). Interpersonal trust, trustworthiness and gullibility. *American Psychologist*, **35**, 1–7.

Rushton, J. P., Chrisjohn, R. D., and Fekken, G. C. (1981). The altruistic personality and the self-report altruism scale. *Personality and Individual Differences*, **2**, 1–11.

Rydell, A. M., Hagekull, B., and Bohlin, G. (1997). Measurement of two social competence aspects in middle childhood. *Developmental Psychology*, **33**, 824–833.

Seligman, M. E. P. and Csikszentmihalyi, M. (2000). Positive psychology: An introduction. *American Psychologist*, **55**, 5–14.

Staub, E. (1978). *Positive social behavior and morality: Social and personal influences: Vol. 1*. New York: Academic Press.

  (2005). The roots of goodness: The fulfillment of basic human needs and the development of inclusive caring, helping and nonaggression, moral courage, active bystandership, and altruism born of suffering. In G. Carlo and C. P. Edwards (eds.), *The 51st Annual Symposium on Motivation: Moral motivation*. Lincoln: University of Nebraska Press.

Steel, J. L. (1991). Interpersonal correlates of trust and self-disclosure. *Psychological Reports*, **68**, 1319–1320.

Swisher, J. D., Shute, R. E., and Bibeau, D. (1984). Assessing drug and alcohol abuse: An instrument for planning and evaluation. *Measurement and Evaluation in Counseling and Development*, **17**, 91–97.

Thompson, R. A. (2006). The development of the person: Social understanding, relationships, conscience, self. In W. Damon, R. M. Lerner (series eds.), and N. Eisenberg (vol. ed.), *Handbook of child psychology: Vol. 3. Social, emotional, and personality development* (6th edn.) (pp. 24–98). New York: Wiley.

Tilton-Weaver, L. and Galambos, N. (2003). Adolescents' characteristics and parents' beliefs as predictors of parents' peer management behaviors. *Journal of Research on Adolescence*, **13** (3), 269–300.

Waters, E., Vaughn, B., Posada, G., and Kondo-Ikemura, K. (1995). Caregiving, cultural, and cognitive perspective on secure-base behavior and working models: New growing points of attachment theory and research. *Monographs of the Society for Research in Child Development*, **60**, (2–3, Serial No. 244).

Weir, K. and Duveen, G. (1981). Further development and validation of the Prosocial Behavior Questionnaire for use by teachers. *Journal of Child Psychology and Psychiatry and Allied Disciplines*, **22**, 357–374.

Wilson, E. O. (1978). *On human nature*. Cambridge, MA: Harvard University Press.

14 Promoting intergroup trust among adolescents and young adults

Rhiannon N. Turner (University of Leeds),
Miles Hewstone (University of Oxford),
Hermann Swart (University of Stellenbosch),
Tania Tam (University of Oxford),
Elissa Myers (Institute of Psychiatry), and
Nicole Tausch (Cardiff University)

Intergroup trust might be broadly defined as a positive expectation about the intentions and behavior, and thus trust, of an outgroup towards the ingroup (Lewicki, McAllister, and Bies, 1998). According to Rotenberg and colleagues' framework of interpersonal trust (e.g., Rotenberg, 1991; Rotenberg and Morgan, 1995; Rotenberg, Fox, Green, Ruderman, Slater, Stevens, and Carlo, 2005), trust consists of three important components: reliability, emotionality, and honesty. In an intergroup context, *reliability* refers to whether promises made by the outgroup are fulfilled; *emotionality* refers to whether the outgroup refrains from causing emotional harm to the ingroup; and *honesty* refers to whether the outgroup is perceived as telling the truth, and behaving in a benign rather than in a malicious or manipulative way towards the ingroup.

Trust is crucial if society is to function effectively, because the formation and maintenance of interpersonal relationships is dependent on our ability to trust one another (e.g., Rotenberg, 1991; Rotter, 1980). Our ability to trust others has diverse psychological consequences, particularly among children. According to attachment theory, the quality of a child's relationship with their caregivers can affect their beliefs about whether others are trustworthy and, subsequently, their ability to have successful relationships (Bridges, 2003). Similarly, it is important for children that they are able to trust their peers, and know that they will be honest, reliable, and benevolent (Bernath and Feshbach, 1995). Children who tend to believe that others are trustworthy tend themselves to be more honest (Wright and Kirmani, 1977), higher in social competence and status (Buzzelli, 1988), better in terms of academic achievements

295

(Wentzel, 1991), and to experience lower levels of depression (Lester and Gatto, 1990) and loneliness (Rotenberg, Fox, Green, Ruderman, Slater, Stevens, and Carlo, 2005).

Rotenberg and Cerda (1992) found that children have a tendency to show a "same-race pattern of trust" (p. 622). That is, they believe that people of the same race are more likely to keep promises or tell the truth, and less likely to behave in a malicious or manipulative way towards them than are members of other racial groups. This ingroup-favoring trust bias helps to ensure the survival of the group because, by ensuring positive relationships between group members, the group remains cohesive. It is, however, imperative that we understand the factors that can help to increase intergroup trust, because research suggests that it may be an important aspect of harmonious intergroup relations. Consequences of trust include enhanced cooperation, information-sharing, improved communication, and problem-solving, all of which are likely to contribute towards successful relations between members of different groups (Hayashi, Ostrom, Walker, and Yamagishi, 1999). Intergroup trust is also recognized as a necessary part of reconciliation strategies which aim to improve community relations in the aftermath of intergroup conflicts. This is because it allows individuals to accept the risk of being vulnerable and to make conciliatory initiatives to the other party, with some degree of assurance that they will not be exploited (Blackstock, 2001; Dovidio, Gaertner, Kawakami, and Hodson, 2002).

Despite its apparent benefits, however, intergroup trust is difficult to instigate. Rothbart and Park (1986) have found that many trustworthy behaviors must be demonstrated before a person is considered "trustworthy," while just one untrustworthy act can deem a person "untrustworthy." Accordingly, in societies characterized by severe intergroup conflict, distrust stemming from intergroup conflict lingers long after the violence itself has stopped (Webb and Worchel, 1986). In sum, the issue of how to create and maintain a relationship of mutual trust and cooperation, in order to ensure harmonious intergroup relations, is one of the major challenges faced by societies, especially post-conflict societies, today.

In this chapter, we outline our program of research which investigates intergroup trust among adolescents and young adults attending high school and university. We focus on this age group for three reasons. First, social development experts suggest that during adolescence and early adulthood, young people go through a process of identity formation, whereby they explore the meaning and implications of their various group memberships (Phinney, 1989, 1993;

Phinney and Chavira, 1992). During this process, their attitudes towards the ingroup and the outgroup are thought to be ambivalent and in a state of flux. Thus, intergroup perceptions may be relatively malleable during adolescence and early adulthood, and processes that generate intergroup trust may be particularly effective (Cairns, Leung, Buchanan, and Cairns, 1995).

Second, the adolescents and young adults who participated in our research were all in full-time education, either at high school or university. Pupils spend on average 15,000 hours in schools (Rutter, Maughan, Mortimore, Ouston, and Smith, 1979) and, if they go on to university, continue to spend considerable time in educational and extracurricular activities with their peers. This provides the ideal opportunity to consider the potential impact of positive social interactions with members of other groups on perceptions of intergroup trust, although it is important to acknowledge that, even outside of the educational arena, opportunities for cooperative intergroup contact can arise in the workplace and local communities.

Third, despite these potential advantages, there has been relatively little research investigating intergroup trust among children. One notable exception to this is a study conducted by Rotenberg and Cerda (1992) with Native American and European American children, with a mean age of 10 years, who were attending either ethnically heterogeneous or homogeneous schools. Participants were shown a photo of a child who was identified as being either Native or European American, and were then presented with a series of scenarios in order to assess how trustworthy this individual was. It emerged that participants from both ethnic groups had lower trust expectancies of an outgroup member than an ingroup member, expecting outgroup members to be less likely to be able to keep a promise or a secret, and more likely to behave in a malevolent way. However, intergroup bias on trust was less evident in heterogeneous than in homogenous schools, suggesting that having the opportunity to interact with outgroup members may increase perceptions of trust. Thus, this study provides some indirect evidence that intergroup contact can moderate the intergroup bias in trust, although it should be noted that it did not directly assess intergroup contact (only the opportunity for trust, provided by a heterogeneous school); nor did it consider other potential predictors, or outcomes, of intergroup trust for intergroup relations. This represents a gap in the literature which we will now address.

In this chapter, we examine the predictors of intergroup trust, focusing primarily on the role of positive contact between members of different groups. We also consider some of the consequences of intergroup trust, and the mechanisms that explain these benefits of trust for intergroup relations. We begin by summarizing research to date on intergroup contact and explaining why it might be an important predictor of trust. We then discuss our work on intergroup trust in three different intergroup contexts: sectarianism in Northern Ireland, race relations in South Africa, and ethnic relations in the UK.

Intergroup contact

Intergroup contact has long been considered a powerful means of improving intergroup relations (Dovidio, Gaertner, and Kawakami, 2003). The contact hypothesis maintains that positive interactions between members of different groups can reduce intergroup prejudice and hostility (Allport, 1954; Pettigrew, 1998). Decades of research have demonstrated that intergroup contact can improve intergroup attitudes in many different contexts – for example, between the young and the elderly, host communities and immigrants, straight and gay people, people of different races and nationalities, and towards people with illnesses such as AIDS (e.g., Allport, 1954; Pettigrew and Tropp, 2006). Studies show not only that positive contact generates more positive attitudes towards outgroups (Pettigrew and Tropp, 2006), but also that it increases perceptions of outgroup variability (Paolini, Hewstone, Cairns, and Voci, 2004) and promotes forgiveness for past wrongdoings (Tam, Hewstone, Cairns, Tausch, Maio, and Kenworthy, 2007).

Cross-group friendship is a particularly effective form of contact, because it implies contact that is not only of a high quality, but also intimate and long-term (e.g., Turner, Hewstone, and Voci, 2007; Turner, Hewstone, Voci, Paolini, and Christ, 2007). Pettigrew (1997) found, in a cross-European study, that having friends in minority groups was a considerably stronger predictor of reduced prejudice than having neighbor or co-worker contact. Subsequent studies, conducted in a range of intergroup contexts, have supported these findings (e.g., Paolini, Hewstone, Cairns, and Voci, 2004; Turner, Hewstone, and Voci, 2007; Turner, Hewstone, Voci, and Vonofakou, 2008). Unfortunately, in highly segregated sectarian areas it may be difficult to establish and maintain face-to-face contact. One solution to this dilemma is to utilize intergroup contact in an indirect manner.

According to Wright, Aron, McLaughlin-Volpe, and Ropp's (1997) extended contact hypothesis, the benefits associated with cross-group friendship might also stem from vicarious experiences of friendship – the knowledge that ingroup members have friends in the outgroup. A number of studies support this premise. Wright, Aron, McLaughlin-Volpe, and Ropp (1997) showed that the more ingroup members White respondents knew who had outgroup friends, the less prejudice they displayed. This relationship has been replicated among Catholics and Protestants in Northern Ireland (Paolini, Hewstone, Cairns, and Voci, 2004) and South Asians and Whites in the UK (Turner, Hewstone, and Voci, 2007; Turner, Hewstone, Voci, Paolini, and Christ, 2007). It has also been developed as an effective intervention with school children, generating more positive attitudes towards refugees (Cameron, Rutland, Brown, and Douch, 2006), disabled children (Cameron and Rutland, 2006), and preventing worsening of attitudes to foreigners (Liebkind and McAlister, 1999). Extended contact is advantageous because one is only observing an ingroup–outgroup interaction, rather than participating in it directly, so it does not evoke the kind of "intergroup anxiety" (Stephan and Stephan, 1985) that often arises during actual contact – that is, anxiety specifically about interacting with members of an outgroup. On a practical level, extended contact may reduce prejudice on a broader scale, as an individual may not need to *know personally* an outgroup member in order to benefit from the positive effects of contact. In fact, the essence of extended contact is that the potential benefits of a single cross-group friendship are shared across many people.

There is reason to believe that both direct and extended intergroup contact may help to develop intergroup trust in contexts characterized by intergroup conflict. Segregation is thought to play an important role in sustaining conflict between groups by fostering mutual ignorance, suspicion, and distrust (Gallagher, 1995). The promotion of direct intergroup contact and desegregation should therefore help establish the trust which may, in turn, promote more positive intergroup behaviors. Research has also demonstrated that multiple positive encounters are required for the development of trust (Rothbart and Park, 1986; Worchel, Cooper, and Goethals, 1991). One might therefore expect that regular, positive intergroup contact that has no negative consequences for either party will help to build confidence among group members, and help to perpetuate the belief that the other group means no harm. Extended contact may also play an important role in establishing outgroup trust, because sharing a network of interpersonal relations with others can increase trust. Individuals may therefore trust others if they know (or believe) that they are directly or indirectly connected to each other through mutual friendships or connections (Maddux and Brewer, 2005). Indeed, there is evidence that a stranger is more likely to be trusted if it is believed that they are a member of one's social network (Yamagishi and Yamagishi, 1994).

We now summarize some of the results of our recent research on intergroup trust, beginning in Northern Ireland, and moving on, first, to South Africa, and then to ethnic relations in the UK. In each case, we focus on the fundamental role of intergroup contact in building intergroup trust.

Intergroup trust in Northern Ireland

In Northern Ireland, approximately 44 percent of the population is Catholic, and many of them believe that the North of Ireland should leave the United Kingdom and become part of the Republic of Ireland. Around 53 percent are Protestant, and most want to remain a part of the United Kingdom (Northern Ireland Statistics and Research Agency). In the late 1960s, the Catholic community in Northern Ireland initiated a civil rights campaign to establish equality with Protestants in employment, education, housing, and voting rights. This sparked sectarian violence, and since then over 3,700 people have been killed and over 35,000 injured as a result of ethno-political violence. Moreover, more than half of the Northern Irish population knows someone who was injured or killed in the Troubles (Smyth and Hamilton, 2003).

In recent years, the Northern Irish peace process has met with great success. Militant sectarian groups have disarmed, stable democratic self-government has been established, and there are now high levels of equality between Catholics and Protestants. But despite this progress, religious polarization continues to be so strong that many central features of social life (e.g., areas of residence, schools, shops, political parties, sports, cultural activities, places of worship, first and last names) can be identified as being either Catholic or Protestant (Nelson, Dickson, and Hargie, 2003). Society also remains fundamentally segregated between Catholics and Protestants. It is estimated that 35 to 40 percent of Northern Irish residents live in completely segregated communities (Whyte, 1986). Moreover, there is evidence of self-segregation when it comes to friendships: 55 percent of Protestants and 75 percent of Catholics report that "all or most" of their friends are of the same religion as them. There is also segregation in the educational system, in which 94 percent of children attend a Catholic or a Protestant, rather than a mixed, school (NICIE, 2008). This segregation allows prejudice and stereotypes to flourish (Whyte, 1986).

Many Northern Irish politicians and policy documents have emphasized the importance of introducing cross-community contact in order to establish mutual trust and generate more positive intergroup relations. In April 2003, for example, the British and Irish governments issued a joint declaration regarding the Northern Irish situation: "A key impediment to completing the evolution to [a stable society] in Northern Ireland is that both major traditions have lacked confidence and trust in each other. The two Governments ... recognise the importance of building trust and improving community relations, tackling sectarianism and addressing segregation, including initiatives to facilitate and encourage integrated education and mixed housing" (Joint Declaration by the British and Irish Governments, 2003; see also Foley and Robinson, 2004; Hewstone, Cairns, Voci, Hamberger, and Niens, 2006; Hewstone, Cairns, Kenworthy, Hughes, Tausch, Voci, von Hecker, Tam, and Pinder, 2008; Hewstone, Cairns, Voci, Paolini, McLernon, Crisp, and Niens, 2005; Mitchell, 1999). Yet there has been a lack of conceptual analysis and empirical research on the subject. Our research addressed this issue by investigating the predictors and consequences of intergroup trust in young people in Northern Ireland. Our initial studies were cross-sectional surveys, which we analyzed using structural equation modelling (SEM) to compare various models of the patterns of association between the variables measured. Although we cannot demonstrate causality with these analyses, we did test a number of alternative models in each case, and the models presented were in each case the best-fitting model of a number of alternatives.

We first conducted two cross-sectional surveys among young Catholics and Protestants who had recently left their almost exclusively segregated secondary schools for desegregated universities (Tam, Hewstone, Kenworthy, and Cairns, 2009). Participants were asked about their frequency of high-quality contact with the other community. They also reported the extent to which respondents intended to behave in positive ways towards the outgroup (for example, spending time with them, finding out more about them, and talking to them) or in negative ways (for example, opposing them, confronting them, or avoiding them). Finally, to assess trust, participants were also asked to indicate their agreement, on a seven-point scale, with the following statements regarding the other community: "I can trust them when they say they are sorry," "I can trust them when they say they want peace," "I trust the other community not to take all the jobs if they had the chance," "I can't trust them because they want revenge for things we have done to them," "I can't trust politicians from the other community to act fairly in the interests of everyone," "I can't trust politicians from the other community when it comes to the issue of policing," and "I can't trust politicians from the other community when it comes to the issue of education" (with the last four items reverse-coded). SEM analyses showed that intergroup trust was a powerful mediator of the relationship between intergroup contact and behavioral tendencies. People who had higher levels of contact with the other community tended to trust the outgroup more. Furthermore, people who were more trusting of the other community were inclined to behave in more positive and less negative ways towards them.

We conducted a second study to replicate these findings with a larger sample, and to address an additional question: Does trust operate in the same way as outgroup attitude in improving intergroup behaviors, or is trust in fact a better predictor of behavior? As noted earlier, trust can be seen as a more demanding gauge of intergroup relations than positive evaluation, because it represents a potential risk to the ingroup in a way that holding positive outgroup attitudes does not. Trust may also be viewed as an emotion (Brewer and Alexander, 2002), and according to intergroup emotions theory, emotions are better predictors of behaviors than are attitudes (Mackie, Devos, and Smith, 2000). We therefore hypothesized that outgroup trust would explain more variance in behavioral tendencies than would outgroup attitudes. We also investigated extended contact as a predictor of intergroup trust.

Catholic and Protestant students (mean age 20 years) from three universities in Northern Ireland completed a questionnaire which assessed direct intergroup contact (frequency and quality of contact at primary school, secondary school, while living at home, and at university), extended contact (how many people in their community have friends in the outgroup), intergroup trust, and positive and negative action tendencies. Outgroup attitude was assessed by asking participants to indicate, on seven-point semantic differential scales, how negative-positive, warm-cold, friendly-hostile, generous-selfish, insensitive-sensitive, and insincere-sincere they thought outgroup members were. SEM analyses showed that respondents who had higher levels of direct and extended contact with the outgroup tended to trust the outgroup more and have more positive attitudes towards them. In turn, trust and attitudes were associated with more positive and less negative behaviors towards the outgroup (see Figure 14.1). Finally, we compared intergroup trust and outgroup attitudes as mediators of the effects of contact on behavioral tendencies towards the outgroup. These analyses revealed that while outgroup trust mediated the effects of direct and extended contact on both positive and negative behavioral tendencies, outgroup attitude only marginally mediated the effects of intergroup contact on behavioral tendencies, and failed to mediate the effects of extended contact on positive or negative behavioral tendencies. Together, these studies suggest that intergroup trust is an important component of conflict resolution and peace-building among young people in Northern Ireland, and may be even more important than reducing prejudiced attitudes.

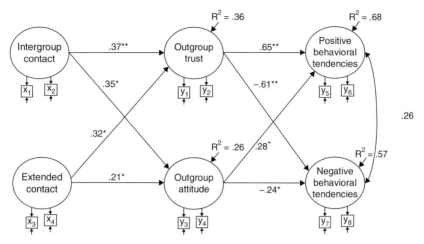

Figure 14.1 Structural equation model of direct and extended intergroup contact, outgroup attitude, outgroup trust, and positive and negative behavioral tendencies. Data from Tam, Hewstone, Kenworthy, and Cairns (2009, Study 2).
Notes: *p < .05; **p < .01; ***p < .001

We next conducted two surveys among Catholic and Protestant university students, with the aim of identifying whether cross-group friendship predicts two important components of reconciliation in Northern Ireland: intergroup forgiveness and trust (Myers, Hewstone, and Cairns, in preparation). Intergroup trust was measured by asking participants three questions, to which they responded on seven-point scales: "Do you think most people from the other community would try to take advantage of you if they got the chance, or would they try to be fair?"; "Would you say that most of the time people from the other community try to be helpful, or that they are mostly just looking out for themselves?"; and "Generally speaking, would you say that most people from the other community can be trusted, or that you can't be too careful?" (adapted from Brehm and Rahn's [1997], measure). We also considered an additional potential predictor of forgiveness and trust: ingroup identification. According to social identity theory (Tajfel and Turner, 1986), the extent to which individuals identify with their ingroup will affect how they react to group-based phenomena. In Northern Ireland, identification with one's ethno-religious community (Catholic or Protestant) has been found to be an important factor in maintaining negative attitudes and is related to ingroup favoritism and outgroup discrimination (Gallagher, 1989; Hewstone, Cairns, Kenworthy, Hughes, Tausch, Voci, von Hecker, Tam, and Pinder, 2008; Trew and Benson, 1996). Individuals with high group identification are therefore more likely to withhold prosocial affects, like intergroup forgiveness and trust, from the outgroup (Myers, Hewstone, and Cairns, 2009).

The research also considered three potential mediators of the relationship between cross-group friendship, group identification, and both outcomes: collective guilt, empathy, and perspective-taking. *Collective guilt* is experienced when the ingroup is seen as deviating from accepted moral norms (Wohl, Branscombe, and Klar, 2006). In Western societies, these norms include social justice, equality, democratic principles and concern for others' well-being (Doosje, Branscombe, Spears, and Manstead, 1998). Collective guilt can be experienced for events that the individual self was not personally involved in when one's ingroup deviates from these humanitarian values. Research has established that once people become aware of their wrongdoing, positive compensations, such as affirmative action and reparations, as well as other forms of prosocial behavior, are common (Iyer, Leach, and Pedersen, 2004; Manzi and González, 2007; Wohl, Branscombe, and Klar, 2006).

There is increasing evidence that empathy plays a key role in improving intergroup relations. Empathy has both a cognitive and an affective component (Galinsky and Moskowitz, 2000; Stephan and Finlay, 1999). The cognitive element of empathy, *perspective-taking*, refers to actively taking the perspective of the other person or group: that is, "putting oneself in another's shoes," whereas *empathic affect*, the affective component of empathy, consists of compassion-related emotions that arise from a feeling of concern for another. Perspective-taking may reduce prejudice because it allows people to view themselves as less different from and more connected to members of the outgroup, and because it improves understanding of the outgroup and thus makes them seem less threatening and "alien." Perspective-taking also allows an individual to anticipate other people's behavior and reactions, which encourages smoother and more rewarding relations (Davis, 1983).

We conducted a cross-sectional survey in which we measured cross-group friendship and ingroup identification as predictors; collective guilt and perspective-taking as mediators; and intergroup forgiveness and trust as outcomes. SEM analyses showed that the more people identified with their community, the less they were able to take the perspective of the other community, and, in turn, the less they were inclined to forgive or trust the outgroup. Cross-group friendship, on the other hand, predicted outgroup trust, a relationship that was partially mediated by perspective-taking. Participants with friends in the other community were better able to take the perspective of the other community, which, in turn, was associated with higher levels of intergroup trust. The relationship between friendship and forgiveness was mediated by collective guilt and perspective-taking. People with friends in the other community had higher levels of collective guilt and greater perspective-taking, which, in turn, were both associated with higher levels of outgroup forgiveness.

In a subsequent study, we developed our model further by including a measure of the affective component of empathy, empathic affect, in a questionnaire again completed by Catholic and Protestant undergraduate students. Empathic affect is brought about by perceptions of attachment (kinship, friendship, similarity, familiarity; Batson and Shaw, 1991). Since cross-group friendship involves attachment, it is likely to elicit the affective element of empathy. In turn, empathy has been shown to reduce prejudice towards outgroups (Stephan and Finlay, 1999). In order to measure empathic affect, Batson, Polycarpou, Harmon-Jones, Imhoff, Mitchener, Bednar, Klein, and Highberger's (1997) measure of emotional empathy was adapted for cross-community relations in Northern Ireland. Respondents were asked how often, when encountering or interacting with members of the other community, they had felt compassionate, sympathetic, soft-hearted, tender, warm, and moved.

SEM analyses showed that identification was associated with lower levels of intergroup forgiveness and trust – relationships that were fully mediated by perspective-taking. Specifically, those who highly identified with their own community were less able to take the perspective of the outgroup, which, in turn, was associated with lower levels of forgiveness and trust. Cross-group friendship was positively associated with forgiveness via two mediating processes: perspective-taking and collective guilt. The more friends in the other community that participants had, the more they took the perspective of the other group, and the more they experienced collective guilt. In turn, perspective-taking and guilt were associated with higher levels of intergroup forgiveness. Cross-group friendship was also positively associated with intergroup trust, this time via both aspects of empathy: empathic affect and perspective-taking. Specifically, people with cross-group friendship experienced more empathic affect and were also better able to take the perspective of the other community, which, in turn, predicted greater levels of intergroup trust.

Finally, we conducted a study to examine Northern Irish Catholic and Protestant students' implicit associations not only with the group labels *Catholics* and *Protestants*, but also with Catholic and Protestant militant sectarian groups (Tam, Hewstone, Kenworthy, Cairns, Marinett, Geddes, and Parkinson, 2008). We did this because focus groups we conducted with people from both sides of the Northern Ireland conflict had revealed that, when considering whether to forgive or trust the other community, not surprisingly, people often bring to mind the actions of extremist sectarian groups associated with that community (McLernon, Cairns, and Hewstone, 2002).

Implicit measures differ from explicit, self-report measures in that they reflect thoughts and feelings that operate outside of conscious awareness (Greenwald, McGhee, and Schwartz, 1998). They reveal unintentional bias, of which those who consider themselves unprejudiced may be largely unaware (Dovidio, Kawakami, and Gaertner, 2002). Implicit measures of attitudes have been shown to predict spontaneous nonverbal behaviors, while explicit measures of attitude predict more deliberative and controlled behaviors towards outgroups (Chen and Bargh, 1997; Dovidio, Kawakami, and Gaertner, 2002). Both are therefore important for investigation in Northern Ireland. Moreover, even though explicit conscious attitudes may become increasingly positive towards outgroup members over time, implicit attitudes may not – especially in areas with residual tensions from the conflict.

We examined Catholic and Protestant students' scores on implicit bias measures, and considered associations between implicit bias, forgiveness, distrust, and behavioral tendencies towards outgroup members. We used the Implicit Association Test (IAT; Greenwald, McGee, and Schwartz, 1998), a widely used implicit measure of bias, to measure the degree to which people automatically associated images of Catholic and Protestant extremist sectarian groups (e.g., the Irish Republican Army [IRA], the Ulster Volunteer Force [UVF], and the Ulster Freedom Fighters [UFF]) with positive and negative words (e.g., rainbow or ugly). Participants' response times, recorded by a computer, provided the measure of implicit group evaluation. We compared the "extremist sectarian" IAT scores with results of a standard Catholic-Protestant IAT, which measured the degree to which people associated Catholic names (e.g., Patrick, Maire) and Protestant names (e.g., Robert, Jane) with positive and negative words. To assess explicit prejudice, Catholic and Protestant student participants were asked to rate the degree to which they felt "cold" or "warm" towards Catholics and Protestants, on a "feeling thermometer" scale of 0° to 100° (see Haddock, Zanna, and Esses, 1993). Both Catholics and Protestants clearly displayed relative ingroup–outgroup bias on both implicit and explicit levels; but on both measures Catholics showed greater bias than did Protestants.

Brewer (1999) pointed out that a positive attitude towards the ingroup does not necessarily imply a negative one towards the outgroup. Ingroup favoritism and outgroup derogation are, in principle, orthogonal concepts, and indeed are often found to be uncorrelated in empirical research. However, because the IAT does not allow for separation of these concepts (Catholic-Good is always linked to Protestant-Bad in the IAT), we used the go/no-go association task (GNAT; Nosek and Banaji, 2001), and had the same respondents complete this additional implicit measure to investigate separately implicit ingroup favoritism (Catholic-Good versus Protestant-Good) and outgroup derogation (Catholic-Bad versus Protestant-Bad). For the GNAT, participants were instructed to respond quickly to items that fell into one of the categories (e.g., "Catholic name" or "Good") by pressing the space bar, but to ignore any item that did not fit either category. Results showed that both Catholics and Protestants displayed ingroup favoritism *and* outgroup derogation on the implicit level.

Further analyses revealed that implicit associations with extremist sectarian groups in particular (as opposed to the outgroup in general) were related to intergroup outcomes, in terms of trust, forgiveness, and behavioral tendencies. The extremist group IAT predicted several intergroup measures that the Catholic-Protestant IAT did not. Negative associations with the outgroup *extremists* were associated with decreased forgiveness towards the other community ($r = -.24$, $N = 56$, $p = .07$) and increased distrust towards them ($r = .33$, $p < .02$). Interestingly, while negative associations with outgroup extremists were strongly related to *aggressive* behavioral tendencies towards the other community ($r = .42$, $p = .001$) (e.g., argue with them, confront them), they were only marginally related to avoidant behavioral tendencies ($r = .22$, $p = .10$) (e.g., avoid them, keep them at a distance). Negative associations with the *outgroup in general* were not associated with these three variables ($r = -.17$, $r = -.04$, $r = .08$, respectively, all *n.s.*), nor were the GNAT measures of ingroup favoritism and outgroup derogation towards the *outgroup in general*. We therefore concluded that implicit associations with the extremist groups from the other community are distinct markers of intergroup distrust, aggressive behavioral tendencies, and a lack of forgiveness. These findings highlight the importance of developing interventions in Northern Ireland that focus on reducing fears and negative feelings about extremist groups specifically, rather than only the outgroup in general, and of targeting implicit as well as explicit biases.

Our final set of findings on intergroup trust in Northern Ireland come from a large sample of young people aged 16–19 years, who completed the 2003 Young Life & Times Survey (The Northern Ireland Life & Times Survey is a long-running, well-established and well-reputed annual "barometer" of social attitudes in Northern Ireland; see www.ark.ac.uk/ylt/). We conducted secondary analyses on this publicly available data set, which includes a number of measures relevant to our exploration of intergroup trust. The original sample was 902, which reduced to 762 when participants who did not identify as being either Catholic or Protestant were excluded (the sample was further reduced, and varied across measures, due to missing data and "don't know" responses). First, we classified respondents according to whether they lived in "mainly ingroup" ($N = 460$), "mainly outgroup" ($N = 41$), or "mixed" ($N = 212$) residential areas (for all respondents who indicated their religious background and area composition). Next, we recorded how many of their "close friends" came from "the other main religious community." Finally, we used two measures from the survey which pertained to different types of trust. These were items in which they gave their level of agreement to the statements that (1) "Most people who live in this area trust one another," and (2) "Would you say that you trust: (i) most of the people in your area, (ii) many, (iii) a few, (iv) you do not trust, or (v) don't know."

Looking first at the mean level of responses, respondents living in areas containing "mainly ingroup members" had, as would be expected, less contact with outgroup friends than respondents living in either "mixed" or "mainly outgroup" areas. Moreover, we found that respondents living in "mainly outgroup" areas showed lower agreement that most people living in their area trusted one another, than did respondents living in either "mainly ingroup" or "mixed" areas. Additionally, there were no reliable differences between areas in the extent to which respondents said that they personally would trust people in their area. Finally, we computed correlations between the number of reported outgroup friends (the most intimate measure of contact) and the two measures of trust (agreement that most people living in their area trusted one another, and the extent to which respondents said that they personally would trust people in their area) in each of the three types of area. There was one especially interesting result. For those young people living in an area dominated by the outgroup, for whom one might expect daily life to contain numerous challenges, there was a highly significant positive correlation between cross-group friends, and agreement that the area was a friendly place to live in.

Summarizing this body of research on trust in young people in Northern Ireland, we have collected extensive evidence of a strong positive association between both direct and indirect intergroup contact and outgroup trust, and between trust and action tendencies towards the ethno-religious outgroup. Young people who identify more strongly with their group, however, are less able to take the perspective of outgroup members, and, in turn, are less trusting of the other group. Nonetheless, cross-group friendships may be an especially valuable resource for promoting prosocial orientations, including empathy, perspective-taking, trust, and forgiveness. Finally, we found that implicit associations with extremist groups were especially strong markers of outgroup distrust, and that respondents' cross-group friendships were associated with their feeling of safety in their neighborhoods, even when they lived in an area where their own group was in a small minority.

Intergroup trust in South Africa

Whereas the situation in Northern Ireland is a classic, dichotomous conflict between ingroup and outgroup, the setting in South Africa is more complex in some ways. South Africa is arguably one of the most multicultural countries in the world (Vora and Vora, 2004). The South African population is comprised of Black South Africans (who make up the majority of the population), White South Africans, Colored South Africans (people of mixed racial heritage), and Indian South Africans (who are predominantly of East Indian descent). South Africa's tumultuous history of intergroup relations is characterized by conflict and distrust. This can be traced back to the arrival of the first Dutch settlers in 1652. They bartered for cattle with the local inhabitants, but what started out as a cordial relationship soon became hostile as the expanding colony encroached upon land used by the locals as grazing land, leading to disputes and open conflict (Thompson, 2001). Poor relations continued over the subsequent decades. In the 1920s, White Afrikaners perceived a threat, or *swart gevaar* (Black peril), posed to the cultural and economic future of White South Africans by continued contact and intermixing with non-White South Africans. This fear, which was manipulated by the Nationalist media at the time into full-blown distrust (even paranoia), was the driving force behind apartheid (Lubbe, 1991), the iniquitous policy to keep members of different racial groups separate from one another.

Apartheid came into being in 1948, under the predominately Afrikaans National Party, and was a grand exercise in racial segregation, which attempted to reduce intergroup contact between Whites and non-Whites to the bare minimum (Lemon, 1987). A host of laws criminalized intimate intergroup contact and drastically restricted social intergroup contact (discouraging specifically the establishment of cross-group friendships). Moreover, apartheid was maintained through warnings from members of the government of the negative consequences that were to be expected from intergroup contact (Kuper, Watts, and Davies, 1958). Accordingly, White South Africans acquired expectations regarding non-White South Africans that were negative in nature, and characterized by prejudice and distrust (e.g., Nieuwoudt and Plug, 1983). On the other side, Black, Colored (the term used in South Africa to describe mixed-race individuals with some sub-Saharan ancestry), and Indian South Africans had undergone almost three hundred of years of exploitation by White South Africans, including 40 years of systematic oppression under apartheid, resulting in very low levels of intergroup trust.

When apartheid came to an end in 1994, the new President of South Africa, Nelson Mandela, embraced the idea of a "rainbow nation," to be characterized by cooperation, sharing, and charity between the different groups, where groups would not feel threatened by one another and would be able to trust one another (Broodryk, 2002; Tutu, 1999). However, a number of indicators suggest that distrust remains among all sections of South African society. As many as 66 percent of South Africans believe outgroup members are untrustworthy (e.g., Gibson, 2004; Mattes, Chikwanha, and Magezi, 2005; Slabbert, 2001), and that outgroup members are more prejudiced than ingroup members (Roefs, 2005).

One explanation for this continued distrust may be a lack of meaningful contact between different groups. There continues to exist large-scale residential segregation in South African towns, which, in turn, translates into racially homogeneous schools, churches, and community groups (Chisholm and Nkomo, 2005). Concomitant with this residential segregation, a national survey found that 15.5 percent of Indians, 32.0 percent of Coloreds, and 37.7 percent of Whites reported having no Black friends, while 56.4 percent of Blacks reported having no White friends. Furthermore, roughly 25 percent of Whites, Indians, and Coloreds found it hard to imagine ever being friends with a Black person, while 50 percent of Black respondents found it hard to imagine ever being friends with a White person (Gibson, 2004).

In order to investigate whether intergroup contact might help to generate intergroup trust in South Africa, Swart and Hewstone (in preparation) conducted a survey with White (mean age 16.83 years) and Colored (mean age 16.93 years) senior high school students in South Africa. Participants completed measures of cross-group friendship, intergroup anxiety, and intergroup trust, and we used SEM to analyze the structural relationships between these variables. The SEM showed that there was a significant path between cross-group friendship and intergroup trust: the more cross-group friends that White and Colored participants had, the more they trusted the outgroup. Further analyses showed that this relationship was partially mediated by intergroup anxiety: participants with outgroup friends were less anxious at the prospect of interacting with outgroup members, which in turn was associated with greater trust of the outgroup. We concluded that it is important to encourage interventions that focus on bringing South Africans together in contact settings that have an atmosphere that is conducive to the establishment of social bonds, as this will facilitate both the reduction of intergroup anxiety and the development of trust.

Intergroup trust between South Asians and Whites in the UK

Finally, we consider intergroup trust in the context of relations between the South Asian and White communities in the UK. South Asians form the largest ethnic minority in the UK (Census, 2001), yet relations between the two communities have not always been harmonious, and in recent times, ethnic tensions appear to have increased. In 2000–2001, police recorded 25,100 incidences of racially aggravated harassment, common assault and wounding in England and Wales. The number of racial attacks reported to the police, however, may be only a fraction of the actual attacks that take place. According to the British Crime Survey (2001), those at greatest risk of racial attacks are Pakistanis and Bangladeshis (4.2 percent), followed by Indians (3.6 percent), and Black people (2.2 percent). By comparison, a tiny 0.3 percent of White people are victims of racially aggravated crimes. The animosity between the Asian and White communities has economic, social, and political antecedents. However, racial tensions may have been exacerbated and maintained by high levels of segregation between the two groups. A number of government reports blamed poor race relations on a lack of social cohesion between different ethnic groups (e.g., Cantle, 2001; Ouseley, 2001). Indeed, a survey undertaken by YouGov (2004) indicated the extent of the divide nationally – what the Cantle Report referred to as living "parallel lives" – revealing that 90 percent of White people have no, or hardly any, non-White friends.

Across three studies, one with primary school children (aged 7–11 years), and two with secondary school children (aged 11–16 years), we found that children who had experienced more cross-group friendships with the other community had more positive attitudes towards that community, a relationship that was mediated by self-disclosure (Turner, Hewstone, and Voci, 2007). Specifically, the more cross-group friendships children had, the more likely they were to have disclosed information of a personal nature to an outgroup member. In turn, the more children had self-disclosed, the more positive their attitudes were to the outgroup in general. We conducted a fourth study to investigate why self-disclosure seemed to be such an important predictor of reduced prejudice, and we expected that intergroup trust might be one factor that played an important role.

Kerr, Stattin, and Trost (1999) proposed that trust develops over time, as a result of experiences that show that a person's behavior is predictable and dependable. The more we learn about someone through their disclosures, the more certain we are that we can predict their future behavior in critical, integrity-testing situations. Accordingly, Kerr and colleagues found that children's self-disclosure to their parents predicted parental trust. Clearly, we are unlikely to disclose personal information to another person in the first place if we suspect that it may be misused. Self-disclosure is, however, a positively reinforcing process as a relationship develops (Altman and Taylor, 1973). Thus, as two acquaintances get to know one another and realize that the information they disclose is safe with the recipient, the intimacy of their self-disclosures and their trust in one another should increase. Trust should, in turn, lead to more positive attitudes; Petty and Mirels (1981) argued that self-disclosure implies a trust and confidence in the recipient, and that people trust and like those who trust them.

We also identified two further mechanisms through which self-disclosure during cross-group friendships might reduce prejudice. Specifically, we expected that self-disclosure might generate empathy (Stephan and Finlay, 1999) and increase the perception that contact is personally important for broadening one's horizons (Van Dick, Wagner, Pettigrew, Christ, Wolf, Petzel, Smith, Castro, and Jackson, 2004).

In order to test these potential mediators of the relationship between outgroup self-disclosure and outgroup attitudes, we conducted a survey among White undergraduate students, regarding their experiences with and attitudes towards South Asians. We found that self-disclosure mediated the relationship between cross-group friendship and trust, empathy, perceived importance of contact, and outgroup attitudes. We then looked at the relationship between self-disclosure and outgroup attitude. We found that intergroup trust, empathy, perceived importance of contact, and outgroup attitude fully mediated this relationship (see Figure 14.2). That is, the more people had experienced disclosure with outgroup members, the more they trusted and empathized with the outgroup, and perceived contact to be important. In turn, trust, empathy, and importance of contact predicted more positive outgroup attitudes. These findings suggest that intergroup trust plays an important role in predicting the positive consequences of self-disclosure during cross-group friendships.

Conclusions

Our research has shown that intergroup trust is an important component of intergroup relations among young people in three very different social contexts: relations between Catholics and Protestants in Northern Ireland,

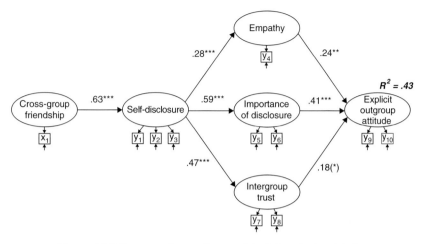

Figure 14.2 Structural equation model of the relationship between cross-group friendship and outgroup attitude, showing mediation via self-disclosure, importance of self-disclosure, intergroup trust and empathy. Data from Turner, Hewstone, and Voci (2007, Study 4). *Notes:* $*p < .05$; $**p < .01$; $***p < .001$

between different ethnic groups in South Africa, and between South Asians and Whites in the UK. In the aftermath of intergroup conflict, and in contexts where levels of intergroup segregation are high, suspicion and distrust tend to be high, and contribute towards negative intergroup relations. By identifying some of the factors that predict intergroup trust, however, we can suggest some strategies for alleviating problematic intergroup relations. Below, we summarize the predictors and mediators of intergroup trust, and make some recommendations for policy and practice.

Predictors of intergroup trust

We have found that three different types of intergroup contact promote intergroup trust: the amount of high-quality contact that participants have experienced (Tam, Hewstone, Kenworthy, and Cairns, 2009), the number of cross-group friends that participants have (Myers, Hewstone, and Cairns, in preparation; Swart and Hewstone, in preparation; Turner, Hewstone, and Voci, 2007), and extended contact – the number of ingroup members participants know who have outgroup friends (Tam, Hewstone, Kenworthy, and Cairns, 2009). The impact of direct forms of intergroup contact emphasizes the importance of introducing contact schemes as a key part of the conflict-resolution process, bringing members of opposing groups together in order to alleviate distrust. If members of different groups are given the opportunity to learn and socialize together in educational settings and beyond, this may provide the greatest likelihood of generating intergroup trust.

Unfortunately, in post-conflict settings there are often high levels of educational segregation (Chisholm and Nkomo, 2005; NICIE, 2008). It is therefore important that policymakers and educators are made aware of the benefits of increasing educational integration. An additional strategy might be to introduce interventions based on extended contact in schools. Such interventions – which involve reading stories about cross-group friendships or sharing information with peers about one's experiences of cross-group friendship – have already been shown to have benefits for intergroup relations, and we now have reason to believe that they will generate intergroup trust too (Cameron and Rutland, 2006; Cameron, Rutland, Brown, and Douch, 2006; Tam, Hewstone, Kenworthy, and Cairns, 2009).

Negative implicit associations held about extremist groups (Tam, Hewstone, Kenworthy, Cairns, Marinetti, Geddes, and Parkinson, 2008) and ingroup identification (Myers, Hewstone, and Cairns, in preparation) were associated with higher levels of distrust. Given that memories of the terror wrought by extremist groups are prominent, and ingroup identification is high in conflict and post-conflict settings, this is problematic. Intergroup contact may, however, provide a potential solution. Positive experiences with outgroup members may "dilute" negative implicit associations held regarding extremist groups. Intergroup contact has also been shown to promote identification with superordinate or "common ingroup" identities, as people realize they share more in common with the outgroup than they previously thought (e.g., Gaertner and Dovidio, 2000). However, it is important to ensure that group members do not feel forced to give up group identities that are important to them, as this can lead to a reactive increase in prejudice (e.g., Crisp, Stone, and Hall, 2006). Encouraging people to hold a "dual identity," whereby they maintain their original group membership but share an additional group membership with the outgroup, can help to circumvent this problem (Gaertner and Dovidio, 2000).

Mediating mechanisms

We have found that intergroup trust is a powerful mediator of the relationship between direct and extended contact on the one hand, and positive and negative behavioral tendencies towards the outgroup on the other. Intergroup attitudes, on the other hand, played a weaker mediating role

(Tam, Hewstone, Kenworthy, and Cairns, 2009). These findings highlight the importance of developing interventions that target intergroup trust, rather than just focusing on improving general positive feelings towards the outgroup, if we are to bring about positive changes in the ways groups treat one another.

Finally, we have also uncovered several mechanisms that underlie the relationship between intergroup contact and intergroup trust. The relationship between cross-group friendship and intergroup trust is mediated by an increase in empathic affect and perspective-taking (Myers, Hewstone, and Cairns, in preparation), and self-disclosure (Turner, Hewstone, and Voci, 2007), and a decrease in intergroup anxiety (Swart and Hewstone, in preparation). These findings highlight the importance of developing interventions in schools and universities. Particularly important are programs involving intergroup contact, which generate cross-group empathy and perspective-taking, reduce discomfort at the prospect of interacting with the outgroup, and provide opportunities for close relationships to develop between members of different groups, whereby they feel able to share their thoughts and feelings with one another.

Caveat and future directions

Notwithstanding the achievements of our research program to date – including multiple replications within and between intergroup contexts – a caveat is in order, and it highlights the need for future research. All of our research to date has been cross-sectional, thus preventing us from drawing confident causal inferences, a concern that is typically raised in the context of intergroup contact research (Pettigrew, 1998). The model we have presented in each case is the best model which has been found superior to theoretically plausible alternatives. This allows us to draw tentative conclusions that the set of relationships between contact, mediators, and trust is, in fact, in line with the causal direction proposed in this paper. Nonetheless, future research must include both experimental and longitudinal designs, which will allow for more confident assessments of the direction of causality, and indeed we have already carried out such research on intergroup contact (although not yet with trust as an outcome), and are currently undertaking new studies that will help to address these lacunae.

Acknowledgments

We gratefully acknowledge the financial support of the Community Relations Unit, the Economic and Social Research Council, and the Russell Sage Foundation, for funding parts of the research reviewed in this chapter.

References

Allport, G.W. (1954). *The nature of prejudice*. Oxford: Addison-Wesley.

Altman, I. and Taylor, D.A. (1973). *Social penetration: The development of interpersonal relationships*. New York: Holt, Rinehart & Winston.

Batson, C.D. and Shaw, L.L. (1991). Evidence for altruism: Toward a pluralism of prosocial motives. *Psychological Enquiry*, 2, 107–122.

Batson, C.D., Polycarpou, M.P., Harmon-Jones, E., Imhoff, H.J., Mitchener, E.C., Bednar, L.L., Klein, T.R., and Highberger, L. (1997). Empathy and attitudes: Can feeling for a member of a stigmatized group improve feelings towards the group? *Journal of Personality and Social Psychology*, 72, 105–118.

Bernath, M.S. and Feshbach, N.D. (1995). Children's trust: Theory, assessment, development, and research directions. *Applied & Preventive Psychology*, 4, 1–19.

Blackstock, M.D. (2001). Where is the trust? Using trust-based mediation for first nations dispute resolution. *Conflict Resolution Quarterly*, 19, 9–30.

Brehm, J. and Rahn, W. (1997). Individual-level evidence for the causes and consequences of social capital. *American Journal of Political Science*, 41, 999–1023.

Brewer, M.B. (1999). The psychology of prejudice: Ingroup love or outgroup hate? *Journal of Social Issues*, 55, 429–444.

Brewer, M. and Alexander, M.G. (2002). Intergroup emotions and images. In D.M. Mackie and E.R. Smith (eds.), *From prejudice to intergroup emotions: Differentiated reactions to social groups* (pp. 209–226). New York: Psychology Press.

Bridges, L.J. (2003). Trust, attachment, and relatedness. In M.H. Bornstein and L. Davidson (eds.), *Well-being: Positive development across the life course: Crosscurrents in contemporary psychology* (pp. 177–189). Mahwah, NJ: Lawrence Erlbaum Associates.

British Crime Survey (2001). Retrieved from www.homeoffice.gov.uk/rds/bcs1.html on August 2, 2005.

Broodryk, J. (2002). *Ubuntu: Life lessons from Africa*. Pretoria: Ubuntu School of Philosophy.

Buzzelli, C.A. (1988). The development of trust in children's relations with peers. *Child Study Journal*, 18, 33–46.

Cairns, R.B., Leung, M.-C., Buchanan, L., and Cairns, B.D. (1995). Friendship and social networks in childhood and adolescence: Fluidity, reliability, and interrelations. *Child Development*, 66, 1330–1345.

Cameron, L. and Rutland, A. (2006). Extended contact through story reading in school: Reducing children's prejudice toward the disabled. *Journal of Social Issues*, 62, 469–488.

Cameron, L., Rutland, A., Brown, R., and Douch, R. (2006). Changing children's intergroup attitudes towards refugees: Testing different models of extended contact. *Child Development*, 77, 1208–1219.

Cantle, T. (2001). *Community cohesion: A report by the independent review team*. London: Home Office.

Census (2001). Office for National Statistics. Retrieved from http://neighbourhood.statistics.gov.uk/ on October 20, 2003.

Chen, M. and Bargh, J. (1997). Nonconscious behavioural confirmation processes: The self-fulfilling consequences of automatic stereotype activation. *Journal of Experimental Social Psychology*, **33**, 541–560.

Chisholm, L. and Nkomo, M. (2005). Bringing the South African rainbow into schools. *HSRC Review*, **3** (3), 15–16. Retrieved from www.hsrc.ac.za/about/HSRCReview/Vol3No3/HSRCReview.pdf on March 3, 2006.

Crisp, R. J., Stone, C. H., and Hall, N. R. (2006). Recategorization and subgroup identification: Predicting and preventing threats from common ingroups. *Personality and Social Psychology Bulletin*, **32**, 230–243.

Davis, M. H. (1983). Measuring individual differences in empathy: Evidence for a multidimensional approach. *Journal of Personality and Social Psychology*, **44**, 113–126.

Deutsch, M. (1973). *The resolution of conflict: Constructive and destructive processes*. New Haven, CT: Yale University Press.

Doosje, B., Branscombe, N. R., Spears, R., and Manstead, A. S. R. (1998). Guilt by association: When one's group has a negative history. *Journal of Personality and Social Psychology*, **75**, 872–886.

Dovidio, J. F., Gaertner, S. L., and Kawakami, K. (2003). Intergroup contact: The past, present, and the future. *Group Processes and Intergroup Relations*, **6**, 5–20.

Dovidio, J. F., Gaertner, S. L., Kawakami, K., and Hodson, G. (2002). Why can't we just get along? Interpersonal biases and interracial distrust. *Cultural Diversity and Ethnic Minority Psychology*, **8**, 88–102.

Dovidio, J. F., Kawakami, K., and Gaertner, S. L. (2002). Implicit and explicit prejudice and interracial interaction. *Journal of Personality and Social Psychology*, **82**, 62–68.

Foley, F. and Robinson, G. (2004). *Politicians and community relations in Northern Ireland*. Londonderry: *International Conflict Research*. Retrieved from www.incore.ulster.ac.uk on January 10, 2006.

Gaertner, S. L. and Dovidio, J. F. (2000). *Reducing intergroup bias: The Common Ingroup Identity Model*. Philadelphia, PA: Psychology Press and Taylor & Francis.

Galinsky, A. D. and Moskowitz, G. B. (2000). Perspective-taking: Decreasing stereotype expression, stereotype accessibility, and ingroup favoritism. *Journal of Personality and Social Psychology*, **78**, 708–724.

Gallagher, A. M. (1989). Social identity and the Northern Ireland conflict. *Human Relations*, **42**, 917–935.

  (1995). Equality, contact and pluralism: Attitudes to community relations. In R. Breen, P. Devine, and G. Robinson (eds.), *Social attitudes in Northern Ireland: The fourth report* (pp. 13–32). Belfast: Appletree Press.

Gibson, J. L. (2004). *Overcoming apartheid: Can truth reconcile a divided nation?* New York: Russell Sage Foundation.

Greenwald, A. G., McGee, D. E., and Schwartz, J. L. K. (1998). Measuring individual differences in implicit cognition: The implicit association test. *Journal of Personality and Social Psychology*, **74**, 1464–1480.

Haddock, G., Zanna, M. P., and Esses, V. M. (1993). Assessing the structure of prejudicial attitudes: The case of attitudes towards homosexuals. *Journal of Personality and Social Psychology*, **65**, 1105–1118.

Hayashi, N., Ostrom, E., Walker, J., and Yamagishi, T. (1999). Reciprocity, trust, and the sense of control: A cross-societal study. *Rationality and Society*, **11**, 27–46.

Hewstone, M., Cairns, E., Kenworthy, J., Hughes, J., Tausch, N., Voci, A., von Hecker, U., Tam, T., and Pinder, C. (2008). Stepping stones to reconciliation in Northern Ireland: Intergroup contact, forgiveness and trust. In A. Nadler, T. Malloy, and J. D. Fisher (eds.), *The social psychology of intergroup reconciliation* (pp. 199–226). New York: Oxford University Press.

Hewstone, M., Cairns, E., Voci, A., Hamberger, J., and Niens, U. (2006). Intergroup contact, forgiveness, and experience of "The Troubles" in Northern Ireland. *Journal of Social Issues*, **62**, 99–120.

Hewstone, M., Cairns, E., Voci, A., Paolini, S., McLernon, F., Crisp, R., and Niens, U. (2005). Intergroup contact in a divided society: Challenging segregation in Northern Ireland. In D. Abrams, J. M. Marques, and M. A. Hogg (eds.), *The social psychology of inclusion and exclusion* (pp. 265–292). Philadelphia, PA: Psychology Press.

Iyer, A., Leach, C. W., and Pedersen, A. (2004). Racial wrongs and restitutions: The role of guilt and other group-based emotions. In N. R. Branscombe and B. Doosje (eds.), *Collective guilt: International perspectives* (pp. 262–283). New York: Cambridge University Press.

Joint Declaration by the British and Irish Governments (2003). Retrieved from www.cain.ulst.ac.uk/events/peace/docs/bijoint010503.pdf on December 15, 2008.

Kerr, M., Stattin, H., and Trost, K. (1999). To know you is to trust you: Parents' trust is rooted in child disclosure of information. *Journal of Adolescence*, **22**, 737–752.

Kuper, L., Watts, H., and Davies, R. (1958). *Durban: A study in racial ecology.* London: Jonathan Cape.

Lemon, A. (1987). *Apartheid in transition.* Hants: Gower.

Lester, D. and Gatto, J. (1990). Interpersonal trust, depression, and suicidal ideation in teenagers. *Psychological Reports*, **67**, 786.

Lewicki, R. J., McAllister, D. J., and Bies, R. J. (1998). Trust and distrust: New relationships and realities. *Academy of Management Review*, **23**, 438–458.

Liebkind, K. and McAlister, A. L. (1999). Extended contact through peer modelling to promote tolerance in Finland. *European Journal of Social Psychology*, **29**, 765–780.

Lubbe, H. J. (1991). *Die Burger en die "Swart Gevaar" – propaganda gedurende die parlementêre verkiesing van 1928 tot 1929 [Die Burger and the "Black Peril" – propaganda during the parliamentary election from 1928 to 1929].* Unpublished master's thesis, University of South Africa.

Mackie, D. M., Devos, T., and Smith, E. R. (2000). Intergroup emotions: Explaining offensive action tendencies in an intergroup context. *Journal of Personality and Social Psychology*, **79**, 602–616.

Maddux, W. and Brewer, M. (2005). Gender differences in the relational and collective bases for trust. *Group Processes and Intergroup Relations*, **8**, 159–171.

Manzi, J. and González, R. (2007). Forgiveness and reparation in Chile: The role of cognitive and emotional intergroup antecedents. *Peace and Conflict: Journal of Peace Psychology*, **13**, 71–91.

Mattes, R., Chikwanha, A. B., and Magezi, A. (2005). *South Africa: After a decade of democracy*. Retrieved from www.afrobarometer.org/Summary%20of%20 Results/Round%202.5/SAFSOR-Round2.5-FINAL.pdf on 9 April, 2006.

McLernon, F., Cairns, E., and Hewstone, M. (2002). Views on forgiveness in Northern Ireland. *Peace Review: A Journal of Social Justice*, 14, 285–290.

Mitchell, G. (1999). *Making peace*. Berkeley: University of California Press.

Myers, E., Hewstone, M., and Cairns, E. (2009). Impact of conflict on mental health in Northern Ireland: The mediating role of intergroup forgiveness and collective guilt. *Political Psychology*, 30, 269–290.

(in preparation). Predictors and mediators of intergroup forgiveness and trust in Northern Ireland.

Nelson, S., Dickson, D. A., and Hargie, O. D. W. (2003). Learning together, living apart: The experiences of university students in Northern Ireland. *International Journal of Qualitative Studies in Education*, 16, 777–795.

NICIE (2008). *Northern Irish Council for Integrated Schools Annual Report*. Retrieved from www.nicie.org/publications on May 19, 2008.

Nieuwoudt, J. M. and Plug, C. (1983). South African ethnic attitudes: 1973 to 1978. *Journal of Social Psychology*, 121, 163–171.

Nosek, B. A. and Banaji, M. R. (2001). The go/no-go association task. *Social Cognition*, 19, 625–666.

Ouseley, H. (2001). *Community pride, not prejudice: Making diversity work in Bradford*. Bradford Vision.

Paolini, S., Hewstone, M., Cairns, E., and Voci, A. (2004). Effects of direct and indirect cross-group friendships on judgments of Catholics and Protestants in Northern Ireland: The mediating role of an anxiety-reduction mechanism. *Personality and Social Psychology Bulletin*, 30, 770–786.

Pettigrew, T. F. (1997). Generalized intergroup contact effects on prejudice. *Personality and Social Psychology Bulletin*, 23, 173–185.

(1998). Intergroup contact theory. *Annual Review of Psychology*, 49, 65–85.

Pettigrew, T. F. and Tropp, L. R. (2006). A meta-analytic test of intergroup contact theory. *Journal of Personality and Social Psychology*, 90, 751–783.

Petty, R. E. and Mirels, H. L. (1981). Intimacy and scarcity of self-disclosure: Effects on interpersonal attraction for males and females. *Personality and Social Psychology Bulletin*, 7, 493–503.

Phinney, J. S. (1989). Stages of ethnic identity development in minority group adolescents. *Journal of Early Adolescence*, 9, 34–49.

(1993). A three stage model of ethnic identity development in adolescence. In M. E. Bernal and G. P. Knight (eds.), *Ethnic identity: Formation and transmission among Hispanics and other minorities* (pp. 61–80). Albany, NY: State University of New York Press.

Phinney, J. S. and Chavira, V. (1992). Ethnic identity and self-esteem: An exploratory longitudinal study. *Journal of Adolescence*, 15, 271–288.

Roefs, M. (2005). Embracing the rainbow nation could help bridge the colour divide. *HSRC Review*, 3 (2), 3. Retrieved from www.hsrc.ac.za/about/HSRCReview/Vol3No2/HSRCReview.pdf on March 3, 2006.

Rotenberg, K. J. (1991). Children's interpersonal trust: An introduction. In K. J. Rotenberg (ed.), *Children's interpersonal trust: Sensitivity to lying, deception, and promise violations* (pp. 1–10). New York: Springer-Verlag.

Rotenberg, K.J. and Cerda, C. (1994). Racially based trust expectancies of Native American and Caucasian children. *Journal of Social Psychology*, **134**, 621–631.

Rotenberg, K.J. and Morgan, C.J. (1995). Development of a scale to measure individual differences in children's trust-value basis of friendship. *Journal of Genetic Psychology*, **156**, 489–503.

Rotenberg, K.J., Fox, C., Green, S., Ruderman, L., Slater, K., Stevens, K., and Carlo, G. (2005). Construction and validation of a children's interpersonal trust belief scale. *British Journal of Developmental Psychology*, **23**, 271–292.

Rothbart, M. and Park, B. (1986). On the confirmability and disconfirmability of trait concepts. *Journal of Personality and Social Psychology*, **50**, 131–142.

Rotter, J.B. (1980). Interpersonal trust, trustworthiness, and gullibility. *American Psychologist*, **35**, 1–7.

Rutter, M., Maughan, B., Mortimore, P., Ouston, J., and Smith, A. (1979). *Fifteen thousand hours*. Cambridge, MA: Harvard University Press.

Slabbert, A. (2001). Cross-cultural racism in South Africa – dead or alive? *Social Behaviour and Personality*, **29**, 125–132.

Smyth, M. and Hamilton, J. (2003). The human costs of the Troubles. In O. Hargie and D. Dickson (eds.), *Researching the Troubles: Social science perspectives on the Northern Ireland conflict* (pp. 15–36). Edinburgh: Mainstream Publishing.

Stephan, W.G. and Finlay, K. (1999). The role of empathy in improving intergroup relations. *Journal of Social Issues*, **55**, 729–743.

Stephan, W.G. and Stephan, C.W. (1985). Intergroup anxiety. *Journal of Social Issues*, **41**, 157–176.

Swart, H. and Hewstone, M. (in preparation). *Intergroup trust in South Africa*.

Tajfel, H. and Turner, J.C. (1986). The social identity theory of intergroup behaviour. In S. Worchel and W. Austin (eds.), *Psychology of intergroup relations* (pp. 7–24). Chicago: Nelson-Hall.

Tam, T., Hewstone, M., Cairns, E., Tausch, N., Maio, G., and Kenworthy, J. (2007). The impact of intergroup emotions on forgiveness. *Group Processes and Intergroup Relations*, **10**, 119–136.

Tam, T., Hewstone, M., Kenworthy, J., and Cairns, E. (2009). Intergroup trust in Northern Ireland. *Personality and Social Psychology Bulletin*, **35**, 45–59.

Tam, T., Hewstone, M., Kenworthy, J., Cairns, E., Marinetti, C., Geddes, L., and Parkinson, B. (2008). Post-conflict reconciliation: Intergroup forgiveness, trust, and implicit biases in Northern Ireland. *Journal of Social Issues*, **64**, 303–320.

Thompson, L. (2001). *A history of South Africa* (3rd edn.). New Haven, CT: Yale University Press.

Trew, K. and Benson, D. (1996). Dimensions of social identity in Northern Ireland. In G.M. Breakwell and E. Lyons (eds.), *Changing European identities* (pp. 123–143). Oxford: Butterworth-Heinemann.

Turner, R.N., Hewstone, M., and Voci, A. (2007). Reducing explicit and implicit outgroup prejudice via direct and extended contact: The mediating role of self-disclosure and intergroup anxiety. *Journal of Personality and Social Psychology*, **93**, 369–388.

Turner, R. N., Hewstone, M., Voci, A., Paolini, S., and Christ, O. (2007). Reducing prejudice via direct and extended cross-group friendship. *European Review of Social Psychology*, **18**, 212–255.

Turner, R. N., Hewstone, M., Voci, A., and Vonofakou, C. (2008). A test of the extended intergroup contact hypothesis: The mediating role of intergroup anxiety, perceived ingroup and outgroup norms, and inclusion of the outgroup in the self. *Journal of Personality and Social Psychology*, **95**, 843–860.

Tutu, D. (1999). *No future without forgiveness*. New York: Doubleday.

Van Dick, R., Wagner, U., Pettigrew, T. F., Christ, O., Wolf, C., Petzel, T., Smith Castro, V., and Jackson, J. S. (2004). Role of perceived importance in intergroup contact. *Journal of Personality and Social Psychology*, **87**, 211–227.

Vora, J. A. and Vora, E. (2004). The effectiveness of South Africa's Truth and Reconciliation Commission: Perceptions of Xhosa, Afrikaner and English South Africans. *Journal of Black Studies*, **34**, 301–322.

Webb, W. M. and Worchel, P. (1986). Trust and distrust. In S. Worchel and W. G. Austin (eds.), *Psychology of Intergroup Relations* (pp. 213–228). Chicago: Nelson-Hall.

Wentzel, K. R. (1991). Relations between social competence and academic achievements in early adolescence. *Child Development*, **62**, 1066–1078.

Whyte, J. (1986). How is the boundary maintained between the two communities in Northern Ireland? *Ethnic and Racial Studies*, **9**, 19–34.

Wohl, W. J. A., Branscombe, N. R., and Klar, Y. (2006). Collective guilt: Justice-based emotional reactions when one's group has done wrong or been wronged. *European Review of Social Psychology*, **17**, 1–37.

Worchel, S., Cooper, J., and Goethals, G. R. (1991). *Understanding social psychology*. Pacific Grove, CA: Brooks/Cole Publishing Company.

Wright, S. C., Aron, A., McLaughlin-Volpe, T., and Ropp, S. A. (1997). The extended contact effect: Knowledge of cross-group friendships and prejudice. *Journal of Personality and Social Psychology*, **73**, 73–90.

Wright, T. L. and Kirmani, A. (1977). Interpersonal trust, trustworthiness, and shoplifting in high school. *Psychological Reports*, **41**, 1165–1166.

Yamagishi, T. and Yamagishi, M. (1994). Trust and commitment in the United States and Japan. *Motivation and Emotion*, **18**, 129–166.

YouGov (2004). *YouGov survey for the Commission for Racial Equality*. Retrieved from www.yougov.co.uk/archives/pdf/RCF040101001_1.pdf on August 2, 2005.

Index

families
  and adolescent trust, 254, 259–261, 264
  and parental trust beliefs in adolescents,
    205
  see also adolescent–parent relationship;
    parents; siblings; significant
    others
fathers, 254, 259–261, 264, 282–285
Finkenauer, C., 205
Fitzpatrick, S., 170
forgiveness, 303–305, 307
Fox, C., 18, 110, 162
Fraley, R. C., 135, 137
Frank, R. H., 42
friends
  best friends, 60, 63, 64, 66, 68–70,
    125–127
  cross-group, 298–299, 303–305, 308,
    310, 311–312
  during adolescent development, 248–249
  prosocial, 281, 282–285, 288
  see also peer relationships; significant
    others
Furman, W., 114
Fusaro, M., 100, 102

game theory, 37–39
gender, 15
  and development of trust, 63
  and effects of social support, 71–72, 78
  and lying, 183
  and prosocial behaviors, 289
  and reciprocity, 126
  and response to life events, 74
generalization of trust, 57
Generalized Trust Beliefs-Late Adolescence
    (GTB-LA), 252–253, 256–259,
    272, 280–281
  assessment of, 261–266
genetics, 47–48
  evolutionary approach to sibling trust,
    137–138, 145, 146
  see also behavioral genetics approach
go/no-go association task (GNAT), 307
Gore, S., 77
Grimbeek, E. J., 167–170
group agreement and disagreement, 100–105
group socialization theory, 60
groups see ingroup bias; ingroup
    identification; intergroup contact;
    intergroup trust
GTB-LA see Generalized Trust Beliefs-Late
    Adolescence

Harris, J. R., 60
Harris, P. L., 90, 100, 102, 173

Hartshorne, H., 16
helping behaviors see prosocial behaviors
heritability, 138
  see also genetics
Hewstone, M., 310
Home:School Linkages Project, 208
honesty, 10, 16, 177–178
  in adolescent relations, 227–228
  and adolescent trustworthiness, 217
  and adolescent–parent relationship, 261,
    265
  in animals, 30–31
  blunt truth-tellers, 194–195
  and children's testimonies, 189–193
  detecting children's, 184–193
  parents' belief in children's, 189
  and promise-keeping, 155, 172–173
  and prosocial behaviors, 277, 282–285,
    287–288
  and theory of mind, 21
  see also disclosure; lies and lying; shared
    information
hormones see oxytocin; vasopressin

Implicit Association Test (IAT), 306
implicit bias measures, 306–307
information see epistemic trust; shared
    information
ingroup bias, 296, 306–307
ingroup identification, 303–304, 305, 314
inhibitory control, 16
insecure children, 92–93, 94, 96
interdependence, 124, 125
intergroup anxiety, 299, 310
intergroup conflict, 299
intergroup contact, 298–299, 313–314
  in Northern Ireland, 300, 302
  in South Africa, 309–311
  see also cross-group friendships;
    racial segregation; religious
    segregation
intergroup trust, 295, 296
  among adolescents and young adults,
    296–299
  future research, 315
  and intergroup contact, 299, 300, 302
  mediating mechanisms, 314–315
  in Northern Ireland, 300–309
  predictors of, 313–314
  in South Africa, 309–311
  in UK, 311–312
internal influences on disclosure, 168,
    171–172
Internal Working Model (IWM), 14,
    56–57, 68, 249
internalized maladjustment, 17